HISTORY OF MANKIND

CULTURAL AND SCIENTIFIC DEVELOPMENT

VOLUME V

THE NINETEENTH CENTURY

1775–1905

PART FOUR

PUBLISHED FOR THE

INTERNATIONAL COMMISSION FOR A HISTORY OF THE
SCIENTIFIC AND CULTURAL DEVELOPMENT
OF MANKIND

BY

GEORGE ALLEN & UNWIN LIMITED
LONDON

HISTORY OF
MANKIND
CULTURAL AND SCIENTIFIC
DEVELOPMENT

VOLUME V

Edited By

CHARLES MORAZÉ

THE NINETEENTH
CENTURY

1775-1905

PART FOUR

EUROPEAN EMPIRES, TECHNICAL AND SCIENTIFIC PROGRESS,
CULTURE CONFLICTS

Prepared under the auspices and with Financial Assistance of the United Nations Educational, Scientific and Cultural Organization

Consultants for Volume V
Professor Asa Briggs
(University of Sussex, Great Britain)
Professor A. A. Zvorikine
(Institute of History, Academy of Sciences of the
Union of Soviet Socialist Republics)

PRINTED IN GREAT BRITAIN
in 11 pt Plantin type
BY W & J MACKAY LIMITED
CHATHAM

CONTENTS

PART FOUR: EUROPEAN EMPIRES, TECHNICAL AND SCIENTIFIC PROGRESS, CULTURE CONFLICTS

ILLUSTRATIONS

*All illustrations are grouped together at the end of the
book, following page 1320*

MAPS

The maps of Volume V were prepared by Hallwag A. G., Berne.

PART FOUR

EUROPEAN EMPIRES, TECHNICAL AND SCIENTIFIC PROGRESS, CULTURE CONFLICTS

EUROPE AND THE COLONIAL EMPIRES

BY CHARLES MORAZÉ

ONE of the singular features of European thought and its literary and artistic expressions in the nineteenth century was the lack of interest taken in other countries, which nevertheless European trade and European armies had overrun. True, we find in England particularly, and also in France, references, descriptions and characters inspired by these lands outside the confines of European culture. A certain taste for exoticism inherited from the previous century faded away and disappeared, then reappeared in a different style. Though Robinson Crusoe had something in common with the heroes of Jules Verne, the adventures of Kim were naturalistic compared with the moral intention of the adventures of Gulliver. In his tales, Voltaire was searching for a certain truly cosmopolitan spirit; the writings of Loti centred rather on the picturesque aspects of circumstances and things. In brief, it might be said that more than a hundred years of experience brought highly specific knowledge to conceptual themes whose relativism was matched by the sentiment of European scientific and technical superiority which was taken as an established fact.

Colonial expansion and the problems connected with development, which had enriched Europe in every way, were not as such the specific subject of any major work or of any profound philosophical renaissance, unless we consider as fundamental certain rather marginal aspects[1] of Marx and Engels on the one hand, and on the other hand the movement of ideas leading from Gobineau to Nietzsche, from racial inequality to the concept of the superman. Thus one of the essential conditions of the progress of capitalism and of its expansion remained practically foreign to those who were benefiting from it.

At a time when there was so much discussion about God and the State, about authority and liberty, and about classicism and romanticism, the tremendous problem of the relationships between the smallest of the continents and all the others which were being penetrated by it did not really arise. True, erudition, history, philology and anthropology took advantage of easier travel and of the material gathered, but the conclusions drawn from all this were not general or urgent enough to force themselves upon the attention of the general public. No doubt a very fine analysis of certain situations imagined by poets or novelists could have revealed systems of relationships comparable with those existing between Europe and the rest of the world; but only in so far as the internal structure of European social groups provided many examples of material or cultural proximities of the same type as those of colonization. Shakespeare's Caliban, Rousseau's Noble Savage, Voltaire's Brahmin and Emperor of China, all reflect an interest in foreign lands much greater than that which prevailed in the nineteenth century. Marx himself provisionally studied the statuses and conflicts of colonial or semi-colonized societies, and referred to them in different terms from those which Europe inspired him to use. The same could almost be said of nations which did not belong to Western Europe proper but shared their culture with the latter. When Tocqueville dealt, sometimes prophetically, with the United States or Russia, he treated them as extensions of Europe, and in the light of developments and institutions of interest to Europe herself.

This point can be generalized indefinitely. The great monotheistic religions of Europe, pondering on the political and social evolutions which touched them, obliged the Roman Catholic Church to adopt new standpoints and encouraged the Protestant churches to develop along certain lines. But no general confrontation took place between Western forms of Christianity and the religions of Asia, much less those of Africa. From the religious point of view, Europe in the nineteenth century was much less penetrable than the Roman Empire had been to Oriental influences. It was even less sensitive than it had previously been to discussions like those to which Chinese rites gave rise. What was more, no notable attempt was made with a view to a rapprochement between Catholicism and Orthodoxy; there seemed to be a resigned acceptance of this age-old schism. And though the High Church in England sometimes felt the need for a reunion, the consequences were not long-lived.

Such a state of mind prevailed also amid populations of European origin who formed national entities, notably in America. Though European public opinion took little interest in events of a cultural nature, public opinion in the new Latin states remained extremely sensitive to aesthetic as well as political events affecting their country of origin, to which they still felt they belonged. When nativist movements led societies descended from the first colonizers to an awareness of their originality and to an exaltation of the specific features of the lands chosen by their near forebears, it was a function of a patriotism whose model was European. It drew only secondary illustrations or references from local conditions; physical conditioning factors did not easily differentiate what the economic and moral intention wanted to identify with a cherished and admired example. Outside Europe, the European remained loyal to the culture of his country of origin, whose attributes he remained proud to adopt. True, the feeling of an original national existence devoid of nostalgia prevailed earlier and to a greater extent in the United States.

But despite this desire to see themselves as directly established in a land with no history, despite this breakaway from Europe, it was with Europe that the Americans claimed kinship in contesting the native legitimacy of the

Indians and in underestimating the value of the contribution of the coloured African and Asiatic people who worked under their orders. All the same, the belief of the first of the Mormons in the existence of an American Saviour and in the preservation in America of a very old golden Bible, though it survived, in no way abolished the forms of Christianity which were attached to the traditions of the Old World. It is possible that the lands of Russia and Siberia were the theatres of more profound integrations of habits and customs; but here again, the opposition still prevailing between Christianity and Islam prevented the Russian expansion from allowing this syncretist result to be fully achieved.

It is understandable that Europeans, thinly dispersed among the hordes of Asia or the tribes of Africa, did not feel inclined to merge with these cultures which were so foreign to them, even when as in the case of the Portuguese they had been led to overcome racial prejudices to a great extent. The case of the French Canadians integrated with the Indians, that of a few enthusiasts who adopted the civilization of Islam or any other civilization by whose discovery they were attracted, remained exceptional and had no collective significance. At the best, among a few élites there was an attitude of esteem or admiration for the lands which they discovered. The European expatriate usually took with him his habits of thought and his way of living to very different climates, and made it a point of honour to keep these habits.

So it was that nobody in Europe expressed, or perhaps even suspected, the possible dangers of this turning in on one's self. This assurance on the part of the West, and of each of its nations, of its own excellence was doubtless the result of the tremendous progress which had been made and which was soon to throw Europe into its own tragedies before non-Europeans prepared their revenge on her. Such a large-scale phenomenon had a profound significance. So many things were happening in this extreme tip of Eurasia, so many scientific, artistic and political inventions, that people's whole attention was riveted on what was happening there and then. Cultural introversion was much more marked in the nineteenth century than it had been in the eighteenth century. Thus the great ethic and aesthetic productions of Europe were much more universal in nature than the sentiments which had accompanied their germination. The spirit shrank in proportion as wealth increased beyond all expectations. Marx, in a way, was sensitive to this phenomenon, which led him to consider the spiritual as a manifestation derived from the material. This may help to explain the recourse to lyricism accompanying romanticism, the persistence of philosophic idealism beyond Kantian objections, and even the strictly relative nature of realisms, more critical than constructive and as it were disillusioned, nostalgic for their own past, and such that they could not succeed in overcoming the forces which were leading blind nationalisms to the explosions which were to claim so many victims in the twentieth century.

It is possible that the sentimental introversion which kept Europeans closed up within their own countries was a condition of any cultural stability. But in the period of rapid transformation and unstable situations which we are dealing with here, the fragility of groups thus affected was aggravated in proportion as they remained blind to the inherent dangers of this attitude. It is remarkable that in about 1900 there should have been so much illusion about the future possibilities of Christian missions or of Western cultural outposts in a world where the material contributions of technology produced much more rapid effects in changing local conditions and in conditioning customs. The intrinsic inadequacies of the things which it was aimed to inculcate in them were attributed to some kind of natural incapacity for educating themselves on the part of the conquered peoples.

Relationships between the West and the rest of the economically and sometimes politically colonized world derived from a misunderstanding, a mutual incomprehension, whose dimensions were very much greater than in the nineteenth century. It was on at least a millenary scale that the phenomenon appeared in its grandiose and tragic simplicity. On the one hand, history had led Europe along the road of operational reasoning, involving the conception of mathematical demonstration and scientific rationalism applied to chains of cause and effect, thereby enabling Europeans to take full advantage among other civilizations of the knowledge acquired in all branches of natural experimentation. On the other hand, at the same time, different preoccupations prevailed among those other civilizations which were more closely linked with social order so as to ensure a certain loyalty to ancient and proven traditions of a religious and moral order. They paid less attention to the mental resources thanks to which abstraction could finally lead to tremendous scientific and technical developments.

Thus non-European cultures were surprised to learn (often through manifestations of violence which, more or less successfully, they seemed to have preferred to avoid) that a new human universe had come into being, quite outside their own. Often numerically stronger, and in some cases rich in resources, they were as though paralysed by this great change of scene. Doubtless they soon attempted to recover from their surprise and understand that this new conceptual and material environment was specifically human and was valid for all men. Far from forgetting on that account the merits of their own personal experience and its philosophical implications, they attempted a conciliation between what they knew and what they had learned.

The history of the nineteenth century reflects significant manifestations of this effort of which European sailors, soldiers, merchants, and sometimes even missionaries, did not always realize the dramatic and voluntary nature, and which was destined to become fecund not only for cultures which were attached to their traditions but for all humanity. In this process and in this conflict some peoples went under completely; all were profoundly affected.

When this period ended, the results of this profound and painful effort were far from being universally perceptible. They did not, in any case, allow

Europeans to gain sufficient awareness of the multiple character of human developments whose diversity is a natural condition of progress.

NOTES TO INTRODUCTION

1. This statement undoubtedly will be challenged as there are many passages in which K. Marx speaks, often prophetically, of the destiny of colonized people. Marx firmly believes that the proletarian revolution would take place in industrialized countries and not in rural colonized areas. He felt, it seems, that pre-industrialized regions would first be colonized and subject long enough to the imposition of urban and industrial capitalism, before a revolutionary proletariat would develop.

CHAPTER XXIII

THE MOSLEM WORLD[1]

I. CROSS-CULTURAL INFLUENCES IN MOSLEM COUNTRIES

Foreign contributions

THE Moslem East of 1700 resembled an open fan: its handle was in upper Asia, its right side to the south of Muscovy, and its left on the Ganges delta. Towards the handle lay the Khanates such as Kashgar, Kirghiz and Uzbekistan and at the broad end of the fan, the ancient Turkish and Mongolian conquerors were under three rulers, the Grand Turk, the Grand Sophy (Persia) and the Great Mogul. Between 1000 and 1500, these tribes gradually abandoned the Shamanism of their forefathers for the Bukharan or Caspian forms of Islam, especially adopting those aspects which resembled their Shaman beliefs. Turanian Islam, political heir of the Saracen Islam of the high Middle Ages, was similar throughout: the same proverbs and legends, songs and dances, customs, musical style and art forms, clothing and utensils; the same trades and professions, manual and intellectual equipment; even the same dishes such as pilaf, yoghourt, shashlik, qaymaq, etc. It was in almost every respect a single homogeneous culture and was to experience more or less the same development.

Just before 1800, this imaginary fan was half closed as if pressed by an invisible finger and thumb. Even the most optimistic Westerners had not expected such a sudden retreat of the Oriental powers. After a gradual reconquest of the lands of the ancient Golden Horde, the Muscovite armies reached the north shores of the Black Sea and the Caspian. The left side of the fan closed even further when Hindustan, the colossus with feet of clay known to Europeans as the Mogul Empire, collapsed under English pressure. By 1774, Warren Hastings had set up his headquarters at Calcutta with the rank of Governor-General. In 1803 Wellesley descended on Delhi. The impetus carried the English as far as the town of Herat in central Asia, where it met the resistance of Persia and Afghanistan (1838–42). Ancient Hindustan was indeed submerged.

France, too, which had become an ambitious power since the revolution, could not fail to seek an outlet in the Orient. In 1798 the Government of the Directory dispatched a military expedition to Egypt and, under Bonaparte, the French army attacked the ancient Turkish province of Egypt, and while encouraging the aspirations of the Persians (1799–1807) and the Sikhs of Lahore sketched in an empire which should lie between Russia and the North Sea. In 1801 the Ottomans, in alliance with the English, drove the French out of the Nile valley; but the military revolt in Istanbul (*coup d'état* of 1862 against the Janissaries)[2] and the naval defeat of Navarino (1827) left the Ottoman Empire defenceless on land and sea. The French took the opportunity to acquire Algeria, while the Russians quietly established themselves in the Caucasus.

The annexation of Algeria (1830) gave the French a window on to another variety of Islam; the mysterious land of the western Maghreb, stretching from the Sudan to the Tyrrhenian Sea, which had, as came to be recognized later, its own characteristics and its own way of life: the spirit of the Jema'a (association), applied equally to agriculture and to crafts, to religion (Maraboutism) and commerce. At this time the French were already in N'Dar (St Louis in Senegal) at the other end of this unknown subcontinent; but in spite of their technical superiority, it took them another century to penetrate as far as Mauritania, the heart of this world in itself. It was only after a long delay that a Resident-General was able to impose the decrees of Paris on the Maghreb itself, the historic home of this form of Mohammedanism. The Niger basin and Lake Chad were conquered only after a similar delay, owing to the impenetrability of the country and to lack of preparation on the part of the French.

Meanwhile, the Russians and the English were in process of invading the Ottoman Empire, their imperial ambitions fired by its successive defeats in Europe: the independence of Serbia (1826) and of Greece (1829). It was a question of who could wrest the richest lands and the finest provinces from their Moslem rulers. The English, who were already masters of Ceylon and the Mahratta states (1815–19), now captured Aden, a strategic point on the route to India (1839) and moving up the Indus valley subjugated the Punjab (1849) and curbed the independence of the Sikhs. The Crimean War (1853–6), undertaken by France, England and the State of Piedmont to defend Turkey against the Russian expansion, did not, however, give back the principalities of Moldavia and Wallachia to the Sultan. The national uprising in India (1857–9) did not stop the English proceeding with their plans for colonial expansion.[3] Persia was attacked in 1856 because she prevented Britain from handing over Herat in central Asia to Dost-Mohammed (1826–63) of Kabul. English protection was offered to and accepted by the Sheikh of Bahrein (1861), while the sultanate of Muscat (Persian Gulf) and the isle of Zanzibar on the African coast passed into the British sphere of influence after a century of independence. By his building of the Suez Canal (1859–69) the Frenchman Ferdinand de Lesseps gave England an inestimable advantage—the short route to India. In 1872 the Khan of Baluchistan came under English protection. In 1877 the Empire of India was proclaimed. This included a number of native states. England did not succeed in conquering Afghanistan because of the strong resistance put up by the population, but she occupied Egypt in 1882, the continued obedience of the native princes being ensured in each case by a system of regular payments.

In the meantime, the Russians had begun the conquest of central Asia, overcoming Khoquend between 1864 and 1866, and reducing to the status of clients the Khans of Bokhara (1868) and Khiva on the Aral Sea (1873). Nor did they overlook the desert areas inhabited by the Turcomans (1881–5); their occupation of this area made the Russians in central Asia the immediate neighbours of Persia and of the Emirate of Kabul. The Shah of Persia thus became the unwilling fulcrum of the Anglo-Russian balance of power, leaning sometimes towards St Petersburg and sometimes towards Calcutta and London.

One result of Russian penetration into central Asia was the tribulations undergone by the Moslem communities of China. There were a few Moslems scattered throughout China, but two large communities existed. First, on the northern frontier of Indo-China, in Yunnan, Islam had become, since the Yuans, the religion of several nations related to the Annamites. These Moslem communities revolted against the Manchus from 1856 to 1873, at the same time as those in Bengal (now Bangladesh) were in revolt against the English. The Yunnan Moslems were in fact in contact with their co-religionists in India by way of Malaya and Java (now Indonesia). Secondly, there existed to the north of China, in Chinese Turkestan, another Moslem community which had close cultural ties with Persia and Turkey. These were the Turks of Kansu and Shen-si, who rose against Peking (1862–77) under Ya'qub Beg (1865–77). This community was regarded by the Manchus as one of the 'Five-Nations' of their Empire, because it had, in addition to its religion and its language (Sino-Turkish), its own script (Arabic characters).

There was, also, Malayan Mohammedanism, which was to make Indonesia one of the great Moslem powers of the twentieth century. By the beginning of the nineteenth century the British were already established in Singapore and in process of subjecting the Malay sultans, but Islam progressed freely in South-East Asia, particularly in Java, where the Dutch were unable to prevent it.[4] The same thing happened in the western Sudan and in East Africa, in spite of the efforts of missionaries, sometimes aided by colonial governments. Far from being able to stop the advance of Mohammedanism among the Africans, the European invasion of the second half of the nineteenth century only served to precipitate it.

Moslem theologians were not entirely opposed to the European advance, which took the form mainly of destroying the power of native rulers and paying the sultans and pashas for loyal support. The mullahs felt themselves unassailable, and the Europeans, knowing the impossibility of converting Moslem peoples, hesitated to attack them. Nevertheless some of the mullahs accused the West of seeking to undermine the basis of Islam by introducing the theory and practice of secularism, of civil rather than religious rule—all the popular connotations of the term 'European civilization'.

Internal reactions

In spite of a few books printed relatively early in the Orient (Jehan-numa,

Mirror of the World; Tuhfet ul Kibar, *History of Ottoman Maritime Expeditions*, Istanbul 1732 and 1729), and the maps contained in them, the Islamic peoples were in 1800 very ignorant of practical geography. They had no idea of the size in territory or population of Islam, which they believed to be the whole world, nor of the power and position of the West. Treatises and maps and a few wonderful instruments were not sufficient for that understanding of the physical nature of the world, now made more than ever necessary by economic circumstances. Even in the West at this time geography was mainly a branch of the art of navigation which held little interest for the mainly continental peoples of the Moslem world. In 1732, a Protestant-converted Moslem, Ibrahim Mutefarriqa, had attempted without success to convince the Ottoman *Divan*, in his *Philosophical Principles of Government Among Various Nations*, that the 'infidels', having rounded the Cape of Good Hope and captured the Indian trade, were preparing to encircle Islam. An understanding of this economic prophecy was impossible to minds with no idea of economics and no conception of the importance of seaborne commerce to the sailors and island peoples of Europe.

They did not in fact discover the West until much later, towards the end of the nineteenth century, and then not so much through its political conquests—which indeed passed almost unnoticed—as through the products of its industry which flooded into the Orient and affected the livelihood of the many Asian craftsmen. The political conquests of the West affected no one but the Moslem potentates, who took some time to assimilate the matter. This phase was followed by a scientific invasion from the West both civil and military, particularly in technical fields such as modern medicine, surgery and pharmacy. This, too, passed unnoticed except by a few intellectuals, whose number increased very slowly during the nineteenth century. The third and final phase of this invasion from the West, that of its industrial products, was of little importance towards the middle of the century, catering merely for the satisfaction of a few individuals who were fascinated by European articles. But towards the end of the century these importations increased to such an extent as to become a serious anxiety to the Moslem craftsmen of Oriental towns, who found themselves losing the trade of their rich fellow-countrymen as the latter gradually became accustomed to European goods. By the beginning of the twentieth century the industrial invasion from the West had already produced its first disastrous results: the reduction of the Moslem craftsman to poverty and imminent ruin, which gave the Moslem struggle against colonialism and imperialism the peculiarly bitter and intensely critical character of a fight by people deprived of their very means of life.[5]

In the two principal Moslem states or 'empires' in the East, Turkey and Persia, the dynasties tried hard to reorganize themselves, fixing and defining their capitals, frontiers, succession, military and diplomatic methods, and setting up the nucleus of an administration. This desire to bring together the elements of a monarchy began in Turkey with Selim III (1789–1807) and in Persia with Feth-Ali (1797–1834); its first successes occurred under Mahmud II (1808–39) in Istanbul and Mohammed II (1835–48) in Teheran. From fluid empires where it was difficult to speak of a state, a capital of frontiers, a regular army or a 'normal' transmission of sovereignty, Turkey and Persia became, during the first three-quarters of the nineteenth century, more like two Western monarchies. This development cost them a certain amount of territory in provinces detached or become independent, but what they lost in barely controlled outlying lands they gained in the strength, stability and centralization of royal power. The feudal lords, representing the ruling class in these countries, were forced to make a number of concessions to the rising national bourgeoisie and to carry out a partial reform of the administration in order to preserve the monarchy.

At this stage in their progress, acute economic problems began to appear in the form of financial difficulties. Any monarchy, however uncomplicated, needs regular revenues to pay its subordinates, who can only be controlled if they are paid regularly in ready money. In short, to maintain the state it was necessary to formulate monetary policies, and to encourage the development of trade, customs policies. The two new monarchies were the less capable of such financial efforts since they could neither close their frontiers to European businessmen nor fight with any success against the commercial energies of the West. Their economic devices, such as tolls and duties, hindered rather than helped the development of trade. Modern machines were introduced for the minting of coins on a large scale (*ghurush* in Turkey, *qeran* in Persia) but the continuing output of piastres merely weakened agriculture—the only real wealth of these countries—for the benefit of a parasitic commerce. There was a sudden growth of usury in the most backward areas, and a whole class of *nouveaux riches* came into being who, after lending money at 100 per cent, began soon after the Crimean War to buy small properties and even feudal estates, and to reduce the peasants to a state of servitude by the suppression of the communal traditions. Many of these money-lenders enriched themselves by the system of 'farming' which became more and more widespread. This parasite class, hungry for titles and honours, became towards the end of the nineteenth century a considerable problem for the Ottoman and Persian dynasties whom it was willing to undermine to maintain its privileges and landed properties.

Until this time neither monarchy had known any but external enemies—the Russians to the north and the English to the south—but the growth of a money economy had created for them a domestic enemy in the middlemen with their bought titles and estates. Though these were few in number, anxious to buy high-sounding titles and rich in rents and 'farms', they never felt at ease in Istanbul or Teheran, where the weight of the monarchy was most heavily felt. The laws—simple decrees by the ruler—were a daily threat to the lives of those men used to being able to buy anything. A feudal chieftain of the old days could disobey the padishah at will, driving his flocks to safety and shutting himself in his stronghold high in the mountains; but the upstart of the latter half of the nineteenth century, living in a fine house in Istanbul or Teheran with his wealth in gold and titles to land, was subject to every whim of the despot. Only the famous 'capitulations', of which this century was the golden age in Asia, gave any guarantee of safety. If the merchant was a Christian or a Jew, then he would put himself under the protection of a foreign consulate. If he was a Moslem, he deposited his money in a foreign bank, and secretly sought the protection of a European consulate, as his only chance of remaining unmolested. Just as this new middle class espoused more or less openly the cause of the West, so the Western powers, and England in particular, felt extremely sympathetic towards these new-fledged capitalists and employed every diplomatic and political means to protect them.[6,7] Their interests seemed to be identical: dissolution of the absolute power of the monarchy, extension of individual liberty, and the removal of barriers to trade and the power of money. The rich and ennobled usurers of Istanbul and Teheran aimed fundamentally at the same object as England and the Concert of Powers when they set out to undermine the monarchy and, by removing the monarch's personal power, to bring the state under the control of their own class.

The career of a prominent member of this middle class in Persia may be taken as an example. Melkom (1833–1908), the son of an Armenian gold-smith, arrived in Teheran in 1851 at the time of the opening of the European-style Dar ul-Funun College, to act as interpreter to the Austrian teachers, who taught in French, the official language (with Persian) of the college. In a few years he had gained so much wealth and influence that in 1857 he was sent to Paris to negotiate the armistice with England: his conduct of the negotiations was highly satisfactory to the English since he made more concessions than they asked for. However he did not return to Teheran with empty hands: he brought a small telegraph with which he connected the college and the palace—a novelty which fascinated the court. Taking advantage of this revival of his prestige he founded the lodge of Jami'a Ademiyyet (Great Mosque of Philanthropy), dividing the initiates into future courtiers, ministers and governors, in the manner of the middle class striving for secret protection. He also prepared the ground for obtaining a concession for the Persian tele-graph from the Shah for an English company whose agent he was, and succeeded beyond all expectations. By 1860 the Indo-European Telegraph Company began to extend its network across Persia. After this, Melkom turned to another task; and with it in mind took up residence in Istanbul for ten years from 1861. Istanbul had become the centre for the new rich in the years after the Crimea and their leaders had just started a newspaper, *Teswir-i Efkar*, in which new writers like Shinasi efendi (1826–71), Kemal bey (called Namiq), and Zia pasha, explained and commented on the new terms now being heard for the first time -*veten* (country), *Meshurtiyet* (constitution), *hurriyet* (liberty), etc. In this Istanbul of Abdul Aziz (1861–76) which had become a centre of thought, Melkom found thinking men with a wealthy middle class following who hung on their writings. In Turkey as in Persia, difficulties had arisen for Islam with the emergence of a new class. Melkom settled down to his task: the Great Mosque of Philanthropy of which he was Director, and also began a newspaper there called *Akhter*, a Persian adaptation of *Teswir*; and he published a series of writings: *The Age of Progress* (*Mebda i Terreqi*); *The Dialogues of the Vizier and the Sheikh ul-Islam*; *The Three Epistles*; *Haji Baba*; *The Voyages of Ibrahim Bey*; *The Cafe of Surate*, etc.

Meanwhile in Teheran, the Grand Vizier Mohammed Sepehsalar (1867–71) spent his time crowning the work of the monarchy with a group of 52 scholars who had now returned after being sent in 1858 to complete their studies in Paris. Teheran was enlarged in 1867 and provided with straight and broad streets; the first main carriage roads in all Persia were also built. After the example of the reformation of justice in Turkey (1861–8) he created fifty chambers of justice (Adliyyeh) and a police force (Nazmiyyeh), thus strengthening the hands of autocracy. But the 'young Persians' on whom he counted to carry through this programme were almost all associated with the Great Mosque of Philanthropy and disparaged the aged Sepehsalar and his 'Turkish ideas'. They spoke highly of the abilities of Mirza Hossein, Persian ambassador to Istanbul and, like themselves, a follower of Melkom, to such effect that he succeeded Sepehsaler as Grand Vizier (1872) and brought in Melkom as the leader of his cabinet and chief adviser. With this, the middle classes began to expand. Melkom represented Persia at the Congress of Berlin, and in return for gifts to the Shah was given the title of 'Reforming Prince' (Nazim ud-Dawlah). But his loyal follower Ali Emin ud-Dawleh (d.1899), Vizier of Posts (1877) called him 'Supreme Wisdom' (Aql-i-Kull) because from London (where he was the Shah's representative) he published anonymously an anti-monarchist newspaper, *Qanun* (The Law), which, banned in Persia, was clandestinely distributed by the Vizier of Posts; all this activity did not prevent Melkom, Emin ud-Dawleh and others of their class from becoming extremely rich at the expense of the Persian people, as foreign merchants had done before them.[8]

What were the reactions of the mullahs, who represented the cultured conscience of Islam, to the cultural and scientific supremacy of the West?[9] We may answer that by another example. The Afghan Jemal ud-Din (1838–96) was a mullah. On his return to Kabul after his pilgrimage to Mecca (1857) and a long visit to British India, he became tutor and vizier to the princes of Afghanistan. As British influence grew, however, Sher-Ali (1863–79), the emir supported by Calcutta, expelled Jemal ud-Din as the vizier of a discredited rival. The exile chose Istanbul as his place of residence, travelling to it by way of India, Mecca and Cairo. Finding that the brilliant city of Sultan Abd ul-Aziz offered him no opportunities, he made his way to the

Cairo of Khedive Isma'il (1863–79) where he found recognition and a liveli-hood as professor of scholastic philosophy. His Arabic culture and many connections made it easy for him to create a school of Moslem reform, midway between the pure scholastic clericalism of earlier times and the ultra-modernism approved by the English materialists, who sought to create a Moslem world without Mohammed. He wished to adopt practical methods from Europe in order to preserve the Moslem character of Islam. The Khedive Isma'il was of the same opinion, but fell back, discredited, after selling his Suez Canal shares to Disraeli. He was removed in favour of an inexperienced young man (Tewfik 1879–92) who let his power fall into the hands of two Western 'managers', first only of the Canal, but then of all Egypt, thus preparing the ground for the appointment of Lord Cromer. In 1879 Jemal ud-Din was compelled to leave his second homeland and again went on his travels (via India) to London where he met Melkom and his group of 'young Moslems', with whom, though, he never entirely agreed. He had his own personal following and a considerable influence in the East, greater than that of the Melkomians by reason of his being a mullah—as were many of his followers. Because of this the Melkomians made use of him, providing him with the means of editing from London two quasi-'young Turkish' newspapers, one aimed at Persia (Dia-ul-Khafiqayn—The Light of the Two Horizons) and the other at the Syrians and the Arab dependencies of the Ottoman Empire in general (Al-Orwat el Wuthqa—The Indissoluble Tie). Melkom's two attempts in 1886 and 1889 to introduce Jemal ud-Din into Persia to make the country rise against the Shah (Nasir ud-Din, 1848–96) were unsuccessful.

In Turkey the disquieting situation under Abd ul-Aziz became rapidly worse. Midhat (1822–83) did not long enjoy the constitution forced from the Sultan (1876) because he aimed too high. Conspirators murdered the unfor-tunate Emperor in his bath and enthroned Murad V, a docile and inoffensive padishah (some said a half-wit) of whom much was expected. But about 100 days later a secretly prepared coup d'état raised to the throne the famous Abd ul-Hamid II, a prince who both believed and practised his religion. Abd ul-Hamid II (1876–1909) dismissed Midhat after the Russian war and the Congress of Berlin (1878) and surrounded himself entirely with conserva-tives, monarchists and Moslems who distrusted British designs on Egypt and Turkey. The new padishah turned out to be a strong personality who took seriously his title of Caliph, spiritual head of Islam, and his task of frustrating his adversary Lord Cromer. To the British policy of economic imperialism he opposed a policy of Ottoman spiritual imperialism: pan-Islam. The Sultan sent for Jemal ud-Din, approved of him and kept him at court (1893–6) as one of the spiritual leaders of pan-Islam. He had formed a favourable opinion of him from his book (written in Persian from the stand of orthodox philosophy and translated into Arabic) The Epistle against Materialism (Redd-i Neychuriyya, 1880).

The object of pan-Islam was to defend Islam both spiritually and politically and to demonstrate its capacity for revival. To the 'reformation' unleashed by the political and cultural successes of Europe, pan-Islam opposed a 'counter-Reformation'. When followers of the West criticized despotism, pan-Islam replied with a criticism of colonialism. When the British and their followers demanded freedom for the subjects of the Ottoman Empire, pan-Islam suggested that they should set an example in India. If it was alleged that Islam had got rid of the priests, they pointed out the atheism and materialism rampant in Europe. To eulogies of Western civilization they opposed articles praising that of the Arabs in the Middle Ages.[10,11]

Thus the Moslem world towards the end of the nineteenth century underwent a double transformation: in economics and in thought. Brought into being by new monetary and banking techniques, the middle class of merchants and officials developed a cultural and national conscience via newspapers and encyclopaedias, and laid the foundations for the political resurgence of Islam.[12] In the independent empires like Turkey and Persia this development took the form of an internal struggle between the bourgeoisie and absolute monarchy. On the other hand, in countries like Egypt openly 'conquered' by Europeans, a more normal development took place, with the liberty-loving enthusiasm of the local bourgeoisie opposing foreign colonial rule. In the independent monarchies of Turkey and Persia the problem was to win small individual liberties—tiny fractions of liberty itself—whereas the Arab countries aimed at total freedom, that of the entire people and its whole culture, not a fractional liberty resulting from internecine struggles within the nation itself. On the one hand, the freedom concerned was that of a single class—the bourgeoisie—on the other, that of a whole country.

The new institutions

To estimate the extent of the change in Islamic institutions between 1800 and 1900, the cases of the Ottoman Empire, the Khedivate of Egypt, or the Persian Empire may be cited, as the only Moslem states both independent and modern at the time. Of these Persia offers the best example because of her situation in the interior of the Asiatic continent, midway between the continental influence of Russia and the maritime influence of Britain. Teheran was situated far enough in the interior of the Orient for Western influences to arrive somewhat modified by their passage through Istanbul and the Caucasus from the west and north-west, or through Calcutta and Cairo from the south. The Teheran of 1800 was a small country town of dirty, narrow, winding alleys, each district being barricaded at nightfall with iron doors and chains. Great boulevards were added to the old town where it began to extend toward the north-west in 1867; by 1889 it was three times as large as it had been 100 years before. It had a network of broad straight roads crossing at right angles, with pavements shaded by plane trees and lit by gas lamps at night. Large numbers of hansom cabs and carriages, previously unknown, passed through the streets, drawn by great Russian horses, carrying the gentry about their affairs. An unusual tramway ran through the main streets of Teheran, whose cars were provided with compartments for the veiled women. At the south end of the town was a railway station serving a nearby suburb. The caravan routes of 1800 had given way to paved roads, for the Persians of 1900 travelled by stage-coach or open brakes. Inns replaced the now almost deserted caravanserais. The Persia of 1800 was still living in the age of the Crusades, that of 1900 in the age of Turgot. The railways, already opening up Turkey and Egypt, had not yet become established in Persia. This was mainly owing to the death of the wealthy businessman Haji Mohammed-Hassen (1833–98) who in 1896 had been forced to abandon his plans for the construction of a line from the Caspian to Teheran owing to the assassination of his patron, the Shah.

The career of this Persian entrepreneur is a typical example of that of the Persian and Moslem middle class of the nineteenth century, brought into being by finance: the piastre and the bank-note. Dealings in piastres made of Mohammed-Hassen—in 1857 merely a small-scale money-changer (*serraf*)— an enterprising businessman engaged in Anglo-Indian trade. Most of his wealth came from taking over the lease of a factory for minting piastres (*qerans*). His projected Caspian–Teheran railway, of which one-third was completed, led to his downfall: the groups responsible for the assassination of the Shah (1896) intrigued against his plans. Envious men who had been unable to turn the late Shah against him had more success with the next, Muzaffer (1896–1907), a mere pawn in the hands of the 'reformers'. They easily persuaded him to put Mohammed-Hassen to the question, and by accusing him of malpractices while farming the mint, succeeded in extorting from the unfortunate man some eight million piastres. Of this, he paid six million in gold ingots from the strongrooms of his palace, and the rest in letters of credit drawn upon various money-changers in Teheran. He died in 1898, a disillusioned and ruined man, and the railway from the Caspian to Teheran was never built.

The piastre and the bank-note had led in Persia to the formation of a small middle class, but this had only been able to develop freely thanks to the enlightened despotism of Nasir ud-Din. His murder in 1896 led to a crisis in the Government, owing to the stupidity and weakness of the new ruler, whose reign was a great misfortune for Persia. He was quite incapable of protecting his merchants against Russian and English influence, which stood in the way of the progress of Persian civilization. The sugar refinery and match factory of Ali Eminu ud-Dawleh (d.1899) hardly maintained their ground; the spinning and weaving enterprises of Haji Mohammed-Hossein Kazuruni (1853–1925) only succeeded because the prince-governor of Ispahan supported them against English and Russian competition. The Persian bourgeoisie, who had no confidence in the Government, invested their capital in land, which was tantamount to burying their talents. This infant capitialism required enlightened protection against both its internal and external enemies; it imagined that a constitutional régime backed by England would be most helpful.

The piastre and bank-note had been only recently introduced into Persia. Good piastres (*qerans*) were first struck in quantity by modern methods in 1857. Before that there was nothing that could be properly called 'currency'. Small quantities of gold and silver were hand-wrought and used as much for royal ornaments and amulets as for coinage. For this purpose each town had its own small workshop. The only wealthy people in the country were feudal magnates whose fortunes consisted of grain, straw and hay. The Shah paid his officials by granting them the right to levy land tax (the only tax then known) on some village or other.

The circulation of money brought into existence by the piastre was increased after 1889 by the introduction of bank-notes by the Imperial Bank, an English company which played a similar part in Teheran to that of the Ottoman Bank in Turkey, founded by the Sultan's creditors. This bank rendered good services but also found it extremely profitable. Thus, for instance, its bills bore the inscription 'payable only in Teheran', or some other city, as if each Persian town issued its own paper money. By this system of internal exchange the foreign company controlled the trade of the whole country, and rather restricted than aided its expansion.[13]

Melkom was for a long time the advocate of concessions to the English. He was succeeded after 1889 by Hossein-quli the Nabob, an Anglo-Indian who became a naturalized Persian. It was thanks to him that the Imperial Bank became established. He was in charge of the department of foreign affairs and persuaded the Shah to grant all sorts of concessions to the English; the Shah let himself be persuaded because he needed foreign exchange badly, not only for himself but for his relatives and courtiers, by this time accustomed to travelling in Europe and to buying European goods. He had already mortgaged the customs revenues from the Persian Gulf. In 1901, for a small sum, he conceded to an Englishman named d'Arcy land (near Abadan) where the presence of oil had already been detected in 1899 by the engineer and archaeologist, Jacques de Morgan. Oil was subsequently struck in 1908.[14]

It was not only to pay for necessities in Europe that the Shah needed currency: there was a desparate need for money within the country itself. The printing of paper money was already an English concession and could not be revoked, while it was difficult to issue false piastres without ruining the credit of the State. The only small change in Persia consisted of old copper coins only worth their weight in metal. The Nabob Hussein-quli had an inspiration: he would sell to the English the right to put into circulation nickel coins at a value well above that of their metal content and, in order to boost their value, he would forbid the circulation of copper coins. If the Russians objected they could be granted the right to establish a Discount Bank in Persia.

The pattern of the future was now clearly visible. The fluid Persian Empire of 1800 was becoming more and more fixed. Its capital was now definitely Teheran. International commissions had delimited the frontiers to within a few yards. After the tragic death of the last Shah in 1896 there were no more royal progresses by caravans consisting of thousands of men. The present Shah had no harem and did not go hunting. Many of the upper class went for cures to fashionable spas in Europe, and their amusements were childish and harmless. The legendary Oriental court of the late Shah had disappeared. Only the public services survived the change of rulers: the Postal Service begun in 1877, the Persian Telegraph Department founded in 1860, the Dar ul-Funun College opened in 1851, the Cossack Brigade, the Persian Sanitary Board, the modern hospital and a few other such institutions.

Between 1807 and 1857, the Persians aimed at building up an army on the British or French model. After several attempts, troops called *serbaz* were recruited and trained by French and English instructors. Textbooks were translated, barracks and forts were built, without any really worth-while results. It was impossible to create a Western-type army with a democratic spirit and quasi-naval discipline in a despotic continental state like Persia. The Persian defeat by the English in 1857 proved the futility of the attempt, while Russian victories over Turkestan in 1864–73 and Turkey in 1877–8 awoke Persian interest in troops of the Cossack variety. By 1879, Cossack instructors went to Teheran with a Russian military mission in order to teach their methods to young Persians in a Cossack military school, Qazaq-Khaneh, where Russian was the language of instruction. Teheran in 1900 now had a modern division (2,000) of Persian Cossacks, trained and dressed like those of Russia.

In a few years Cossack instructors had succeeded where the English and French after two generations had failed—probably because of some natural affinity between Persians and Russians. The Persian Cossacks were certainly closer in spirit to the Janissaries than to the French Republican Guard; they were trained to serve a despot and had no national or democratic feelings. After the Treaty of Berlin in 1878 the Sultan Abdul Hamid also rejected Western military training, but being unable to tolerate Cossack instructors, turned to the Prussians. Yet there was a considerable difference between the pupils of von der Goltz Pasha and those of Colonel Liakhov: the former were patriotic Turks who would if necessary sacrifice the Sultan's cause to that of their country; Liakhov's forces despised Persia and would have sacrificed her not only for the Shah but for any other tyrant if he were a Cossack who provided them with food and lodging.[15]

In order to further these military reforms, the Persians introduced the modern teaching of mathematics in 1851. They translated the textbooks of an Austrian officer, A. Krziz, who taught at the Dar ul-Funun College, on arithmetic and on mechanics and physics (1858); on infantry manoeuvres (1853) and exercise for heavy artillery (1854). These were followed by other translations and original works, such as *The Elements of Algebra* (1888) translated by Aqa Khan, a *Plan of Teheran* (1891) drawn up by Suleiman Khan, and a *Treatise on Geology* (1882) by Yussuf Khan. The Egyptians and Turks had already progressed further than the Persians in modern mathematics as in all other fields. Unfortunately, in Persia, as in Egypt and Turkey, too much time was lost in comparing modern mathematics with ancient Arab treatises, making dictionaries and establishing terminologies, in order to produce really good translations into Arabic. It was a praiseworthy task, but the concentration on lexicography and history of science held up the progress of practical mathematics. The Japanese, who were free from such philological preoccupations, were able to advance much more quickly. What was the importance, for example, of knowing that in the Middle Ages the Arabs had taught all Europe mathematics if Arabic numerals were unpopular and little used in Moslem countries today ? The Persians held to a middle way between the radicalism of the Turks and the (sometimes rather bogus) conservatism of the Cairo Arabs. In Egypt all the modern mathematical symbols had been translated into Arabic letters and signs, although it was well known that medieval Arab algebra did not use many symbols. The Turks and Persians, lacking strong 'Arab' feelings, adopted the Western symbols in their entirety, not only in algebra but in chemistry—where, again, the Egyptians had turned everything into Arabic letters!

The method of measuring time gradually changed. Beginning in the early nineteenth century, clocks and watches ceased to be regarded as rare treasures and came into everyday use. But until 1925 time was calculated from the hour of sunset, as it always had been. The public clocks struck the hours in the ordinary way, of course; but up to 1925 the five most important moments of the day were announced, as they had been for over a thousand years, by the blare of trumpets, pipes and drums from the top of a high tower in the town. Dawn and dusk during the ninth moon (Ramazan), and noon at all other times of the year, were proclaimed by loud cannon-shots.

After 1849, when Sayid Kemal ud-Din published his solar calendar of Jelalian type, at Lucknow, the question of officially introducing a solar year arose in Persia: this was done from 20 March 1878. The months were named after the signs of the zodiac, but the solar years were counted from the Hegira. The Turks had done the same in 1830, giving the months Chaldean-Syrian names, but adopting Gregorian rather than Julian months. After 1881-2, the British firmly introduced the Gregorian calendar and the Christian method of dating into Egypt, but in Persia, Turkey and Egypt the Arab lunar calendar was used by the people and in religious practice. The reform spread very slowly, with the growth of State authority.

The Persians had very soon become interested in Western medicine, and from 1810 sent students to Europe to learn from France, which they regarded as politically neutral. For the same reason, they appealed to Austrian doctors to treat the Shah Mohammed (1835–48) and to teach medicine at Teheran from 1851 onwards—in French, the language of instruction. They felt that the British and Russian 'doctors' who were so anxious to treat the Shah and his courtiers were less interested in medicine than in bolstering up the political influence of St Petersburg, London or Calcutta. The Shah Nasir ud-Din (1848–96) also took great care to choose his own doctors in Paris. The medical faculty in Teheran was founded in 1849 and the first modern hospital, directed by the Austrian doctors Polak and Schlimmer, was built in 1868: in 1880 this was enlarged and Dr Albo became director. Dr J. L. Schlimmer produced in 1874 a medical and pharmaceutic dictionary in French, German, Persian and Arabic, and Dr Polak wrote a treatise on ophthalmics and a dictionary of anatomy (1861). A Dr Joseph Tholozan produced works on hospital organization, surgery, and many other subjects. All these books were translated into Persian by the writer's pupils.

Dr Joseph Tholozan (1820–97), an army doctor from the Val de Grâce hospital, entered the service of the Shah at an early age and died in Teheran. He was the Shah's chief medical adviser, professor of medicine, and director of the hospital. He was, however, unable to maintain the political neutrality expected of him. His daughter married in 1892 Harry Lionel Churchill, who had been British Consul from 1880 to 1883, and he himself was so much in the company of British diplomats in Teheran that he was finally knighted. After the opening of the Suez Canal (1869–70) and the proclamation of Queen Victoria as Empress of India in 1877, Sir Joseph took up the cause of the International Sanitary Board, so much the object of suspicion to the Shah, who had even closed its branch in Teheran in 1875. The Board had confided to England the task of supervising the health of Islam and of Persia in particular by the establishment of quarantine centres at transit points, and it was thought that the British used these to hamper Persian trade and develop their own. The spectre of Indian cholera since appearing for the first time on the route to India in 1817 had caused innumerable deaths. Teheran had epidemics in 1829, 1833, 1846, 1852, 1861 and 1869. South Persia and the Ottoman province of Iraq became gradually depopulated and practically reverted to desert. Cholera was rampant on the coasts of the Persian Gulf from 1817. The Sanitary Board of Teheran, which sat permanently after the assassination of the Shah in 1896, was occupied with other things than cholera. When Dr Koch discovered the bacteria of Indian cholera and the way to eliminate it, he unwillingly struck a blow at 'medical imperialism'. Up to the time when the Persians were able to demand of British ships the 'rat-free' certificates offered by other nationalities, quarantine stopped at the Persian frontiers. In 1899 the Russians on their side had set up their own quarantine regulations in the north. Thus Persia in 1900 was surrounded by a *cordon sanitaire* which was really a one-way economic barrier, for the English, the Russians and their trade passed easily through it, while it was extremely difficult for Persian goods to pass out.

Although the art of printing was known in the Orient, it was not really taken up in Persia until the beginning of the nineteenth century. Mirza Salih, who studied in London from 1810 to 1814, returned to Persia after the battle of Waterloo, bringing with him a printing-press. An Englishman, Major D'Arcy, helped him to publish the first Persian newspaper, which even then was anti-Russian. After a temporary eclipse under the Shah Mohammed (1835-48) the newspaper reappeared with the help of another Englishman called Burgess who collaborated with the Grand Vizier Mirza Taqi, one of the fathers of the Reform movement in Persia. Like the Egyptian reform newspaper (1828)—the first to appear in Arabic—and like the one which appeared in Turkey in 1830, Mirza Taqi's publication was called *Weqayi* (News). Its opponents were treated as mortal enemies, for the press, borrowed from the West like the cannon, was equally a weapon of war. The *Weqayi* of Istanbul approved the massacre of the Janissaries, that of Cairo the massacre of the Mamelukes (1811) and that of Teheran the slaughter of the Babis (1852) and of all its opponents. It was in short an official journalism destined to survive all vicissitudes and thanks to which royalist opinion grew in Persia just as in Cairo and Istanbul.

After the Crimean War the growing middle class felt the need for its own press to defend its interests. The authorities took offence, set up a severe censorship and suspended the independent newspapers, which were forced to appear abroad. In spite of the ban, the bourgeoisie had its own methods, inside the country and out, of obtaining the periodicals it desired. Forbidden papers like *Qanun*, published in London, were distributed regularly in Teheran with the connivance of Ali Emin ud-Dawleh, the Minister of Posts (1877) and sometimes the help of Englishmen like Harry Churchill, director of the Persian Telegraph Department from 1880, and his brother Sydney, both diplomats. After the assissination of the Shah in 1896 a number of opposition journals appeared in Teheran. In spite of strict censorship, Abdul Hamid's Turkey was also inundated with Young Turk publications, edited in Cairo or in London and smuggled into Istanbul with the help of secret societies and Western diplomats, equally hostile to the Ottoman monarchy.

It was thanks to its secret press that the middle class gained some liberties. In Persia in 1888 they extracted from the Shah an edict guaranteeing protection of life and property, but two months later liberty of property was annulled. In 1890 they secured the abolition of the tobacco monopoly which had been conceded to the Englishman Julius Reuter. Finally, in 1899 they secured the abolition of tax-farming in the important provinces of Azerbaijan and Kermanshahan. The press was a powerful lever, and the middle-class zeal for reform could not be satisfied without the complete destruction of the monarchy and its replacement by their own Government.

In Turkey and Egypt the development was more striking: the monarchy was tottering, true feudalism had disappeared, and the middle class, emerging in the second half of the nineteenth century, began to realize its strength and to demand 'national' institutions. The titles of Bey and Pasha were now for sale, and in both Istanbul and Cairo everyone wore a fez and expected to be called 'effendi'.

The origin and development of social classes

In Iran and the neighbouring countries during the nineteenth century, society was divided into three clearly differentiated classes—the nobility, the serfs, and the middle class. To discover how they originated we must go back to the fourteenth century.

The nobility

Writing about 1666, Chevalier J. Chardin describes all the 'Persian seigneurs' as still retaining a definitely Mongol cast of features—yellow skins, slanting eyes, etc.; but a few generations later, after successive marriages with wealthy Alide families, the Mongol type became less marked. Feudal discipline, too, was relaxed during the eighteenth century. The 'cadets' (*ayni*) of the feudal families became known as 'elders' (*aghas*), for the right of primogeniture, firmly prescribed by the Mongol code, was not recognized by Moslem law, which was then coming back into force. In the eighteenth century 'agha' meant 'lord'; by the nineteenth century it had been degraded to mean no more than 'Mr'. Its equivalents in central Asia and India—'mizra' and 'sirdar'—and in the Ottoman Empire—'effendi' and 'bey'—came down in the world in the same way. Simultaneously, the Mongol Islamic empires were declining, the indigenous warriors harrying the imperial dynasties on all sides—in the East, the Afghans, Baluchs, Sikhs, Rajputs and Mahrattas; in the centre the Caucasians, Kurds, Lurs, and the Bedouins of the Arabian plateau; and in the West, the Montenegrins, Albanians, Serbs and Berbers, were sapping or overthrowing the feudal empires established in the sixteenth and seventeenth centuries. In every region a struggle had broken out between the hereditary but enfeebled rulers and the indigenous leaders who were not yet strong enough to oust them. Even the nobility, so proud of their family trees in the seventeenth century, had vanished by the end of the eighteenth. Gobineau, in the 1850s, found not only an aristocracy of quite recent origin, without lineage or nobility, but living in feudal style nevertheless.

There were certain economic reasons for these developments. During the same period in which the feudal system was introduced in Islam, the export of silver to China was intensified, and there was a consequent dearth of that metal in the Moslem countries. In the seventeenth century this situation gradually altered, as supplies of silver began to arrive from the New World. An urban economy thus developed, to the disadvantage of the feudal economic system. In the eighteenth century the empires of the Great Mogul and the Grand Turk were weakened as a result of this, and even in Persia the piastre began to undermine the foundations of Mongol feudalism (collapse of the Grand Sophy's administration).

Then, in the middle of the nineteenth century, there was a sudden glut of silver. Equipment for the mass-production of piastre was set up for the first time at Istanbul (1848), Cairo (1855) and Teheran (1857). This gave the death-blow to the post-Mongol feudal system which had replaced the great Mongol system in the last years of the eighteenth century. In the latter half of the nineteenth century even these minor feudal landowners came thronging to settle at Istanbul, Cairo and Teheran, where they could enjoy a luxury never experienced in their country residences.

The entire economic system of Islam was disrupted by this mass circulation of piastres. In Persia, for instance, 37 per cent of the population died in four successive years of famine (1869–72) brought about by speculators. Brokers (*serrafs*) bought up the feudal estates for a song and compelled the peasants to stop growing food and cultivate raw materials for Western industry—cotton, tobacco and opium. The modernist Vizier Emin as Sultan sold the unoccupied fiefs (*khalissas*) to 'aristocrats' for ready cash (*tes'ir*). Between 1878 and 1888, nearly all the former feudal estates were thus disposed of by the Shah to private 'landowners' who were simply titled money-lenders. At the same time and for the same reasons, the Khedive of Egypt, the Bey of Tunis and the Sultan of Turkey were behaving in the same way. And in all these countries the peasants were losing their status as ordinary serfs. The various 'revolutions' at the beginning of the twentieth century merely legalized the existence of the new-rich aristocracy at the top.

The serfs

In the Moslem territories conquered by the Western powers, a few of the feudal nobility were clever enough to come to terms with their imperialist conquerors and keep their estates, thus forming a 'native aristocracy'. In the more firmly established Moslem states, such as the Turkish Empire, where Christian *rayas* lived side by side with the Moslems, Western pressure was at first exerted solely to liberate the Christian *rayas*, who in some cases even secured territorial independence. But the tendency inevitably spread in due course to the Moslem *rayas* as well.

The trend of development of serfdom in nineteenth-century Turkey is instructive. The first necessity was to do away with the feudal system of land tenure; this was achieved by the *Ottoman Land Code* of 21 April 1858. The freedom of the individual was ensured, in theory, by the *Ottoman Civil Code* (1869–76); but it proved impossible to enforce the constitution promised on 23 December 1876, so that the feudal aristocracy and the institution of serfdom continued to flourish in the Turkish provinces bordering on Iran. In all other areas the landowners lost the right to raise taxes and render justice, even if they did not actually give up the habit of doing so. Liberalism proved so contagious that after making some half-hearted tax reforms in 1885, the Shah of Persia himself was compelled in 1888 to grant freedom of life and property to all his subjects—though two months later a decree was issued, restricting those freedoms to the aristocracy and making the *corvée* system more stringent. Feudalism was gradually being transformed into the rule of an aristocracy and serfdom into local slavery—all this in defiance of laws that were ostensibly fairly modern. There was a wide gap between theory and practice. Even when, in the twentieth century, the new owners of the latifundia began to refer to themselves modestly as landowners, they continued to behave like feudal nobility; by appointing 'sound' members of parliament and local prefects they were able to keep the peasants at the level of the 'good old days', with bastinado and *corvées*.

The middle class

Prior to 1220, the Islamic middle class had been based on the different guilds. These, grouped in unions (*futuwwa*) which had a mystical stamp, had played an important part in politics under the caliphs. The Mongols did not massacre the craftsmen, though they put all other town-dwellers to the sword; but they deported them, as *oez* (specialized serfs) to places many hundred miles from their native towns—which in any case were razed to the ground. The craftsmen thus lost not only their freedom but their social and mystical organizations, and their customers. Many of them fled to the southern regions of Islam which had not been invaded—Lahore, Delhi, Ormuz, Aden, Cairo. Though the survivors ultimately succeeded in emerging from the category of 'specialized serfs', they were never able to re-create the *futuwwas* of the period before 1220. They entered the nineteenth century in a wretched and disorganized condition. The feudal police prevented them from re-organizing on a firm basis, and the nobility seldom paid them properly for the beautiful work they produced, which was regarded as their normal output under the *corvée* system. The result was that when Western industry began to expand, the Moslem craftsmen could not compete with the European products even in quality—much less, of course, in quantity.

While large-scale trade fell into the hands of the southern Europeans and the Hindus, all of whom were superseded in the nineteenth century by the English, the smaller trade was taken over by Greeks, Lebanese, Armenians and Banians, who competed for it with the Parsees, Jews and Copts. To the Moslems—traders from Bukhara who dealt with Kashgaria, Persians from the Caspian who travelled up and down the Volga—they left the more dangerous and less profitable routes. The Persians who dealt in caviare from the Caspian were forced by Cossack bayonets to hand over their ancestral trade to Russian nationals.

In order to wage the Crimean War the Sublime Porte raised a loan in the West (1854), in exchange for various political and economic undertakings which were confirmed by the *Khatt-i Humayun* (August Edict) of 18 February 1856. The protection granted to the middle classes was extended by further measures (1854, 1861) and by the separation of the judicial power from the executive (1868). The half-hearted attempt made in 1869 to revive the old pre-Mongol legal system—the Hanefite code—was firmly opposed by this middle class, whose foreign origin made it completely alien to Islam and which definitely preferred the jurisdiction of the foreign consulates to that of the Turkish State, however liberal.

The most that the helpless Porte could do was to induce 'its' bourgeoisie, when involved in legal proceedings with Moslems, to accept the jurisdiction of 'joint tribunals' (1860); for the so-called Turkish middle class, who wrote the Turkish language in Armenian, Greek, Hebrew or Western script, regarded the privileges they wrested from such liberal Ministers as Mustapha Reshid Pasha (d.1858), Ali Pasha (d.1871) and Fuad Pasha (d.1869) as very insufficient. Were they yearning for a liberal monarchy or a socialist republic? Not at all; their almost unconcealed aspiration was no less than the complete and final expulsion of the Moslems from Europe, and ultimately from Asia. At the demand of the West, the Turks recognized the economic and ethnical privileges of the Armenians (1860), the Lebanese (1861 and 1864), the Jews (1864), etc.; but the Armenians were dreaming of an Arsacid Empire, the Lebanese of a Phoenician Empire, the Jews of a new Solomon and the Greeks of another Constantine.

The hopes of all of them were suddenly shattered: the constitution promised on 23 December 1876 was contemptuously revoked by the 'Caliph' Abdul Hamid II who was determined that the *tanzimat* should be beneficial, first and foremost, to Turkey and Islam. At this the bourgeoisie rose in protest, declaring that the forced resignation of its chosen Vizier, Midhat Pasha (1879) would bring financial disaster; and the 'Bank of Turkey', founded in 1856 —after the Crimean War—went bankrupt. The 'Imperial Ottoman Bank', for which a concession had been granted to a group of foreign financiers on 4 February 1863, and had long been held in reserve for just such an occasion, came into action on 20 December 1881. The international consortium on the 'Ottoman Debt', meeting in London, instructed it to represent the creditors of the Sublime Porte.

The fact that the middle classes in Turkey were of foreign race, anti-Moslem and cosmopolitan, was largely due to the Turks' own inability to form a national bourgeoisie, for which they were as yet by no means ripe. Even the civil service instituted in 1839–40 was slow to develop and numerically small, and not until the early twentieth century did it develop into an 'intelligentsia'. The nineteenth-century bureaucrats were ill-educated, entirely militarized, and still rooted in the prevailing feudal system. Before the Crimean War the pasha who had been through primary school and the bey who could write were by way of being rare birds. Consequently, primary education on European lines was introduced and expanded between 1853 and 1862; but as the problems were becoming increasingly complex as the century advanced, the translation of French textbooks was undertaken in course of time followed by the foundation of a secondary school (1868), a school of law (1870), and a civil service college (1877), the last of which trained *efendis alla franca* whom Abdul Hamid II found extremely inefficient.

The Sultan discovered that the beys of the period prior to 1840 had been slowly transformed into literate effendis who regarded themselves as an exclusive cast; whereas he was desperately anxious to build up a 'national' middle class which could counterbalance the cosmopolitan, anti-Moslem bourgeoisie. The nineteenth-century Turk disdained craftsmanship and despised trade; his dream, now that he could no longer become a bey, or feudal aristocrat, was to be a pasha, or courtier. Advised by Wilhelm II and a group of German professors, the Sultan founded colleges of engineers, schools of agriculture, commercial schools; and these institutions were to result in the emergence—long after the death of the 'Red Sultan'—of a non-Koranic intelligentsia from which the followers of Kemal were recruited in due course.

In Persia the development of the middle class was hampered by similar difficulties. By the end of the eighteenth century Persian trade was concentrated at Bender Bushir, where the British from India opened an 'agency' in 1779. The remnants of the original Persian middle class were suffering hardship owing to the political crisis involved in the transition from feudalism to monarchism; so they again began to emigrate to India, following what was by now a traditional route. These vestiges of the bourgeoisie were the survivors of the Isma'ili, a Shi'ah sect which had originated in the twelfth century not far from the shores of the Caspian Sea. In 1834, Shah Kajar, regarding this sect as the equivalent of a feudal 'clan', granted to its 'noble chief' the hand of a princess, together with the domains of Kerman and the personal title of Aga Khan. But though he was regarded by the Turkoman court at Teheran as a feudal aristocrat, this man was in reality the hereditary president —the *Imam*—of a guild of merchants whose business lay in India and whose interests were at times identical with those of the East India Company, which was trying to spread its political and economic empire from the Persian Gulf to the whole hinterland of Persia: a cold war was in progress between the court at Teheran—which had recently established its suzerainty over Afghanistan and what was left of Baluchistan—and the British-Indian interests in the Persian Gulf; disturbances broke out in the domains of the Aga Khan (1841–2), the Chancellor, Haji Mirza Agassi, accusing him of playing the game of the English. The Aga Khan defended himself by force of arms, was defeated, and fled to the English at Bombay, followed by all his circle, who thus swelled the already considerable ranks of the 'Iranite' merchants established on that coast. The first Aga Khan was followed by the Aga Khan II (1881–85) and the Aga Khan III (1885–1957), Sir Sultan Mohammed.

With the assistance of the British in India, from 1842 onwards, the bourgeoisie resumed its anti-feudal campaign, to which it naturally gave a mystical flavour. On 11 June 1844 a 23-year-old member of this bourgeoisie, Ali Mohammed, declared himself to be the Lord's Anointed (the Bab), the

Messiah who was religiously awaited. Small tradesmen and craftsmen believed in him, more particularly in the very towns where the supporters of the former 'Divine Lord' lived. The court took objection to this, but the affair of the Messiah dragged on for six years, for he had protectors among the new nobility who were just emerging. His followers preached rebellion and there were armed uprisings. In the end the Bab was shot at Tauris on 6 July 1850, on the order of the Chancellor, Mirza Taqi (1845–51).

In his 'Holy Book' (*Beyan*, p. 155), this reformer bears his bourgeois ambitions well in mind, particularly his economic mission: he demands entire freedom for trading and the conclusion of agreements, and declares that it is lawful to charge interest on matured bills (usury). He also exhorts his middle-class followers to wear silk and jewels and to enjoy the luxuries discouraged by the Moslem religion (ibid. p. 162). He replaced the Islamic religious penances by fines paid into the community's funds, and instituted a 20 per cent tax on income from investments (the *Quint*). In fact this prophet—who was prompted, in taking up the pen, by bourgeois more experienced than himself who remained prudently in the background—was obviously attempting, not without success, to establish a middle class which, though still based on mysticism, would be better organized and more modern than that led by the Aga Khan at Bombay. Former Parsees and Jews joined his sect.

His successor, Beha (1850–92) came closer to this form of 'protestant' liberalism. Exiled from Persia (1852), he went to Istanbul, in the traces of the merchants belonging to his sect; but the Sublime Porte felt it safer to insist on his living at the little seaport of Acre (Akka), in Palestine (1868). His propaganda spread in Persia, and in the Persian 'colonies' of the Levant. During the patriarchate of his son, Abdul Beha (1892–1921), it spread to the U.S.A., making, in all, a few thousand bourgeois, grouped in branches strictly closed to outsiders.

At a distance from northern Islam and its feudal system, the Moslem middle class was also able to develop along the southern sea routes—the Persian Gulf, the Sea of Oman and the Indian Ocean—and did so whenever circumstances were auspicious. The bourgeois who lived along the Persian Gulf—known as Kharejians—had suffered a semi-eclipse as a result of the Portuguese invasions in the sixteenth century, but that experience had been a lesson to them. Once the Portuguese had been driven out of Ormuz (1621), the Kharejians recovered most of their former 'colonies' along the Arabian and East African coasts which the Portuguese had usurped for a time.

In the reign of Sayyid Said (1804–56), the Kharejian domains had two centres—Muscat, the capital, and Zanguebar (the island of Zanzibar), its colony. In the metropolitan region the feudal Government of Teheran gave the Kharejians (1797) a concession comprising the stretch of Persian coast opposite the peninsula of Oman, and in 1856 the agreement was extended, under British pressure, for a further twenty years (1856–76), so that the mainland territories included the coastal strips along both sides of the straits of Ormuz. The colonial portion extended from Zanzibar right along the African coast from Bab el Mandeb to the Mozambique Channel.

Merchant caravans travelled every year from the coastal bases into the interior of Africa to exchange Asian products for those of Africa. Religion and trade kept pace with each other, and the trade and civilization of the Persian Gulf penetrated to the African Great Lakes and the Congo. Mohammedanism reached the court of King Suna of Uganda (1833–60), whose successor, Mtesa (1860–84) was converted and adopted Islam as the State religion (1880). By the reign of Mwanga (1884–94), three provinces of Uganda had thus been entirely converted to the Moslem religion. The same success was achieved throughout the hinterland of East Africa. The old-established Kharejian bourgeoisie was extremely adaptable and adjusted itself to historical developments such as the cutting of the Suez Canal, the introduction of the telegraph, steamboats, British imperialism, Protestant and Catholic missions, and so forth. It coexisted and progressed.

By planting 4 million clove seedlings in the island of Zanzibar in the early nineteenth century, these merchant princes established a perpetual revenue for their descendants and retained control of the world trade in cloves. In 1854 the colony secured its autonomy, but continued to pay an annual tribute to its former metropolis. Thanks to a sagacity and flexibility born of long experience, the Moslem bourgeoisie, organized in its various groups, continued to expand even under the British flag. Its financial interests spread north and south to the sources of the Nile and the Congo, and east and west from Madagascar to the Cape. Its culture and its second language, Swahili—an inextricable mixture of the Kharejian dialect (an Arabic-Persian derived from the islands in the Persian Gulf) and the original Bantu dialect of Zanzibar, gradually spread through the eastern half of Africa. The other merchants—Hindu and Protestant, Parsee and Catholic—who came to trade in East Africa were obliged to learn it, as did all East African Negroes who needed to speak any language other than their own tribal dialect.

This long-established Moslem bourgeoisie made Zanzibar the intellectual centre of East Africa, where people went in order to study Swahili, and an economic clearing-house as well. For instance it was from Zanzibar that the whale-boats sailed on their annual voyage to the Antarctic. The Moslem bourgeoisie thus constituted almost the whole of the middle class which was interposed, in this region, between the Negro workers and the upper class of British bankers and naval personnel. Its experience and enterprise had no equivalent in northern Islam, where from the mid-nineteenth century onwards a middle class had grown up which was openly hostile to Islam.

2. CHANGES IN AESTHETICS AND RELIGION

Art and thought[16]

Sir William Jones of Calcutta, an orientalist in the service of the famous Governor-General Warren Hastings (1774–85), together with his pupil and successor Whitney, was already, in 1800, of the opinion that the Koranic alphabet should be replaced by the Latin. They urged the forcible introduction of 'Christian' letters. But the East India Company, whose interests were commercial rather than cultural, were quick to abandon any plan which would involve seriously alienating the Moslem clergy.

Fath-Ali Akhundov (1812–78), a Persian of Russia, developed Jones' thesis further when, soon after the Crimean War and the Indian Mutiny, in his Treatise on Writing (*Risala i Resmul-Khatt*) he agreed with the orientalist's criticism of the Koranic alphabet, but contented himself with suggesting the minor reform of inserting short vowels between the long vowels and consonants. Since this was very logical, it had no more success with the orientalists, who were attached to their own Western script, than with the nineteenth-century Moslems, wedded to the elegance of the Arabic characters. The root of the matter was a disinclination to exchange a centuries-old practice for a foreign one. Writing was in fact not purely a mechanical problem, but more a matter of psychology and art. More, it was a religious problem. Akhundov, having no success among the Persians in Teheran, put his proposals in 1863 in Istanbul. But Fuad Pasha (1814–69), the reformist Vizier, would not countenance the scheme.

Melkom Khan (1820–1908), editor and proprietor of the London-Persian journal *Qanun*, also thought he could carry out this reform. In 1884–5 he edited in a single volume, in characters of his own invention, the favourite writings of the three principal Moslem nations of that time: *The Turkish Proverbs* of Shinasi, the *100 Maxims* of Al-Gahizh, and the *Garden of Roses* of Sa'di, in order to attract the Persians, Turks and Egyptians all at the same time. To the Turkish, Egyptian and Persian viziers, who were all associated with the Great Mosque of Philanthropy, he confided the task of presenting the volume to the Sultan, the Khedive, and the Shah and warmly recommending it. The viziers did so without success. Only the Sultan Abdul Hamid II declared in the *Memoirs* that he favoured the Latin alphabet because being phonetically simple the Turkish language was easily adaptable to Roman letters.

In Egypt, the heart of the 'Arabic Renaissance', the Latin alphabet had not the slightest chance of success, for the Arabs are conservative in matters concerning their philological traditions, and the Arabic alphabet was perfectly suited to the peculiarities of phonetics, syntax and etymology of Arabic. In any case it was the language of the Koran, and it was not the place of a khedive or a caliph to wish to change the script.

It was not however for such practical reasons that in 1885 the Shah Nasir ud-Din, after briefly considering it, threw Melkom's book back at the feet of Emin ud-Dawleh, the vizier of Posts. The Shah and his Vizier were amateurs of fine Arabic calligraphy, as were all nineteenth-century Persians, for this art took the place of painting in the Near East, just as 'Persian composition' took the place of music. Melkom Khan, who was only on the fringe of Islam or of Persian culture, could scarcely succeed where twenty years earlier Feth-Ali Akhundov had failed in carrying through even the mildest reform.

The interpreters (*drogman* in Egyptian, *dilmandj* in Turkish) called upon to play such an important role between Islam and the West were simply *Ciceroni* of the Levant: Greeks, Armenians and Maltese, with an equally superficial knowledge of European languages and outlook and of the theological and literary classics of Islam. They spoke, in fact, only lingua franca (a corrupt form of Italian used on Levantine ships) and Turco, a hybrid and uninspired language. Both were still in use at the time of the Crimean War (1854-6) and it was mainly through their coarse medium that the ideas and thoughts of the West had to pass from English and French to Persian and Arabic. Naturally these ideas emerged practically unrecognizable.

When it was a matter of concrete things such as *inversion* (photography) or *rectangle* (bank-note), they finished by understanding what was meant, and the oddness of the words passed unnoticed; but in the case of abstractions or political or scientific theories, false analogies continually crept in. Older men reared in the traditional language of the Orient could not help smiling at this flood of incomprehensible words, but the younger generation, more interested in being modish and much less scholarly, adopted all the new expressions uncritically and they became a characteristic language of the *efendis alla franca*. In addition to 'translated' expressions, the *efendis alla franca*, after the Crimea, began to use a great many 'Frankish' words, slightly mispronounced but in most cases used in their Western sense.

In Persian literature of the end of the nineteenth century appeared two literary forms, unknown in the Moslem Orient and copied from European models—the philosophical novel and the comedy with a message. During the years 1863-6 a 'reformed' Persian (*babi*) of Istanbul, Sheikh Ahmed Ruhi, translated into Persian *Hajee Baba of Ispahan*, a novel satirical rather than critical, which had been written at the beginning of the century by a British consul. This man, James Morier, was a humorous writer who according to an account of the journal to England (1810-14) of a Persian student of the period, Mirza Salih, disliked the Persians. Sheikh Ahmed imposed on James Morier by adding offensive details which were not in the original. This novel was altogether new both in its material and in its direct English style and was widely distributed, judging by the numerous editions which appeared in Istanbul, Bombay and Cairo, since it was banned by the Persian censor. The same direct style of reportage appears in *The Seventy-two Sects*, the work of another reformed Persian from Istanbul, the other son-in-law of Subh-i-Azel. This account of a journey among religions was also written in

Istanbul in 1863 and was inspired by a piece of imaginary reportage which was found among the posthumous works of Bernardin de St. Pierre and is quite different from his other writings. In any case *The Seventy-two Sects* was no more than a fairly free Persian adaptation. (After the Crimea, under the title *A Café in Surata*, three other versions had appeared, one in Russian attributed to Tolstoy, a shortened one in Turkish and an Arabic one by the Egyptian Khayret Bey.) Aga Khan Kermani, the editor, had intended this novel as criticism of Persian religion and its sects, which it broadly caricatured rather than portrayed. In any case, these two works furnished the tone and style of the modern novel in the Moslem East.

Under Abdul Aziz (1861–76) comedy had already reached Istanbul, some French plays having been adapted for the Turkish stage. The adapters and actors were always Levantine, usually Armenians. From the *ville lumière* of Abd ul-Aziz comedy reached Teheran. Turkish plays could be easily adapted into Persian, and were often played in Azerian Turkish, a language midway between Ottoman Turkish and Persian. In Persian, the authors whose works had been published were Fath-Ali Akhundov (1812–78) and his colleague or rather master, Melkom (1820–1908).[17] Mention should also be made of the Qajar prince Haji Mohammed-Tahir (1825–98). Under the influence of his master Melkom, a student of Fine Arts, Muzayinu ud-Dawleh, on his return from Paris, set up in 1871 in the Royal Palace at Teheran (Ergh) a theatre seating 300 people, but it was closed when the Shah did not approve of the comedies played there. There were already in Teheran, however, secret theatres, stages built on trestles out of doors in parks or in the private houses of such influential citizens as Emin ud-Dawleh, the Vizier of Posts. The audiences were entirely composed of the discontented middle class and the plays were performed in great secrecy.

These satirical comedies were sometimes directed against the mullahs (*Mehemet Celebi*, the 'Reverend Mohammed', Vienna 1866) or against the Government (*Beqqal-bazi der Huzur*—'Jolly Wares for the Shah', about 1869). The authors admired Molière, but in fact they were fundamentally indebted for their philosophies to Beaumarchais and Voltaire; they knew nothing of the conventions of true comedy and leaned more to the vulgar style of contemporary clowns such as Kerim Shireyi, Ismail Bezzaz, etc. The bourgeoisie of that period had more taste for buffoonery than for true comedy. Neither the novels nor the comedies circulated much beyond a small group; the mass of the people, the Old Turks, continued to amuse themselves as they had done for centuries.

One of the surprising things about Islam in the nineteenth century is the change in their conception of history. The Persian Chronicle (*Nasikhu 't-Tevarikh*) written between 1840 and 1870 by the historian Sipihr, and much appreciated by Gobineau (1816–82), scarcely differed in its basic conception and method from the work of a Eusebius or a Bossuet. Sipihr regarded the Shi'ite Persians as the Chosen People and the Qajars as ruling by divine right. In this type of history, founded on so-called Chaldean astrology, where the finger of God appeared on every page to cure the wounds made by the Devil's claws, the historian concerned himself only with the marvellous—a comet, an epidemic, the emergence of a heresy, or the birth of a goat, with two heads, the murder of a king, illness of a religious leader, a great fire, etc.: a collection of events appearing like Acts of God, or determined by the movements of the Sphere of Human Destinies. Behind all this lay the determinism of the ancient inland peoples, superstitious observers of a sky which was almost always cloudless.

During the nineteenth century, European explorers worked their way through the East by the new methods. For the convenience of their Western customers, the shopkeepers in the bazaars, mostly Levantines, made it their business to conceal the curios obtained about 1800 from mosques, churches and synagogues. They also began to abstract 'curios' from the palaces. Bonaparte removed libraries and archives from the mosques of Cairo and carried off as many non-Moslem curios as possible, from scarabs to obelisks. During the wars of Greek Independence (1827–9) the British spared neither Doric capitals nor Attic drachmas. The Levantines set up markets for antiquities (atiqah) to satisfy the demand. Here and there were small factories producing forged antiques of all kinds. In an attempt to control this, Western museums bought the privilege of searching for antiques from Moslem princes. The latter were only too pleased to agree, stipulating only that precious stones and metals be reserved for themselves, and that tombs and other Islamic monuments should be left untouched. This last point must be remembered: the application of this method to Islam created the impression that the Moslems were either of the race of the Pharaohs (Egyptians), or the seed of Attila (Turks) or the breed of the Guebres (Persians).

Jean August Mariette (1821–81) and Gaston Maspero (1856–1916), directors of the Boulaq Museum in Cairo, taught their art to Ahmed Kemal pasha (1850–1922), an ex-Ottoman who finally became the leader of a 'pharaoh' school. Marcel-August Dieulafoy (1844–1920) and Jacques de Morgan (1857–1924), agents of the Louvre in Persia from 1881 onwards, began by influencing the Shiraz poet Mohammed-Nasir Furset who started Guebrism with his Açar-i Ajem (Monumenta Zoroastrica, Bombay 1896). This was a considerable work in which appeared, immediately after the death of Nasir ud-Din, the leitmotifs of Iranian neo-guebrism: illustrations of old Persian monuments, the Aryan source of Persian, Sanskrit, the Alma Mater of Aryan philology, the distrust of Moslem chronicles whose archaeological foundations were long unknown owing to lack of research into Mohammedan monuments. Thus, if we only consider Persia, the chronicles, living sources of the history of the kingdom, were being more and more abandoned and forgotten by the end of the nineteenth century; and twentieth-century Persia, even more cut off from its hereditary history, today vainly strives to understand a mute and fossilized past. Barely freed from astrology, history stumbled into a morass of geology. It was a fall from the sky into the depths of the earth, with no thought for the surface, the only intelligible and realistic part of history.

The gradual appearance of feminism is another unexpected part of nineteenth-century Islam. The medieval culture of Eurasia classed women with children as unable to bend bow or draw sword in their own defence. In China their feet were bound to keep them small; in Tibet their faces were blackened, and in Islam they were veiled. They were treated as defenceless, the 'weaker sex', and hidden behind walls to protect them from abduction and outrage. Conscious of their weakness, women accepted the idea that this was the price of civilization. In the Persia of Shah Nasir ud-Din (1848–96) the poetess Tahira was executed in 1851 after undergoing terrible tortures. 'One cuts the throat of a crowing hen', a Greek author makes Darius' Persians say. Even the Shah's wives, if by any chance they had managed to learn to read and write, concealed the fact carefully, as something forbidden. However, the Shah's extensive travels in Europe, of which he wrote an account, made some slight change in his opinion. The travels of Sultan Abd ul-Aziz and Khedive Ismail about the same time had similar results. Reform crept in imperceptibly. The Shah's daughter, the future Mme Majd ud-Dawleh, acted as secretary to her royal father. She wrote quickly—having perhaps learned shorthand—and could write down the romantic novels which a titled story-teller told from behind a screen to amuse the ladies. These novels were *Zerrin-Melik* and *Emir Arslan*, edited and re-edited for the pleasure of women and children. Naturally Mme Majd ud-Dawleh did not allow her name to be made public on account of possible scandal, but the rumour spread and everyone knew that for the first time a Persian princess had published novels. Mu'ayyirul Memalik had good reason to believe that the odalisques and concubines considered illiterate by the Shah secretly kept a diary and noted down the idle remarks he made in the intimacy of the harem, which they passed on to the leaders of the opposition, who in their turn told the foreign consuls. The shorthand adapted for Turkish in the reign of Abd ul-Aziz (1861–76) had also been adapted to Persian, and it was used from the inception of the Dar ul-Funun College (1851) and the Great Mosque of Philanthropy (c.1857). This Turco-Persian shorthand, like the Russian, was developed more from the German than the French type.

Another distinguished lady, Mme I'timadu's-seltena (d.1913), whose husband was Vizier of science and first French interpreter to the Shah (replacing Melkom Khan), was the first woman scholar in Teheran. She had a fine collection of Persian and Arabic works which she left to the Rezewiyeh Library of Mesh'hed and was part-author of 'Beautiful Souls' (*Khayirat-i Hisan*), a collection of biographies of famous and virtuous Moslem ladies printed in Teheran between 1887 and 1890 in three volumes and at the time attributed to her husband. In fact the book was Ottoman and the original was the work of Mehemet Zihni, a young Turkish writer, but Mme I'timad completed it, adding biographies of the 'Khanoms' of Teheran, wives and daughters of nineteenth-century Qajars or their viziers.

The assassination of the Shah in 1896 was a blow to the life of the harem. This had comprised some fifty sultanas, each having her own income, her carriage, her apartments and her eunuchs. The succeeding Shah Muzaffer ud-Din (1896–1907) had no harem. Moreover, in order to marry his daughter to Mohsen, the son of Ali Emin ud-Dawleh, now grand vizier, he insisted that his future son-in-law should repudiate his first wife (Bibi Khanom, daughter of Mushir ud-Dawleh, a diplomat and friend of his father). This was done and Mme Fakhr ud-Dawleh (d.1955), model for the new women of Teheran and with a considerable fortune, never had any official rival throughout her married life (1898–1955). This gave her almost as much authority as her great wealth. From 1898 onwards, middle-class women began to follow her example.

In the nineteenth century, the mystical and subjective classical painting of Moslem Persia—the so-called *miniature* which sometimes covered several square yards!—could no longer compete against the encroachment of the objective and personal style of the West. This style had been rapidly popularized during the nineteenth century by the multiplication of examples of lithograph, chromograph and other processes on wood, copper and zinc, whereas the Oriental tradition of painting was the jealously guarded possession of a few masters, its rare examples being hidden in the depths of treasure houses. The eclipse of the *miniature* by cheap engraving is another aspect of the retreat of aristocratic continental culture before the prodigality of Western industrial democracy.

In Teheran about 1900 the doyen of painting was Kemal ul-Mulk (Mohammed of Kashan, 1862–1930) a man of 38. He was a member of a family of miniaturists (the Ghaffari), but his father had abandoned miniature to copy English and French chromographs depicting princes, in hussar's jackets complete with epaulettes and braid, standing in truculent attitudes, or viziers in Persian dress enthroned in European arm-chairs, all wearing astrakhan hats and surrounded by an English landscape treated in Western style and lighted to give relief and perspective. By 1851, Abu Turab Ghaffar and Mirza Ismail Jelayir began drawing in pencil and ink with a view to reproduction as lithographs in school-books, and later in the illustrated journals of Teheran, which were copied from Western models. The popularization of lithography for the reproduction of works of art brought about at the same time the debasement of calligraphy and classical drawing, which was impossible to carry out in ink.

During his travels in Europe, the Shah acquired a taste for Western furniture, pictures and statues. He sent two students to Paris. One, the *ustad* Mohammed Ali, studied furniture-making in the Faubourg St. Antoine and on his return to Teheran set up a studio and took orders for the royal palaces. Kemal ul-Mulk studied painting in Paris under Fantin-Latour

(1836–1904) and sculpture under Rodin. He was the first to take up sculpture, and the bronze statue of the Shah on horseback, still to be seen in the Bagh-i-Shah Park in 1925, is attributable to him, as are several bronzes representing wild animals such as stags, ibex, etc. But in oil painting he had had predecessors in Muzayyin ud-Dawleh, who studied fine arts in Paris (1858–77), and the *ustad* Behram, who decorated the Pavilion of Sleep in the Ergh at Teheran. As court painter, Kemal ul-Mulk left mostly portraits of princes, the only sitters possible at that time. Neither he nor any other modern Persian painter had the desire or the audacity to treat imaginary, amusing or religious subjects: nor did they dare, except occasionally, to paint portraits of women, or sacred scenes, although the miniaturists had done so before them. Consequently modern painting did not become a popular art, even when political influence gained Kemal ul-Mulk official recognition and permission to start an Academy of Fine Arts in 1906. To be taken up and enjoyed by the mass of the people, this style of painting would have had to use subjects dear and familiar to Persian Moslems instead of slavishly imitating European subjects, and the painters would have had to think and feel in an Oriental rather than a Western manner. The most successful of Kemal ul-Mulk's imaginative paintings, for instance his 'Saqqa' (Religious Beggar selling Iced Water) was at best a photographic work and possessed no Moslem feeling. His sculpture had worse faults. His 'Gach-kub' (Plaster-crusher) is a naked Hercules who has taken the pestle for the club, and in spite of its subject, this Michelangelo-type statue had nothing which recalls a Persian crusher of plaster. This pseudo-Renaissance sculpture was even less adapted to Islam and remained something artificial and foreign, the more so as the doors of the mosque were firmly closed to it.

What has been said about painting is equally true of the artless music of the Moslems, without large instruments or notation, linked with mysticism, its technique that of a craft passed from one to another. This was swamped in the nineteenth century by the Occidental music which was linked with applied physics, mechanizing the voice and remodelling hearing to achieve the heights and depths where voice and ear exceed their range. About 1890 an official school of Western music flourished in Teheran and middle-class hearers became as accustomed to Western tunes from Istanbul and Baku as to the 'Theatre' of Islamic Mysteries (the Takiyeh-i-Dewlet).

It was through military reforms that Western music appeared in Persia. After a few brief experiments with Western military music about 1830, the Shah ordered Mukhber ud-Dawleh to found the Teheran School of Music (Medressah-yi Muzik) in 1868–9. A French officer, Lemaire, was put in charge of it and remained in the Persian service until his death. There were only eleven pupils in fifteen years (1868–83) and instruction was given on wind instruments only. Another French master, Duval, taught the violin for two years only. Lemaire died towards the end of the century and instruction ceased, but one of his pupils, a Persian cossack named Gulam-Reza

Minbashiyan, finished his studies in St Petersburg (1907–12). When he returned to Teheran in 1913 he started a new basic course in a reorganized School of Music (1914), similar to the old one except that the son of the director, Nasrollah Minbashiyan, taught the piano. By Gulam-Reza Minbashiyan's death in 1928, several classes of students had graduated, all soldiers and all experts in martial music. For the final exmination each student had to compose a march and conduct its performance by a band.

Oriental musical scales did not possess the modulations introduced in the West during the eighteenth century and brought to perfection by the piano in the early nineteenth century. But wind instruments, whose scale was said to be derived from Pythagoras, had nothing to shock Oriental ears. At the time of his entry into Cairo, Bonaparte ordered several pieces of classical music to be played—probably on the harpsichord—in order to please the 'Arabs' (Turks), who were disagreeably surprised; when the band played marches, however, they were pleased. 'In that case,' said the future Emperor, 'play them *Malborough s'en va t'en guerre*—it's all they are fit for.' As often happens in contacts between different cultures, this remark was only a half-truth. What displeased the Turks were the modulations of the harpsichord, which were not produced by wind instruments or violins. It was owing to these that Europeans had the impression that Asians used quarter-tones, and Asians had exactly the same impression when hearing the piano for the first time. In fact the idea of quarters and smaller fractions of tones came from the speculations of Greek philosophers, since the Greeks, unlike the Chinese who started with the flute—so like the human voice—began with monochords which are infinitely divisible.

What pleased the Persians most was undoubtedly what Mirza Salih (*Travels*, 1815) saw for the first time in Moscow: the orchestra. He described orchestration as *Destebend-i Musici*, using the old word *destebend* (rondo, farandole) to give an idea of the movement of the ensemble. In instrumental music, an orchestra presupposed the existence of a system of music notation. But in music as in other things in the Orient, musical theory—Greek in origin, and practice—of Chinese origin, were never co-ordinated into a single technique, and theory and practice remained apart. Borrowing a system of notation would have been a great advance, if the notes had been written from right to left in the Koranic manner so that the words could be written down as well. The old obstacle arose, however, of Arabic figures, known in Persia since the fifth century but not popular because they were read from left to right, in contrast to the script.

Western musical notation was in the same situation, and from 1868 it has not passed beyond the circle of the initiated.

Another problem, that of harmony, was solved by 1913/14 by Gulam-Reza Minbashiyan (d.1928), who harmonized several *rengs* and *peshderameds*, but he greatly scandalized the Asian classicists.

The same may be said of musical time: that of the march, two beats, was universal and did not shock Persian ears, but the more complex Western pieces, accented in a seemingly barbarous manner, had nothing in common with the Asiatic 'cycles' (*daours*) which went back to the rhythm of Chinese poetry, in absolutely symmetrical rhythms, but often so complicated that it required a whole section to tap out the measure, sometimes in such a manner as to drown the sound of the stringed instruments. Here as in painting, the schematic nature of continental music—the note buried in the rhythm—was in complete contrast to the Western style in which the note appears unadorned against its harmonic background. Apart from the question of the natural sound of wind instruments, the Persians found European march tunes not unpleasing because of the percussion which accompanied them. Fundamentally this was an Asiatic form returning from a long journey through the West, enhanced with a system of notation. No one was shocked in 1870 to hear the band play some European march during the Persian religious mysteries.

New manifestation of faith

As examples of the nineteenth-century Moslem revival, the cases of Wahabism in Arabia and Shi'ah in Persia may be cited.

Wahabism

The founder of Wahabism,[18,19] Mohammed ibn al-Wahab (1703–92), was a member of the strict Hanbelite sect (madhab) which derived from Ahmed Ibn Hanbel (780–855), and whose doctrine, since the time of Caliph Harun al-Raschid, represented the extreme right of Islam. The early life of Ibn Abd al-Wahab was therefore influenced by extremist literature. The decadence and impotence of the Ottoman Empire in the eighteenth century led Ibn Abd al-Wahab to take part in politics. According to him, the decadence of Islam was due to the decline of authority—in fact to the absence of that strictness so dear to Ahmed Ibn Hanbel and his party. To revive Islam, Wahab contended, one must revert to the spartan régime of earlier times, to the ox-sinews (*derra*), the cadi's sabre, stoning, to complete theocratic rule. From its strict religious beginnings, Mohammedan law had become 'laicized' in the thirteenth century by the Mongols, until finally sixteenth-century Turks had seized the Government and the police and abolished the Arab caliphate. Although among the Arabs from the seventh to the fifteenth century the two had been closely bound up with one another, during the eighteenth century Arab Mohammedanism became simply a kind of religion. The cadis, who were responsible to Allah alone, did not possess political authority in the Arab villages. Thus, in the Arabian provinces of the Ottoman Empire, from the sixteenth century onwards, the Turkish pasha took over the ancient functions of the Arab cadi. The Arab cadis had not even retained their old religious importance, since among the Turks religion was the province of the dervishes. The arrival and spread of 'Sufism' paralleled the arrival and triumph of the Turks; even in the Arab provinces of the Ottoman Empire, the cadi or imam who wished to retain some religious influence was obliged to become a convert to Sufism, that is, the Turkish brand of Mohammedanism.

Mohammed ibn Abd al-Wahab was a true-bred Arab from the Persian Gulf, and far from adapting himself to the dervishes, he set out to oppose them. He was able to do this because he lived in the Arabian desert on the skirts of Ottoman Iraq, where the climate was so repellent that only its natives could bear it. The military weakness of the Ottomans at the end of the eighteenth century allowed this desert religion to encroach on the more cultivated provinces, to cover them like the *simoom* and spread towards Damascus, Palestine and the Hedjaz.

Ottoman Sufism is connected with the tombs of saints: Wahabism condemned this cult of the saints and preached the destruction of mausoleums—even those of the Friends of the Prophet, and that of the Prophet himself! Sufism was strongly influenced by Turko-Persian art and decorated its mosques with carpets, faience, wood-carvings, *mihrab*, minarets and chandeliers, while Wahabism demanded the destruction of all these ornaments and a return to the bare-walled huts of primitive Arabia. It condemned in its entirety the Mohammedan civilization of the Turks and Persians and preferred the primitive and simple life of the Bedouin. The forty strokes with an ox-sinew, prescribed by Mohammed ibn Abd al-Wahab as punishment for smoking the *narghileh* was indeed a death-warrant for every non-Bedouin Moslem, an excommunication of all Turks and Persians.

Wahabism, which had great appeal for the Bedouins, converted a Bedouin chief named Saud who became the patron of Mohammed ibn Abd el-Wahab, and this was the origin of Saudi Arabia, a small 'state' whose capital was the tiny oasis of Darija. From here Saud, Ibn Saud I (1745–1803) and Ibn Saud II (1803–14) launched fanatical attacks on the Persians of Kerbela (1801), on caravans of Persian pilgrims (1785, etc.) and on the Turks of Baghdad, Damascus, Medina and Mecca itself (1822). The Persians were busy in the Caucasus (1779–1834) and preoccupied with quarrels between church and state; the Ottomans were involved in wars against the Russians in the Crimea, at Odessa, then against the Janissaries, the Greeks, the English and even the French, so that only Ibrahim, the son of Mohammed-Ali, encamped in Syria, had any opportunity to fight the Wahabites. Held in check by Sultan Abd ul-Mejid (1839–61) the Wahabites were three-parts annihilated under Abd ul-Aziz (1861–77) who finally succeeded in retaking all the maritime fringe of Arabia except Oman and Aden, where the British had established protectorates.

The extreme climate of the region, the almost total lack of water and the absence of known tracks prevented the Turkish troops from conquering the central desert of Arabia, where two small Wahabite tribes, Ha'il and er-Riad, kept up a continuous feud throughout the second half of the nineteenth century. On one occasion (1884–97) Ha'il heavily defeated er-Riad. In 1901, the heir of the er-Riad tribe, Ibn Saud the Great, reconquered the ancestral oasis, restored the Wahabite state in 1904 and mastered Ha'il (1921).

Shi'ah

At the end of the eighteenth century another Mohammedan reformer arose, at the other extreme of Islam—the Shi'ite reformer (*mujeddid*) Mohammed Baqir Behbahoni (1707–96) who was almost the contemporary of Mohammed ibn Abd al-Wahab. Behbahoni founded the school of rationalists (Osuliyya) which opposed the traditionalists (*Akhbarriya*). To understand Behbahoni's reformation, the nature of Shi'ah must be recalled.

Alongside the Arab chiefs who took the title of 'suppliants' (Khelifa, caliphs) there was also a spiritual inheritance, a 'divine' descent both of blood and of testament, belonging to the heirs of Mohammed, by his daughter and his cousin, son-in-law and executor Ali I, who because of their spiritual qualities were called *imams*, religious leaders. Those who acquired the political succession to Mohammed by usurpation were naturally hostile to his actual descendants, the Impeccable (Ma'sums) Imams, the guardians of the prophet's spiritual inheritance. One after another they were murdered, imprisoned or poisoned until the last of the race, Mohammed IV, then a child of five, was by order of the Caliph el-Mu'temid thrown down the ventilation shaft of an underground room (*serdab*) in Samerra (Iraq) in 873/4. But the Shi'ites have never ceased to keep watch over the shaft where their Imam disappeared—their *Mahdi* or Messiah whose return they await. He was the twelfth of Mohammed's successors. Excluded from orthodox Islam by the caliphs, the religion of the Impeccable Imams developed on the fringe of political events. It confined itself to Mohammed's spiritual doctrines. The Shi'ah or Imam doctrine had adherents in Iraq and in the Iranian countries which were much visited by the Imams and their disciples.

As a universal doctrine of salvation for the human soul, Shi'ah was not a national sect but appealed to Moslems of all races—Arabs, Turks, Persians, Indians and Africans. However, since the Imams mostly taught in Iraq and Persia, and their tombs and those of their disciples were in these countries, there were always more Shi'ites there than elsewhere in Islam. For this reason alone Shi'ah found itself situated in the geographical centre of Islam.

The tradition (Akhbars) or 'news' of the Impeccable Imams, as well as their theological teachings, were not codified until the second half of the tenth century, one of the most brilliant epochs of Islam. The characteristics of this golden age, freedom of thought, positivism, etc., continued to be attributed to Shi'ah and made of it a sort of 'Renaissance heresy'.

Thus Shi'ah, in spite of its basis in asceticism and puritanism, always had a leaning towards philosophy and the sciences, arts and letters, the old schooling of its youth. The obverse of this picture was the continuing political weakness of Shi'ah, since puritans, scholars and artists, always seeking their ideal world, did not concern themselves with the frivolous and unfeeling world about them.

It was at this point that Mohammed-Baqir Behbahoni (1707–96) began his reforms during the second half of the eighteenth century, leaving Ispahan and its magnificent mosques rich with faience for the true source of Shi'ah at Kerbela in Iraq, a simple collection of houses round the tomb of the Imam Hussein. He rejected too the mass of sacred stories, the whole theological equipment of the Historicalism (*Akhbariyya*) of the seventeenth century for the rational principles (*Osul*) of the tenth. This was a genuine return to the sources, a rebirth of Shi'ism. The Reforms (*Tejdid*) however, far from being supported by the Persian Shahs, were strongly opposed, as much by the nineteenth-century officials such as Mirza Mohammed Neishaburi (1764–1817) a strict 'Akhbarist', as by the Qajar shahs who were systematically hostile to the independence of Shi'ah. Nevertheless, the personality of Behbahoni and the success of his Osulist school at Kerbela were such that even the small school of Sheikh Yussuf Bahreini (1695–1774), an attempt at compromise between *Osul* (rational principles) and *Akhbar* (sacred legends), was abandoned. The murder of Neishaburi in 1817, the expulsion of the doctors from Teheran in 1829 and the continuing hostility of the Qajars only served to increase the reputation of the Osulist school of Kerbela, brilliantly represented during the nineteenth century by its great teachers Mohammed-Hassan Najefi (d. 1851), Mohammed-Hassan Shirazi (1815–94) and Mohammed-Kazhim Khorasani (1835–1911) who followed one another as leaders of the Shi'ite world.

From the second half of the eighteenth century Shi'ah once more became, through Behbahoni and his followers, a purely democratic organization, and its adherents found themselves free to choose as spiritual director the doctor (*mujtehid*) whom they preferred, and the doctors were in their turn free to choose as their leader the one amongst them whom they most respected. In this way Shi'ah gave a practical example of its doctrine of free will (*ikhtiyar*), i.e. that man is responsible (*mukella*) for his own salvation and that he is master of his own actions (*mukhtar*), his happiness or misfortune. This Shi'ite teaching of the tenth century, reappearing in the nineteenth, was directly opposed to the usual teaching of Islam, the only form known in the Mediterranean countries, in which man is the slave (*abd*) of God, a creature whose actions he predetermines (*mektub*). For the Shi'ites Mohammed taught free will, and the well-known fatalism of the 'Turks' or Mediterranean Moslems was, like that of the Greeks and Romans, simply a pagan survival.

The freedom preached and put into practice by Shi'ah was the more unwelcome to the nineteenth century Persian rulers in that Shi'ah regarded them as tyrants and usurpers (*zhelema*), forbade its adherents to serve the kings, and considered taxation and the pensions and rewards offered by rulers as plain theft. Anxious to establish its legitimate right to rule in Persia, the Qajar line were exasperated and annoyed to find themselves thus practically excommunicated. The war between religion and the throne waxed sometimes hot, sometimes cold.

Shi'ah was only able to resist the temporal power of the Persian state by the fact that its headquarters was outside the Persian kingdom, in Ottoman Iraq, where the Ottoman Government, hostile to the Qajar shahs and well aware that since 1736 and more particularly since 1779, Shi'ah was no longer the political tool of Persia, were glad to tolerate the Shi'ites. Western ideas of reform and freedom which filtered into Turkey were also welcomed by the Shi'ite doctors in Ottoman Iraq and were defended by their leaders Mohammed-Hassan Shirazi and his successor Mohammed-Kazhim Khorassani. In 1890 the former telegraphed a few words forbidding Shi'ites to smoke, and this religious command was so scrupulously obeyed that in the spring of 1892 the Shah of Persia found himself compelled to cancel the concession granted on 21 March 1890 for £15,000 to the second baron Julius von Reuter of the Persian tobacco monopoly. In fact on 5 April 1892 the Shah had to agree to pay £500,000 damages for breach of contract. The second heavy blow to the Qajar shahs was the *fetwa* put out in 1906 by Mohammed-Kazhim Khorassani in favour of constitutional government, which was enough to break all the resistance of the reactionaries. Thus in Persia it was religion which undermined the royal power by its spiritual influence.

If the history of Shi'ah before, during and after the nineteenth century shows its divorce from politics, and its inability to acquire temporal power without betraying or denying its puritan origins, this same history illustrates its continual ascendancy in the realm of ideas, arts, letters and science.

In art, as in thought, Shi'ah never failed to produce first-class men, and to show great power of revival—this fecundity was due to the fact that, irrespective of place or time, it produced its distinctive type of mind and background. In the nineteenth century Shi'ah, which had never ceased to encourage philosophy, produced Haji Mulla Hadi Sabzewari (1797–1872), a follower of the great Mulla Sedra, by way of the Shi'ite philosophers of the eighteenth century, Mulla Isma'il and Mulla Ali Nuri. Sabzewari published his *System* (*Menzhuma*) in 1824 and added a commentary (*Sharh-i Menzhuma*) in 1845. The number of editions of this work indicates the interest of Shi'ites in his philosophy. His larger work, *The Secrets of Wisdom* (*Asrar*) was printed in two volumes (Teheran, 1869 and 1905) and his commentary on *The Four Latitudes of the Soul* of Mulla Sedra was published in 1904 in Teheran in four splendid volumes. It may be recalled that Avicenna, the greatest Arab philosopher of the eleventh century, whose ideas were famous at one time among both Moslems and Latins, was a Shi'ite. The Shi'ites themselves never ceased to study *their* philosopher, as is shown by the *editio princeps* of his *Physics of the Shifa* in Teheran in 1885–7, with a commentary by the famous seventeenth-century Mulla Sedra. Another remarkable fact is that, with very few exceptions, all the manuscripts of these Arabic philosophers have been copied from the tenth century to the present day by Shi'ite scribes for their co-religionists.

Shi'ah alone of all the Mohammedan sects possessed a dramatic tradition. Islam in general is rich in burlesques, farces, a kind of Guignol, in small-scale comedy and comic types, but only Shi'ah had a drama which could stir the emotions of its audience. An agent of the East India Company, William Franklin, was present at some of these performances in Shiraz about 1770. The play (*Waqi'ah*) was performed in a square theatre called Tekiya; the stage, also square and raised, was in the centre of the theatre, and round it, separating it from the audience, was a gangway representing the street, where the actors could move about on horseback. A second stage for the actors and extras who took the parts of princes and their courts was up on the Tekiya, like a Western stage. Entry to the theatre was free. A huge canopy covered the court of the Tekiya in place of a ceiling. All round the theatre were rows of boxes whose proprietors furnished them with carpets, chandeliers, potted plants and mirrors, but the majority of people watched from the pit or gallery. The plays were evidently rhymed in the popular language of the region, sometimes in Turki, sometimes Urdu, at other times in the Arabic of Iraq, or in some Persian dialect; they were in no way literary works, especially not Persian literary works, but consisted of songs in special metres and scales, chants in which the language—whether Turkish, Iraqi, Hindi or Persian—was of no consequence.

In the nineteenth century, by the goodwill of the Qajar shahs, Teheran was one of the vital centres of this form of drama. The authors, who were anonymous, were the dervishes of the Ne'meti Order founded in the fifteenth century by Shah Ne'metullah. In fact it was one of them, Nur-Ali-Shah of Tebes (d. 1797) who first turned into verse the famous *Burial Garden of the Martyrs* (*Rawzet-ush-Shuheda*) of the fifteenth-century Mulla Hussein Khashifi, a Shi'ite 'evangelist'. King Aqa-Mohammed (1779–97) had close ties with Nur-Ali-Shah, for the Qajars were all followers of the Ne'meti Order. Aqa-Mohammed in a letter to his 'confessor' Nur-Ali-Shah asked the latter to establish a Tekiya in every Shi'ite town, although this was not accomplished without opposition. The heir to the throne, until then called Baba Khan, took on his accession in 1797 the mystic Ne'meti title of Feth-Ali-Shah. During his reign (1797–1834) the versification of the *Rawzet* was completed by two Ne'meti dervishes, Rawneq-Ali-Shah (d. 1810) and Nizam-Ali-Shah (d. 1826). Rahmet-Ali-Shah (1793–1861) was on the best of terms with his penitent king Mohammed II (1835–48) of the Qajar dynasty, while the dervishes Munewwir-Ali (1809–83) and Sefi-Ali (1835–99) had the same influence with the succeeding rulers, Nasir ud-Din (1848–96) and Muzaffer ud-Din (1896–1907).

Although apparently anonymous, the texts brought back from Teheran by Alexander Chodzko in the reign of Feth-Ali-Shah (1797–1834) can be attributed to one or other of the Ne'meti dervishes of the time. These dramas were in fact such that the words, verse or prose could be in Turkish, Parsee (Persian) or any other tongue, but the songs and music never varied. The Tekiya-i Dewlet (State Theatre) in Teheran was the most opulent of these establishments, of which there were many in Shi'ite towns. The first performances were given there about 1849 and the last in 1909.

About 1850, however, in the golden age, 'theatre managers' (*ta'ziyeh-gherdan*) such as Mirza Mohammed-Taqi and his son Mu-in-ul-Buka, or the two Bekhtiyari, father and son, Seyid Ahmed and Seyid Abd-ul-Baqi, collected eighteenth-century and perhaps seventeenth-century tunes, searched unceasingly through the Shi'ite world for the best basses (*shimr-khôn*), tenors (*imam-khôn*) and, what was most difficult in view of the ban on actresses, the few men who could sing contralto or soprano (*zeineb-khôn*). Horsemen always escorted, from his village of Saveh, Haji Mulla Hussein Zeredi, the soprano who sang the part of Zeineb, Imam Hussein's sister. Choirs of small girls and boys, the girls as fairies (*paris*), the boys as angels (*ferishtehs*) grouped by voice, formed the background of these operas from start to finish.

The official snobbery and anti-clericalism of the twentieth century allowed all these treasures to seep away into the depths of the provinces. Even the opera *Koeroghlu*, so popular in Iran in the eighteenth and nineteenth centuries, which was translated into English by Alexander Chodzko, suffered the same fate—both words and music—although its subject, loyalty to the Shah Abbas II (1641–66), could hardly be called religious. During the nineteenth century *Koeroghlu* was played at court in Teheran; in the twentieth it is barely possible to find a few *Koerughlu khôn* (*Koerughlu* singers), on the northern borders of Iran.

3. POLITICAL AND SOCIAL EVOLUTION

The recognized states:
Persia[20]

Few statistics exist for Persia, and those only for the later decades of the nineteenth century. Customs figures for the last thirty years show that by 1900 48 per cent of Persia's imports consisted of European cotton cloth, a further 47 per cent was made up of tea and sugar, and the remaining 5 per cent a mixture of goods, including silver. The majority of the people who, in 1800, wore Indian cottons or Persian materials now dressed in cottons imported from Europe. Tea and sugar catered for the tastes of the new Persian middle classes, who had adopted the habit from the English after their defeat in 1857. Sugared tea began to rival the age-old coarse salted tobacco in *narghilehs* (pipes) as a luxury for the people. In the years preceding the Crimean War the words *samovar* and *astakan* (tea-glass) were adopted from the Russian. Tea brought by caravan from China (called Moscow tea) was, however, rapidly giving way to tea from Assam (called Calcutta tea);

stearine candles, which also began to be imported after the Crimean War, were by 1905 yielding place to lamps burning paraffin from Baku. Bohemian lustres and candelabras disappeared from the houses of the rich and were replaced by lamps; by 1905 these were quite common in the towns and were spreading to the countryside taking the place of the traditional castor-oil lamps.

Persia had, of course, to pay for all these luxuries, and from about 1858, in addition to exporting her famous carpets, she exported two new raw materials: firstly, raw cotton, to meet the English demand, and secondly, poppies for opium. By 1881 Persia was already exporting nearly 500 tons of this subtle poison. This was a remarkable achievement if one considers that it was only in 1857-8 (after the defeat of Persia) that the Ispahan peasants were taught, at a model farm, the Anglo-Indian art of rolling the poppy-juice in the standard shape of batons. It was thanks to this commercial technique that the export of opium passed from 30 cases in 1858 to 3,000 cases in 1885. From that date exports rose annually, and in the same way the pernicious habit of opium-smoking became diffused throughout Persia.

The cultivation of cotton and opium-poppies, while enriching one class of the people, began to replace the growth of foodstuffs: cotton was grown instead of rice and poppies instead of wheat. This partially accounts for the numerous serious famines which ravaged the country between 1860 and 1882. According to German travellers, the famine of 1869-72 alone killed one in four of the inhabitants (about 1·5 million men). Thenceforward, for the first time in her history, Persia began to import cereals and flour.

In 1905, 49 per cent of Persia's trade was with Russia, 35 per cent with England, and only 16 per cent with the rest of the world. With the growth of a mercantile middle class exporting raw materials, towns expanded in North Persia; after the October Revolution in Russia their growth ceased abruptly. The south Persian towns, despite their situation on ice-free seas, were in a state of decay from 1857 onwards; at Abbassi and Bushire whole bazaar quarters had been deserted by the shopkeepers. This was due to the superior organization of the English who skimmed the best of the trade from the Persian Gulf. The *cordon sanitaire* set up in 1870 to protect Persia and Europe from cholera was also a handicap to the Persian traders. By the treaty of 1857 with its 'most favoured nation' clause, the English were able to regulate the exchanges.

By 1900, too, the immense gulf between the mass of the people and the small ruling middle class was very apparent. The former worked long hours for a few yards of cotton and a cup of tea—both of these being heavily taxed. The usurers, who were generally Jews or recent converts to Islam, lent money at 70 per cent; by 1900 they had become owners of large amounts of rural and urban property, either acquired from the small proprietors or 'inherited' from indebted feudal landlords. The rural population, engulfed in debt, were eventually forced to cultivate cotton or opium under threat of the whip.

The revolution of 1906, which brought into power middle-class people born since the 1858–81 famines, did not yield the expected benefits. On the contrary, it aggravated the lot of the people, 'democratically' represented in 'parliament' by their employers.

The formation of the kingdom of Afghanistan

Under Ahmad Shah, in the eighteenth century, Afghanistan had been a mere confederation of tribes, each of which retained full sovereignty within its own borders; but Dost-Mohammed, taking the proto-monarchical policy of Teheran as his model, intervened repeatedly in the internal affairs of all the clans, and thus built up a kind of central authority. If he had imitated Teheran in every respect, he would also have ensured the survival of his state by settling the question of the succession; this he unfortunately neglected to do, and at his death (1863) his heirs began a violent war of succession. Aware of this situation, the British seized the opportunity to invade Iran by the 'hot road' via Baluchistan. They recognized the administrative authority of Teheran over western Seistan (1873) and west Baluchistan, and thus obtained a free hand in the eastern part of the plateau, where they fought a victorious campaign against the Afghan tribes of Kandahar (1878–80). Left alone, the Amir Sher Ali and Yakub Khan abandoned their capital, Kabul, to the British.[21]

Adb ur-Rahman (1880–1901), an elderly man rendered docile by many years as a refugee in India, recognized the 'Kaisr-i-Hind' as his overlord instead of the Shahan-Shah of Teheran, whose position had by that time considerably declined. The English equipped him with up-to-date artillery, and let him lay waste (1891–2) the border region of Herat, whose people were Moslems of the same creed as those of Teheran. In his memoirs Abd ur-Rahman, an enlightened despot, confesses himself ashamed of conducting a religious war of this type. But he also waged a war to the death against his fellow-countrymen of Kandahar whose social and military power was a factor of unrest. But Abd ur-Rahman was rewarded; to forestall the threat of a Russian advance south of the Amu Darya, the English helped to occupy the *pamir* of Vakhan—in which region he was, as the crow flies, a neighbour of the Chinese—and the district of Kafiristan (1896), which made him the neighbour of Little Tibet and Kashmir.[22]

Turkey

In Jerusalem, in the Christian holy places, the Ottoman rulers held the balance between the various Christian nations. At the same time that the Europeans believed that they could decide the life or death of Turkey, the rulers of Istanbul felt themselves the arbiters of Christendom—a heterogeneous world ever on the alert, and very much divided against itself. The monuments in Istanbul show that the Turks of the nineteenth century were convinced of their moral superiority over the various champions of Europe.

Far from feeling 'sick', they believed themselves full of strength. The least Anatolian peasant thought himself superior to a Greek or Armenian millionaire, for he lived in a world of sentiment and dreams. For him, the *padishah* was the ideal Turk; the legitimate sovereign, protected by heaven. As for the Ottoman ruler, when he modernized his state he had no intention of changing anything of the sacrosanct constitution of the Empire. His reforms were no more than *tenzimat-i-askierie*—'military reorganization', the creation of an army, and of a body of civil servants in the modern style. In many respects the work of the Sultan Mahmud II (1808–39) resembled that of Peter the Great. His destruction of the Janissaries, a feudal militia, and their replacement by the *nizam-i-djedid* or Napoleonic troops strongly resembles the suppression of the *Strelitzy* by the Tsar, who substituted an army based on that of Charles XII. Abd ul-Medjid (1839–61), who succeeded his father, issued the imperial edict of Gulhane, an administrative charter which went much further towards reform than the work of Catherine the Great.

This state of affairs lasted until the Suez Canal was built, an epoch-making event in the history of the nineteenth century. England took on an importance equal to the tonnage of her shipping and finally settled in Egypt, thereby becoming a great threat to Turkey. The Sultan Abd ul-Hamid II (1876–1909), however, was neither less able nor less energetic than his famous predecessors. Like them, he desired no more than to consolidate his throne by military and administrative reforms.[23] A glance at the building of Istanbul would show that he achieved more than the other two! But the Empire was threatened, no longer by Russia but by the infiltration of the British Empire—officially proclaimed in 1877, the second year of the reign of Abd ul-Hamid II—and by English propaganda no longer confined to the Christians but reaching those Moslems less rooted in Turkish culture; the Albanians and the Arabs.

The way in which France and England took possession of Tunisia and Egypt, the secret correspondence which they kept up with the Greeks in Turkey, the Lebanese, and the Armenians could only lead to a reaction against all democratic reform. The weakness of Abd ul-Hamid was that he had never left Istanbul; he was ignorant of the diversity of his great Empire. Hard as iron, he believed in Islamic unity. He surrounded himself with Arab advisers and bodyguards, causing discontent among the Turks although the Arabs were flattered. He thought it wise to take the title of Caliph seriously. It is not surprising that the power of the idea of nationalism should have eluded Abd ul-Hamid. The sultan had always led a retired, quasi-monastic life. The Turkish monarchy had had its day. The entire continent was on the verge of revolution brought on by a sort of historical fatality. On the Bosphorus, in his Yildiz palace (Star of the North, guiding light of the world) Abd ul-Hamid II seems like the hero of a tragedy. In his last years (after 1896, when the Shah of Persia was assassinated by a group of Istanbul reformers), he lived like a hunted animal. Abd ul-Aziz, his uncle and predecessor, had been assassinated in his bath by reformers (1876), who had put on the throne a simpleton (Murad V) whom they wished to make a constitutional monarch. A *coup d'état*, or rather an old Turk counter *coup d'état*, had put Abd ul-Hamid on the throne in place of the half-witted Murad. From that moment there existed the 'Young Turks' for whom the new *padishah* was the man who must be assassinated. Abd ul-Hamid thought the 'Young Turks' were the tools of England, but he was mistaken, for when they came to power they proved very hostile to the allies and in fact followed the very policy outlined by Abd ul-Hamid.

In 1876, when he came to the throne, Abd ul-Hamid promised a constitutional charter to all his subjects 'without distinction of race or of religion'. He made the promise because he had a Russian war on his hands (1877–8), but once the Berlin Treaty relieved him of his military troubles he postponed the charter indefinitely and exiled the first 'Young Turks'. Turkey was in great need of reform but, the sultan thought, reforms which would consolidate the monarchy: military and civil arrangements of the kind which existed in Russia. Indeed, in this sphere alone, there was a great deal to be done: education, the civil service, the judiciary, the police, reorganization of the army, and sanitation. What was needed most of all were men able to carry out this vast programme efficiently. The Sultan obtained genuine results. In 1909, when he abdicated, after the revolution of 1908, he left the Empire almost intact, as he had received it thirty-three years earlier, with a State machinery almost entirely created by himself, a respectable army, police, roads, railways, mines being worked, a system of civil and military officials. His fall was the beginning of anarchy, the signal for the break-up of the monarchy created by Mahmud II and of the old Ottoman Empire.

The aged but still energetic Abd ul-Hamid II still ruled over a sprawling Empire, which in his eyes and in those of his subjects was one of the six great world powers. The official religion was Moslem and the Sultan, whose kingdom was 600 years old, was also regarded as Khalif or successor to Mohammed. But in reality this immense Empire of 2,735,000 square miles and 43,106,000 inhabitants was in a shaky condition. To begin with, it was a loose collection of provinces: of these Bulgaristan (Bulgaria), Buena (Bosnia), Hersek (Herzegovina), Crete, Cyprus, Egypt, Tunis, and Tripolitania had already been lost or were about to be. The capital, Istanbul, had a population of 1 million, and its immediate surroundings (Rumelia) about another million. This area, geographically part of Europe, belonged to the Anatolian demographic pattern and remained attached to Turkey. Almost half the population of Istanbul was made up of soldiers or civil servants; among the latter were some non-Moslems, but the soldiers, who were mostly Turks or Kurds, were all Moslems. The Turkish army, organized and officered by Germans, was one of the largest in the world.

Trade, which had expanded a good deal since the Crimean War, was mainly in the hands of unbelievers—Greeks, Armenians, Jews, Lebanese, etc., who made up the only middle class in Turkey. There were 2,120 mosques in the

Empire, and attached to them were 1,780 primary schools. Education in these schools was mainly religious, as it was in the Christian and Jewish schools, run by Western missions. Catholic and Protestant schools totalled 36,200. About thirty technical schools, high schools and colleges were an exception to this rule.

After the Charter of 1839 the civil laws were reorganized in a more modern form; in 1905 the codes of 1869–76 were still in force. The civil courts were on the French model, but side by side with them were religious courts (*sher'i*) and the apportionment of cases between the two was not very well defined.

Turkey found herself in no position to pay off her war debts and on 20 August 1881 she was forced to dedicate the customs revenues of Cyprus, Bulgaria and east Rumelia, her income from the so-called 'Persian' tobacco (*tambeko*) and the £18 million sterling which Egypt paid her annually to the service of the 'Ottoman debt'—62 per cent of which was owed to French and 29 per cent to German creditors.

Abd ul-Hamid II was greatly concerned with the construction of railways of which 3,890 miles had been (or were about to be) completed. It was hoped by the Turks that it would soon be possible to travel by train from Istanbul to Mecca, and (by the Germans) from Istanbul to the Persian Gulf. The chief towns of Asia Minor were already linked by railways, but only 31 per cent was actually owned by the Turkish Government: 37 per cent of the capital was subscribed by French and 20 per cent by German investors. There were also 28,000 miles of telegraph wires, 1,000 telegraph offices and 1,800 post offices in the Empire. Many of these also belonged to foreign companies.

Industry was still, with few exceptions, medieval. Here and there could be found a glass or soap factory, a spinning-mill, a factory for making military cloth, etc. Mining, which was developed at the same time as the railways, was more active; in various parts of the country chrome, manganese, zinc, antimony, silver, copper, borax, lithographic stone, oil, etc., were to be found. Some of these had hardly been explored; others were just being worked for the first time.

Turkey was still a pastoral country with subsistence agriculture. Exports included cereals, tobacco, dried fruits, wool, carpets and Angora goats' hair. In 1905 the peasantry lived very abstemiously on barley-cakes, onions, milk and butter and a few fruits. In many secluded valleys of Asia Minor, for example in Kurdistan, the shepherds lived on acorns, eked out with millet and turnips when they had them. In the country districts tea, sugar, paraffin for lamps, cotton cloth and soap were regarded as luxuries. Only the better classes could afford the famous coffee. The break-up of the Empire had not diminished the war charges which weighed so heavily on the Anatolian peasants, who in addition had to spend their youth in the army. The population of Anatolia began to fall: estimated at 13 million in 1878, it was only 10 million on the eve of the First World War. Turkish immigration from Europe and the Islands helped partly to counteract this decline. Meanwhile, the population of Egypt was increasing rapidly.

But behind the scenes a tremendous ferment was at work in Turkey: the question was, must all the traditions on which Ottoman greatness had been based be abandoned blindly for the progress of the West? In Istanbul, it was a matter of immediate choice, of action. The Sultan and his circle were opposed in principle to all Western ideas.

The 'Young Turks', who contented themselves with urging 'constitutional reforms', in fact wished to abolish all traditional habits and beliefs and replace them by those of the West.[24]

While on the one hand enlisting German aid in the modernization of his state, on the other the Sultan reinforced religious traditions by creating the Pan-Islam movement. To this Pan-Islam, which was a purely religious movement, reformers in Egypt replied with a similar movement which was racial, linguistic and irreligious. This was to arouse great discontent against the Khalif in Istanbul both among the Arabs (who were caught up in a Pan-Arab nationalist movement unconnected with religion) and among the Kurds and Albanians who were nationalists pure and simple.

Egypt

Ancient Egypt was described as the gift of the Nile to the pharoahs; the Egypt of 1900 seemed to be a gift of the Suez Canal to the English. The Isthmus was cut through in 1869; barely ten years after this event, the Khedive, who had just turned over his shares to Disraeli, was 'sold up' by his creditors as a bankrupt. From 1879 to 1883 two 'comptrollers general'— one English and one French—governed the Nile valley. The unimportant revolt of the Khedive's guard in the summer of 1882 gave the English an unhoped-for pretext for firing on Alexandria and taking over the Cairo Government. On 18 January 1883 they wrested from the Khedive an order which abolished the Anglo-French 'joint control' by purely and simply expelling the French. The Right in France protested in vain. By the London Convention (1885) England forced France to give up its 'rights' in Egypt. At the same time as they dispossessed the French, who were undesirable in the Orient, the English tied the hands of the Khedive, Mohammed Tewfik (1879–92) whom they forced, on 1 May 1883, to relinquish all real power to various 'advisory bodies': a 'General Assembly', a 'Legislative Council' and certain 'Provincial Councils'.

On 8 June 1873 the Viceroy Ismail had obtained from the Emperor Abd ul-Aziz (1861–76), for a large sum, permission for his semi-independent pashalik to maintain its own army and to sign its own treaties with other powers. From that day, the house of Mohammed Ali went out of control, despite the Sultan's efforts to restrain it. This voluntary abandonment of suzerainty brought into Istanbul a yearly tribute of £692,350 sterling. In

1882 the English found a legal means of gaining hold of this tribute by assigning it to the service of the 'Ottoman Debt'. So well did this work out that from that time on there was only one privilege remaining to the Sultan: that of being Caliph of the Egyptians, who were obliged to mention his name in public prayers. As has been seen, the Sultan set great store by this privilege, which was of course recognized by Mohammed Tewfik and Abbas II (1892–1914).

By means of violently despotic measures, the Egyptian Government, from the time of Mohammed Ali, had devoted itself to the promotion of industrial crops, principally cotton. This latter became particularly widespread in Egypt during the American Civil War. In 1881, on the eve of the English invasion, cotton already represented 66 per cent of the value of Egyptian exports. With British colonialism, this cotton policy became daily more important, so much so that in 1900 cotton represented 77 per cent of the total value of exports. By 1924, it had risen to 86 per cent! In Egypt, cotton was developed to the detriment of food crops such as rice, wheat, beans, sugar, etc.

The tyrannical evolution towards monoculture put the farmer into complete dependency on the 'lord' (*pasha*) who, by about 1900, was in most cases a Levantine hostile to Islam. The farmer (*fellah*) would have liked to devote himself to the cultivation of foodstuffs, or to some production remunerative to himself. A law expressly forbade it. The mercantile régime preferred to import flour, rice and tobacco; the poor *fellah* toiled for the price of a single piece of corn bread a day!

As a result of the contact with Europe, the small properties were disappearing. By about 1900, out of 100 landowners, one owned 50 per cent of the land, while 61 owned but 7.7 per cent between them. There were few, if any, medium-sized estates. Twelve thousand landowners held half of Egypt for themselves. Sixty per cent of the growers were former, dispossessed small landowners reduced to the condition of impoverished rural serfs by Copt usurers and Greek shopkeepers. Thus, a thousand foreigners had each taken over from 500 to 600 *feddans* of land.

Before 1885 the landlord was almost always a Turk. Having a 'medieval' mentality, he did not insist on monoculture. A Moslem, like the *fellah*, he used, but did not abuse the whip (*kurbash*). Under the Levantine 'pashas' (*bashawat*), non-Moslem foreigners who gradually ousted the Turks after 1883, this was changed. From 1888 on, the English forbade the whip, but they established 90 summary courts with jurisdiction in cases involving less than 150 Egyptian pounds; these courts sentenced the *fellahs* to forced labour for trifling misdemeanours. Labour camps arose with prisoners cultivating the cotton fields under the supervision of armed guards.

In Egypt the era of non-Moslem 'pashas' dawned in 1876, at which time the Armenian vizier from Smyrna, Boghos Nubar Pasha, avowed enemy of the Turks and 'right hand' of Khedive Ismail (1863–79), persuaded that monarch to establish 'joint tribunals' to try 'international'—that is, inter-community—cases. Installed at Alexandria, these comprised three courts of first instance and a court of appeal which judged civil or criminal cases between Moslems (Egyptians or Turks) and non-Moslems (Armenians, Jews, Greeks, Lebanese, etc., not excepting the Maltese, Italians, French, and English). Seventy per cent of the cases that came before these courts, where foreign judges were in the majority, dealt with bankruptcy proceedings: Turks or Egyptians who had borrowed money at 60 per cent or more from some usurer whom they were incapable of repaying. The joint tribunal then decided on the seizure of their rural or urban properties, which fell into the hands of their creditors. This 60 to 70 per cent interest rate was not excessive —in the Orient, everyone, borrower as well as lender, thought it fair enough. True, there were half a dozen pawnbrokers and a loan association which, in principle, lent at 8 per cent, but their capital was small, and the needs of Egypt were enormous.

If the statistics are to be believed, the population of Egypt doubled between 1860 and 1900, rising from 4 million to 10·5 million. What is more certain is that poverty more than doubled. Ease and luxury were to be found only among the bourgeoisie—the 260,000 non-Moslems, 60,000 Greeks, 30,000 Jews, 30,000 Armenians, as many 'Syrians' (Lebanese), 30,000 'Italians', etc. The 700,000 native Jacobites ('Copts') were no richer than the native Moslems.[25]

And what was the level of education towards 1900? Students in theology and Moslem canon law were still much more numerous than the students of modern disciplines. Nevertheless, two tendencies were coming into evidence: there were more and more applicants for study in technology, medicine and modern law and, thanks to 300 young women who took up the teaching profession, it was finally possible to organize elementary schooling for women.

Morocco

Morocco in the nineteenth century was a country of ancient traditions. The guilds of Fez still worked to ancient formulae and processes learned from the Orient more than a thousand years before. The Moroccan minaret, of which the Giralda of Seville is a good example, was similar to those constructed in the East in the seventh century. This was no doubt because only the first wave of Asiatic culture in the eighth century reached the Atlantic Ocean. The other two did not get so far: the Seljuks stopped at the Levant, and the Tartars did not even reach the Mediterranean. Hence the archaic appearance of Morocco which followed its own path. Its towns, above all Fez, were almost as crowded with monuments as those of Italy or Spain. In spite of a certain desire to modernize and adapt, it remained a fortress of conservatism because it clung to its traditions. Morocco, somewhat like Japan, was open to the raids of European naval forces. In the nineteenth century, it also had opened only one port to the foreign enemies, Tangier, and the inhabitants were forbidden to leave the country.[26]

In its great days, Morocco had held sway not only over the whole of Moslem Africa, but even over the Iberian peninsula. At other times it had hardly stretched beyond the palace of the Caliph and the ramparts of the chief cities. The formidable walk, pierced here and there by gates and surmounted by towers, guarded not only Fez but every one of its quarters, and perhaps, too, the medieval style of government.

Morocco still had no capital—or rather it had at least four: Fez, Marrakesh, Meknes and Rabat. The *makhzen* occupied now one, now another in winter and when the weather was bad. At other times he lived in a mobile camp, a vast canvas capital of about 50,000 tents. It was an army perpetually in the field, either for fighting the rebels (and there were always some) or for collecting the taxes, which were paid as often as possible in kind, and consumed on the spot.

The Emperor Sliman embellished Fez at the beginning of the nineteenth century and built bridges across the river as well as the Bab el-Ftouh and Bu-Djida quarters; the embankment mosque and that of the Customs House (*el Diouna*), the college of Ech-Cheratine, and the mausoleum of Sidi Ali Bu-Ghalib, his favourite saint.

Desaulty, under the name of Abd er-Rhaman became converted in 1834, during the reign of the prince Abd er-Rhaman (1822–59) whose name he took, and entered the service of the Makhzen. The Emperor gave him the task of making the first carriage road of the Empire: between Fez and Meknes. He served several Moroccan rulers and built a number of bridges: that on the Fez wadi and those of N'aja, Wislan, Mahdouma and Mikkes. The New Meshwar, i.e. the 'Champ de Mars' of Bab Bu-jat was also laid out by him.

The Arsenal (*el-Makina*) or mechanical workshop was erected in 1886 by Italian engineers in the service of El-Hassen. They were still at work in 1889 when Pierre Loti visited Fez. There they had under Moulay El-Hassen three turbines, several power-hammers, and machine tools for the construction of rifle butts and barrels; a foundry for small artillery; a minting machine for coins, and a generator. In the twentieth century, when Morocco became a protectorate, nothing remained but a spinning machine and a mechanical loom. The fact remains that among the Moroccan rulers in the nineteenth century there was none to compare with Mahmud II (Turkey), Mohammed Ali (Egypt) or Abbas Mirza (Persia)—who from the first were in the forefront of the reform movements.

There was a free circulation both of goods and of ideas between Fez and foreign countries. But Moulay Sliman (1794–1822) closed the gates and during his caliphate the tendency towards isolation, already in existence, grew stronger. The freedom of the Jews to come and go had already been suppressed: they were forced to choose whether to leave Morocco, become

Moslems or live in the *mellah,* or ghetto which was to the south of the Middle City. The Christians, who were mainly Italian merchants, all left Morocco except for those who became Moslems.

Finally, there was the slave market in Fez. Pierre Loti and another French-man, disguised as Moroccans, visited it in the spring of 1888. They saw one day a young Negress, and another day a troop of thirteen Ghana women just imported from the Sudan. Like all the African countries, with the exception of Egypt, Morocco in the nineteenth century was a centre for the slave trade. The soldiers of the Makhzen, in their red livery, were slaves; and so were the menservants and maidservants in almost every middle-class house. Society was made up of three classes: the patricians or 'sharifs', the plebeians, and the slaves. There were also some freed slaves.

The roots of future states[27]

After the First World War, and again after the Second, Islam gave birth to several new states, nearly all of them Arab-speaking and most of them former Turkish possessions. In the nineteenth century some of these new states, such as Iraq and Syria, were simply provinces of the Ottoman Empire, while others, such as Tunisia and Lebanon, were in the nature of 'dominions'. What had been their respective situations during the nineteenth century?

Iraq[28]

Before it fell into the hands of the Ottoman Turks, Mesopotamia had formed part of the Persian Empire. The southern part of the territory, Basra, did not escape from the Persians until 1779. It was later occupied by dissident Turks from Cairo (1832–40) who had to defend it against Wahabi Bedouin, and not until 1884 did it come under the authority of Istanbul. The first attempt to modernize Mesopotamia was made during the administration of the liberal-minded Pasha Midhat (1860–71). Baghdad, until then an unas-suming provincial town, was subjected to a town-planning campaign, its medieval walls pulled down and some of its winding alleys widened to allow the passage of a horse-drawn tram. The three vilayets, Basra, Baghdad and Mosul, were linked by a telegraphic network. The Pasha approved a scheme submitted by the Lynch Steam Navigation Co. and started a service of Turkish steamers on the Tigris between Basra and Baghdad. Trade expanded, and Babylonia was very soon an economic appendage of British India. The Jewish and Christian minorities enriched themselves and attained a new importance.[29]

From 1860 onwards the province of Iraq had been governed judiciously by the Ottomans. It was the fourth military district of the Turkish Empire, and four divisions were permanently stationed there. The Pasha was thus enabled to keep order protecting the settled plain-dwellers (1·5 million) against half a million Bedouin from the Arabian plateau and half a million Kurdish mountain-dwellers. Order was also maintained among the Moslem sects and the religious minorities—40,000 Jews, 70,000 Assyrian Christians, 20,000 Yezidi Kurds and 4,000 Mandeans.

The majority of the inhabitants were of the Shi'a creed, which was followed by 24,000 Turkomans and many Persians and Arabs. Under the rule of Turkey holy places were allowed a relative autonomy. Vast numbers of pilgrims, including 150,000 Persians, visited Najaf, Karbala and other holy cities every year, from the beginning of October to the end of May. Karbala, a small town, was visited in 1890 by 15,567 Persians. At some of the Shi'ite festivals, the dates of which were determined by the Moslem lunar calendar, Karbala, Najaf, Kazhimain and Sanarra were literally flooded with pilgrims from Iran. Persian was spoken in all these towns, and only Persian currency was accepted there.

Confronted with this torrent of Shi'ite devotion, the Turkish authorities tried to create a Sunnite counter-current. It encouraged Turks to visit the tombs of the medieval mystics, such as Hallaj, Junaid, Ma'ruf, Abd-el Kader Jilani, etc. Rural life was thus entirely dominated by religion, there being as yet no 'Iraqi' feeling. An Arab nationalism, already prompted by Iraqi officers in the Ottoman army (members themselves of the Arab secret society, al-Ahd), went on developing.

The provinces of the Arabian peninsula

Its centre, south of the tropic, is the uninhabitable 'Rub 'Khali', the Arab plateau mainly populated along the coasts. The two camel routes respectively linking Medina with the Euphrates and Mecca with the Persian Gulf, have to cross a high, waterless plateau that resembles the Sahara. This region—the Nejd—never tempted the settled empires that followed one another in the East; they left it to the nomadic Arabs who led much the same life as the Touaregs of the Sahara. During the nineteenth century the Wahabi Bedouin controlled the route from Medina to the Persian Gulf, and the Shammar Bedouin the route from Medina to the Euphrates. The Turks were satisfied with the North, East and West of the Arabian peninsula, a region shaped like an inverted U, which they found difficult to defend effectively against Bedouin invasions and British infiltration. For the English were protected by their natural element, the sea, and the Bedouin enjoyed complete impunity thanks to their element—the desert. These geographical circumstances reduced the Turks to impotence and enabled the Arab 'feudal lords', the sheikhs, to maintain connections with the Bedouin of the interior and with the English on the coast.

To consolidate the Turkish authority, Emperor Abd ul-Hamid II decided to link Istanbul by rail with Mecca and with the Persian Gulf. The latter line—the Baghdad Bahn—was the pet project of Wilhelm II of Germany, while the Ottoman Caliph himself was particularly enthusiastic about the Istanbul–Mecca line, which he hoped would form a spiritual link between the various parts of his incongruous Empire. The Sultan had carried his much-loved railway only as far as Medina, several days' journey from Mecca. The trains consisted chiefly of tankers full of fresh water. Wilhelm II therefore regarded this line as an economic folly, though the Sultan saw it, through the eyes of a mystic, as the most noble of undertakings!

This road to paradise, this 'celestial route', was threatening certain privileges: those of the British, of the sheikhs of Heja who had been holding poor pilgrims to ransom for centuries: but both were already in secret league against the Turks.

Arabia felix, the south-western part of the peninsula, is a case of its own. Bordered by the sea and cut off on the landward side by uninhabitable desert, it forms a kind of mountainous, well-watered island, which has always been open to Persian influences. This region remained under the religious influence of the Zaidi, a Shi'a sect which flourished in Persia from the ninth to the fifteenth century. Like all Shi'a, the Zadi rejected Sufism, and the mystics as propagators of the Ottoman creed have never made any impression on them. Moreover, the Zaidi belief preserved even in the nineteenth century the esoteric character which the Shi'a of the twelve infallible Imams lost as early as the seventeenth century.

The sultans spent years between 1849 and 1873 in perfecting their military organization and in striving to make a reality out of their administration, which had so far been purely nominal. This led to the outbreak of nationalist revolts of a religious character in all parts of *Arabia felix*, particularly in 1892 and 1895–6. In 1904 the Imam Yahia, the Zaidi high priest, went so far as to declare a holy war on the Sunni of Istanbul. He succeeded in buying modern armaments from the Italians in Eritrea and the English at Aden. In 1905 he captured San'a and drove out the Turkish garrison.[30]

Syria and Lebanon

The province of el-Sham, comprising Syria, Lebanon and Palestine, with Damacus (Sham i Sherif) as its chief city, came under the domination of the Ottoman Turks in 1516 and was included in the Turkish Empire until after the First World War. In the nineteenth century Damascus was the headquarters of the Turkish Fifth Army Corps. It was not only an important stage on the route from Istanbul to Mecca, but was also regarded by the Turks as a holy city; during the centuries of their rule they built many mosques there in the Ottoman style, and an even greater number of monasteries.

During the nineteenth century the fortunes of the province fluctuated considerably. After being in danger from the French (1799) and from the Wahabi Bedouin who came down from the Arabian plateau (1810), it was occupied for some years (1832–40) by the 'Egyptians', i.e. the dissident Turks of Cairo—who drove back the Wahabi. Later the 'Egyptians' returned to the Nile valley, leaving Istanbul in control.

The mountainous regions of the province, several of which were populated by Syrian Christians, had been governed on feudal lines from 1697 to 1841 by two Shi'a families (Druze) of Turkoman origin, the Yazbeg and the Janpuladh. The Syrian Christians had finally rebelled, at the instigation of France, but a combined Austrian, English and Turkish fleet bombarded Beirut from 10 September to 14 September 1840, and the nationalist revolt was crushed.[31]

Having thus rid themselves of the Wahabi, the 'Egyptians' and the Syrian Christians of the mountainous regions, the Turks from 1841 to 1860 attempted to establish direct monarchist government in a province which was religiously divided and had so far been ruled entirely by feudal principles. In 1860 the international situation was propitious for France, where Napoleon III was posing as the secular arm of Catholicism and even of Christianity (Russia was still licking the wounds inflicted by its recent Crimean defeat): a feudal dispute between certain Shi'a (Druze) nobles and some Christian (Maronite) leaders provided Napoleon III with an excellent pretext for defending Christianity against Islam. The Turks were astonished and disconcerted, but a French expeditionary force obtained their consent and landed at Beirut. On 9 June 1860 the sultan accepted the administrative 'settlement' proposed by France on behalf of the Syrian Christians in the Lebanon. The Maronite districts were placed under the authority of a Maronite governor (Mutesarrif). On 6 September 1864, similar rights were extended to all Christians in el-Sham, so that any Lebanese traders and merchants, Maronite or other, who visited Damascus or settled there for business reasons received preferential treatment in political and economic matters.

Beirut thus became the Shanghai of the Arab world—the shop-window for Western trade and the platform for the 'progressives' who were trying to bring about a philological-political and an economic (secularized) 'renaissance' in the neighbouring Arab-speaking provinces. By 1850 there was known to be a 'Syrian Secret Society', and by 1857 a 'Syrian Scientific Society', which were undoubtedly making active preparations for the events of 1860–1 and those of 1864—which, as already mentioned, came as a great surprise to the Turks, since the members of the two societies were ostensibly concerned only with science and literature. At Beirut, Yazidji Bustani, Khazen, Ma'luf, Mashaka and Dahdah, and at Damascus Shidyak, Jazayiri, Kawakibi, etc., were making names for themselves in encyclopaedism and journalism.[32]

Midhat Pasha, who had first been governor of Damascus and now controlled the whole of el-Sham, believed himself to be paving the way for the early establishment of a liberal constitutional government for all Turkish subjects, and failed to anticipate that in the long run a fatal cleft would split 'Arab nationalism' from 'Turkish nationalism'—not to mention the national aspirations of the Kurds, Armenians, and Jews, which could have no satisfaction while the Turkish Empire lasted, but were fulfilled once it had gone.

Abd ul-Hamid II lost no time in getting rid of Midhat. He failed, however, to maintain the dignified attitude of a caliph, a supreme arbiter; he sided with the feudal reactionaries. His pan-Islam policy was seen as a defence of Turkish despotism rather than of the Ottoman community. The favours the sultan heaped upon the Arab sheikhs were taken as evidence of indulgence towards feudalism, and his harsh treatment of the young Arabs, whom he regarded as a southern offshoot of the Young Turks, was stigmatized as a persecution of the Arab race. He thus defeated his own aims.

Abd ul-Hamid II placed all his hopes in the railway by which he planned to link up the widely dissimilar regions of his huge Empire. Damascus, which had already been considerably modernized, was connected in 1894 with the Hauran, in 1895 with Beirut, and in 1905 with Haifa; and before long the line was extended in one direction to the Asian station at Istanbul and in the other to Medina.

Tunisia

The family of the Beys of Tunis goes back to 1705, the *beylik* being at that time a feudal dependency of Istanbul. Under Ali Bey (1759–82) and Hamuda Bey (1782–1814), Tunisia enjoyed a certain prosperity, which survived the war with Venice (1784–92). In the nineteenth century the situation changed. In anticipation of danger from Russia, the Turkish Empire sought to Westernize itself. Emperor Mahmud II introduced reforms and pledged himself, first at Vienna (1814) and afterwards at Aix-la-Chapelle (1824), to forbid his subjects to indulge in the corsair warfare which had hitherto been the pride of the whole coastal region of Berberistan (el Maghreb), including Tunisia. Husein Bey (1824–35) was faithful to the Emperor and even sent part of his fleet to fight on the Turkish side at Navarino (1827). The French invasion of Algeria (1830) strengthened his devotion to Istanbul, and his attitude was continued by Ahmed Bey (1837–55), who sent troops to fight beside the Turks in the Crimea (1854).

Ahmed Bey had the virtues and failings which were common to most Moslem and Arab rulers during this period. He tried to 'modernize' along the same lines followed at Cairo and Istanbul, Teheran and Kabul. But instead of modernizing, he aped the French: he prohibited slavery, 'restored' the liberties of the Jews, and paid a visit of admiring curiosity to Louis-Philippe (1846). He built the arsenal of Porto Farina, brought his army up to date, built palaces and public buildings, and raised money by adopting capitalist methods—setting up monopolies and imposing a number of taxes. His successor, Mohammed Bey (1855–9) found himself compelled to carry on the same programme, and promulgated a charter (*'ahd el-'amân*) guaranteeing freedom of trade for Jews and Westerners. Mehmet Sadik Bey (1859–82) was so alarmed by the helplessness of his suzerain, the Sultan of Istanbul, by the diktat imposed by Napoleon III at Beirut (1861) and by the French advance into Algeria, that he embarked upon a frenzied campaign of liberalization; on 26 April 1861 he proclaimed a constitutional charter and took immediate steps to enforce its provisions.

French and Italian consuls tried to secure concessions for public works. In 1869 an 'international' financial commission took over the finances of the little state. Another Turkish defeat, in the Balkans (1877–8) enabled France to make plans for the invasion of Tunisia (1881). France absorbed Tunisia by easy stages. The first measure (1883–4) was to abolish the concessions that had been granted to London and Rome. In 1885 (23 June) the French consul assumed the title of 'Resident-General'. In return, France acknowledged the supremacy of the English in Egypt and the Italians in Ethiopia. In 1891 the franc took the place of the Turkish piastre (*gurush*). In 1896 France withdrew the preferential tariffs hitherto conceded to the Italians. At this, 5,000 Italian Jews established as traders at Tunis applied for French nationality and obtained it. The Moslem religious authorities had enormous revenues (*aukaf*) in Tunisia, as in the rest of the Turkish Empire; France was afraid to confiscate these outright, but introduced ingenious methods in 1896 and 1898 to turn these ecclesiastical funds to other than their traditional charitable uses. For France, despite its non-denominational constitution, favoured the Catholics and Jews.[33]

Some economic progress did, however, take place in Tunisia: phosphate deposits began to be mined (1885) and agriculture was developed. Tunisia recovered some of the prosperity it had known in the Middle Ages, from the ninth to the fourteenth century. But most of the profits went to the French and Italian colonists—the indigenous population became the pariahs of the new social system.

Algeria

The occupation of Algeria, initially brought about by circumstances rather than by deliberate decision, was a long, costly and murderous undertaking. From its outset, considerations of prestige rather than of economy prevailed. The attempts at colonization which followed were for long unpopular in France. Tough work, hazardous living conditions and a high mortality rate were all to this country's discredit, and it was not until the last decades of the century and after great efforts had been accomplished that its reputation improved. These very difficulties, far from uniting the peoples whom the conquest had brought into contact, led to mutual incomprehension. Arrivals, whom the original occupants did not welcome, arrogated excessive privileges to themselves on the pretext of the hard and risky conditions. The development of Algeria was achieved at the cost of this terrible discord, most of whose many victims were initially among the native population.

Numerically speaking, the Europeans in Algeria were in a minority in comparison with the Moslem population. The few thousand who had arrived in the wake of the first French troops had huddled together in the big cities; only a handful were interested in agriculture. In 1841 there were 27,024 Europeans; by 1850 their number had risen to 112,607, and they already included a considerable proportion of foreigners—55 per cent in 1841 and still over 48 per cent in 1850, although the French Government had founded agricultural settlements in 1848 and 1849. The increase in the number of foreigners was due to the flow of immigrants who came to Algeria expecting to make their fortune there. Between 1850 and 1872 the European population increased from 112,607 to 245,117 (index-figure 100 = 218 per cent), and by 1901 it had reached 576,718. A large proportion of this number was still constituted by foreigners—Spanish, Italians and Anglo-Maltese; the number of Spaniards and Italians, which stood at 50,350 in 1856 (when the French population amounted to 92,738) had risen by 1886 to 188,845 (French population, 219,071) and was causing concern to the French administration.

As early as 1843, Bugeaud had perceived that their number constituted 'a perpetual scourge and danger', and in 1846 he had expressed the wish to 'gather up the whole of this mixed population, this mob of foreigners from here, there and everywhere, and fuse them inextricably together with the French elements, in the crucible of the law'. The first step towards carrying out Bugeaud's scheme was taken in 1865, when the Senatus Consulat adopted measures to facilitate naturalization after three years' residence in Algeria; but the foreigners showed no greater alacrity than before in applying for French nationality. So in 1889 came the law of 26 June.

This was a law big with consequences. For one thing, it conferred French citizenship upon foreigners who knew nothing whatsoever about France; these 'Frenchmen' formed 'an artificial, Algerian nationality, French only in name' (Larcher, *Traité élémentaire de législation algérienne*, vol. 2, p. 636). For another thing it granted these foreigners political rights which enabled them to seize the lion's share of political and administrative influence in Algeria. Being French by law, they soon obtained a monopoly of parliamentary and municipal representation and used it to secure budgetary appropriations, roads and railways, schools and a water supply. By that time they held the country in the hollow of their hand, as they soon showed.* By 1901 these French citizens of foreign origin constituted one-fourth of the European municipal population in the settlements (21,400 inhabitants out of 81,516) and formed large colonies in the cities—the Spaniards in Oran and Algiers and the surrounding districts, the Italians in and around Algiers and Constantine, and the Anglo-Maltese round Constantine (chiefly at Bone).

This influx of Europeans had changed the face of the Algerian towns; those along the coast had grown rapidly, whereas those in the interior (Constantine and Tlemcen, for example) showed a slower growth. Algiers, which had some 30,000 inhabitants in 1830, had 174,000 by 1906; the population of Oran rose from 10,000 to 106,000 in the same period. But Constantine,

* It is significant that at this period the local folklore gave birth to a character known as Cagayous, a 'new Frenchman' who speaks a jargon entirely alien to French; except for a few words borrowed from that language, it is a compound of Italian, Spanish, Maltese and Arabic put together with no regard for syntax and bristling with elliptical expressions that no one outside Algeria would understand.

which had 25,000 inhabitants on the eve of the French conquest, had only 54,000 in 1906.

As we have already said, the French administration established settlements for colonists in the interior of the country. Until 1846 they were confined to the vicinity of the coastal cities, Algiers, Oran and Bone; in that year there were 48 of them. A law promulgated in September 1848 announced the creation of 42 settlements in different parts of Algeria (12 in the department of Algiers, 21 in that of Oran, and 9 in that of Constantine). These experienced numerous vicissitudes before they began to prosper. The villages which the big colonization companies were obliged to create during the Second Empire (for instance, those built by the Société Gnvoise in the department of Constantine) foundered with equal rapidity. In fact, as is clear from the population figures given just now, the bulk of the extensions and new establishments took place between 1871 and 1900, 228 new settlements being established and 90 existing ones enlarged during that period. Irrespective of whether they were new or enlarged, many of them were gloomy, stagnant places. The first settlers went away, abandoning their concessions; others, scorning the law requiring them to live on the spot, took up their quarters in the nearest market town or city. The decline was hastened by economic crises and fluctuations, particularly in the last twenty years of the century.

Colonial expansion depended on a number of circumstances, the effects of which were cumulative. Up to 1870–5, colonization failed to strike deep roots. The concessions, even the large ones, were neglected by their holders, who thought only of making as much as possible out of them with the smallest possible capital investment, and did this either by simply selling the hay and other forage which grew in natural abundance in moist ground, or by farming out their land to the former peasants. Besides, considerable capital was required for agricultural development, and here the lack of specialized credit organizations to work with the farmers was a grave impediment, especially in years when the harvest was bad owing to climatic conditions. It had originally been supposed that Algeria would be able to supply France and the rest of Europe with the tropical products which had ceased to arrive in the eighteenth century; but this hope soon proved illusory and a switch had to be made to cereals, which did not yield the anticipated profits.

The colonial income began to increase encouragingly in 1871, thanks to sequestration and the land laws, to the military contributions and fines levied on the fellaheen, the expansion of the credit organizations, and the cultivation of vines, the last measure being actively stimulated by the administration and by the opening of the French market (the French vines were ravaged by phylloxera in 1875–80). But the tenuous nature of this new prosperity was suddenly revealed by the results of speculation, the first appearance of phylloxera in the Algerian vineyards, and the great depression which affected agriculture in Algeria in the last twenty years of the century.

The Europeans were completely bewildered, and looked for scapegoats—selecting the Algerian Jews, and launching violent demonstrations against them in the large towns. The most impassioned demonstrators were the 'new French', who were a source of tumult for several years until, somewhat late in the day, the French authorities adopted a firm attitude towards them.

The conquest and colonization of Algeria had very serious consequences for the Algerian population. In legal matters, individual rights were determined by measures derived from Koranic law and from French law. Generally speaking, the former applied to the Algerians in civil matters, and the latter chiefly in penal matters; but in this respect the French legislation was simplified to such an extent that the most elementary safeguards provided by French law were usually ignored when the defendant was a Moslem. The civil law was administered by the Kadis. From 1886 onwards, the Justice of the Peace became the common-law Judge so far as the Moslems were concerned, and the Kadis had no more authority except in personal matters (marriage and divorce) and questions of inheritance. In penal matters the Algerian 'native' was at first subject to martial law; after 1870 the military tribunals were changed, in name though not in nature, into Native courts (Indigenat), Disciplinary Commissions and Criminal Courts. They could impose a variety of penalties, ranging from the death sentence which was very often carried out, to fines, by way of hard labour, transportation to a penal colony, imprisonment, deportation and internment. The charges in many cases were not taken from ordinary common law, but from the 'native' code; and it was common practice for the adminstrative official of the 'Commune-mixte', a civil servant, to take the place of the judge in trying and punishing offences.

In fact, the French administration put safety before justice, and was always ready to ignore French legal precedent in order to strengthen the domination of the European minority.

The Senatus-Consult of 14 July 1865 declares that 'the Moslem native is French' as is 'the Jewish native' (Art. 2), but that both are to be governed by their respective laws until 'at their request, they desire to enjoy the rights of the French citizens', whereupon they 'shall be governed by the civil and political laws of France'; but only a few score Jews and Moslems took advantage of the provisions of this Senatus-Consult. On 24 October 1870, Cremieux, a minister in the Government of National Defence, decided to grant French citizenship to all 'Jews who are native of the Algerian departments', which left only the Moslem natives outside the French community. A few years later, on 23 March 1882, a law was passed by which every Moslem native was required to possess civil status like that of the French citizen and the rest of the population of Algeria. This law was the natural corollary of the land law of 26 July 1873, which put the finishing touch to the economic disruption of the tribal system which had been initiated by the Senatus-Consult of 22 April 1863.

Despite the *attachements* policy, which bound Algeria more closely than ever to France, and despite the demands of the Moslem élite, who claimed admission to the French community, the Europeans inexorably refused.

French legislation disrupted the property system even more completely than it upset personal status.

Immediately after the conquest, and regardless of the pledges given by Bourmont on 5 July 1830, considerable changes were introduced. The French administration resolved to transfer to the ownership of the French State: (1) all property belonging to the Dey and the Beys; (2) religious property and the pious donations (*Habbous*) collected in towns and villages for the upkeep of the mosques, schools and benevolent institutions. In the beylik of Constantine alone, 146,000 hectares were thus requisitioned by the State.

Almost at the same time tremendous speculation developed in the towns, concentrating on buildings and landed property, for there was no law to prevent this. Some of the property thus 'sold' had never existed. To clear up a situation which was becoming more confused as time went by and to increase the area available for colonization, Louis-Philippe's Government issued decrees, in 1844 and 1846, by which all uncultivated land was confiscated by the State. This deprived the fellaheen in the Mitidja of 95,000 hectares, and in the province of Constantine 54,000 hectares were very probably taken over by the public authorities. But it was not always easy to enforce these decrees, and the attempt was abandoned in some cases (e.g. the outskirts of La Calle).

Although a law of 1851 declared that the rights of ownership and enjoyment of land remained undisturbed, the French administration began in 1854-5 to allocate 'districts' to tribes which were considered to own too much land. Although no legislation empowered them to do so, the authorities continued these measures, drawing up plans which involved considerable areas. Wherever this system was enforced (in the Cheliff valley and the Philippeville district) it deprived the fellaheen of their best land, to a much greater extent than was admitted by official declarations. In 1861 the Imperial Government contemplated issuing a decree on this confinement to districts; but in the summer of 1862 it withdrew this, replacing it in April 1863 by a Senatus-Consult.

This Senatus-Consult of 22 April 1863 was the first and most important of the legislative measures intended to restore the confidence of the fellaheen and make their land available for purchase by the European colonists in normal conditions. Going beyond this principle, the law broke up the old tribal structure and replaced it by a new unit which was too often artificial. This was the douar, whose existence was less firmly founded than that of the tribes. All land within a douar was to be divided into 'arch' holdings, so that each member of the douar would have his own land, defined in title-deeds. This measure also had political aims, the desire being to reduce the authority of the great Arab chiefs once and for all. Be this as it may, the tribal system began to disintegrate in 1863, putting an end to the fellowship which formerly united all the members of a tribe and enabled the poorer tribesmen to survive periods of famine with the help of their wealthier fellows.

In 1873, a new law was passed by which French civil legislation was henceforth to supersede the traditional system of land ownership. There would be no more arch or melk land, but only one system of land tenure, with two alternative forms—'collective' and 'individual'. This led to a series of contrary interpretations, and above all to manoeuvring and measures of spoliation at the expense of the fellaheen. Other laws, enacted between 1887 and 1897, accelerating the process of dispossession, were supplemented by further legislative measures providing (1) for sequestration and (2) for eviction from forest areas. The principle of sequestraton made its first appearance in 1840, when the fellaheen, fleeing from the French troops, abandoned their land; but it was not extensively applied until after Moorani's uprising in March, 1871. It came to a head in July of that year, when the formalities were simplified and extended to the collective sequestration of land belonging to the tribes in the province of Constantine alone, the tribes were made to give up over 568,000 hectares to the State, the greater part of this being fertile land. In 1885, a law virtually abolished all rights of user and all title to the cultivated enclaves on the part of the fellaheen. The results proved so disastrous that a further and more liberal law was promulgated in 1903 to clarify the situation of the Algerian forests and their inhabitants.

A further result of the military conquest was to compel the Algerian population to pay large sums, by way of military contributions and fines, to the commanders of the expeditionary forces. To these cash payments were added the losses due to deliberate acts of destruction by the soldiers, the pillaging of crops and orchards and the raiding of flocks and herds. Furthermore, the Algerians were the only members of the population who paid direct taxes (the Arab taxes) in addition to the indirect taxes and customs duties paid by all inhabitants of Algeria. From 1845 onwards the French administration demanded payment in cash instead of in kind, and increased taxation above its level under the Turks. We shall not be far out in saying that the *per capita* figure of taxation increased threefold between 1830 and the end of the century.

The conquest had considerable repercussions on the demographic situation. Between 1830 and 1856 the Algerian population was greatly reduced by the hard fighting, by certain other episodes (such as the scorched-earth policy applied to Dahra and Sbeha), and by the many epidemics that devastated the country during that period. It is impossible to estimate the loss of life among combatants and non-combatants, including that caused by epidemics —of plague, cholera, vomito negro, and typhoid. The combination of war and natural disasters caused such havoc in Algeria that in 1849 'some *douars* in the province of Constantine are literally depopulated'.

Not until 1886 did the Algerian population revert to the figure at which it was estimated on the eve of the French conquest; in that year it reached 3,264,000. By the beginning of the present century it had topped the four million mark (1901: 4,063,000 inhabitants). This increase gave rise to a number of problems, aggravated by the fact that the entire basis of the traditional rural economic system had been changed, and that France, immediately after setting foot in Algeria, had drawn that country into new international circuits and given a new and unfamiliar trend to economic activity.

The conquest of Algiers and the other chief cities caused a rise in prices which varied according to the locality and the products concerned. The price of wheat rose by 259 per cent in Algiers and 357 per cent at Constantine; that of barley by 254 per cent in Algiers and 314 per cent at Constantine; that of wool by 461 per cent at Constantine and that of dates by 1,600 per cent in the same city. Moreover, the introduction of French coins, with their intrinsic value, led to speculation which lasted for a long time. And lastly, a state of economic crisis was endemic throughout Algeria during the first twenty years of the conquest. Matters reached a climax between 1845 and 1850. The economic situation in Algeria made a slight recovery as a result of the Crimean War and the relaxation of restrictions on trade; but the improvement was ephemeral and could always be cancelled out by fluctuations in the climate. The terrible years from 1866 to 1870 gave striking evidence of this; and when the depression of 1873-5 broke out in Europe, its repercussions were soon felt on the other side of the Mediterranean.

The last twenty years of the century were very difficult ones for the Algerian economy, owing to competition from the newly developing countries, the ravages of phylloxera, and several dry seasons. Colonists and fellaheen, townspeople and farmers, complained with one voice, either in the newspapers or in petitions to their Members of Parliament. The administration tried to improve matters by setting up institutions to help the fellaheen, but these administrative measures were completely ludicrous and inadequate; usury continued and little or no technical progress was being made.

Yet the French colonization of Algeria had transformed the face of the country. New towns had sprung up and old ones had grown larger; new districts now rubbed shoulders with the old ones; the old streets had been widened, thus disturbing the traditional layout of the towns. Harbours had been extended and provided with wharves and quays, lighthouses and sheds to facilitate the work of a port; roads had been laid down, at first by the soldiers and later by the Public Works authorities, to link the cities and connect them with the colonists' settlements, and had often contributed to the conquest (e.g. in Kabylia). But there were extensive areas which were still without carriage roads, and their isolation added to the distress of difficult years. Under the Second Empire railways were built, connecting Algiers with Oran and Constantine and Constantine with Bone and Biskra; but they did not prove as useful as had been expected.

Beginning in the years of the Second Empire, schools and hospitals were built, priority being given to the settlements and colonial towns; funds for school building in the '*communes-mixtes*' were very inadequate. At this same period Algeria began to set up large banks—the Banque de l'Algérie, the Crédit Foncier and the discount banks; but the crises of 1870, 1873–5 and 1880–90 made it clear that these were not geared to meet the needs of Algerian agriculture.

As for agriculture, many of the colonists had technical equipment of a high quality, but at the end of the nineteenth century the fellaheen were still working with their traditional implements; in the province of Constantine, less than 5 per cent of the Algerian peasants had exchanged their ancient swing-ploughs for the French plough.

Thus, at the beginning of the twentieth century Algeria displayed two very different faces. On the one side there was a population of European origin which had seized the best land, was paying no direct taxes, but was receiving considerable grants, concessions and loans because it was able to make its voice heard. These people were in sole control at municipal, departmental and national level, the successive crises of the past twenty years having eliminated the weaklings from their ranks and increased the power of the strongest among them.

On the other side there was a population consisting chiefly of peasants, who had been steadily driven back into the least fertile or the most southerly and therefore most arid regions. They had suffered all the effects of the conquest and were supporting the greater part of the burden of taxation. Despite the French presence and example, their techniques had remained unchanged since before the conquest. They had no political influence and could not gain a hearing. Their traditional tribes, disrupted by legislation and by the inclusion of Algeria in the international circuit of the capitalist economic system, had now split up into individuals—who had lost their traditional culture and not yet acquired the European and French culture, which was apt to be dispensed with a grudging hand.

The origin of Pakistan

West Pakistan (now Pakistan) covers an area eight times that of East Pakistan, (now Bangladesh) and its principal city is Karachi. Any study of its history during the nineteenth century is thus tantamount to a study of the Indus valley. When Canning (1856–62) crushed the Indian 'Mutiny'—which was partly incited by Teheran—and brought East Pakistan under the direct rule of the British Empire, West Pakistan was still experiencing the last throes of a dying feudalism. Even today, the traveller in the Indus valley can see here and there the ruins of Baluch forts, castles and mosques, destroyed by the British guns in the 1840s. It was during the conquest of Baluchistan in the fifteenth and sixteenth centuries that the population of Jats, who were small farmers, were reduced to the condition of serfs and gradually converted to Islam by the missionary Orders.

King Shah-Alam (1759–1805), who was at war with the Marathas, had recognized the 'suzerainty' of the East India Company in Bengal, Bihar and Orissa, in return for an annual subsidy of 2·6 million rupees (1764). When the Marathas took him prisoner the Company saved him (1805), but he was persuaded to make over Delhi to them, in return for a further annual subsidy of 960,000 rupees. In the reign of King Bahadur (1837–57), the Company, which had hitherto acted in the guise of a Mongol vassal, felt strong enough to forsake (1837) the language of its overlord—Persian—in favour of its own English speech.

Already in 1821 the English, again taking advantage of the quarrels between Moslem and Hindu feudal states, had seized Karachi; afterwards, advancing up the Indus with a flotilla of gunboats, they demolished (1843), one by one, the castles of the Baluch nobles of Sind, and in 1849 those of the Indo-Afghan potentates in the Punjab. Nasir II (1840–57) had not even time to put his fortresses in a state of defence; they collapsed like cardboard under the fire from the British gunboats. His despairing appeals to his feudal chief, Dost-Mohammed (1826–63) met with no response, and even the Shahan-Shah at Teheran was powerless, for Persia had no navy. The only Moslem fleet which could have come to the help of the Baluch ruler was that of Sayid Said (1804–56), with whom he had quarrelled over Karachi and other harbours on the coast of Baluchistan which were a perpetual subject of discord between the two states. By the time of Khadadad (1857–93) the great territory had shrunk to the little district of Kalat; but even this remnant, a head without a body, was invaded in 1875 and its ruler was compelled to surrender to the British his few estates in Upper Baluchistan in return for a pension politely camouflaged as 'annual tribute'. He then looked on with helpless bitterness while the Shahan-Shah of Teheran, in complete disregard of feudal rights, annexed the western domains under the name of 'Persian Baluchistan'. This was the end of feudal Moslem India; all that now remained of Moslem India was its Indo-Persian language, with its religious institutions and local customs. The Moslem middle classes, divided into a number of economic and religious groups, had long grown accustomed to living in a kind of 'dispersion' in the big merchant cities and had no political ambitions. Moreover, they were satisfied with the English Government, under which trade prospered more than it had done during the feudal period. The serfs too, whether Hindu or Moslem, had every reason to welcome the English, for they were now no longer subject to the jurisdiction of their former owners except in a few districts and to a very limited extent; in most of India the English controlled finance, the police and the law courts, and had reduced the duties of princes to what was almost a sinecure.

The only 'class' to which the interference of Britain brought real hardship was the Moslem intelligentsia, the literate part of the population. It was they alone who lost their source of income owing to the policy of Lord Canning (1856–62). After the Mutiny (1856–7) the English authorities, mistrusting the educated Moslems, dismissed large numbers of them from their employment, replacing them by educated Hindus whom they regarded as devoid of political ambition. Sir Sayid Ahmed (1817–98), leader of the Moslem intelligentsia, undertook to save the situation. He made it his mission to change the English attitude towards their Moslem employees (1860); and when the last of the Mongols, the unfortunate Bahadir—who in 1857 had looked in vain for help to the Persians and to the Tsar—died in captivity (1862), Sir Sayid Ahmed urged the educated Moslems to collaborate with the English (1868) on the principle enunciated in old times by the poet Saadi: 'if you cannot cut the hand off, kiss it'! He was so upright and so shrewd that he managed to convince both the English and the Moslems. His great achievement was Aligarh College (1875), founded to train Moslem clerical staff for the English. Meanwhile, freed from the feudal system imposed by Islam and favoured by their English liberators, the literate Hindus were making tremendous strides; side by side with the growth of a Hindu middle class, a pan-Indian Hindu bureaucracy was rapidly created, already confident that one day it would be strong enough to take over from the English. At this period the English hardly realized the situation, though the Moslems were well aware that the Hindu menace was imminent. They already apprehended the day when the British would withdraw and Moslem India become the scene of a murderous *reconquista* by the Hindus. Plans must be made without loss of time for living in the post-British India.

The man who was needed arrived towards the end of the nineteenth century in the person of Sayid Amir-Ali. In 1877 he founded the Central National Mohammedan Association, which at its third session (Lucknow, 28 December 1887) took the name of United Musulman Patriotic Association. The results were far from encouraging, owing to the extreme caution of old Sir Sayid Ahmed and those of his generation who still remembered the dark days of Lord Canning and who advised their juniors against following Sayid Amir-Ali, on the ground that he was still 'inexperienced'. But the old men were mistaken: the world was moving so fast that their experience could not always be of use to the young. Sir Sayid Ahmed had been right in 1857— when he was 40 years old; but now, in the last quarter of the nineteenth century, it was Sayid Amir-Ali whose views were correct. So in 1898, when the old leader died, the young men founded the All-India Muslim League, with a programme which was reasonable for that period. At their Dacca meeting they suggested to Lord Minto that he should take some Moslems into his Legislative Councils (1906)—which he did without too much demur.

All clear-sighted Moslems were aware by this time that once the English left, the Moslem territories would be divided from the Hindu provinces. They must therefore make plans to establish reunification on religious principles, beginning with the Indus valley, the cradle of Islamic India.

Here there arose the problem of the Punjab, with its capital, Lahore, where Hindus and Sikhs had settled in the late eighteenth century, when the

Mongol power began to decline. The ruler of Afghanistan, Ahmed (1747–73) had fought them and his successor, Timur (1773–93), had taken Lahore and Multan from them; but the internecine warfare that broke out in Afghanistan after the death of Zeman (1793–1800) had left the field free for the Hindus and their friends. The Moslem population was obliged to put itself on a footing of self-defence (1826) and to make a spiritual reconquest of the Punjab by a puritan revival on the Wahabi model. In any case the military occupation of the Punjab by the British as a result of the Anglo-Sikh war (1849) left no possibility of armed attack, so that organization of missions was the Moslems, only remaining hope of eliminating the Hindu religion from the Punjab. The weak point of the Hindu system being the division of the community into castes, the Moslems proceeded to convert the 'low caste', the unfortunate proletariat of every organized Hindu community. They met with remarkable success. By about 1900 all the 'low caste' inhabitants of the Punjab had seceded to Islam, which constituted a far more brilliant and decisive victory than any in the tournaments held by the Afghan and Baluchi chivalry and recorded by poets in their epics.

NOTES TO CHAPTER XXIII

1. V. V. Tsybulski, Doctor of Geographical Sciences, points out that this chapter covers by no means all the Moslem countries though, in view of its title, it should do so. There is, for instance, no mention of one of the largest Moslem countries—Indonesia. Moreover, the author speaks of all Moslem trends in one breath, without making any distinctions between Sunnites, Shi'ites, Ismailites, and so on; though such distinctions are important for the study of the cultures of countries like Turkey and Iran, for instance.

E. A. Beylaev, Doctor of Historical Sciences, emphasizes that the author attaches no importance to society as such, and that the chapter deals mainly with outstanding personalities. There is no mention of the people, who really make history. The author evinces no interest even in such popular movements as, for instance, Babiism in Iran—the most important movement in the Moslem countries in the nineteenth century.

I. M. Filshtinsky, Candidate of Historical Sciences, remarks that the author has not mentioned the main reasons for the cultural decline of the Moslem countries of Asia and Africa at the beginning of the nineteenth century: the maintenance of patriarchal-clan relations, the continuance of feudal inter-clan warfare, the merciless exploitations of the peasants and the supremacy of Islam in all spheres of life.

The author does not mention the fact that the colonial expansion of the European powers in the nineteenth century, made possible by the economic and political backwardness of the Moslem countries of Asia and Africa, subsequently became one of the main factors responsible for intensifying their backwardness and for the abnormal, lopsided development of their economy.

In addition, A. A. Popova, Candidate of Historical Sciences, writes: when speaking of countries like Turkey and Persia, the author says nothing about the fact that, at the end of the nineteenth century, they had become dependent on foreign capital and had become semi-colonies of the European powers. In general, the author is not familiar with the concept 'semi-colonial'. 'Semi-colonial' countries, a characteristic feature of imperialism, are countries which are nominally politically independent, but actually dependent economically and diplomatically. The usual pattern in such countries is for the imperialist powers to control all the economic structure, impose unequal economic and political treaties, arrange for foreigners to enjoy immunity in relation to local tribunals, grant loans under crippling conditions, demand low tariffs on imports and take over control of the country's customs machinery. Another usual feature of a semi-colonial régime is the appointment of foreign political, military, financial and economic 'advisers', 'observers' and 'experts'; and the exercise of military and economic pressure for the purpose of obtaining economic privileges and territorial settlements for foreigners to live in, under the protection of the imperialist powers. Semi-colonial countries are stakes in warfare between the great powers, and are divided into 'spheres' of political or economic influence, and 'regions' of special interest. The history of Turkey or Persia at the end of the nineteenth and beginning of the twentieth century provides a good example of this process.

2. A. A. Popova writes, firstly, there was no *coup d'état* in 1827 against the Janissaries' corps. The rising of the Janissary corps in Istanbul, followed by its destruction, took place in June, 1826. Moreover, there are no grounds for saying that the elimination of the Janissary corps, which was already in a state of disintegration, weakened the Ottoman Empire. On the contrary, this step was taken for the purpose of reorganizing the Turkish army and saving the Empire from destruction.

3. Professor Asa Briggs feels that the reference to the national uprising in India squares with nothing else that is stated in the book about 1857; whatever its effects were upon British policy, they were different from what is stated in this paragraph.

4. Professor Briggs does not believe that the Dutch tried seriously to prevent the spread of Islam.

5. E. A. Belyaev comments that the penetration of European capital to the countries of the Moslem East not only had economic and political consequences but also exerted an ideological influence on these countries. This influence comparatively easily affected the liberal landowners and the bourgeoisie. The Moslem clergy, interested in the preservation of the feudal system, feared that the influence of European ideas and innovations would weaken their spiritual domination over the ignorant and oppressed masses.

6. A. A. Popova, observes that the author misinterprets the significance of the so-called 'capitulations' in the case of Turkey and Persia. The capitulations, which by the eighteenth century, through unequal treaties, had placed the countries of Asia in a position of dependence vis-à-vis the capitalist states, whose representatives and citizens were granted special privileges, constituted a means of helping the European states to control the markets of Asia. Under the Capitulations régime, the consuls of the states concerned were granted plenipotentiary rights—administrative, police and legal (consular jurisdiction)—over their own nationals, rights of settlement, immunity of foreign persons and property from the jurisdiction of the local courts, tax exemptions and privileges, fixing of customs tariffs, etc.

A. A. Popova's comments are endorsed by I. M. Filshtinsky who writes that the author regards the Capitulations régime (in particular, consular jurisdiction) as a means of guaranteeing European merchants against the despotism of the Oriental rulers, whereas in fact this régime, by instituting special privileges for Europeans, facilitated the colonial subjugation of the Eastern countries.

7. A. A. Popova states that the author's statement, to the effect that the interests of the growing bourgeoisie in Turkey and Persia were identical with those of the foreign powers, especially England, is incorrect. England, whilst stating that she was in favour of constitutional movements in these countries, was in fact concerned only with strengthening her positions there. The members of the national movement, even those in favour of British assistance, strove actively for the abolition of the privileged régime for foreigners in their country, and were opposed to its subjugation by foreign capital.

8. A. A. Popova considers that the author gives a completely one-sided account of the actions of Melkom Khan, whom he represents as being virtually a British agent, but who in fact, in his writings, protested against the subjugation of the country by foreign powers.

9. Professor Briggs wonders whether all the mullahs represent the cultured conscience of Islam. The very odd and inadequate discussion of Egypt on this page misses the most historical points.

10. E. A. Belyaev states that the Afghan Jemal ud-Din, together with the Egyptian Mohammed Abdo, was the founder of the politico-religious conception of pan-Islamism: all the people professing the Moslem faith ought to unite into a single state under the rule of the Moslem Caliph (at that time the Sultan of Turkey). The followers of pan-Islamism were hostile

to the national interests of some of the Moslem peoples (e.g. the Asian Arabs and Kurds who strove to free themselves from Turkish rule). They were resolute opponents of any social struggle by the working people since they denied the existence of class contradiction among Moslems, proclaiming that all Moslems (regardless of social origin or status) were brothers.

11. I. M. Filshtinsky points out that by no means all Moslem movements supported the struggle for national liberation. An example of this is the Pan-Islam movement. The preachings of one of the main theorists of the Pan-Islam movement—Jemal ud-Din— who advocated the amalgamation in one state of all the peoples supporting Islam, ostensibly for the purpose of resisting the penetration of foreign capital into the countries of the Moslem East, were subsequently endorsed and widely used by the Turkish Government of Abd ul-Hamid II in his campaign to reinforce his own political authority in the Moslem countries and gain power over many of the countries of Asia and Africa inhabited by a Moslem population.

12. A. A. Popova points out that the author is wrong in describing Turkey and Persia, both here and in other places, as independent empires. They were nominally independent but in fact, by the end of the nineteenth century, they had become semi-colonial powers.

13. A. A. Popova thinks that the description of the Imperial Bank in Persia, founded by England in 1889, is one-sided. This bank was in fact an important tool for exploitation of the country by British capital. This must be stated.

14. To Professor Briggs the reference to oil should be greatly expanded. This was one of the most important hidden events in the century.

15. A. A. Popova states that the author attempts to demonstrate that the results of the activities of Liakhov in Persia and General von der Goltz Pasha in Turkey were different; but he is wrong. In point of fact, Liakhov in Persia and von der Goltz in Turkey were pursuing the same aim: to subjugate the armed forces of those countries in the first case to Russia, in the second to Germany.

16. I. M. Filshtinsky considers that, when describing the cultural development of the countries of the Moslem East, the author should begin by stating that one of the main cultural phenomena was the emergence of the new contemporary literature in the nineteenth century. This literature took different forms in the various countries (Iran, Turkey, Egypt, Syria); but there was one feature common to them all, namely the rejection of the traditional forms and themes and an interest in the new problems arising from real life. The new Iranian literature (which developed on a large scale in the second half of the nineteenth century) dealt with public topics and important political questions, advocated special changes within the country, democratic reforms and even the transformation of Iran into a constitutional monarchy. Poetry which had always, hitherto, predominated in Persian literature, now began to be overshadowed by prose; and prose writers began to adopt a simple concise style making literature accessible to the ordinary reader.

17. I. M. Filshtinsky points out that Melkom Khan is described as the 'teacher' of Akhundov. This is not correct. In fact, the great Azerbaijanian writer Mirza Fath-Ali Akhundov, whose plays, translated into Persian, together with translations from Molière, laid the foundations for Persian drama, exercised a great influence on the development of Persian literature, including the literary productions of Melkom Khan, the great Persian educator and writer.

18. Professor E. A. Belyaev writes: The Wahabites were the most representative of Moslem puritanism. This movement, in Islam, clearly formulated ideologically in the words of Ibn Teivniya (thirteenth–fourteenth century), was one of the forms of passive protest against economic and social inequality in Moslem society. The Moslem puritans contrasted the avarice, greed and corruption of the feudal lords and the rich townspeople with the piety and asceticism which, in their opinion, were characteristic of early Islam. At the end of the eighteenth century, in backward Arabia, this doctrine was used by the local feudal lords as a means of affecting tribal unification in their interests. A way out of the crisis which these tribes were then experiencing because of the lack of means of production was found in the raids and conquests of the Wahabites. The rich and powerful Turkish and Iranian feudal lords, townspeople and clergy were proclaimed to be bad Moslems and disloyal to the faith. Because of their extreme poverty, the nomads of Arabia were fanatical in their

morals and, therefore, the teachings of Wahabism on self-denial and the rejection of an elaborate religious cult met with favour among them.

19. In addition I. M. Filshtinsky points out that the author says nothing about the social conditions which were the cause of the emergence and development of Wahabism, but mentions simply its 'gnosiological roots'. It should have been said that the strict monotheism and 'puritanism' of the Wahabites, as well as the other features of this politico-religious doctrine, stemmed from the desire for unity inspiring the tribes of the Arabian peninsula; also that the Wahabites' rejection of 'Turkish' Islam which, they maintained, had deviated from monotheism by instituting the worship of Mohammed and the cult of the prophets, was closely linked to the struggle of the peoples of Arabia against Turkish rule.

20. A. A. Popova points out that the paragraph about Persia in the section 'Political and Social Evolution' deals only with certain aspects of Persia, and says nothing at all about the country's political structure and social institutions. The accounts of Afghanistan and Turkey are quite different in character.

21. A. A. Popova emphasizes that the Second Anglo-Afghan War (1878–80) was not a victory for England as the author makes out. In the first stage of this war, England succeeded in defeating the Afghan troops and forcing on Afghanistan, in 1879, the unequal treaty of Gandamak. But this roused the opposition of the Afghan people. There then occurred, throughout Afghanistan, an anti-English rising, as a result of which England was obliged to forgo her plans for conquering and partitioning Afghanistan, and to make a compromise agreement with the Emir Abd ur-Rahman, recognizing England's right to control the foreign policy of Afghanistan but leaving the Emir independent as regards domestic policy.

22. A. A. Popova remarks that the author's assessment of the activities of Abd ur-Rahman is not entirely correct: the result of his policy (enlarging the army, opposing the separatism of the feudal lords, introducing a single monetary system, etc.) was to facilitate the liquidation of the feudal clan system and reinforce the country's economy.

23. A. A. Popova thinks the author's assessment of Abd ul-Hamid II is incorrect: his policy of oppression of the peoples of the Ottoman Empire and, in particular his programmes against the Armenians, earned him the nickname 'bloody sultan'.

24. A. A. Popova does not agree with the author's statement that the Young Turks wanted to introduce Western traditions instead of the national ones. The Young Turks were in favour of giving Turkey a constitution and introducing progressive reforms into the country, but they were never opposed to Turkish traditions. On the contrary, they proclaimed the theory of the unity of all Ottomans—subjects of the Turkish Sultan—including the non-Turkish peoples of the Ottoman Empire.

25. L. N. Kotlov, Candidate of Historical Sciences, points out that the author's explanation of the reasons for the social and economic processes in the Middle East and North Africa in confined to superficial phenomena of secondary importance. This is illustrated by the account given, on these pages, of social and economic changes in Egypt. The author states that one of the basic reasons for progress in that country was the replacement of the old Turkish, Moslem landowners with their 'medieval outlook' by non-Moslem, Levantine *bashavati*. This is true, but it was a reflection of more fundamental changes. And the 'old Turkish' Moslem landowners, including members of the royal dynasty, also adopted the new methods. The author attributes more significance to changes in the matter of money circulation, but without justification.

Professor Briggs cannot see what the author means by 'poverty more than doubled'.

26. N. A. Ivanov, Candidate of Historical Sciences, maintains that if the author is putting forward the theory of the isolation of Morocco, he should make some endeavour to explain the causes and character of Morocco's isolation.

27. L. N. Kotlov writes: This work takes no account of many very important sources on the history of the Arab countries of Asia. This is, obviously, due to the fact that far too little space is devoted to these countries in comparison with that allocated to Persia, Turkey and North Africa. Various vitally important problems which would throw light on the fundamental theme of the history have been omitted; and there is only a passing reference to the question of Moslem reforms, the activities of the Syrian Government associations, the ideology of developing Arab nationalism, and questions of Arabo-Turkish relations, Pan-Ottomanism and Pan-Islamism.

'Since the field covered by the work does not include a description of the historical processes throughout the territory of the Near East and North Africa, it is incomprehensible why the author should give an account of the history of Yemen, which throws no light on anything. But since Yemen is touched on, then there should be two or three pages giving a clear and concise account of recent events in that country.'

28. L. N. Kotlov remarks that, in the section on Iraq, when describing the vicissitudes of the struggle for power over this region between Turkey and Persia, the author has said nothing about an important period in the history of Iraq: that when Baghdad and the whole of Iraq were ruled by the dynasty of semi-independent pashas (from the beginning of the eighteenth century until 1831). The rulers of this dynasty virtually followed an independent domestic and foreign policy, possessed their own army and strove to eliminate even the formal trappings of submission to the Porte.

29. L. N. Kotlov points out that the author, when speaking of Pasha Midhat's reforms, omits to mention that they were, in addition to everything else, anti-Arab, thus leading to considerable reinforcement of the burden of taxation, and were the cause of mass popular risings. For example, it was during the reign of Pasha Midhat that there were created, to the detriment of the peasants, the first large feudal estates which were characteristic of Iraq in the first half of the twentieth century.

30. L. N. Kotlov objects that the account of Yemen does not describe the most important historical events in that country:

(1) It says nothing at all about the period of the existence of the independent Imams of Yemen, who throw off the Turkish yoke at the beginning of the seventeenth century, and survived until 1873. During that period, Yemen established the first direct economic and political contacts with the West, and came under pressure from Western colonizing forces, which seized parts of Yemen's territory (Aden, Perim) for the purpose of establishing themselves on the shores of the Red Sea.

(2) There is no mention of the significance of Mohammed Ali's campaigns into Yemen.

(3) The Imam Yahya was proclaimed after the defeat of Turkey in the First World War, not before.

(4) It is not correct to say that religious dissensions were the cause of the anti-Turkish risings: they were only the ideological aspect of more fundamental contradictions of an economic and political character. Note that, even after the Young Turk revolution and the secularization of the Ottoman Empire, the rising (in Yemen) continued for about three more years, and was settled only as a result of a series of domestic and foreign factors (including the incipient Italo-Turkish conflict).

31. L. N. Kotlov maintains that the author has no justification for describing the Anglo-Austrian action in Beirut in 1840 as being directed against a 'nationalistic' (a term which he finds unacceptable) rising. The fact is that the Anglo-Austrian fleet carried out this operation against the troops of the Egyptian Pasha Mohammed Ali who, incidentally, had just put down a rising of the Christians of the Lebanon. England had supported the rising, in the Lebanese mountains.

32. L. N. Kotlov points out that the author, when describing the history of Syria and the Lebanon after 1840, and the restoration of the power of the Porte in these countries, says nothing about the extremely strong peasant movement in the region.

33. N. A. Ivanov considers that, if the question of the liberalization and Europeanization of Tunisia is touched on in this section, some mention must be made of the reforms, the situation in the country, the roots of liberalism and the general features of the development of Tunisian society. We cannot agree that the liberal reforms were the result of the weakness of the Turkish sultan and of French successes in Algeria; not can they be considered as an imitation of France. The reforms carried out in Tunisia in the 1850s were part and parcel of the reforms carried through in the Ottoman Empire in the Tansimat period (1839-70), and were a concession made by the feudal state to the growing bourgeoisie. It is absolutely inadmissible to represent the application to Tunisia of the principles of the Tansimat as a guarantee of freedom of trade for Jews and Western Europeans. Why are trade monopolies —a typical Oriental form of economy—alleged to be the upshot of acceptance of capitalist practices ? And lastly, it is not at all clear why the author decided, in this section, not to mention either the restoration of the French protectorate or the Treaty of Bordeaux in 1883.

CHAPTER XXIV

THE BRITISH IN INDIA[1]

Introduction

INDIA can be said to have entered into the world in the nineteenth century in the sense that the interdependence between India and other countries then became infinitely stricter. Until that time commerce, in the broader sense of the word, formed the only link. In the eighteenth century, Western merchants and adventurers had just begun to play a role in the distribution of political power in the country; in exchange for her exports India imported, as she had always done, precious metals. Nevertheless, Indians and Europeans knew little of each other. With the conquest by the East India Company, all this changed. India was compelled to import manufactured goods and to export raw materials. While the rhythm of Indian economy had been and continued until the end of the nineteenth century to be dominated by periodical famines of a regional character, in the twentieth century, on the contrary, it will be seen that the crises are those of world economy: from 1850 onwards the world market commands to a large extent the fate of Indian productions. First of all, Indian economic development remained, up to the end of the century and beyond, dependent on the will of the British masters of the country.

The same is not quite true in the realm of politics. Toward the end of the century, the masters had already to take into account Indian demands. It is true that they were presented by a numerically insignificant intelligentsia. But this minority claimed to speak in the name of the people, and this claim was to be vindicated later on, thanks mainly to Gandhi. Still, even in this sphere, India was acted upon more than she herself acted: she was present on the world stage only by proxy.

Not so in the sphere of thought. There, India was free at the end of the nineteenth century. The interaction with the West was then complete: it had matured into an Indian ideology which was to result in political victory half a century later, and which combined two components, namely the assimilation of Western political values on the one hand, the renaissance and reform of traditional Hindu religion on the other.

I. THE WESTERN ONSLAUGHT

Invasion and resistances

When Warren Hastings became governor in 1772, England had overcome France and the East India Company had acquired, under the nominal suzerainty of the Mughul Emperor and the Nawab, the province composed of Bengal, Bihar and Orissa. Trade was still the order of the day, which, for the servants of the Company, did not exclude the unfettered acquisition of wealth by fair means and foul. With Warren Hastings began the *administration* of territories which increased throughout the first half of the century, while the second half was to see the growth of nationalism, together with a more systematic and expensive administration.

The invasion developed slowly, as it were reluctantly, as many British authors have said. The conquerors felt compelled to go ahead. In the first decades both the Board of Directors and the Government in London were opposed to aggrandisement, and while the governors in India were generally more inclined to intervention, the only avowed imperialist among them was Wellesley. Since the time of Clive, the British were aware of their military superiority, but systematic conquest was set aside for commercial and financial reasons, in view of the expense and the long-term obligations and risks involved. On the other hand, the unsteady situation resulting from the decay of the Mughul Empire and the risk of an anti-British coalition being possibly formed by some younger power such as the Marathas, the need for stability as a condition of the satisfactory exploitation and orderly administration of the Company's territories, even an often sincere indignation at the extortion and carelessness of the native rulers led the governors to intervene again and again. The Company acquiesced, but only within certain limits, as is seen from the indictment of Warren Hastings and the recall of Wellesley. Thus periods of war alternated with periods of non-intervention and of administrative consolidation. And in actual fact this slow process was the best way for firmly establishing foreign rule. The cautious, empirical, measured continuity displayed by Britain recalls the imperial genius of ancient Rome.

Two limits of this continuity, the one internal, the other external, may be described. First of all, a critical development of divergent views among the rulers—chronic among the French in India in the eighteenth century—such as prevailed under Warren Hastings; then, the Indian resistance after Dalhousie: within a few years a number of drastic measures had been enacted regarding the Native States, and the Mutiny broke out, with those princes who had been the victims of this policy taking leading roles.

If the rule of Warren Hastings (1772–85) was warlike, it did not result in important extensions of territory or of the Company's influence. Apart from the expedition undertaken against the Rehillas for the Nawab of Oudh (1773), Hastings was mainly busy restoring a situation jeopardized by the thoughtless initiatives of Bombay, the near-anarchy in Madras, and the uncompromising opposition of his own Council. After he had been impeached for exactions England was at last compelled to acknowledge that, at a time of great reverses (the War of American Independence), and in an administrative situation well calculated to lead to disaster, he who had maintained her position in India was indeed a great statesman. Bombay, supported by London, had decided to come

INDIA (1753-1890)

SHOWING THE SEQUENCE OF TERRITORIAL ACQUISITION

INDIAN STATES

Cartography Hallwag Berne

to terms with the Marathas (Treaty of Wadgaon, 1779), when Warren Hastings was eventually able to assert his authority and restore 'peace with honour' (Salbai, 1782). In the south the Nawab of the Carnatic had been left in power and, as individuals vied with the Company in exploiting him, corruption continued in Madras.

A serious threat came for a moment from the coalition of Haidar Ali with the French. While Haidar Ali, the brilliant usurper of Mysore, defeated though he was at Porto Novo in 1781, had become practically master of the south, the French fleet under Suffren was master at sea (Cuddalore, 1782). Fortunately for the British Haidar Ali died in 1782, and peace with the French was signed at Versailles in 1783. Finally, but against Warren Hastings' advice, a compromise treaty was concluded with Haidar Ali's son, Tipu (Mangalore, 1784).

Cornwallis (1786–93), a man of peace, intended to follow conscientiously the policy forbidding all wars of conquest as laid down by Pitt in the Act of 1784. Yet he was led to isolate and then attack Tipu (1790–2), and wrested from him half his possessions, a part of which he gave to the Marathas and the Nizam of Hyderabad.

The conquest was systematically resumed with Wellesley (1798–1805). Stimulated by the threat of Napoleon and by the presence in the courts of many Indian princes and of French adventurers acting as military advisers, Wellesley resolved to establish British supremacy in India. He set to work methodically and vigorously. He conquered the south of the Deccan by crushing the domination of Mysore; in the north he conquered a large part of the Gangetic plain; in the centre he seriously weakened the Marathas but was recalled before he could completely subdue them. Tipu was seeking an alliance with the French. Wellesley upon arrival isolated him by compelling Hyderabad to disband its troops and place itself under the protection of the British. The campaign was short, Tipu was killed while his fortress, Seringapatam, was taken (1799). The kingdom of Mysore was diminished, cut off from the sea, and restored to the Hindu dynasty. In 1801 the Carnatic was annexed. The Company then ruled directly over the southernmost Deccan, except for some enclaves. Ceylon, save the centre of the island, had been conquered in 1798.

In 1801 Wellesley forced the Nawab of Oudh to cede by treaty to the Company almost half his territories, including Rohilkhand and the lower Doab. The principality was now hemmed in by British territory, and the way was clear for dealing decisively with the Maratha Confederacy, which had been the great rival of the Company since the decay of the Mughuls. Wellesley made use of the differences that had opposed the main princes. The nominal head of the Confederation, the Peshwa Baji Rao, fled to the English, who gave him their protection, subordinating him the while (Treaty of Bassein, 1802), reinstating him in Poona in the following year. Then, in a vast combined campaign, two of the three great Maratha leaders were defeated. Arthur Wellesley, the future Duke of Wellington, attacked in the south, was victorious at Assaye, and obtained from the Bhonsla of Nagpur, by the Treaty of Deogaon (1803) the cession of Cuttack, completing the conquest of the eastern coast. In the north, Lake attacked the Sindhia, the Raja of Gwalior, taking Aligarh and Delhi and completing his victory at Laswari. By the Treaty of Arjangaon, Shindia abandoned his possessions in the north (the upper Doab between Ganges and Jumna) and his interests up to the Stlej (1803). A little later Sindhia's rival, Holkar, took up arms. His initial successes led to the recall of Wellesley, whose policy was thought in London to be adventurous and costly. Finally, however, Holkar was defeated and took refuge with the Sikhs.

Wellesley's successors, Cornwallis and Barlow, made concession after concession, and India was at peace until the end of Napoleon's Empire. Activity was diplomatic and external: there were dealings with Persia and Afghanistan, a treaty with Ranjit Singh, the Sikh leader who was busy uniting and organizing the Panjab and expeditions to drive the French from the islands of Bourbon, Mauritius and Java (1810–11). At this point the French disappeared as a political force in India.

Hostilities were resumed under Lord Moira, with the war against the Gurkhas (1815–16). Nepal was not only contained, but reduced in size, and actually became an ally. More important was the war against the Pindari bandits in which the Marathas took arms and saw their influence reduced to nil: the Peshwa surrendered and his lands were annexed. Bhonsla, Sindhia and Holkar were beaten and subjugated (1816–18). Only the north-west of India—i.e. with Sind, the Panjab upon which, together with Kashmir, Ranjit Singh held sway—was still independent.

There followed a period of peace until 1839, except for the first Burmese war of 1826. A disastrous expedition into Afghanistan led to the resignation of Governor Auckland in 1842, but prestige was restored by his successor, Ellenborough. Sind, whose territory had been violated by the army on its way to Afghanistan, became a protectorate, and was finally conquered by Napier in an operation which he himself described as 'a very advantageous, useful, human piece of rascality' (1843). After the death of Ranjit Singh in 1839, the Panjab with Kashmir was conquered in two short, very hard campaigns against the excellent but badly commanded Sikh army (1845–6 and 1848–9).

The conquest proper was then ended. Henceforth all wars would take place on the frontiers in connection with imperialist rivalries: second Afghan war (1878–9) against Russian influence; second and third Burmese wars (1852 and 1885), the latter, linked with the French conquest of Indo-China, ending in complete annexation.

A few words remain to be said, first, about the Company's policy towards the States over which it was content to exercise a kind of protectorate, and secondly about the Mutiny, or Revolt, of 1857. To begin with, the protected

States were considered as buffer states; their rulers paid for the maintenance of the Company's troops designed to ensure both their defence and their loyalty to the British alliance. This was the case for Oudh, and the Carnatic. Then the habit was introduced, if the State could not afford the tribute, to replace it by a cession of territories. Wellesley, who created the first general bond between the main States and the Government of British India, expanded the system: the Peshwa, Hyderabad and Mysore had to agree not only to pay for the maintenance of troops, but to submit their foreign policy to the Governor-General's control. Wellesley wanted to go further and establish the Company's right to supervise the internal affairs of the protected States which, as a result of this artificial situation, were often badly managed. He was, however, able to do it only for Mysore, which he had almost re-created; and Bentinck, in 1831, took advantage of this disposition to drive out an incapable ruler. The note of subordination became further stressed under Lord Hastings, and little by little, as the authority of the Mughul Emperor died out, the Company came to consider itself as having a right of suzerainty —'paramountcy'—over most of the Native States. Dalhousie is known for his 'doctrine of lapse', according to which the succession of dependent princes dying without heirs, or the adoption of heirs by such princes, was subject to the approval of the Company, which might choose to annex their territories. The theory was not new, but Dalhousie systematized it and used it intensively. Among other States annexed in this way were Satara in 1848, Nagpur in 1853 and Jhansi in 1854. According to the same principle pensions were suppressed, as for instance that of Nana Sahib, the adopted son of the Peshwa, who was to play, with the Queen of Jhansi, a leading part in the Mutiny of 1857.[2]

Also a theory of the 'welfare of the governed' was often used to justify intervention in the affairs of the States, and even annexation. In the case of Oudh, the British had tried for half a century to obtain some improvement in the administration, until finally Dalhousie proposed to take the matter in hand. The Court of Directors went further and in 1856 decided to annex Oudh, although the Nawab had always been loyal and had believed his throne guaranteed by a treaty of 1837. The annexation was immediately followed by a 'summary settlement' of the land revenue which went against the interests of the local chieftains or 'talukdars', and which resulted in the alienation of the whole aristocracy of Oudh. This policy was one of the main factors of the Revolt. Once the Revolt was quelled, the Government returned to a more conservative and cautious policy towards the States. Thus the State of Mysore was given greater autonomy in 1881.

The revolt of 1857–9 has for long predominantly been called the Sepoy Mutiny, after the 'sepoys', that is the Indian soldiers of the East India Company, who made up one of the two mainsprings of the military rebellion, the other having been provided by dispossessed and discontented princes and chieftains who supplied the leadership for the sepoys as well as their own troops and levies, including the Oudh army. The mutiny of the troops was a change of allegiance: they fought under other rulers against the British. Smouldering disaffection in the Bengal army was set ablaze by the threatened introduction of cartridges that were to be bitten with the teeth and greased with animal fat—cow's as well as pig's—so that the Hindu soldiers were afraid of losing caste, and the Moslem soldiers of forgoing their religion. On 10 May 1857 the sepoys mutinied at Meerut, where they massacred their officers and other Europeans, set out for Delhi, where many European soldiers and officers were also killed, acclaimed the Emperor Bahadur Shah and took possession of the city. They were to be dislodged only months later, in September, after a long and extremely hard struggle. The movement spread rapidly to other cantonments, among them Allahabad, and to Cawnpore—all too famous for the massacre and reprisals which took place there—and to Lucknow, where the British forces were besieged in the Residency but were at last relieved. All these towns had to be reconquered by troops, many of them European, brought from the Panjab and elsewhere. Then the rebel detachments had to be pursued and reduced, especially in Oudh. Protracted operations also took place in Bihar. In central India troops from Bombay besieged Gwalior and Jhansi. The rebel Queen of Jhansi died a soldier's death. The Emperor was deposed. After the first excesses in repression, Canning, nicknamed 'Clemency' Canning, restored order with moderation. The army was reorganized, the recruitment of Indian elements modified, care being taken always to maintain a certain proportion of European personnel, which controlled in particular the artillery.

The revolt remained localized. The Bombay and Madras armies did not mutiny; Sikhs from the recently conquered Panjab and the Gurkhas of the King of Nepal greatly helped the British. (Pl. 76d) The military operations were limited to a large area in north India, comprising the Gangetic plain from Delhi to the western confines of Bengal and a part of central India. Within this area, the people's participation varied. Oudh seems to have risen as a body for its independence under its traditional leaders. In Bihar a ruined prince and landlord, Kunwar Singh, led a movement which, in one district at least (Shahabad) assumed, according to a British official, 'all the dignity of a national revolt'. In the North-West Provinces, along the Ganges and the Jumna, the situation was more varied, but no sooner was the British power regionally in abeyance than a great agrarian discontent came to the fore. The rights of big landlords, revenue farmers and local chiefs, had been disregarded; rent-free lands had been resumed; for default in paying the land revenue; land had been auctioned and bought by townspeople, merchants and money-lenders. In every district headquarters the Treasury was plundered and the jail opened, the Government Land Records were burnt; less frequently, usurers and land purchasers were attacked for the recovery of the bonds and titles held by them.

While there had been, or were to be, isolated mutinies as well as localized peasant disturbances, the convergence of the two elements over a wide area is characteristic of 1857. We may note that the three kinds of discontent which we can distinguish, political among the rulers, agrarian among the peasants, religious among the soldiers, were intimately linked. A big landlord was at the same time a political chieftain, and he could often enlist the services of individual peasants, as in Oudh. Also, the sepoys of the 'Bengal' army were mostly recruited from the disturbed areas, and often enough had their cantonment very near the residence of their peasant relatives. More-over, there had been, if not a centralized and planned conspiracy, at least more than 'understandings' between sepoys of different regiments. A patient propaganda against the British power had been carried out by some fanatical Moslems on the one hand, by agents of certain rulers on the other. This explains the 'outburst of terrified fanaticism', for, whatever can be said about the technological innovations (railways then just in the making, the telegraph), the missionary activities, and some blunders such as the affair of the cartridges or the messing and drinking arrangements in jails, it is obvious that nobody had planned the massive conversion of the people, and that it existed only as a belief worked up in ignorant men by interested propaganda and obscurantist zeal. This belief united a part of the population and made sense of each isolated incident. It explains, as an instance, the extreme popular reaction at Arrah regarding drinking arrangements in the jail. The belief can be traced to earlier Moslem utterances.

On the whole, and though much has been recently written to the contrary, there is reason to maintain that the revolt was more the last struggle of the old powers buttressed by traditional beliefs than the first act of the new, more strictly national consciousness, although the latter was, at the beginning of the twentieth century, to see in the Mutiny its own beginning.[3] Otherwise the movement is misunderstood not only in itself, but in the context of the general history of India in the nineteenth century. The classes that were later to take up the struggle for independence, i.e. the modern intelligentsia and the mercantile classes, at the time of the Mutiny much less numerous, were unanimously opposed to it. It was also natural for the Moslims, more closely tied to the old order than the Hindus, to play a predominant role in the revolt, a fact which, although well known of the British who had experi-enced the event, has been of late somewhat understressed.

The revolt led to the end of the annexation of States and to the suppression of the Company, India coming directly under the Crown. How far 1857 represents, as is often assumed, the great dividing line in the nineteenth century and in the history of British India in general, will be judged from what follows. For the present writer at any rate, the fundamental fact is precisely that while all military resistance had been crushed, the future independence of the country arose from other quarters. India's most powerful reaction to conquest was to issue, not from the power of arms, but from the slow and irrepressible work of the mind.

I. A MODERN DESPOTISM: THE RULE OF LAW

Main features of policy and administration

With the nomination of Warren Hastings as Governor in 1772 and the Act of 1773 which introduced government control over the Company, the latter began the orderly administration of its territories. This meant in the first place collecting the land revenue and administering justice. The administrative branch of the Company was separated from the commercial, whose monopoly of trade between England and India was supressed in 1813, and which disappeared in 1833 with the end of its exclusive right to trade with China. To ensure the quality and integrity of civil servants, a college was founded in England and excellent salaries and prospects were offered. One result of this was to separate, more and more as time went on, the social life of the administrators from that of the country and even of European businessmen and planters. The latter were few, especially in the initial stage: no more than 1,324 residence permits were issued between 1814 and 1832. Pitt's India Act of 1784 strengthened the control of the Company: its Court of Directors was subordinated to a Board of Control, a government body comprising six Commissioners. At the same time, the authority of the Governor-General in India was strengthened, and Madras and Bombay came under his control. As Governor-General, Warren Hastings laid the foundations of Indian administration. His policy belongs to the eighteenth century in that it shows the humanistic respect for Oriental civilizations and religious neutrality. The latter was actually well in keeping with commercial good sense; profits would be endangered if Indian values and prejudices were attacked. To ascertain native law, Warren Hastings encouraged research, which led to the systematic study of Sanskrit. Up to 1813, the English Baptist Mission had to settle in Danish territory, in Serampore near Calcutta. But even later, religious neutrality was always to remain a principle of government; in general, and although there were to be many changes, the British preserved their basic conservative caution in their relations with Indian society. They have of late been criticized for having hampered necessary changes, but it was perhaps, on the contrary, a happy aspect of their domination to have led India to a point where changes appeared desirable while leaving it to the Indians to realize them.

As in England, the first third of the nineteenth century had a different ideological climate, with a marked moral, or moralizing, tendency. The components combined into what has been called liberalism: Free Trade, Evangelicalism, and Philosophic Radicalism (i.e. political economy and utilitarianism). It has recently been most forcefully emphasized that the administrative history of India in the century is dominated by the conflict and interplay between this current, which was on the whole victorious, and another which tempered and modified it to a large degree and never entirely disappeared, the 'paternalism' of those who felt the same horror as Burke at 'the idea of destroying an immemorial social system in the name of speculative principles', in short the *conservatism* of conscientious and devoted administrators, the greatest of whom, Thomas Munro, Mountstuart Elphinstone, Malcolm, Metcalfe, the Lawrences, England is justly proud of. The liberalism of the time, tinged with conservative caution and paternalist care, found its perfect expression in the governorship of Lord William Bentinck (1828–35): he preserved peace, reduced expenses, abolished 'suttee' (*sati*), i.e. the burning of widows, in 1829, ordered the police campaign against the murderous Thugs, fought female infanticide, and, after a report by Macaulay (1835), laid down the principles of higher modern education in English. This liberal movement was by no means confined to the English; it found an eminent representative in the great Ram Mohan Roy, the pioneer of Indian awakening. Decisions which interfered with recognized Indian customs, like the abolition of *sati*, were taken only after long consultation, but they rest in the last analysis upon a strong feeling of the social, political, and even moral, superiority of Western culture. However, that culture was conceived in this period as being, in its essence, universal. Indians had to be educated in order to be able to share that superior culture, and the final disappearance of British rule would be the normal end of the process.[4] For instance, the contradiction between non-representative, or, as it was then called, 'despotic' government on the one hand and freedom of the press on the other did not frighten Metcalfe, who introduced the latter in 1835. In actual fact, together with the English political literature, often exaggeratedly critical of British dealings in India, philosophical radicalism was the staple of modern education in India in the nineteenth century.

In governing circles, however, the dominant tone changed. Very soon, in rough synchronism with the accession of Queen Victoria (1837), it became 'imperialistic', without liberalism disappearing for all that, as is seen from the viceroyalty of Lord Ripon (1880–4).[5] It seems that at this stage, the idea of their superiority led the British to see themselves as predestined rulers; they drew back upon themselves, at times considering their acts as being beyond moral standards; they resisted the increasing claims made by Indians as a result of the latter's liberal education, and they even justified British isolation and domination by something approaching a racial theory. It appears that the superiority of the Western ruler, already postulated in some measure in liberal thought, hardened in losing its universalistic basis. Moreover—and this is important—this universalistic basis was not directly attacked, but rather discarded in the name of 'experience'. Imperialism was not an ideology in the full sense of liberalism. It did not operate on a universal and ideal plane, but on a practical, personal, almost apologetic level; and for this reason it was finally to be beaten by the Indian form of liberalism. Let us take as an instance the belief in the natural superiority of the whites, used to justify segregation and, if not the exploitation of the country, at least the exclusion of Indians from the higher posts in the administration. This belief is hardly to be found in documents; that it existed is only known from witnesses. It is significant also that, in the struggle for representative government which began at the end of the century, the English, who did not believe in the practical feasibility of a Parliament like their own, had nothing whatever to oppose to the liberal principles on which in the final analysis the claim rested.

Attempts have been made to explain the growing separation between the English and the Indians by reference to different circumstances and events. For some authors, the administrative circles became a self-sufficient society when English women could join their husbands, and this was made possible, even before the opening of the Suez Canal, by improvements in transport. For others the Mutiny increased the distance between rulers and ruled and the proud isolation of the English community, deeply shocked by the event. Still others, who refer to the belief in the civilizing effect of railways, think that technical developments would have lent tangible support to the notion of Western superiority.

The Statutes of 1858, suppressing the Company, put an end to the duality of powers in London. A Secretary was now responsible for the whole business of India. He was assisted by the Indian Council, which had no right of initiative. In India the Executive Council of the Governor was enlarged. The Governor-General, now mostly called the Viceroy, saw his initiative reduced through the telegraph. These administrative changes, in the words of Maine, 'swept away the obstacles to a transformation as remarkable as has been the development of any western country' (6, p. 483). The administration of the country was considerably intensified by the sudden application, as Hunter puts it, 'of our own English ideas of what a good government should do' (40, p. 177). The revenue, from a total amount of £22 million in 1837, jumped to £71 million in 1884. The cost of justice, police, education, increased. Eight districts, which had 176 courts of justice in 1850, had 288 in 1870. The Penal Code, ready since 1835, was promulgated in 1860, and codification went on. James Wilson reorganized finances and introduced new taxes (1859). The Rent Act of 1859 laid down the rights of tenants in Bengal. Annual 'Moral and Material Progress Reports' were submitted to Parliament.

After Lord Mayo's administration (1869–72), Lord Northbrook (1872–6) resigned rather than obey the instructions of the Government in London regarding the customs duties. This was a characteristic incident of the period which saw disagreements between the Government in India and the Indian Civil Service, both taking up the interests of India—or rather, of India as they conceived it, i.e. Anglo-India—against the Secretary of State, who was often strongly influenced by English industrialists. Lord Lytton (1876–80), under a Conservative Government, passed an Act for the control of the press in vernaculars. Under a Liberal Government his successor, Lord Ripon (1880–4), repealed it; he also developed representative local government (municipalities, etc.) in which he saw a means for the political education of the people. Lord Curzon (1899–1905), in spite of his eminent qualities, gave offence to the nationalists, his plan for the administrative partition of Bengal (1905) provoking the first deep agitation among Bengali Hindus. On the whole, British administration has been recognized as praiseworthy. To quote an author who is not suspect of partiality:

'It is in the field of administration that Britain was able to demonstrate her ability and proclaim to the world her achievement' (K. M. Panikkar, x, p. 153).

As in the central Government, changes occurred in local administration. At the level of the district, executive, judiciary and police, functions were now united, now separated. On the whole local administration remained personal rather than institutional. This was in keeping with the paternalist tendency of the civil servants, as well as with the traditional Indian pattern. The administrator, 'Collector' or 'District Magistrate' toured his district in the cool season and kept an eye on everything. Much depended on the quality of these men, and indeed Britain produced here an admirable body of men—hard-working, devoted, and shrewd—whom the Indian peasant has not yet quite forgotten. The series of writings giving the results of their inquiries and observations (*Settlement Reports* relating to Land Revenue, *District Manuals* and Gazetteers) are indispensable for a knowledge of the country, and form a unique monument. But this good government had disadvantages. It has been said that the Indian peasants came to look upon the State as a sort of Providence, or as their 'father and mother' (hence the name of *mām-bāpism*), but surely the matter has deeper and older roots.

The land revenue

While becoming *diwan* of Bengal, the Company acceded to one of the essential prerogatives of the Indian sovereign, namely the connection of what has been called the 'Land Revenue', which was to constitute about a half of the State income. This did not go without much trouble, and it affords the most remarkable example of the contrast between the traditional Indian and the modern mentalities. Notwithstanding their deep prejudice against innovation, the British were compelled to alter radically the existing rights in land (or, more precisely, the rights in connection with the land). This was not due to lack of inquiry or to precipitation in exploiting the country. It is true that the local officials had to conciliate the demands from London, which asked for as much money as possible, and their zeal for the interests of the Indian peasant, but it was thought that the development of agriculture would be served by a just taxation. In order that it might be established, the administrators worked strenuously for more than half a century, trying to unravel an extremely complex fabric in one region after the other, and this gigantic work resulted in mapping parcel by parcel a large part of India.

An initial period, when the rule of thumb prevailed, with attempts to farm the revenue, etc., led to a settled organization. The State, armed with appropriate sanctions, would itself collect the revenue, but the question arose: who ought to pay it? Certainly those who owned cultivated land. Hence the dominant preoccupation of the administration in Bengal and elsewhere: to establish who was, or might be declared to be, the owner of the land, in order to put the revenue on a firm basis. Unfortunately, no real 'land-ownership' existed in India. As it has been subsequently recognized—very clearly by Baden-Powell at the end of the century—the rights that were defined in India in general were rights to a part of the *produce* of the land, including the sovereign's rights. The cultivator kept what was left of the crop after the king and other claimants had received their share. What the British administration actually did was to choose, from among the number of right-holders, one person and to give that person an exclusive property right. The choice was to vary from one province to another, and according to the ideas prevailing in the Government at the time.

The difficulty of the choice had already appeared in Bengal, during the preparation of the Permanent Settlement of 1793, in the controversy between two experts, Grant and Shore, the former favouring the State, the latter the 'zamindars', i.e. the quasi-feudal landlords or tax-farmers. Beyond the question of fact, there was question of policy. Even if there was no recognizable owner, assuming that there could be no order, nor progress, without a clear definition of the rights of the State and of the individual, who was it equitable, and useful, to declare as the owner? In Bengal the zamindars, whether ancient lords or tax gatherers of recent origin, were recognized as proprietors subject to the payment of the Land Revenue, here conceived as a tax. They thus acquired complete freedom towards the peasants who became their tenants. Furthermore, the State, through the Permanent Settlement of Bengal, fixed the tax assessment in perpetuity in the hope that, understanding their true interest as well as the big landowners of eighteenth-century England, they would employ themselves in raising the yield of their own estates. But the State demand was high and, for the first time, was accompanied with drastic sanctions. Many estates were auctioned for default and numerous zamindars were ruined. Later on, the rise of prices lowered the relative rate of the tax, whose amount was fixed in money, and those zamindars who had been able to retain their lands became prosperous, while the peasants in their turn suffered. The Government, despite its disinclination to intervene, finally took the first effective steps towards safeguarding the tenants' rights with the Rent Act, Act X of 1859. Another Bengal Tenancy Act was passed in 1885. Thus the social reality that the legislator had disregarded avenged itself, and the British had to recognize and uphold by a complicated legislation that plurality of rights which they had thought to reduce to unity for the sake of their conception of order.

The other provinces, settled at a later date, had other systems.[6] In Madras, Sir Thomas Munro succeeded in establishing the '*ryotwari*' settlement, in which the individual peasant ('ryot') was recognized as proprietor. Bombay followed, with a different terminology (while borrowing from the following). In the North-West Provinces (later called United Provinces) and the Panjab, on the contrary, the settlement was made predominantly with joint communities as proprietors, whether or not their estates coincided with a village. The Oudh system as finally adopted after the Mutiny was more like that of Bengal. In these later cases, however, experience had taught the authorities to recognize several kinds of rights. For instance, while settling with the 'village communities', they fixed the percentage due to the persons who, until then, had acted as intermediaries between the communities and the State, or again the position of 'under-proprietors' or 'tenants' was more or less protected.

It is widely believed that British rule, through the Revenue Settlements in particular, destroyed the 'village communities' which would have existed all over India. This belief seems to have little foundation in fact. Let us in this respect recall the conservatism of Elphinstone and his contemporaries and, in general, the care with which existing rights and institutions were registered.[7]

Without going into too much detail, it must be added that the Land Revenue was the main field of controversy between the paternalist and the utilitarian tendencies. From this point of view, Cornwallis and Munro belonged to the same school, as both attempted, although in different ways and degrees, to create a private property in the soil. On the other hand, the adepts of Malthus's Law of Rent, as amended by Ricardo, held in principle that the State was entitled to the full rent, and could consider itself as the sole owner of the land, each peasant holding from it as tenant. In the first case, the Land Revenue was considered to be a tax, in the second a rent, and discussion on this point ran through the whole century. The rent theory was assiduously recommended by James Mill, who was Assistant Examiner to the Company in London from 1819 onwards. It had a large measure of success, but it was counteracted by, and blended with, paternalist empiricism. This was fortunate because, taken by itself it would have led and in some instances did actually lead, to severe over-assessment. Long after it had been recognized that the theory did not apply to a non-capitalist agriculture such as that of India, it continued to be upheld. On the whole, the theory seems to have provided a rationalization of an old institution in terms of modern political economy, and a justification for the British domination relying on that institution for its main source of income.

The rates of the Revenue were high to begin with. Reference was made to the 'demand' of previous rulers, which was sometimes increased. For the later settlements, the rent theory also favoured high rates, as it was believed that the Land Revenue was the best possible kind of tax and that the State could, without doing any harm, appropriate the totality of the 'rent' or 'unearned increment' otherwise going to the landlords. In general, the lessons of experience and the efforts of the local administrators led to reductions of the rates.

The British Revenue was paid uniformly in cash and, for the first time, it was unalterable once fixed, except for exceptional remissions, as in the case of famine. Default in payment was sanctioned by the loss of property. Moreover, the creation of ownership in land naturally entailed the introduction of the right for the owner to alienate his property, and alienation could in fact be forced upon him not only by the State, but by a creditor taking advantage of the judicial machinery set up by the British power. All these factors produced changes in the ownership of land that sometimes led to disturbances, and which the British, although reluctant to intervene, saw themselves compelled to restrain. This was especially the case when the changed circumstances were taken advantage of by urban money-lenders and speculators who succeeded on a large scale in dispossessing the small peasant owners and reducing them to the condition of tenants. Agrarian discontent is evidenced by several disturbances, the most important of which took place in 1855, 1857, 1860 and 1875. In 1855 the Santals, a tribe widely spread in Bengal and neighbouring areas to the West, rose in the Rajmahal Hills against the zamindars and the money-lenders, and against the Government which, in their idea, protected the formers' encroachments and exactions. In 1857, taking advantage of the Mutiny of the troops, the people burned the Government records and recovered the lands that had changed hands recently, attacking money-lenders and merchants. The movement of the tenants in the indigo plantations in Bengal is a special case. In 1875 the Maratha peasants, in numerous villages of the two districts of Poona and Ahmednagar, used coercion against the usurers in order to deprive them of recent title deeds and to get back their debt bonds, exerting no further violence when this aim had been reached. A similar movement took place in Panjab in the nineties. The Government finally limited the power of the creditor and protected the improvident peasant by the Deccan Ryot Act, 1879, and the 1900 Act in the Panjab. An agrarian element has been found in the revolts of the Moplahs in Malabar.

Laws were also passed to prevent the fragmentation of holdings (Settled Estates of Oudh, 1868 and 1900; Impartible Estates of Madras, 1902–4) and to protect the big owners against the results of improvident management.

On the whole, this array of legislation is evidence of a contradiction in British policy to which the Government's belated intervention in favour of the peasant more closely testifies. The Government that had introduced the conditions of a capitalist economy in agriculture shrank in the end before the social consequences of its action and turned more and more to a paternalist conservatism.

It is hard to say whether the peasant was on the whole better or worse off than before. It is easier to state a qualitative change in his situation. While he had previously been in the hands of the general and local rulers, exposed to their depredations, their arbitrary will and their greed, but nevertheless found in the social network of close interdependence an insurance against excessive individual hardship, he was now protected by an orderly and just government only to be made more dependent upon himself and to be exposed to a new enemy, an enemy which was the more dangerous for his having little experience of it: the power of money[8] (Thurburn, *41*). *Justice, Laws and Codes* (see esp. *8, 29*).

The authority of the Company was originally partly derived from the British Crown, and partly from the Mughul Emperor and other princes. In the Judiciary this led to a dualism which lasted for a long time. While on the one hand, in accordance with the principle established by Warren Hastings in Bengal, courts sat in each district, and there were corresponding Courts of Appeal, on the other hand Crown Courts called Supreme Courts existed in Calcutta, Bombay and Madras. The former administered local law, the latter English law (except for the application of private law to the natives). This duality was suppressed only after the cessation of the Company when, in 1861, thanks to the introduction of the Codes, the old Courts of Appeal and the Supreme Courts were amalgamated under the name of Provincial High Courts themselves in the last instance under Her Majesty's Privy Council.

Warren Hastings laid down the principle, which remained unaltered, that *personal law*, whether Hindu or Moslem, must be applied by the Courts in all actions relating to family and religion. The first necessary step was, then, to ascertain those laws. Warren Hastings, who had tried as early as 1764 to introduce the teaching of Persian at Oxford, encouraged the linguistic researches of Wilkins, Jones and Colebrooke. William Jones came to Calcutta in 1783 as a Judge of the Supreme Court and, taking advantage of Wilkins' research, founded the Asiatic Society of Bengal. This marked in practice the discovery of Sanskrit, the real beginning of classical Indology. At the outset it was a question of collecting and interpreting the laws and usages of the Hindus (and the Moslems). The first book, the *Code of Gentoo Laws*, was still translated from Persian, but gradually the treatises and commentaries in Sanskrit came to light.

Up to 1864 Hindu law was applied literally; a Hindu scholar, attached to each Court, was to decide which precept of the law was applicable in each case; this division was of course often arbitrary given the lack of precision and the discrepancies in the texts. The judge confined himself to ratifying the expert's opinion. (Pl. 76a) At first, the texts were taken as containing the positive law applicable to all Hindus but, apart from other imperfections, it was at length recognized that they were rather a 'mixture of religious, civil and moral ordinances that the priestly order considered proper to be observed but which, as a whole, were never administered as law' (Lindsay, in *8*, p. 108–9) (see also Barth 28). Indeed, as we see more clearly today, custom varied, not only from region to region but, in the same region, from one social layer to another. It was only in 1868 that the Privy Council advised the Courts to avoid taking as laws injunctions that were more of the nature of moral precepts, and decided that clearly established custom should take precedence over the letter of Hindu law (a principle which is in no way opposed to the spirit of Hindu law itself).

For a long period, government was improvised by means of 'Regulations' issued by the Governor-General. Codification became a recognized objective only with the Charter of 1833. Macaulay was appointed as Law Member to the Governor's Council. From 1834 onwards he presided over the work of the Indian Law Commission which was to prepare a body of laws showing, in his own words, 'uniformity when you can have it, diversity if you must have it, but in all cases certainty'. The Commission set up a penal code, different from the English and generally considered to be excellent, but which was not promulgated until 1860. Later, a Commission sitting in England prepared two codes of procedure, civil (1859), and criminal (1861). These codes were the outcome of tremendous work, and they were corrected and recast several times. To obtain certainty and simplicity, English law was used on a large scale, but in an adapted and simplified form, and then only when there was no risk of coming into conflict with native laws directly linked with religion. In particular, personal law was not touched, which is why no civil code was drafted. The codes were completed in subsequent years by a certain number of laws in which dispositions relating to property were sometimes made more precise or modified. One notices especially the extension of the rights of the individual to property, which was indispensable for adapting the law to modern conditions. Several provisions encouraged the decline of the joint family (although the feeling of solidarity remains very strong even today); the faculty of making a will—previously unknown, we are told, outside Bengal—finally became, after some opposition, as widely used as in England.

However cautious the British strove to be, however scrupulously they maintained a religious neutrality, and quite apart from any modification of the law, they unwittingly made a profound impact on Indian society. Brahmanical precepts had never been as powerful as they were made to be in being taken as principles of law, in being extended as such to all Hindus, in being applied in a uniform and strict judiciary system buttressed by the accumulation of case law. The policy of non-interference had here unexpected conservative effects. On the other hand, the British achievement in this sphere, and its progressive effects, have often been celebrated. According to Maine, India at the end of the nineteenth century was one of the rare countries where the law was (in conformity with Bentham's wish) not beyond the grasp of an intelligent person (6, p. 447). According to a modern critic:

'The first and perhaps the most abiding influence was in the sphere of law ... the great principle of equality of all before law ... The imposing and truly magnificent legal structure ... has changed the basis of society in a manner which few people realize ...' (Panikkar, 10, p. 497).

British and Indian authors alike insist on the importance of the establishment of the 'rule of law'. And surely the fact that the law is sovereign, and that the individual can maintain his rights against the State itself, marks a complete transformation of political power. This revolutionary change would not have been possible if the Indians had not been prepared for it by a number of elements present in their own culture. In particular, and apart from the traditions of the king's justice, each caste had an elaborate body of custom and many castes doubtless a much more detailed procedure than has been generally believed. There was also a taste for argument, and even for legal quibbles; respect for learning at least under its religious forms; and a feeling for oratory.

On the other hand, the judicial system is often criticized as having grown into a parasite of the social body. It is argued that by its complication, by the physical and social distance separating the courts from the village, it led to an increase in litigation which impoverished the peasants and enriched the lawyers. There is certainly much truth in this criticism, but the persons who proffer it commonly idealize the system of village justice or *panchayat*, which is taken as having been uniformly the self-sufficient antecedent of British courts, just as they may underrate the importance of conflict in the village, irrespective of its judicial aspects. Another criticism claims that the theoretical equality before the law actually favours the rich. The situation is still more complex: the introduction of equalitarian institutions certainly favours wealth, in particular against the old caste status distinctions, but the latter have not disappeared either. We shall have to look at the combined effect of economic and juridical changes against the general social background.

Education

Three phases have been distinguished in the Government's policy on education. The first phase was marked by some interest in traditional Oriental studies. Macaulay's Report in 1835 marks the beginning of the second, during which the Government developed the teaching of European culture and science through the medium of the English language. This was higher education for the few. Finally, the problem of mass education, and hence of teaching in local vernaculars, was energetically posed by Sir Charles Wood's report in 1854, and some progress was made in this field during the ensuing decades.

Warren Hastings' interest in Oriental learning has already been singled out. He founded the Madrassa for Moslems in Calcutta in 1782 and, in 1792, a Sanskrit College in Benares. The idea of education in English advanced at the beginning of the century thanks to individual initiatives. Charles Grant, a former employee of the Company, campaigned in England and obtained the support of Wilberforce. In Madras, official help was granted to the mission school, but in Bengal the Baptist missionary Carey had to establish schools from his private resources. A rationalist, David Hoare, and Ram

Mohan Roy opened schools which led to the foundation of the Hindu College in Calcutta.

The Charter of 1813 envisaged a minor part for education in the Budget. The Company here was in advance of England. In 1823 a Commission prepared to found a Sanskrit College in Calcutta, but Ram Mohan Roy in a famous petition protested against the project and demanded the introduction of Western science for the sake of the country's progress. Textbooks in English, published by the Missions, met with great success. This was the beginning of a controversy between 'Orientalists' and 'Anglicists'. The latter gained ground owing to Alexander Duff, a missionary, to Lord William Bentinck, who founded the Medical College at Calcutta, and to Macaulay. The Governor and Council decided that henceforth all available funds should be devoted to education in English (1835). Macaulay's Minute is famous for its cutting condemnation of oriental erudition, but

'It is the genius of this man, narrow in his Europeanism, self-satisfied in his sense of English Greatness, that gives life to modern India as we know it' (Panikkar, 9, p. 208).

It has been said that this education was mainly designed to produce subordinate employees, and also that it laid too much stress on literature as opposed to science. Certainly, in the minds of the liberal administrators of the period, it was first of all a question of opening India to Western values by educating an élite, in full knowledge of the fact that this would one day lead to the end of British rule. According to Macaulay, that would be 'the proudest day in English history'. Universities, colleges and examinations were organized on the English model. The three Universities of Calcutta, Bombay and Madras were founded in 1857, two others later. In 1901, there were 149 arts colleges and 46 vocational colleges, Bengal being in the lead with 64 colleges.

The supporters of education in English had believed that enlightenment would 'filter down' from a university-trained élite to the mass of the population. Even so, the Government began to take an interest in primary education, attempting to make a census of old-type schools (Adam's reports in Bengal), and to increase and improve them (Elphinstone in Bombay). Mass education became the order of the day with the dispatch of 1854 from Sir Charles Wood, President of the Board of Control, to the Governor-General, Lord Dalhousie, who was in agreement with this policy and took the first steps. Progress was slow for several reasons. The subject-matter was far removed from village life, and primary education was not free, since it was thought that it would be too heavy a charge on the Budget. By 1901 there were 98,000 schools with 3·2 million pupils. Teaching was given in the vernaculars, which meant a promotion of those tongues, previously humbled under the prestige of the two learned languages.

Lastly there was an intermediate teaching, called 'secondary', mostly given in English, which cut down its syllabuses and increased its numbers as more colleges were established. Of course, education was very unevenly distributed among the various castes and in different areas. Compared with that of the boys, the education of girls lagged far behind. In general, India owed much to missionaries for their initiative in the establishment and maintenance of teaching institutions, for the training of teachers and for the level of instruction.

The new education exerted a complex action on Indian society. One of its major long-term effects was to foster nationalism in several ways: it unified the intelligentsia all over the country through the use of a common language, English; it made for the penetration of Western ideals and modes of thought; it led to the growth of an educated class of civil servants, lawyers, and also physicians and journalists, whose background was mainly literary and humanistic, with a fringe of young unemployed degree holders.

2. A DEPENDENT ECONOMY

In terms of the stages of economic development, the economic transformation of India in the nineteenth century has been characterized as follows:

'The developments to be described consist not so much of a transition from one stage to another as of the gradual extension to an ever greater proportion of the population of economic features and organization, such as the use of money and of capital, division of labour, and economic diversification, which are characteristic of modern economic life, but existed in India in certain areas, or in embryo, before the British era . . . Production has been substantially commercialized, the use of money predominates, and approximate economic unification has been attained, (Vera Anstey, in O'Malley, 8, p. 259).

Change was greater in the forms and volume of exchange than in modes of production. Therefore the growth of transport and trade will be considered first.

Transport
Steam navigation, tried in 1825, brought India close to Europe. In 1843, the P. & O. (Peninsular and Oriental) Company opened a regular service between India and Europe, via Suez and Alexandria, but due to the necessary transhipment from the Red Sea to the Mediterranean, trade continued to use the Cape route until the opening of the Suez Canal in 1869, which reduced the duration of the voyage from three months to one. Steam navigation on the rivers began in 1828. Later, a regular service was opened on the Ganges, but it still took 25 days to travel from Allahabad to Calcutta. It was on the Brahmaputra that water transport was to play the most important role by opening communications with Assam.

When the British arrived, roads were very few, and passable only in the dry season. Most of the provinces had few vehicles and transport was mainly by pack-animals—hence slow and expensive. Matters slowly improved in the second quarter of the century, and a road was constructed over the Ghats from Bombay to Poona in 1830. In 1839 the decision was made to rebuild the great Mughul road from Calcutta to Delhi and to macadamize it, but without bridges over the bigger streams. This was the Grand Trunk Road, of which about two-thirds was completed in 1852. Other roads connecting the larger centres were added. Later the development speeded up under the stimulus of the railways, which had to be connected with the hinterland. Up to the middle of the century the quickest mode of travel was by palanquin, for which the postal service provided the bearers. Correspondence went by couriers in relays, and it took eleven days for a letter from Bombay to reach Calcutta, the tariffs varying according to distance and from province to province. The modern postal service, the electric telegraph and the railways were all introduced at the same time (1854). In due course, for a half-anna stamp, a letter was to go from one end of the country to the other, and postal traffic to reach vast proportions, including money orders and parcels as well as letters.

Objections to the building of railways included the surmise that caste regulations would prevent the Hindus from using them. Dalhousie's Minute of 1853 carried the decision. In 1855, with 200 miles of track, there were already a million and a half travellers, and by 1869, with 4,000 miles of line, external trade had tripled. In 1891 the railway system, which was mainly constructed for strategic purposes and to serve the requirements of external trade, included 12,000 miles of track, increasing to 25,000 miles in 1901. The greater part of the lines was under private ownership, with a small part being State-owned. Invested money, essentially English, reached £226 million in 1901. The State had guaranteed a fixed interest to the stockholders from the start (Thorner, 42).

It should be noted that modern transport was introduced when India had already been administratively organized, and that, contrary to the order of events in Europe, it preceded the needs of industry. On the whole, the railways acted less radically as agents of economic progress and of social transformation than some had hoped. In particular, they did not provoke a rapid and thorough industrialization of the country, due partly no doubt to their being geared to the interests of the ruling power (Thorner, 43). However, they had sizeable results: they helped the unification of the country and the development of outlying regions. The role they played in the growth of external and internal trade, in the change in agriculture from subsistence crops to cash crops, in the uniformity of prices, is obvious. Railways made possible effective relief in famines, which were always regional. Regarding the population, they increased the physical mobility of the people and weakened, within fairly narrow limits, the prejudices of caste, while they considerably increased the frequenting by pilgrims of the Hindu holy places.

Trade

Brooks Adams has drawn attention to the synchronism between the arrival in England of the 'treaure' plundered in Bengal, around 1760, and the beginnings of the industrial revolution (*34*, pp. 313–14). Investment of wealth brought from India would have permitted the exploitation of technical innovations and led to the development of the modern textile industry. The idea is tempting and has been adopted by several authors (Nehru, *7*, pp. 296–7; Panikkar, *10*, pp. 484–5); unfortunately the fact has not been proved and accepted by economic historians.[9]

At any rate, the needs of the new industry were antagonistic to the activity of the East India Company: the Company traded fabrics from India, while the new English industry wanted to export its products. Clearly, the days of the Company as a commercial organization were numbered. In 1813 they lost their monopoly of trade between England and India; in 1833, with the abolition of their monopoly of trade with China (where they exported opium grown in India), they ceased all commercial operations, and became, as it were, merely a governing concern. From then onwards, the English members of the Government of India were able to identify themselves with what they conceived as the interests of India in opposition to the interests of English industrialists. This was seen in matters of commercial policy, especially in questions of customs duties, where the British Government was strongly influenced by the textile interests of Lancashire. On the whole external Indian trade was governed by the will of England.

To enter into detail, several periods may be distinguished. In the first, from 1780 to 1813, about one-third of the territorial revenues of the Company in Bengal—some £1·3 million—was used to purchase goods for export (this was called the 'investment'). The Company, alarmed by the progress of the textile industry in England, tried to develop and improve Indian production excluding silk weaving, by means of loans, and by grouping the workers in manufactures. The Company was unsuccessful, for English industry had for long been protected by duties, and even by pure and simple prohibitions, against the import of textiles from India. These paid a duty in London and were for the most part re-exported: France, for instance, had long preferred Indian to English silks. But at the same time the British forced upon India almost Free Trade; while Indian silks paid 20 per cent import duty into England, English silks paid 3·5 per cent on entry into India. For wool textiles, the corresponding figures were 30 and 2 per cent. English import duties were increased in 1813, so much was the Commission concerned with opening up the Indian market, and they were to be notably reduced only around 1830. Meanwhile, the current had been reversed: in 1813, Calcutta exported to London £2 million worth of cotton fabrics; by 1830, she imported a similar amount. In 1825, India imported about 2,000 tons of cotton yarn. This was a great blow to Indian hand weaving. The population of Dacca fell from 150,000 to 30 or 40,000. In the textile industry in 1830, only silk fabrics maintained their exports, while the export of indigo had increased.

For a long time India exported raw materials and agricultural products, and imported manufactured goods. Trade increased rapidly.

	Exports	Imports
	(£ million)	
1834–5.	8	6
1849–50	18·2	13·6
1858.	28·2	31 (*)
1869.	54	51
1877.	65	48
1901.	81	80

(*) The excess of imports over exports is exceptional and due to the Mutiny.

The composition of trade changed between 1850 and 1901. On the export side, cotton, chiefly raw, but with some development of manufactured goods, held its place (14 per cent of the total value in 1901). Opium fell from 35 to 8 per cent; sugar, which accounted for 11 per cent of exports in 1850, was on the contrary imported for 7 per cent of the total in 1901; indigo, 11 per cent in 1850, was finally supplanted by chemical dyes. Against these losses, new exports were developed: jute, raw, but also woven, 15 per cent in 1901; cereals 11·5 per cent; leather 9·5 per cent; tea, and oil seeds about 8 per cent each. On the import side, cotton cloth decreased a little, from 45 to 34 per cent; metals and metallic products accounted for 9 per cent only in 1901; sugar for 7 per cent. World events had an influence on trade. The Crimean War (1853–4) blocked the supply of Russian hemp, and increased the demand for jute, from which sacks were made in Dundee and later in Bengal. Likewise, the American Civil War (1861–5) caused a boom in Indian cotton. With the return of peace, American cotton with its longer staple again took first place. There was a financial crash in Bombay, and despite all its efforts British industry did not succeed in drawing from India in a lasting manner the main part of its raw material. Nevertheless, the events had brought on the birth of a modern textile industry. It was only a beginning, but sufficient at any rate to frighten Lancashire into action. In 1876, after a long controversy, the small Indian tax on the import of cotton was suppressed. Later, when all import duties had been abolished by Lord Ripon in 1882, the Manchester industrialists succeeded in obtaining the creation of a tax of 3·5 per cent on the production of all cotton textiles in India. Another result of industrial competition was the early introduction of labour legislation into Indian factories.[10]

Internal trade increased alongside external trade, particularly after 1850, thanks to internal security and the improvement of communications. Internal duties were not abolished until rather late (from 1836 to 1844), and the 'salt wall', which separated the Native States from British India, where the Government had a monopoly and levied a tax on salt, disappeared much later still. The prices, hitherto regional and fluctuating, became more uniform and nearer to world prices.

Regarding external trade, the demand for iron, steel and machines was small, while the Indian industrial production of these remained insignificant. At the same time, the exportation of cereals from a country where many people were underfed is striking. R. Dutt saw therein an effect of the Land Revenue; to pay it, the peasant had to sell a part of his crops, and India to deprive herself of staple foods. Hunter on the contrary, estimating the exports at about $\frac{1}{35}$ of the total consumption, remarked that at the same time India was importing a comparable amount of bullion, and concluded that it illustrated a vicious distribution of income (Dutt, *38*, II, 349; Hunter, *40*, p. 118).

Industry

Before looking at modern industry, a word has to be said about the decline of traditional handicrafts. This is often exaggerated, as when, according to somewhat popular contentions, it is thought that Indian handicrafts were utterly ruined by the concurrence of British industry. It should be remembered that until our own times, the great bulk of the population went on using for the most part native products, the village artisans catering as of old to the village needs. On the contrary the market for luxury goods almost disappeared with the end of the power of most of the local rulers and the decay of the old artistocracy. Skilled craftsmen who lived near the courts and who were patronized by the Grandees lost their extravagant, if sometimes brutal customers, and their crafts dwindled.

Even in the case of hand-weaving, which was the most severely hit of all handicrafts, the ruin was not so universal as if often supposed. Let us come back to the reversal of external trade which marked the first third of the century. India ceased to export cotton goods, which meant the end of that part of Indian skilled hand weaving that had worked for export; at the same time India began importing a part of the cloth needed for her own consumption, and this again reduced her own production. The change is significant, but it should not be imagined that at any time hand weaving ceased to be practised in India on a considerable scale, or that British imports entirely replaced native products.

The Tamil country is admittedly a relatively conservative tract; there, in 1950, while men wore almost exclusively machine-made cloth, the bulk of the women still wore the traditional hand-woven saris,; this fact may help to form a more adequate idea of the general situation during the nineteenth century.

On the eve of the twentieth century, Indian modern industry was still of little importance. British commercial policy was no doubt chiefly responsible, but the reluctance of Indian capital towards long-term investments has also been noted.

Coal-mining, long handicapped by the position of the coal deposits, which were difficult to reach, was the only industry that attained a notable development (6·8 million tons in 1901). This development was made possible by the railways, in spite of high freight rates, which aroused complaints. In 1900 the railways used almost exclusively Indian coal, which also ran the textile mills. While gold-mining was notable, iron works were founded only in the first years of the twentieth century by a Parsi and with the help of Indian subscriptions, whipped up by the nationalist campaign for self-sufficiency. Jute weaving began in 1854. The first cotton mill was opened by a Parsi in 1851. In general, the cotton mills, located in western India (Bombay, etc.), were owned by Indians and run with the help of British technicians. In 1901 they employed 237,000 workers as against 262,000 in agricultural industries and 600,000 in tea plantations.

Agriculture

A basic fact of Indian agriculture, at least from 1880 onwards, is the pressure of population on land. It is sometimes contended that, then and even later, the cultivated area could have been substantially increased. While it is true that according to agricultural statistics the proportion of 'culturable waste' to the cultivated area appears considerable (about 10:24 in 1900–1), Hunter nevertheless remarked in 1880 that the greater part of the available land was situated, apart from Burma, in a few relatively sparsely populated provinces; Assam, Panjab, and also Central Provinces. So far, the problem was one of settling in those regions people who had to be removed from the densely populated tracts, as was done, for instance, with the irrigation and colonization of large tracts in Panjab. For the rest of the land, said Hunter, the 'culturable waste' was made up of small patches scattered throughout the other provinces; he added that in this matter the increase of cultivation had, if anything, been too rapid (e.g. in Madras): trees had been felled, pastures converted into fields, and this was regrettable (40, p. 154). Hunter was right, he foresaw the degradation of agriculture, the 'bankruptcy in the soil', which is an all too familiar fact today. A category of 'cultural waste' that does not allow for pastures, and which does not state whether and under which conditions water can be made available, is simply misleading.

In point of fact, the land as it stood was, in most provinces, fully occupied at the end of the nineteenth century. While a century earlier much land had been lying fallow, manpower being scarce in relation to land, so that the problem for the landlord was to get tenants to cultivate the land, a century later the situation was reversed; there was not enough land for all the village people to live from, manpower being in excess of the land (this is said as holding within the given technical and social framework). Hunter, who knew Bengal well, wrote:

'a century ago one-third of Bengal lay unoccupied; but since then the population of Bengal has increased not by one-third, but threefold; and the area which had to feed twenty-one millions in 1780 has in 1880 to feed over sixty-three millions of mouths' (*40*, p. 138).

The pressure on land is often attributed by Indian authors to the lack of sufficient non-agricultural employment resulting from the decline of handicrafts and the slow growth of industry. This is certainly true to some extent, but it should not obscure a far more cogent factor, namely the growth of the general population, which was the first and most sweeping of all the unintended consequences of British rule.[11] The fact stands beyond doubt, if only because of its dimension, although there was no general census before 1872, when the population amounted to 255 million, and although the increase was small, owing to famines and epidemics, from 1872 to 1881 and again from 1891 to 1901. According to more or less reliable estimates the population would have been about 100 million under Akbar, and 150 million at the beginning of our period. Apart from some progress in prophylaxy, and while famine control was in its beginnings, the fact has to be attributed mainly to the maintenance of peaceful and ordered government over most of the country. As early as about 1815 the view of the Abbé Dubois, who had witnessed the change from war to peace, and who detected the change among a tiny portion of the population and even foresaw its probable development, was the following:

'From such observations as it was given me to make upon the Christian portion of the population in Mysore and in the districts of Baramahal (Salem) and of Coimbatore, it appeared evident to me that the population had increased about twenty-five per cent within the course of twenty-five years ... I have every reason for supposing that a substantial increase in the population must be thought of as being rather a curse than a blessing. Now, given the present state of things, in the midst of peace ... the population must inevitably continue to grow; and this growth may well become dreadful' (*37*, 1825, I, pp. 117–18).

Still, famines continued to exercise their terrible check on population growth. In 1770 10 million people died in Bengal, and one famine succeeded another; 1783–4 in Benares, Oudh, Madras; 1803–4 in Bombay and the north; 1813 (Bombay); 1807, 1823, 1833 (Madras); 1837 and 1860 (United Provinces); 1866–7 (Orissa); 1874 (Bengal); 1877 (Madras); 1897 (widespread, followed by a return of plague in Bombay); 1900–4. In 1833, in a part of the district of Guntur, one-third or more of the population died. In 1837, the Ganges plain witnessed sights as horrible as those of Bengal in 1770. When that region was struck by famine again, but less seriously, in 1860, relief was for the first time organized on a grand scale, including the opening of works for the unemployed. Baird Smith, who was asked to write a report, concluded that the resistance of the population after bad harvests depended largely on the amount and distribution of the Land Revenue, and that the famine was less a question of food shortage than of the people's inability to procure food. Relief was less successful in Orissa in 1886 and in Madras in 1877. The Government set up a whole organization with a special fund, which functioned satisfactorily in 1897, except perhaps in the Central Provinces where conditions were particularly severe.

Given India's climate, the availability of water for irrigation is the basic means of increasing agricultural output. Here, as in general, the Company was content with a policy of *laissez-faire*, and it was only after the Government had been transferred to the Crown that a more active course with more generous investments was pursued. Many of the old irrigation works had been badly maintained in the recent past; a beginning was made by repairing some of them, such as the Jumna canals. After 1850 new works were constructed, for which Baird Smith and Sir Arthur Cotton are well known: the Ganges Canal, the Bari Doab in the Panjab, the systems of the Coleroon, the Godavari, the Krishna, the Periyar. In Madras, the area irrigated by State canals increased by 41 per cent between 1852 and 1890. The effort was intensified so that from 1894 to 1913 the irrigated area over the whole of India grew from 24 to 47 million acres. There was some controversy between the supporters of railways and those of irrigation; Indian opinion favoured the latter and found the expenditure on irrigation insufficient. There were sometimes additional problems: in the Doab between the Ganges and the Jumna an excess of irrigation sent up alkaline salts, which had to be eliminated.

Considering the economy of the country as a whole, the main event of the period was the increasing change from a subsistence to a market economy. As for the individual village, it was not so self-sufficient as it had hitherto been. The cultivation of cash crops increased, which resulted in some diversification.

Opium poppy was grown for the Company and under its control in north and north-east India. The crop was delivered to the Company who prepared the opium, imposed an enormous tax on it, and auctioned it (after the end of the monopoly) for trade to China.

After the revolution in Santo Domingo, there was a greater demand for indigo. Production continued and increased until about 1890, reaching some 50,000 tons, when it was hit by the production of chemical dyes. Cultivation was chiefly confined to Bengal and the lower Ganges valley, the industry being under European control but employing some local capital. European manufactures, by means of a system of loans, often brought pressure to bear on the grower, forcing him to produce at a fixed price more than he wished to grow. Abuses had led to demonstrations and to some violence in Bengal, when in 1860 hundreds of thousands of peasants sternly refused to grow indigo any longer. The Government sided with the peasants against the planters, and a Commission of Inquiry was appointed which concluded that the cultivation had become unprofitable to the peasants. Indigo was later to give occasion to Gandhi's first *satyagraha* in India, in Bihar in 1917.

The cultivation of tea, which increased tremendously after 1850, was slow in starting, in spite of the perseverance of British pioneers. Until 1833 the Company saw in it a threat to their Chinese trade, and as such had opposed it. Bentinck ordered an inquiry, and in 1839 the Assam Tea Company was founded. In difficult climatic and hygienic conditions, this was to lead to the prosperity of the province, thanks to European initiative and to Indian labour imported from other provinces. Indian opinion protested against the long-term contracts by which the coolies were bound, calling them 'slave-law'. Coffee, introduced in the high Deccan (Mysore and Coorg), suffered setbacks. A large number of the plantations were in the hands of Indians.

Finances

British firms adopted the practice of conducting their Indian business through 'managing agencies', and the system became general, first for the British in Calcutta, and later for the Indians in Bombay, as a flexible and practical method combining at need banking facilities, commercial management, and technical advice. In particular, the combination made possible, once a particular venture was launched, an appeal to Indian capital which, although little inclined to long-term investments, was attracted by the proved competence of the agency. The Indians had their own banking system, but it was ill suited to modern conditions in that it preferred the short-term operations and speculative rates of agricultural credit, while giving credit only to individuals. We have already seen that the railways were built with British capital to which the State guaranteed an interest—an arrangement which was much criticized by Indians. The State itself built some of the lines, and for the others it took advantage of a purchase clause, so that after some time the Indian railways were to a large extent nationalized.

It was not until 1835 that a uniform currency was established for the whole of India. This was the silver rupee. The minting of gold coins remained free for a time. In the last quarter of the century, following the world movement of silver, the value of the rupee fell from 23 to 14 pence between 1871 and 1893. This favoured the export trade, but the British officials, who had to make payments to England in gold (the 'Home Charges', below), at once tried to persuade London to stop the fall in currency. London resisted, but eventually decided to stop the issue of coins so as to stabilize the price (1893) and finally to make gold legal tender at the rate of a sovereign for 15 rupees (1899).

The manufacture and sale of opium at a high price was the only remnant of the commercial activities of the Company after 1833. It was a very lucrative item in the Revenue, and it was considered as a 'most unexceptionable' one, being 'a tax levied on the Chinese for the general benefit of the State' (Campbell, *36*, pp. 388–9). How the Chinese were compelled by war (1840–2) to accept the import of the drug is well known. In 1850 opium represented about one-seventh of the Government's income. The trade went on without change until 1907.

The Act of 1833, which put an end to the commercial activities of the Company, settled that a dividend of 10·5 per cent would be paid to the shareholders from the territorial revenues. When, in 1858, India passed under the Crown, the State took charge of the dividends. According to R. Dutt, 'the Empire was thus transferred from the Company, but the Indian people paid the purchase money'. From 1813 the territorial revenues were used to pay for the civil and military administration and for the Indian debt (and also, until 1833, for the maintenance of commercial establishments). Periods of war generally led to deficits, and even when, as under the wise administration of Lord Bentinck, there was an excess of receipts over expenditure, the balance was not always enough to pay for the Indian debt in England. This debt increased from 27 million sterling in 1807 (and the same amount in 1836 after Bentinck's rule) to 69 million sterling in 1857-8. In the middle of the century the dues in England, or Home Charges, were made up of three almost equal parts: dividends to shareholders, leave and retirement pay of personnel, and costs of the Indian administration in England. Later, the debt increased considerably, partly as a result of the Mutiny, but mainly because of investments of British capital, chiefly in railways. It reached 139 million in 1876-7 and 226 million in 1901-2.

The British tendency throughout the period was to make India pay for all expenses having any connection whatsoever with India, without England contributing anything in proportion to her own interests. Thus, not only all civil servants on the spot, but also the Indian administrations in London, were paid for by India. There, too, the total cost of the maintenance and campaigns of the Indian army was borne by India alone. However, English protests against this treatment were not lacking, and Indian critics soon echoed them. The latter went further, sometimes considering the total debt as it appeared at the end of the century as being an unacceptable 'tribute' or 'drain' without distinguishing the productive role of invested capital, mainly in railways. In 1914 British investments in India and Ceylon amounted to 379 million sterling.[12]

A committee appointed by Gladstone to study Indian finances sat in 1871-4. Before this committee, Sir Charles Trevelyan in particular, an old member of the administration, former Minister of Finance for India, repeated his earlier protests against the increase in expenditure under the Government of the Crown.[13] He asked that some representation be granted to Indians so that they might have some control over expenditure. Again, in 1895, a Commission of Enquiry was set up, which recommended that England should share in the expenses of the India Office in London, and in those of the Indian army.

3. THE GENERAL IMPACT OF BRITISH RULE

Every aspect of British policy has acted on the society, not in isolation, but in conjunction with all others and with the basic fact of British domination. Therefore, to follow up the consequences of every innovation we must take a general point of view. The general impact is reasonably clear in parts and within certain limits. Beyond these, it has been assessed in the most varied manners and raises important questions. Let us begin with the most obvious.

First there appeared new, for the most part urban, professions. These professions were not always new in their function, but they were so in their numbers, in the fact that their members were more or less Western-oriented, had in the higher levels a university education, and functioned either on an all-India level or within the new economic and social make-up. They were first of all servants of Government and of the national services (railways, post offices, public works), then teachers and professors, lawyers and physicians, journalists. It was this new 'middle class', for a large part dependent on the Government, that carried in the main the new reformist and nationalist aspirations.

In the villages, where an increased population competed for land to till, land had become to a large extent a commodity, while the land revenue, high to begin with, payable uniformly in cash, was for the first time but for exceptional remissions, fixed and inexorable. This seems to have acted powerfully to draw the village into the market economy. It created golden opportunities for the money-lender, who might rely on the courts to dispossess his debtor, and led to the acquisition of much landed property by usurers and town merchants. The peasants' discontent was evidenced in several regions by disturbances, and the Government was compelled to intervene to check the evil.

This situation is an index of the new freedom and power acquired by (movable) wealth as distinguished from landed rights and political power. To measure the change, we must contrast it with the former situation, in which the merchant and the possessor of money in general were at the mercy of the arbitrary will of those retaining force and political power. This was clearly the case under the Mughuls. The first result of British order and the 'rule of law' was to emancipate wealth from its subjection to brute force, and to create the possibility of economic power. This is bourgeois revolution, at least in part. Thus, the mercantile classes were the great beneficiaries of British rule. They became, in their particular way, together with the professions, the main agents of progress and of political assertiveness.

If certain professions or classes benefited from the changes introduced under British rule, is it conceivable that the condition of other categories of people became worse? Even apart from the rulers or landed aristocrats and persons attached to their fortunes, some good observers have thought that such was the case for the poorer portion of the agricultural population. Abbé Dubois, speaking for the first years of the period, concluded that while most of the people were better off than before, the most miserable part of the population, on the contrary, might have been left even more destitute (37, ed. 1825, I, 116). Hunter's testimony is still more conclusive. I have quoted him as stressing the growth of population in relation to the land. He goes on to say that his growth must have worsened the situation of the poorer peasants who were competing for land to till. He also insists that the food supply of India, sufficient absolutely, is insufficient because it is not evenly distributed:

'... of the 63 millions of Bengal ... 40 millions, as nearly as I can estimate, are well fed; 10 millions suffer hunger when the harvest falls short; and thirteen millions are always badly off—in fact, do not know the feeling of a full stomach except in the mango season' (40, p. 150).

Recognizing that things are at their worst in Bengal, he generalizes by saying that

'Two-fifths of the people of British India enjoy a prosperity unknown under native rule; other two-fifths earn a fair but diminishing subsistence; but the remaining fifth, or forty millions, go through life on insufficient food' [this was written in 1879] (40, p. 151).

How is it that the enfranchisement of money, coupled with the introduction of modern means of transportation, has failed to produce a more pronounced and more rapid economic progress, and to transform to any appreciable extent the social fabric, namely, the caste system, which is generally thought to rest on a different type of economy?[14] Regarding the economy, this sort of question is most often answered by referring to British policy itself: India was managed for the benefit of foreigners who did not favour industrialization and even did something to prevent or retard it. Hence a lopsided, unbalanced development. The same contradiction, the same juxtaposition of progressive with conservative aspects, is found in the British social and political policy, and results in what has been called euphemistically a 'differential' diffusion of modernization (Thorner, 44, pp. 104-5). Socially, we have referred to the conservative attitude which, regarding religion and personal law, was maintained throughout. Politically speaking, a large part of the country was maintained under the personal rule of a great number of seemingly independent princes. The maintenance of order under a foreign rule, and also, as we have seen, the paternalism of an influential fraction of the administrators, led to upholding institutions which, in a greater or lesser degree, went against change.

This is doubtless true, but is it the whole truth? To come back to our merchants and moneyed people, I have refrained from calling them capitalists because, as we have noticed in relation to agriculture in Bengal and with productive investment in general, they showed a marked reluctance to turn to properly capitalist pursuits, and did so belatedly and in small numbers, at least up to the end of the century. This seems to show that economic conditions are not sufficient to create capitalism, but that something like a particular spirit is also necessary, as Max Weber attempted to show. Everything looks as if British rule had found, as it were, an accomplice in the prominently conservative character of Hindu society itself. In other words, our question cannot be argued *in abstracto*, as if 'economic forces' acted uniformly in all kinds of society. Account must be taken of the general social background, i.e., in this case, of the caste society *and its values*. The point has to be indicated here, although it cannot be sufficiently developed. Avowedly vague formulas give an idea of what is in question here. First, we may say that caste society is remarkably resilient and integrative, in the sense that it can stand a considerable injection of heterogeneous features without alteration of its general form. This will be seen from the modern religious and political development. As an instance, the claim of political independence is foreign to caste society and seems contrary to its ethos, and yet India could make it hers successfully without notably altering her social order. Or again, we may say that the areas of change were, and are, surrounded by, and encapsulated in, an unchanging social framework. The principle of 'quality before the law', important though it is, did not impair the traditional recognition of caste inequalities and disabilities in social life at large.

This being so, we may surmise that a more coherent general policy might certainly have accelerated economic changes, but would not have had much influence on the social organization. This is confirmed by two facts: first that apparently revolutionary measures, such as the transformation of rights in connection with land, had no consequence of that kind; second that economic changes were more pronounced in the twentieth century under British rule and still more in independent India, once again without entailing, until now, any marked decline of the caste system. This fact can be understood if it is remembered that 'ultimate values' are everywhere, by definition, far removed from the realities of everyday life, that in Hindu India the social system is based on religious values, and far from rejecting what is not religious accommodates it in subordinate positions. Apparently radical changes, such as the emergence of a new kind of power or the creation of rights in land, the economic rise of one community or the ruin of another, strike in the first analysis in the vacuum, because they are not meaningful for the system either as a change within it or as a threat against it. With what subtlety and integrative power the system can react to a threat will be seen in the section dealing with religious reform. And in point of fact, British power refrained from intervening in this sphere, and located the changes in indifferent areas. Moreover, not a single reformer has ever advocated that the British should have disregarded Abbé Dubois' warning and have attempted to destroy the caste system. The timid policy of Gandhi and of independent India regarding untouchability convinces us that, short of disastrous bloodshed, India was bound to remain very conservative in the nineteenth century.

This is not to say that the changes had absolutely no effect on the social system, but only that they have failed to alter it visibly. It may well be that the effects have been accumulated somewhere and will act some day through their gathered pressure, but we need more sensitive instruments to detect them than we have at present.[15]

II. THE INDIAN RESPONSE[16]

The Indian intellectual response to Western influence has been positive. This is shown by the tale that will now be briefly recalled, a tale of revival and awakening. This is because, at the root of all the movement, whether literary, religious, social or political, there lies the common factor of an almost unanimous acceptance by the new Indian intelligentsia—the people immediately concerned—of some fundamental ideas offered by the West, and the rejection, implicitly at least, of corresponding Indian ideas. This is graphically emphasized by Indian historians:

'Reason and judgement took the place of faith and belief; superstition yielded to science; immobility was replaced by progress . . .' (Advanced History *1*, p. 812).

This might be missed because the religious and political movements, looked at in the totality of their development, appear increasingly directed against the West.[17] Yet many things which later came to be questioned were at first accepted without reserve or ulterior motive. And even where the reaction appears to be most radical it will invariably be based on an acceptance of certain fundamental principles or a transformation of traditional Indian points of view by those principles. The initial acquiescence was fortunate from the point of view of the relations between the two civilizations, because it was the condition of later syntheses. Everything looks as if India had instinctively perceived that, in order to remain herself, she must first resolutely enter the modern stage. To forget this general design would lead to attributing an exaggerated importance to certain aspects such as Gandhi's spinning-wheel in the twentieth century. It must be remembered that in the initial stages we have to deal with a progressive élite, which is not always followed even by all the educated class: the movement had to change somehow when it spread among the public. Anyway, the Indian intelligentsia fulfilled its historic function in a manner which does it great honour.

In the field of letters, the idea of a literature which would be public and autonomous (public rather than confined to specialists; autonomous of religion, but also in some measure of such arts as music); in religion, monotheism; in politics, the ideas of the rule of law and of representative government are some of the new features which imposed themselves as a result of the Western contact. This enumeration is of course inadequate, since it leaves out what is essential, namely the relations between those ideas as they appeared to the Indians; but this is a question which must be left out here.

Literary renaissance

In the nineteenth century India experienced a whole series of changes bearing on languages and literatures as well as on the role of writing and of literary education in culture as a whole, this last element dominating. It is not enough to speak of the replacement of the oral tradition by the printed word. The real change, as it is still going on, is clearly perceptible. As is well known, India has had adopted its own scripts and literatures since ancient times. If it had not yet the printing-press it was probably in part because there was no need for it. Written culture was specialized, but a part of it spread among the mass of the people by word of mouth, the specialists being so to speak in charge of reading certain texts aloud to the public. The modern requirement of general literacy suppresses this kind of specialization. This has to be borne in mind in order to understand what follows.

In the matter of languages, the first event was the replacement of Persian by English as the official language; English was taught to the new élite and began to spread. But Persian was after all only a foreign language introduced by Moslem rulers, and the English language and Government were to have a much deeper effect. Sanskrit, the sacred language of Hinduism, was at the same time the literary language *par excellence* for the Hindus; it was to India what Latin used to be for Europe; moreover, it was reserved to a small class. The living tongues of northern India, related to Sanskrit which was recognized as their corresponding literary medium, could hardly be called languages although some of them had an old literature, it was exclusively poetical and religious, often stereotyped and copied from Sanskrit. The new climate reduced the prestige of Sanskrit and gave increased impetus to vernaculars. The use of English in higher education did not exclude, but rather encouraged, primary teaching in the vernacular. Charles Wilkins, one of the founders of the Asiatic Society of Bengal, cast Bengali types which enabled Halhed to publish the first Bengali grammar in 1783. (In the south, missionaries had already issued a Tamil grammar.) William Carey, founder of the Baptist Mission in Bengal, and others, were to print in Nagari (the script for Sanskrit and Hindi). Thanks to printing, and in part to the missionaries, textbooks, translations of the Christian Scriptures, dictionaries and grammars for the vernaculars, and finally newspapers were to give the local languages an unprecedented boost.

We shall concentrate on the Bangali linguistic and literary revival because it was in Bengal that Western influence first penetrated and made the most rapid and deep impact. Other Indian literatures followed suit, but with some delay, and by 1900 they had reached a development comparable to that of Bengali literature.

While the English language largely concerned itself with matters of libel, the press in Bengali, whether published by missionaries or by Hindus, took seriously its role of education; this was important as public instruction was still in its infancy. In 1818 Marshman launched the first stable Bengali periodical: *Semacar Darpan* or 'News Mirror', which also appeared in Persian and was for a long time the first of the Calcutta papers; it met such a success that it was made a weekly. In 1821 the great reformer Ram Mohan Roy brought out another weekly, the *Sambad Kaumudi*, and in 1822 a Persian language newspaper. The Conservatives, in turn, produced a rival paper. Ram Mohan Roy played a considerable role in the creation of the Bengali press. His prose was still 'dry and heavy', but it must be borne in mind that he had to work on the one hand in a peotical language loaded with Sanskritisms, on the other, from a spoken tongue unadapted to the propagation of ideas. He literally had to teach his readers to read, especially to understand punctuation, which was borrowed from English. Here, English had a direct and general influence, as the Indians who succeeded Ram Mohan Roy in this task were all bilingual. Other newspapers followed. In 1825 there were about 1,000 subscribers in all, and by 1830 there were eight Bengali newspapers in existence. By 1878 there were 230 newspapers in the Indian languages.

English influence on the new Bengali literature is evident in the appearance of two new literary forms: the novel, and a new theatre distinct from the classical; both new forms met with great success. The plays had a social, almost a national tendency; thus *Kulina-kulasarvasva* (on the polygamy of Kulin Brahmans) was still close to the Sanskrit drama (1857), while the *Sarmistha* of Madhu Sudan Dutt was modern. In 1860, Dinabandhu Mitra, a post office superintendent, published *Nil Darpana*, depicting the exploitation of the tenant-farmers on the indigo plantations. In 1873 Girish Chandra Ghosa, author, actor and producer, founded the first public theatre in Calcutta. Later, Rabindranath Tagore wrote a number of plays, more lyrical than dramatic.

In fiction, Tek Chand was followed by Bankim Chatterji (1838–93), an outstanding author, probably the most popular writer of the whole period. He has been called the Walter Scott of Bengal, 'rhetorical in style and romantic in his view of history'. Bankim directed three newspapers and wrote fourteen novels, from *The Daughter of the Fort Commander*, in 1865, which has wrongly been called an imitation of *Ivanhoe*, to the *Cloister of Happiness* (*Ananda Math*) in 1882, which, though not his very last work in date, can be considered as Bankim's testament from the national point of view. It contains the quasi-religious hymn, 'Hail Mother', *Bande Mataram*, which was in its day very nearly the Indian national anthem. Bankim was influenced by Auguste Comte and others; his work had a religious, moral and philosophical impact. In *Ananda Math*, an ascetic guided by a mysterious master leads a victorious revolt against the Moslems; when he fails against the British troops, his master enjoins him to stop fighting and to learn from the West in view of the future.

A critic understood this to mean that 'India is bound to accept the scientific method of the West' (Chaudhuri, 47, p. 419).

Lastly, it was in poetry that the Bengalis excelled. Here, in spite of technical borrowings, the core remained essentially Indian. As in other spheres, Westernization was at a peak at the beginning, as is shown in the work of Madhu Sudan Dutt, a convert to Christianity, and particularly in his epic poem in nine cantos based on an episode from the Ramayana, but profoundly original: *Meghnadbadh*.

'The noble characters, the magnificent style match the greatness and sweep of design. This work by a Christian inspired by Homer, Virgil and Milton is one of the major masterpieces of Indian literature of all times' (Jules Bloch, *46*, p. 1034).

Madhu Sudan had reversed the traditional view of the struggle between the Hindu hero Rama and the demon-king Ravana with his son Meghnad. The effect of the poem on the young Bengalis is described in his autobiography by N. L. Chaudhuri, who insists in general on the depth of English and Western influence on the Bengali intelligentsia, comparing the movement with the renaissance of European letters under the influence of the ancients.

Madhu Sudan was followed by other poets, among whom were Nabin Chandra Sen, patriot and humanist, and Bihari Lal Chakravarti, who directly influenced the greatest of them all, Rabindranath Tagore. Rabindranath Tagore was born in 1861 of an intellectual as well as aristocratic, although more or less ostracized, family. He was to live until the Second World War, but by 1905 he had already produced a considerable part of his work. He can be historically situated by saying that with him assimilation of Western culture no longer implied any estrangement from the Indian legacy. The form and technique are European, while the content and essence have remained profoundly Indian. Tagore wrote some 2,000 poems, more than 30 plays, and novels, short stories as well as essays of every description. In 1913 he was awarded the Nobel Prize for literature for his translation into English of his own *Gitanjali* or 'Lyrical Offering', which aroused the enthusiasm of Yeats; from that time it was the habit in the West to look at him mainly as a mystic. In fact his inspiration, and even his language, are of an extraordinary variety. His poetry is intimately linked with music, which he composed while writing, or more accurately, he did not write, he sang.

Around 1900 Tagore founded Santiniketan, 'The Abode of Peace', which became the most Indian of all Indian universities. At the time of the agitation against the partition of Bengal he took part in political action for a short time and his novel, *Gora* (1907) was a dramatic presentation of the conflict between traditionalism and reform. Tagore made a personal synthesis of East and West. 'This great humanist has acquired a world-wide audience, he takes his place among the small team of poets who are at the same time national and universal' (J. Bloch). Tagore's fame was to grow in India in the twentieth century, while contemporary European influence continued to be felt in Indian literature. 'Indian literature has become a province of universal literature' (J. Bloch).

Religious reform
Ram Mohan Roy (1772–1833). Ram Mohan Roy was the pioneer of all

Indian progress in the nineteenth century, not only religious but also social and even political progress. His father, a Bengali Brahmin of high status, sent him to Patna for a Moslem education in order to prepare him for the civil service. There, from the age of 12 to 15, he studied Arabic and Persian, and became intensely interested in Sufism, from which he retained a belief in God and a hatred of idolatry. Later, he studied Sanskirt at Benares, and then English. In 1804 he published a rationalist pamphlet in Persian. For ten years he served in the British administration, familiarized himself with the West, and learned to overcome his instinctive hatred of the foreign rulers. He left the service with a fortune in 1814 and settled in Calcutta to devote himself exclusively to his religious convictions. For four years he directed a 'Spiritual Assembly', preaching the abandonment of idolatry and a return to the pure theism of the Upanishads, and publishing an abridgement of the Vedanta and English translations of several Upanishads. Coming into contact with the missionaries of Serampore, he became interested in Christianity, studied Greek and Hebrew and, in 1820, published *The Precepts of Jesus*, a collection of extracts from the Gospels. Christ was a theist after his own heart, and he condemned the Church. This led to a controversy with the missionaries, and in the end Ram Mohan Roy, who had been much criticized, not to say persecuted, by his fellows, found himself completely isolated. In 1828 he founded the Brahma Samaj (Brahma Society), which was open to all and met each week for an oral rite. The Samaj had a theistic creed and Christian ethics. Two years later, Ram Mohan set sail for England, where he died in 1833.

One aspect of Ram Mohan Roy's thought is essential for it is not peculiar to him but will be found all along the course of the Hindu reform. He criticized contemporary Hinduism and condemned certain aspects of it, but these he held to be accretions and perversions; in the ancient texts—the Upanishads in the present case—he found the Hindu religion in its pure state, needing to fear nothing from critics and having nothing to learn from other religions. Ram Mohan was his own exegete, but in general the reform owed much to Western scholarship which revealed, spread and admired the creations of the ancient Indian genius. Thanks to the exegesis, the Hindu who criticizes the present state of society and religion does not for all that abandon Indian religion. The critic does not desert India, there is no conversion, but reform.

At the same time, the tendency appears to reduce also the other religions to theism, declaring that in essentials all are identical.

Finally, more than religion, it was the political and social creed of the period which was decisive for Ram Mohan. (It is clear that the Indians see our civilization from the outside, and so are able better than we to perceive the relations which obtain between the different domains of Western thought.) Thus Ram Mohan wrote:

'The consequence of my long and uninterrupted researches into religious truth has been that . . . I have found the doctrines of Christ more conducive to moral principles, and better adapted for the use of rational beings, than any other which have come to my knowledge.'

and later:

'I regret to say that the present system of religion adhered to by the Hindus is not well calculated to promote their political interest . . . It is, I think, necessary that some changes take place in their religion at least for their political advantage and social comfort.'

As D. Pocock says, commenting on these two passages: 'This cool presentation of utilitarianism was never so explicitly put forward in India again, but its effects may be noted throughout the century' (52).

In this social action, including his moderation, Ram Mohan Roy appears in perfect agreement with the British liberals of the time. He opposed polygamy, and the burning of widows, while advising against the abolition of this custom in the immediate future for fear of reaction; he supported the law once it had been passed by Lord Bentinck. He was a prime mover in founding the Hindu College at Calcutta, opposed traditional Indian learning and spoke in favour of modern education as did Macaulay. He condemned caste in principle, but did not consider it wise to offend his own people on that point. His lack of nationalism astonished Jacquemont but in this also he agreed with the British:

'India requires many more years of English domination to that she may not have many things to lose when she is reclaiming her political independence.'

His political protests, if they inaugurated what the Indians later called 'constitutional agitation', were based on the same principles. In 1823 he took the initiative of a petition against an ordinance setting up control of the press:

'The appeal is one of the noblest pieces of English to which Ram Mohan put his hand . . . it invokes against the arbitrary exercise of British power the principles and traditions which are distinctive of British history' (Miss Collet, quoted in 1, p. 814).

Similarly, on the occasion of the Jury Act of 1827, he wrote that it had,

'. . . by introducing religious distinctions into the judicial system of this country, not only afforded just grounds for dissatisfaction among the natives in general, but excited much alarm in the breast of everyone conversant with political principle'.

Finally his journey to England, a bold venture for an Indian in those days, adds the last touch to his portrait. Charged with a mission by the Mughul Emperor, he rejoiced on every occasion when freedom triumphed. Invited to appear before the Committee which was preparing to renew the Company's charter, he declined, but sent his views to the Board of Control. He asked for measures in favour of the tenant-farmers of Bengal, oppressed as they were by the big landowners; he campaigned in favour of Indianization of the army, of the codification of laws. He further advocated consultation before the promulgation of new laws and the substitution of the English language for Persian in the courts. Roughly, this parallels the programme of British action and of Indian demands for the century. The fact that this great man, a whole-hearted convert to liberalism, chose to remain a Hindu contains a lesson which casts much light on later developments.

Keshab Chandra Sen (1838–84). After Ram Mohan Roy, the Samaj continued thanks to Dvarkanath Tagore and then to his son Debendranath, the poet's father. It became better organized and developed a missionary aspect with stress on prayer and devotion. At first the Samaj admitted the authority of the Veda but it abandoned its view in 1850. This shows a highly developed critical sense, due perhaps to the publication of the first part of Max Muller's edition of the Veda. The Samaj tended to a kind of traditional monotheism and lost its interest in Christianity and social reform. It was Keshab Chandra Sen who, after joining the movement in 1857, revived this aspect of Ram Mohan's thought. He was at first supported by the devout Debendranath. The Samaj subjected the Hindu sacraments to criticism, then repudiated caste: Keshab, who was not a Brahmin, became the priest of the association, which led to resignations. Keshab developed the movement's propaganda and preached with great success as far as Bombay and Madras. He was strongly influenced by Christianity and urged religious and social reform. At last Debendranath gave up supporting him and a split resulted, Keshab setting up a parallel organization, the 'Original Society', which gently faded away (the 'Brahma Samaj of India'). This was in 1865 when Keshab was 24. He published a collection of texts borrowed from all religions for use in the association's services and introduced new practices inspired by *bhakti*, the doctrine of loving devotion to God and divine grace, derived either from the Bengali Vaishnavism of Chaitanya, or from Christianity. Also, the Society introduced a new marriage ritual, and celebrated marriages of widows and marriages between persons of different caste; the latter were legalized as civil (non-Hindu) marriages through a special law passed in 1872 at Keshab's request. He also worked towards the emancipation of women and the education of girls. The society had its daily paper. Keshab and other 'missionaries' preached with success and recruited members.

However, disagreements arose. A radical group criticized Keshab for dividing all property and claiming to be divinely inspired. Perhaps under the influence of Ramakrishna, whom he discovered about 1875, Keshab turned to asceticism and allowed social work to decline. The marriage of his 13-year-old daughter to a Hindu prince caused a scandal, and resulted in a split. In 1878 was founded the 'Common Brahma Samaj', which took over the influence of the movement. In 1881 Keshab founded the 'New Dispensation Church', of which he was the inspired prophet, proclaiming at the same time the supremacy of Christ as God–Man, and the deep unity of all religions; these two teachings did not appear contradictory.

Keshab must be admired as the reformer who dared to fly in the face of caste. Max Müller, who met him in England, wrote that he was more truly Christian than many professing Christians; he was a Christian at heart at any rate; Max Müller thought that, but for their lack of generosity and imagination, the representatives of Christianity might have united with men like Ram Mohan Roy and especially with Keshab Chandra Sen.

The numerical insignificance of the Common Brahma Samaj should not hide their lasting influence towards the liberalization of Hindu society.

Prarthana Samaj. Founded in Bombay in 1867 under the influence of Keshab, the 'Society of Prayer' or Prarthana Samaj was intimately connected with the preceding movements, but its members always considered it as being *within* Hinduism. It bears the stamp of the practical character of the Marathas, as the Brahma Samaj did that of the emotional Bengalis. Bombay was, after Bengal, the Indian province where the impact of the West was deepest and best assimilated. Here stress was placed on social reform, on intermarriage and interdining between different castes, on the remarriage of widows, on the improvement of the condition of women and of the oppressed castes, and on social work in general. The Society was dominated by the great figure of Justice Mahadev Govind Ranade, a pure theist who devoted his life to reform. He was one of the founders of the Association for the Marriage of Widows (1861) and of the Deccan Education Society. A man of great culture, he understood the problems which arose from the interaction of India and the West, the interdependence of the various aspects of social life, and grasped the conditions needed to make reform effective: 'The true reformer has not to write on a clean slate. His work is more often to complete a half-written sentence (quoted in, *1* p. 882).

Dayananda Sarasvati. Dayananda Sarasvati and the Arya Samaj which he founded in 1875 reveal another aspect of India; this movement also can be considered as a new phase in the response of India to the Western challenge. The centre of the movement was in Panjab. Dayananda did not know English, he was a Brahmin who had chosen to become a *sannyasi*, a renouncer, in the traditional manner unlike Ram Mohan Roy, he did not choose to study Islam and Christianity, but ignored, or opposed them. But however different the message there is a common movement—towards the past.

'The watchword of Luther was 'Back to the Bible'; the watchword of Pundit Dayananda was 'Back to the Vedas'. With this religious watchword another watchword was implicitly, if not explicitly, combined, namely 'India for the Indians'. Combining these two we have the principle, both religious and political, that the religion of India as well as the sovereignty of India ought to belong to the Indian people . . . In order to accomplish the first end, Indian religion was to be reformed and purified by a return to the Vedas, and foreign religions as Islam and Christianity were to be extirpated' (D. S. Sarma, 54, p. 184).

Now for the first time a Hindu movement concerned itself with converting, or rather re-converting, Hindus who had turned to another religion. Further, Dayananda not only considered the Vedic hymns as revealed, but his exegesis was so personal, so willed, that considered by itself it might lead some to doubt his seriousness or his sanity. To understand this exegesis, we must look at what it set out to accomplish. Foreign religions could not be stamped out without reforming Hinduism, and Dayananda, more realistic than the Brahmasamajists, felt the need for solid foundations. This was to be 'the Veda as the Book of Life, the Rock of Ages' (ibid.).

Of course the Veda could by itself lead to rejecting a large part of Hinduism, but in actual fact, Dayananda found in the Veda exactly what he wanted, including—strange as it may seem—monotheism. From Hinduism he kept transmigration, but he condemned not only idolatry, but also animal sacrifices, pilgrimages, temple offerings, ancestor worship, the caste system, untouchability and child-marriage. It is remarkable how well all this fits with the needs of the times and all the critical work of the Brahmas, itself the result of confrontation with Christianity, a religion which Dayananda professed to ignore.

Dayananda was an aggressive, irritable character; he attacked orthodox Brahminism and the other religions with equal violence. The Arya Samaj, militant and nationalist as it was, emphasized social work and won a much wider audience than the other movements already mentioned. After the Master's death, his disciples separated into two different groups, one, with a more modern outlook, founded the Anglo-Vedic College at Lahore, the other the Gurukul at Hardvar, an original creation in the 'Vedic' spirit.

Ramakrishna and Vivekananda. Ramakrishna was a more typically Indian figure. A poor, illiterate Brahmin of Bengal, he was a mystic of a type India has liberally produced, a lover of the divine, a *bhakta.* For the greater part of his life he cultivated the vision and manifestation of the divine within himself, making a tremendous effort of will and spending whole days in trance, possessed at first by the goddess Kali, whom he called his mother and thought of as the supreme deity. His biographer explains, through Ramakrishna's occasional contacts with the outside, his acquisition of a vedantic doctrine.

'The original feature is that he was keen to know the mystical ways offered by the other religions, especially Islam and Christianity. He thus passed through various experiences which confirmed his opinion of the need to establish a mystical plane above all particular religions, a sort of synthesis which was in no way the product of intellectual reflection, but the result of an inner realization' (Renou, *53*, p. 118).

In the last years of his life, visitors came from the near-by city of Calcutta to listen to him, and he communicated his wisdom to them in short, evocative, often caustic, sentences, all of them breathing, as Max Müller put it, the same familiarity with the unseeable. Keshab was among his audience, but Ramakrishna's favourite disciple was a student, later to be known by the name of Vivekananda, who from his teachings drew a doctrine for the physical and spiritual regeneration of India. He founded a quasi-monastic order and the Ramakrishna Mission, which multiplied its educational and philanthropic activities while spreading the gospel even to the West.

Vivekananda eliminated the kind of 'inferiority complex' which affected Indians. In Chicago in 1893, speaking to the Parliament of Religions which was to spread his name, he exclaimed:

'Brothers and sisters of America . . . I thank you in the name of the most ancient order of monks in the world; I thank you in the name of the mother of religions; and I thank you in the name of millions and millions of Hindu people of all classes and sects.'

Vivekananda's teaching was buttressed by the Theosophical Society attitude towards Indian religions and particularly by Annie Besant whose eloquence, devotion to India and energy made her extremely popular. For the sake of these qualities, the Indians were ready to overlook her many weaknesses. D. S. Sarma's judgement is fair and lucid:

'It ill becomes a man who has been rescued from a cruel and unjust prosecution to turn round on his counsel for defence and accuse him of having overstated his case' (*54*, p. 214).

At the dawn of the twentieth century, the movement which had started in the times of Ram Mohan Roy had gone full circle:

'The fact is that Hindu leaders in the twentieth century, strange as it may sound, were firmly convinced of the superiority and catholicity of their own beliefs and felt only a tolerant and mildly benevolent interest in Christian teachings' (Panikkar, *10*, p. 447).

The challenge which finds its answer here is not only that of religion proper —such as the challenge of the Christian missionaries, although a word will have to be said about these, too—it is the challenge of the social and political values imported from the West. We have seen how those values were first accepted, later to be assimilated and integrated as belonging to Indian tradition, in such a way that the reform came to appear as a return to the past, to one of the many potentialities that Indian sages had of old recognized. Not only did this integration give birth to neo-Hinduism, but it laid the foundations for a religio-political movement which, for lack of a better term, we must call Indian nationalism, and for the final eviction of the British.

We must now return to religion *stricto sensu*, and stress the part played by the missionaries in this development. The missionaries failed in what they believed to be their central task: they succeeded in converting only a small fraction of Indian population. But their real historical function has been to develop education and charitable institutions, and to contribute to the awakening, the widening of consciousness among Hindus that has been outlined here. In particular, their action among untouchables and low castes not only lead to conversions, but stirred the desire among those who were not converted to improve their condition. It fell to the non-Christians to make this seed fructify, in the nineteenth century and later, mainly through the Untouchables' movement, Gandhi's action and finally the legal abolition of untouchability as a first step towards its actual disappearance.

Finally, it should not be imagined that neo-Hinduism, important as it is in other respects, immediately transformed the religious practice of the people as a whole, the Hinduism of the masses; seen within this wider framework, the developments we have examined appear to be situated on a narrow fringe.

Political awakening

Religion and politics are here closely intertwined. In the last section, we saw how the adoption of modern social and political ideals led to a reinterpretation of traditional Hindu religion. The advent of neo-Hinduism in turn paved the way for the uncompromising assertion of India's independent personality against British rule. This trend materialized at the end of the century in the struggle between two political leaders, both Chitpawan Brahmins of Poona, the radical Tilak eventually superseding the reformist Ranade.

Largely leaving aside the ideological and the social backgrounds, this section will concentrate on the main events and currents of social and political action. We hardly need to repeat that to begin with and for a long time the creed was entirely Western. English political writing was taught in the colleges, and even critical estimates of British rule were most often based on the exaggerated and misleading judgements of authors like Burke and James Mill (Maine, 6, p. 507; Strachey, 14, p. 215). Except perhaps in Bengal, it is difficult to trace any continuous development of political aspirations and national consciousness from the time of Ram Mohan Roy through the 1850s. From 1837 onwards an Association of the Zamindars of Bengal existed, and in 1843 George Thompson founded a 'Bengal British India Association'. The two combined in 1851 to form the 'British Indian Association', entirely composed of Indians, and in which the zamindars's interests did not outweigh the general interests until 1861 (B. Majumdar, 51, pp. 179 sq.).

A meeting was held in Bombay in July 1852 in connection with the expected renewal of the Company's Charter in 1853, bringing together representatives from all communities except the Christians. Its object was to set up an association to ascertain the country's needs and present them to the authorities. Dadabhai Naoroji, a Parsi, later a Member of the Commons, declared that the real need existed to supply information to the British Government who, in spite of their good intentions, often decided on unsound measures from sheer ignorance. Of course, the Association had to remain on good terms with the authorities, as long as it was active for the recognition of its claims. It submitted two petitions, both strongly critical of the system of government and putting forward a number of claims which were later to be taken up by the Congress. These included the demand for wider Indian representation in the Services, the reduction of administrative expenditure, the decentralization of power between Calcutta, Bombay and Madras, etc. The petition had an echo in England, where an 'Indian Reform Society' was created to support the Indian claims.

Thus began the first period of political agitation, characterized by the continuous confidence that Britain herself would act justly once she was made aware of the actual facts. But on his return to India in 1869, Dadabhai Naoroji admitted that the Indian patriots aimed at the creation of an Indian Parliament.

During this period the Government took a few cautious steps towards Indian representation. In 1861, under Canning's Indian Councils Act, Indians were first admitted into the councils of government. The act provided that the Legislative Council would be increased by 6 to 12 members, of whom at least half were not to be civil servants, and three Indian members were immediately appointed. The Council was concerned with legislation—with some reservations—but had no power to discuss administrative matters or the Budget. Provincial Councils were later created along similar lines.

About the same time, specialized local committees were sometimes appointed to exercise supervision, under government control, over health, education or communications. In 1882 Lord Ripon put forward a resolution which intended to further political and popular education; it posed the principle of local boards, autonomous and partly elected, designed to deal not with a district, but with a smaller area so as to provide contact with the public. Thus the towns were managed by councils some of whose members were chosen by election.

Starting in 1871, Ranade, who has already been mentioned as the founder of the Prarthana Samaj, was active in the Maratha country as the very prototype of a militant social reformer. To him, social reform, economic uplift and in general the political education of the public were the conditions of political progress. He was the moving spirit of the Public Society, which soon launched a periodical. Among other things, the society was interested in the development of representative institutions at the local level and campaigned for their representation in the legislature. It played a considerable part in bringing the Government, which it advised, closer to the educated public which it aimed to keep informed. Ranade tirelessly worked in all sorts of societies and groups, some pursuing commercial and industrial, others educational activities.

From early times in Bengal, the educated Indians had asked for greater proportional employment of Indians in the Government's services; this now became a burning demand. In 1871 a young Bengali, Surendranath Bannerjee, returned from England. Having passed the examination for the Indian Civil Service, he had been unjustly excluded and became the leader of political agitation on an all-Indian basis. In 1876, in Calcutta, borrowing from Mazzini, he launched the idea of a United India, and founded the 'Indian Association', destined to be the centre of a pan-Indian movement. The members belonged to the Bengali intelligentsia, but wished to create an enlightened public opinion by direct appeals to the people. An opportunity for agitation arose in 1877. On many occasions the British had recognized in principle the right of Indians to a career in the administration. The Queen's proclamation of 1858 stated that

'It is our further will that, so far as may be, our subjects of whatever race or creed be freely and impartially admitted to office in our services, the duties of which they may be qualified by their education, ability, and integrity, duly to discharge.'

Indian opinion was particularly sensitive to the British failure to apply this promise to the upper posts in the administration. When, in 1877, the age limit for entry to the examination for the Indian Civil Service was lowered from 21 to 19 years, which meant an additional handicap to Indian candidates, Surendranath and the Indian Association launched a campaign, first in Calcutta, and then over the whole of northern India, to awaken a spirit of solidarity in the country. A petition addressed to the House of Commons asking for this measure to be cancelled, and for examinations to be held simultaneously in England and in India, was entrusted to an orator who toured England with the assistance of John Bright. The claim was only partly satisfied when a separate branch for Indians, the Statutory Civil Service, was set up. Agitation followed against laws concerning the possession of firearms and the control of the vernacular press. There was further agitation in 1883 following an incident. A judge had ordered an idol from a temple to be produced in court; this was looked upon as desecration; Surendranath, who protested vehemently, was sent to jail; a vast demonstration was staged when he was released.

In the same year, the Ilbert Bill aimed at cancelling the long-standing privilege of Europeans to be tried outside the capitals exclusively by European judges. The British community, particularly the planters and traders who were then very proud of their 'racial' superiority, protested vigorously and forced the Government to compromise. But the growing self-consciousness of the Indians, especially of the educated classes, led to a counter-agitation; the Indian nationalists drew the lesson from the British success by uniting more closely. A first Indian Conference was held in Calcutta in 1883; a second meeting coincided with the first session of the Indian National Congress.

This was the 'Congress' or 'Congress Party' meeting annually, which was to become the main actor in Indian political life until independence and after. Its foundation was due to the initiative of Allan Hume, a former civil servant, who in 1883 burningly appealed to the graduates of the University of Calcutta to serve the destinies of their country. Hume meant it to be concerned rather with social than with political questions; he further wanted each meeting to be presided over by the governor of the province where the meeting was held. Lord Dufferin, the Viceroy, thought differently, and his view prevailed: it was decided that the Congress should include in its agenda anything that concerned the country's administration and there should be no high official representation as this might make members feel hampered in their freedom of speech. The first Congress, held in Bombay in 1885, brought together seventy-two delegates, mainly lawyers, journalists, and teachers, including only two Moslems. It put forward three main demands: the extension of the Lesislative Councils, simultaneous civil service recruitment examinations in India and in England, and the reimposition of the customs duty on imported cotton. In general, the Congress in its beginnings was loyal to the Crown and moderate in its claims.

In 1888, at the Fourth Congress, held in Allahabad, appeared the first signs of friction with the Government caused by the mass propaganda which Hume had tried to launch in preparation for agrarian reform. Thanks to campaigns in England and the collaboration of Charles Bradlaugh, the Congress' request regarding the Legislative Councils was partly satisfied by the Indian Councils Act of 1892. The demand for the employment of Indians in the upper administration, on the other hand, was never really granted, and the Congress patiently repeated it for some twenty years. The Congress also asked for a reduction of military expenditure and for the admission of Indians to the higher ranks of the army. (We have seen that the question of military expenditure had already been raised by the Commission of 1892.)

Every year after 1887 an Indian conference was held to coincide with the Congress. It was founded by Ranade, who up to 1899 was its most active member. He also played a determinating part in shaping the economic policy of the Congress in those years. In 1892 he attacked the policy which allowed a purely agricultural India to feed Europe with raw materials: the country, he argued, must become industrialized or perish; the Government must do for industry what it had done for the railways, it must set itself to creating new industries in order to remedy the lack of capital and of private initiative. It was not until after the First World War that the Government decided to follow this sound advice to a certain extent.

The decade 1890–1900 saw the rise of a new political tendency within the Congress, weak at first but which was eventually to prove of great impact. This was an uncompromising nationalism which opposed reformism just as the counter-reform of the Arya Samaj type had opposed the reformist Brahma Samaj. Its founder was Bal Gangadhar Tilak, a Brahmin born in 1856 in the Maratha country. He belonged to the same caste as Ranade, and the two men, who represented the two opposed tendencies faced one another in Poona, particularly between 1891 and 1896. Tilak had founded two newspapers, including *Kesari*, in 1880, and in 1882 he had been sentenced to four months' imprisonment. He was one of the founders of the Deccan Education Society and of Fergusson College, which he was obliged to leave in 1890. In 1891, in opposition to Ranade, Tilak campaigned against a bill which intended to raise the legal age for marriage, for he regarded this as an intervention in the religious customs of the Hindus. A little later after riots between Hindus and Moslems had occurred in Bombay and Poona, he organized communalist festivals in Poona, one in honour of Ganesha—the elephant-headed god, patron of beginnings, revered throughout India—the other in honour of Shivaji, an adventurous Maratha King of the seventeenth century who had fought the Mughuls by means fair and foul and of whom he made a Hindu hero.

The Congress of 1895 was to be held in Poona, and Tilak, fighting reformism, led a campaign against the holding of the Social Conference in the premises of the Congress as usual. The same year, Tilak obtained a majority in Ranade's Public Society, and Gokhale, Ranade's prominent disciple, resigned. In 1896–7 plague succeeded famine in Bombay and Poona. The British, in isolating the stricken and in searching the houses, disregarded caste etiquette. Tilak joined the conservatives' chorus of reprobation. As a result of his propaganda, two British officers were murdered. He was sentenced to eighteen months' imprisonment. Tilak also founded a Society for the Protection of the Cow, whose spread was widely signalled by Hindu-Moslem riots.[18]

Tilak was certainly very gifted as an agitator. Indeed, if sowing hatred in prejudice were not the easiest thing in the world, he would be a genius; he was successful in instigating hostility between the orthodox Hindus on the one hand, and the British, the Moslems, and even Hindu reformers on the other. For him, reform entailed a kind of collaboration with the infidels; the most obtuse fanaticism suited him best. But he went to his task with energy and intelligence. He tried to base his policy on a reinterpretation of Hindu ethics, and for the purpose he wrote a book called *The Secret of the* (Bhagavad) *Gītā*, in which he did not hesitate to reverse the traditional perspective in order to proclaim that of the three modes of union with God, it is neither love nor knowledge, but action (subtly transformed from war as the vocation of the warrior into religious crusade) which is supreme. It can be observed that the Will to Action expressed here takes on a very personal form and is much more Western than traditionally Indian. One cannot but think of the physical, muscular side of Vivekananda's teaching; Tilak also created gymnastic societies to teach young Hindus to fight. Vivekananda knew that he was borrowing from the West and, strange as it may seem, Tilak, was more Westernized than the reformists. At any rate, he exemplified an unfortunate combination of Western and Indian elements; it fell to Gandhi to transcend this stage by imbuing action itself with truly Indian values, through nonviolence. It must be added that, years later, Tilak returned to more statesmanlike policies.

Being based entirely on religion, the group consciousness which Tilak wanted to promote is exactly what later came to be called communalism. He is actually the founder of communalism in India. But his uncompromising attitude certainly made him popular, and for some of the Hindus Gandhi appeared as his successor; Gandhi himself preferred to trace his ascendance to Gokhale, while the men who murdered Gandhi can be said to have been in the line of Tilak's influence.

The partition of Bengal in 1905 was to set off a wave of popular agitation, of boycott of foreign goods, and of a terrorism partly inspired from Tilak, but this belongs rather to the twentieth century.

The Moslems. Up to this point, our summary of the 'Indian response' has been almost entirely confined to what was in fact the reaction of the Hindus. This is legitimate in so far as this development began earlier among the Hindus and predominated over that of the Moslems. Moreover, the question of the Moslems' reaction to British conquest and rule and of the evolution in this period of their relations with the Hindus is of extreme importance in view of the developments which followed and led to the partition between India and Pakistan in 1947. This course of events is most often exclusively attributed to a policy of division pursued by the British; in actual fact, it was to a great extent determined by a set of historical conditions, some of them going very far back, others arising in our period. Three main factors can be isolated following Beni Prasad (57): the social heterogeneity of the two communities, the different impact upon them of the change in political power and their different reaction to it, and the 'revivalist' tendency on which first the Hindus, and later the Moslems built their response to the new conditions.

Even at the height of Mughul power, the attitude of the two communities towards one another had not ceased being one of compromise and juxtaposition rather than of understanding and combination. There was a great deal of interaction between the two cultures, but the social values remained heterogeneous and opposed, and no effective synthesis occurred. Two sets of values existed side by side, each of them naturally tending to rule the whole population. Two contrasting social principles coexisted in a single society, but one which was *one* only on the level of fact, and not on the level of norms. This can be seen from the point of view of either community. As far as the Hindus are concerned, they were ready to recognize any political power, provided the rulers acknowledged Hindu values and paid homage to the Brahmins as repositories of all truth and wisdom. But this the Moslems would not do, and the Hindus were forced to accept a situation normatively impossible in their system, and to submit to a power which they did not recognize as their own. (It has been pointed out that this situation has probably, by reaction, contributed to increasing the rigidity of the caste system.) To the Hindus, the Moslems were impure people who ate beef and killed the cow. Therefore they deserved to be treated as the worst of Untouchables, were it not for the fact that they *had to* be treated differently. The attitude of the Brahmin employed by the rulers is characteristic:

'Although it was not forbidden to work for the foreign ruler or wear his dress when worldly interests required these, the foreign costume had to be discarded in the outer house when one returned home and the wearer to purify himself by touching Ganges water before he could go into the inner house ... The more thoroughgoing his external and interested servility the more complete was also his emotional disaffection' (N. C. Chaudhuri, *46*, p. 406).

The unstable equilibrium on which rested the situation of the Moslems in relation to the hierarchical Hindu society was to be destroyed with their loss of power. The Hindu values which tended to bring them down remained in operation when the power-force which had until then supported them disappeared. Even cultural elements which had been borrowed from them were threatened, such as the use of Persian in poetry and even, at a further stage, the Arabo-Persian vocabulary in the language of northern India. No wonder that the Moslems should have felt under a growing threat as the Hindus increasingly asserted themselves more strongly in the new political order. Tilak's 'Cow-protecting Societies', which in fact represented an attack against Moslem custom, are an instance of this threat.

If this is true in some degree of Moslems in general, it applies less to Moslems of the lower class than to the Moslem aristocracy, which suffered directly from the conquest since it depended for its subsistence on the Moslem State. For Bengal, Hunter has described (*49*, chap. IV) how the Moslem aristocrats lost their means of livelihood one by one: first the income from land, derived from benefices or tax-collecting functions, as the English preferred to recognize their Hindu subordinates as zamindars, and later as owners; at the same time the military, and later the civil functions. When the Persian language disappeared from the courts, the Moslems commented that the British had 'closed every honourable walk of life to professors of their creed'. With characteristic pride and indolence, they refused for several decades to change with the times, in particular to take to English education. They withdrew into themselves, thus becoming backward in comparison with the Hindus. The fanatical *wahhābī*, or *farāizi*, conspiracy, although it seems to have recruited from the lower class, embodied the same refusal to accept the new state of things (Hunter, *49*). The conditions varied from one province to another, but on the whole this negative attitude predominated until the Mutiny.

At the same time, as we have seen, political power changed in its nature, for the greatest advantage of the mercantile classes. But it was precisely these classes that were predominantly made up of Hindus. The revolution is prefigured in the very conquest of Bengal, which has been described as the

'overthrow of foreign (Moslem) government, by the trading and financial classes, native (Hindu) and British' (Roberts, *11*, p. 130).

In short, the Moslems lost power and they were outdistanced by the Hindus in the development of the professional as well as of the mercantile classes. Even the lower-class Moslems were at a disadvantage as compared to the Hindus, for under Moslem law daughters inherit equally with sons, which made for a more rapid fragmentation of holdings; further, usury was forbidden them, so that the money-lender was most often a Hindu.

A third general factor of the 'estrangement' of the two communities is what B. Prasad has called the 'revivalist' tendency. We have seen how the Hindus found the elements of their response in what they conceived as their own Hindu past. The Moslems in turn later did the same. The result was to make abstraction of the recent past, the very period in which Moslems and Hindus had lived *together* in India, the only one on which a really Indian (Hindu-cum-Moslem) nationalism could have been founded. Perhaps this was inevitable, given the deep cleavage on which we have insisted from the start. But, at any rate, these factors taken together throw light on subsequent developments. For instance, the introduction of a separate electorate for the Moslems in 1909, whatever its effects may have been, does not appear as the creation, but rather as the expression, of a gulf between the two communities. Far from having been demoniacally introduced, or suggested, by the British at the beginning of the twentieth century, as has often been implied, it was demanded by Moslems in Bengal as early as 1882–3 (B. Majumdar, *50*, pp. 396–8.

After the Mutiny, a great modern leader arose among the Moslems, who pointed out the danger of their backwardness, called upon them to awake to the Western message, and turn to Western education. This voice was that of Sayyid Ahmad Khan, who in many respects did for the Moslems what Ram Mohan Roy had done for the Hindus much earlier. Sayyid Ahmad Khan, by a rationalist interpretation, strove to reconcile Islam with Christianity and with modern science. In 1885, after a stay in England, he founded the Anglo-Mohammedan College at Aligarh on the pattern of the older English universities. He took great care to maintain the religious education alongside the new teaching. The new college not only reopened access to administrative careers to the local Moslems but it played a great role in helping the Moslem community adapt to modern conditions; it should be added that the college was open to non-Moslems.

Sayyid Ahmad Khan was a little perturbed by the beginnings of the Indian National Congress. In the political progress of the Hindus he saw a threat to the Moslem minority. In general the last quarter of the century witnessed a change in the three-cornered relationship between British, Hindus and Moslems. Up to that time, the British had been more favourably disposed towards the Hindus than towards the Moslems, but now the Hindus began formulating their political demands against British rule while Sayyid Ahmad Khan, in the interests of his more backward community, brought the British the loyalty of his fellow Moslems; thus the British came to regard the Moslem community with greater favour. The Arya Samaj introduced a militant attitude against Islam, and Tilak followed suit. In the last thirty years of the century, seven serious riots took place between Hindus and Moslems. The Moslems, who had been attracted by the Congress in spite of Sayyid Ahmad Khan's warnings, withdrew from it. Their participation, which had been of 3 per cent in 1885, 22 per cent in 1890, fell to seventeen delegates only out of 756 in 1905. The attitude of the Moslem League, founded in 1916 while the Hindus were agitating against the partition of Bengal, was very much like that of the Congress twenty years earlier.

III. INDIA'S INFLUENCE ON THE WEST[19]

Western culture and the discovery of Indian civilization

> Since we are a dialogue
> And can hear from each other
> Hölderlin.

While the impact of the West on India was global in that it affected all aspects of social life, and compelled the whole country to adapt itself to new conditions, Indian influence on the other hand affected the different spheres of social activity in the West very unequally. In the sphere of ideas, at least three different attitudes can be distinguished among the Europeans who came into direct or indirect contact with India.

British officials established immediate contact with living India, and looked at it primarily from the point of view of their professional tasks. We have stressed the fact that many of them were led by genuine interest to study the people and in due course, in service or in retirement, to become the pioneers of a better knowledge of contemporary as of past India. Then, by and large, slowly perhaps but inexorably, the British in India recoiled upon themselves and developed a belief in their own superiority which was not exempt of some taint of racism. We can conclude that protracted contact in this particular situation has not been favourable to interaction, but has bred estrangement. After the first brilliant generation which created the Asiatic Society of Bengal, Sanskrit studies declined in England while they prospered on the Continent. The public remained relatively indifferent and the effort in the universities limited.

Some Westerners, dissatisfied with their own civilization, simply converted to Indian values. The Theosophists, with Annie Besant, provide a prototype. Upon such minds, the action of India was as central as was the Western impact upon India as a whole. They were not numerous, but there was probably an uninterrupted trickle of them. This radical attitude could not be very popular in Europe, it was rare among the intellectuals proper, Schopenhauer being an exception. Also the matter is to a large extent subjective, and there might be some question as to whether they did not continue, willy-nilly, to belong to the West.

The reaction of the educated European public to the revelation of Sanskrit literature was, in turn, very different. In the first half of the century, this public was greatly interested, often even enthusiastic. But, if India was intimately linked with that public's own preoccupations, she did not replace them. Friedrich Schelling converted to Catholicism in 1808, the very year in which he published his essay, *Uber die Sprache und die Weisheit der Inder* (On the Language and the Wisdom of the Indians). It is this action of India on the intellectual level that deserves our attention. Here India represents a particular case, though perhaps a privileged one, in a much wider movement. At this time the discoveries of Orientalism follow upon each other at an extraordinary tempo: the decipherment of scripts, the archaeological finds, the translation of literatures suddenly reveal a gigantic and diverse Orient, from Egypt to India. The image of the world was changed by these discoveries; the writers pounced avidly upon these new riches, and conceived the hope of a second Renaissance, which Edgar Quinet called the Oriental Renaissance. In this India played an important, but not the only, role. This can be readily shown by summing up a remarkable book, Raymond Schwab's *La Renaissance Orientale*. In this book Schwab sets out to study the living texture of Oriental, and particularly Indian knowledge and influence in Europe and particularly in France, from one book and one *salon* to another, among orientalists, publicists, historians, writers and poets.

The story begins with Sanskrit, which had virtually been discovered by the Asiatic Society of Bengal, founded in 1784. Through the efforts of the Society, three translations of Sanskrit texts were published. Of the three founders, Colebrooke, the best philologist, lived long enough to give surveys of the Veda and of the classical philosophical systems. A chair of Sanskrit was created in Paris in 1815, and two more in Germany in 1818. With Burnouf, who taught from 1829 to 1852, a rigorous philology established itself. Bopp created the comparative grammar of Indo-European languages, which substituted scientific analysis for speculations on the unity of all languages. Buddhism entered the domain of scientific knowledge about the middle of the century thanks to Burnouf who deciphered *Pāli* and to Hodgson who provided Europe with texts from Nepal. At the same time, that is to say a little after the great advances in philology, the two keys to ancient history, Indian archaeology and epigraphy, were founded by Prinsep. Archaeology was to develop, but Indian art never received in Europe the resounding reception which Indian literature was granted from the start. With comparative linguistics, the discovery of Vedic religion led to the comparative study of religions, in the first place of the religions of Indo-European-speaking peoples. This comparatism in the field of religion was less successful than in linguistics: it was in fact to suffer an eclipse. Further, the study of comparative law was launched by Sir Sumner Maine on the basis of the encounter with India. Of course, in one sense, the development of comparative disciplines was imposed by the widening of the world. But India was its main ferment, largely for subjective reasons. In her ancient or Vedic guise, India appeared not as different from the West, but rather akin to it, with a kinship which was at first perceived intuitively, particularly by the German Romantics, and then established scientifically, thanks to the advances in comparative grammar.

The discovery of Sanskrit literature was an extremely important event in contemporary European literature, although the fact is not pointed out in the standard histories of Western literatures. The newly discovered texts were made available to the Continent with striking speed, notwithstanding the troubles and wars of the period. They had been expected with much impatience and are now zealously retranslated. True, they are worthy of such a reception. They were, first, the *Bhagavad Gītā* or 'Song of the Blessed One', translated by Wilkins in 1785, the admirable philosophical poem extracted from the great Indian epos, certainly one of the messages most apt to stir the West; then the *Gītagovinda*, a mystical song, and then *Sakuntalā*, a drama translated by W. Jones in 1789. Its fastidious graces could not but appeal to eighteenth-century minds. It enchanted Goethe and, of the three works, had the greatest literary impact.

These first texts created such an enthusiasm that a whole world of speculations, expectations and hopes arose, often anticipating real knowledge. Schlegel's essay constituted an attempt. He wrote in 1800, 'It is in the Orient that we must seek for what is in the highest degree Romantic'. In Germany, interest in things Indian was a part of Romanticism, from J. P. Richter's *Hesperus* to the 'Enchantment of Good Friday' in Wagner's *Parsifal* (Wagner also sketched a Buddhistic drama). In France, the influence is seen from the place afforded to Orientalism in learned circles and in the *salons*, as well as from the authors' statement that a second Renaissance was expected in which Sanskrit would play the role Greek and Latin had played in the first, on the eve of a new humanism. In his preface to *Les Orientales* (1829), Hugo writes that 'the Orient, either as thought or as image, has become . . . a kind of general precocupation'. In *Louis Lambert*, Balzac proclaims: 'It is impossible to doubt the priority of the Asiatic Scriptures over our Holy Scriptures. For one who recognizes this historical point, the world gets strangely widened' (1832). Lamartine, deciding to compose long poems, says that he wants to write 'Hindustany poetry', or that 'the key to everything is in the Indies' (1853).

Edgar Quinet's *Genius of the Religions* (1841), and Michelet's *Bible of Humanity* (1864), which he wrote to oppose a more ancient revelation to Renan's *Life of Jesus*, reflect widely spread tendencies.

That poetry in the English language owes much to India can be seen from William Jones' writing to begin with, but still more from Shelley's and Wordsworth's pantheism and further, but chiefly through a German intermediary, from the writings of Coleridge and Carlyle, Emerson and Whitman.

However, this ardour was to subside. In 1884 Bergaigne, a Sanskritist, remarked that Sanskrit literature had ceased to interest the educated public. As to the new disciplines, though they had won recognition, they came toward the end of the century to play the role of secondary specialities, essentially unrelated to the core of the culture. This held true of all Europe, Germany excepted. The excessive hopes of the early nineteenth century were forgotten, and if Orientalism has in fact entered into our modes of thought, we are not fully conscious of the fact. How is this to be explained ? What has happened ? To begin with, a number of tendencies were active from the start, besides those which have just been mentioned. In literature, Goethe and Victor Hugo were cautiously reserved; Hegel, who knew only Colebrooke's exposé, found nothing in India worthy of the name of philosophy, and he declared Indian religions—including Buddhism, still little known in his time—to be inferior to those of Persia, Syria and Egypt. There were also the uncompromising traditionalists, and the sceptics. Another remark: broad circles of intellectuals were actively preoccupied with Orientalism, just at a time when Orientalist science was still in the making. The picture of India that emerged from study was different from the expectation. India appeared as more strange, as further removed from us than had been anticipated. From Vedism, which was still Indo-European, the focus moved to Buddhism and Hinduism; the accumulation of sources and the inevitable specialization on the one hand, the diversities of Indian culture on the other showed the all too simple initial views to be obsolete. Comparative mythology found itself in difficulty and saw the problems multiply where it had hoped for easy certainties. This was not all, and the disappointment has a deeper reason. At the source of the 'Oriental Renaissance', R. Schwab often discovers a coincidence between the revelations of Sanskrit and the contemporary tendencies of the West. For some time, people saw in the Indian civilization of the past precisely what they had wanted to find in it; this was the reason for its extraordinary success in Europe. Clearly the progress of knowledge would not long allow the two images to coincide. Let us try to sketch some aspects of this remarkable, if short-lived, marriage. Basically the nineteenth century kept to the rationalism of the eighteenth, yet in another respect it escaped from it. It yearned for something new and strange, a wider sensitivity, a return to the 'deep springs': and these it found in the Orient. As early as

1762, Herder recommmended 'crusades to the Orient'. In 1784, in his *Ideen zur Philosophie der Geschichte* ('Ideas for a Philosophy of History'), he celebrated primitive, popular, spontaneous poetry as opposed to the waning elegances of classicist literature: this in the very year when the Asiatic Society of Bengal was founded. At the same time, speculation thrived regarding the original unity of all languages and a primitive and universal religious revelation. The new Oriental discoveries came just in time to satisfy those cravings and to confirm those dreams. Here was a language whose affinities with the classical languages of antiquity were being announced, and would soon receive confirmation. Here was an old epos which had flourished between Homer and the Nibelungen. Here was the *Bhagavad Gītā*, a poem of sublime thought steeped in religion. And here were the Vedas, descried rather than known, embodying the primitive religion of the human race. Even in philosophy the coincidence was almost miraculous: while absolute idealism was being elaborated in Europe, the Upanishads brought absolute monism; there is a difference, no doubt, but the two are as close as the difference in the civilizations allows.

It is not surprising that the new Orientalism received its warmest reception in Germany. This was due not only to special affinities, to a common inclination to metaphysics, as has often been said since Madame de Staël, but also to the historical situation of the German intelligentsia, then busy shaking off the yoke of rationalism and founding the German nationality against the Napoleonic domination. This involved the rehabilitation of everything medieval, popular and primitive against the narrow claims of classicism; the widening, that is, of the cultural outlook. The same need was felt elsewhere, in France in particular, though more vaguely; there a Lamennais thought that the primitive universal revelation, as found almost unaltered in Vedic India, might enter into the conception of a more embracing Church.

What began as speculation ended as sober science. It is worth while to ask in what measure science has succeeded in answering the questions that were first asked of it, and in what measure it has modified them. It is perhaps in this modification that the action of India on the West, though indirect, was deepest. The initial search was for origins, *common* origins of languages and religions. It is from this that comparatism developed. But the main result has been to lead us to recognize *diversities* and to turn away more and more from questions of origins—a process which certainly had not yet been completed, especially in the case of the public, at the end of the century. Comparative grammar has demonstrated the 'common origin' of the languages called 'Indo-European'; at the same time essential corrections have been introduced regarding the initial speculations on two points: first it has been recognized that, besides these languages, many others existed which were absolutely and irreducibly different. In the second place, while languages, civilizations and races were supposed to go together, it appeared that these were three heterogeneous wholes. On this point the disappointment was so great that some lent a deaf ear, labelling 'Indo-Germanic' the languages generally called 'Indo-European', and basing on linguistic truth a racial myth which can be regarded in this respect as an aberrant reaction to the discovery of India. Did not Gobineau write (in 1865) 'Everything that we think and all our manners of thinking have their origin in Asia'? Except racism, for sure.

The adventure has been much less successful in so far as the study of religions is concerned. The symbolism of Creuzer as well as Max Müller's 'naturistic' reaction were born from German Romanticism; but the latter did not live to survive as a science. The initial insights were superseded more drastically than in the matter of languages: the discovery of religions had just begun and, especially in the case of the theory, it is still going on.

To sum up, the West at first approached India's past civilization with a will to widen its outlook, but within a unitarian framework which in the last analysis was based on religion. At the same time, the West looked at this *Other* in an objective way, and it set up particular disciplines for its study. And the discovery itself destroyed the very hope which had led to it. Childhood dreams are over: the adult mind now knows that the unity of mankind can be based only on the very diversity of cultures. We see at the same time to what degree the enthusiasm of the romantics led to a dead end, and how far it can be said to have been founded in truth. Also, there is a parallel to be drawn between the attitudes of both our protagonists: in India as in the West, *One* borrowed from the *Other* just what it needed, in a particular context, to remain itself. The difference is that India integrated everything within an unchanging form, while the West widened a movement which was rooted in its principles but which did not admit of any permanent framework.

From the specific point of view of mankind and its cultures, what I have described here is the beginning of a dialogue. There is no dialogue without misunderstandings—misunderstandings which are such only in appearance. For the dialogue to go on, it is not sufficient merely to rule out all dreams of domination, temporal or spiritual. We must also keep from falling into the facile illusion of the unity of the partners, of the identity of different cultures. This would constitute the one real, unredeemable misunderstanding. As Hölderlin implies, we must—with passion and caution—work at bettering our mutual understanding.

NOTES TO CHAPTER XXIV

1. In the opinion of Candidates of Historical Sciences E. N. Komarov and A. K. Vafa, the author has produced a circumstantial and well-informed account of the historical development of India in the nineteenth century. Characteristic of the author's whole conception is his analysis of the British administrative and political system in India. Whilst quite rightly remarking on the desire of the British authorities to find the most acceptable forms of administrative system, the author gives rather a tendentious account of the administrative system and of British policy in India. He claims that throughout the first half of the nineteenth century this policy was typified by a humane attitude towards Oriental civilizations. Although he singles out a number of instances of colonial exploitation

in India and certain of the adverse consequences of colonial rule, the author nevertheless tries to convince the reader that British rule as a whole had a favourable effect on Indian society. One may ask the author why, then, half a century of 'humane' and 'neutralist' policy produced the mighty explosion of the anti-British War of 1857–9. If the colonial authorities in India ruled so well, how is one to explain the undeniable fact that almost from the very beginning of this rule it was so strongly opposed in India; and why did this struggle become more and more intense, finally leading to the annihilation of that rule ? What is the explanation for the fact that after the end of British rule India made a quantitative forward stride in its economic, political and cultural development and acquired international authority ?

Soviet scholars consider that the system of colonial rule had no other aim but the economic exploitation and political subordination of the Indian people. It did not correspond with the national interests of the country and of its development. The bourgeois law and order which British rule brought with it, although historically progressive in themselves, could not find a favourable soil in the semi-feudal conditions existing in colonial India. Colonial exploitation, like the whole system of British rule in India, was based upon the social and economic backwardness of the country and therefore tended to preserve backward relationships.

2. Since the first draft of this chapter was prepared for circulation, a number of books have appeared on the subject to mark the centenary of 1857. These would call for longer consideration than is here possible. Some titles will be found in the reference list.

3. *The Indian War of Independence* is the title of a militant book published anonymously by Savarkar in 1906. As to the origin of the legend of the Mutiny in Bengal, see N. C. Chaudhuri, *The Autobiography of an Unknown Indian*, New York, 1951.

4. It is often assumed that this awareness disappeared with the Mutiny, and that thereafter Englishmen imagined themselves to be in India for ever. That is certainly not true of the best minds, as for example John Strachey: 'if our dominion should last sufficiently long' (*India* [2nd edn, London, 1894], p. 325, see also p. 308), and Maine: 'What reason can there be for supposing that the British-Indian Empire will continue at all except a reason furnished by experience of a very particular kind?' ('India', in T. Humphrey Ward, *The Reign of Queen Victoria*, [London, 1887], vol. I, pp. 460–522). What is possible, and likely, is that this awareness had been common in the first part of the century (cf. *India Gazette*, Calcutta, quoted in Bimanbehari Majumdar, [*History of Political Thought from Rammohun to Dayanada*, 1821–84, vol. I, Bengal–Calcutta, 1934] p. 73) but later became much rarer (cf. Maine, ibid. p. 486: after the Mutiny, the Stock Exchange had the 'practically new conviction that the British . . . dominion was likely to be of indefinitely long duration').

Charles Trevelyan, returning to India after the Mutiny, found that there was less intercourse between English and Indians than before (Henry Sumner Maine. *Village Communities in the East and West*. London 1890, p. 292). But the process began earlier than the factors alleged. Three examples of friction between Indians and English officials in 1843 show a haughty attitude on the part of the latter (Bimanbehari Majumdar, ibid.).

F. J. Shore, in his *Notes on Indian Affairs* (2 vols., London 1837) describes and deplores at great length the insufficient intercourse of British officials with the people. He explicitly contrasts this with the state of things prevailing around 1780. This book gives a clear idea of the growth of bureaucratism and of a kind of caste pride affecting all but the best of the British; a growing disaffection on the part of the Indians is also diagnosed. As early as 1821, in the Minute quoted above, Malcolm warns his subordinates against a wrong notion of their superiority and refers to the advantages they enjoy as against Indians. English aloofness seems to have developed with a necessity of its own. As Griffiths remarks, integrity guaranteed by high salaries, non-admission of Indians to higher posts, and Anglicization, if taken together, lead logically to aloofness (Percival Griffiths, *The British Impact on India*, London, 1952).

In general, there was a contradiction between the egalitarian principle of a modern government and the hierarchical principle of the caste system of Indian society. This contradiction could not but create a tension in men who were in charge of such a government and who at the same time had to respect the values of such a society. As Maine put it: 'the rulers of India are like men bound to make their watches keep time in two longitudes at once' (Henry Sumner Maine, ibid. (p. 528).

5. In Professor A. Briggs' opinion, the reference to imperialism being 'in rough synchron-ism' with the accession of Queen Victoria seems to be quite wrong. There were new signs of 'imperialism' in the sense in which the term seems to be meant here until after 1857. It would be very helpful if the author could clear his mind of this important subject. Unfortunately there is no account in the chapter of special effects of late nineteenth-century English imperialism in India and in general the section is stronger on the early part of the period than on the later part.

6. A criticism from the U.S.S.R. suggests that the British were prevented from extending the Bengal system to Madras and Bombay 'by the disturbances among the peasants, who de-fended their land rights'. No evidence at the authors' disposal seems to support this statement.

7. E. N. Komarov and A. K. Vafa object to the fact that the author disagrees with the wide-spread belief that British rule destroyed the village community in India. The only argument which he advances is the 'care with which existing rights and institutions were registered' by the colonial revenue authorities. In the first place, this 'care' was by no means universally shown. It was not shown when the Permanent Settlement of Bengal, Bihar and Orissa was introduced. Here, as is well known, the colonial rulers completely ignored the rights of the various categories of landowners, particularly the peasants, in the interests of the zamindars. Secondly, the British authorities by no means confined themselves to register-ing existing rights and institutions where such registration did occur. The authorities pursued their own agrarian policy, which changed from time to time. In the areas where the ryotwari system prevailed (Bombay and Madras) private, not communal rights and duties were institutionalized and registered. Communal rights and duties were either ignored or deliberately done away with. The legal conditions of landownership and use ceased to depend on community membership. The collective responsibility of community members for payment of land tax was done away with in places where it still survived. The former community officials (headman, scribe) became revenue clerks of the State. Thirdly, and most important, the general effect of colonial exploitation was such as to undermine and destroy the village community, making this process, which was inevitable anyway as a result of the collapse of medieval relationships, particularly painful. Initially, the sharp increase in land revenue and the methods used by the British authorities to obtain it led to a situation where existing rights to land, including community rights, were to a great extent undermined and sometimes destroyed, particularly in Bengal. As India was turned into a market for British products and a source of raw material, the further development of money-exchange relationships also began to undermine the ties holding communities together. British land and revenue policy in the middle of the nineteenth century particu-larly favoured the conversion of community members' lands and rights into objects for buying and selling and this further weakened the village community in India. Various historical materials, in particular the reports on the establishment of land taxation in accordance with the 1833 decree, show clearly how a considerable section of community members were ruined and their rights and lands taken over by traders and money-lenders. Hence, if certain relics of the institutions of the village community did continue to survive, it was not due primarily to 'registration' but to the general social and economic conditions in a country where various pre-capitalist relationships and institutions, although under-mined and seriously damaged, could not become entirely extinct whilst colonial rule con-tinued to exist.

8. E. N. Komarov and A. K. Vafa note that the author says it is hard to say whether the peasant under British rule was on the whole better or worse off than before. He empha-sizes a qualitative change in the peasants' situation in that he was 'exposed to a new enemy . . . the power of money'. The mass of the Indian peasantry was in a more un-favourable situation to meet this enemy precisely because of the country's colonial situa-tion. Colonial exploitation, the slowing down of industrial development by foreign capital, the support whole-heartedly given by the colonial authorities to an outmoded feudal system of landownership and the rural over-population which resulted from this, all made the Indian peasant particularly vulnerable to the growing power of money and made the collapse of the medieval relationships a particularly painful process, at the same time causing unprecedented poverty among the great majority of the country's population.

9. Professor Asa Briggs points out that a similar problem is posed in the economic impact of slavery in the West Indies.

10. In Professor A. Briggs' opinion the section on cotton seems to be inadequate and somewhat misleading since it does not distinguish clearly between cotton growing and textile
production. There always was a powerful pressure group from Manchester pressing for
more cotton to be grown in nineteenth-century India.

11. For E. N. Komarov and A. K. Vafa, in explaining the enormous rural over-population in
colonial India by mainly demographic factors, the author is flying in the face of established
historical facts. According to generally accepted estimated and statistical data, in the
period between 1750 and 1900 the population of Europe increased by 186 per cent, whilst
that of India increased only by 104 per cent, and that of Asia as a whole by 96 per cent
(*Census of India 1951*, vol. I, part IA, 1952, p. 136). Only since the 1920s has the rate of
growth of population in Asia and in India in particular caught up with that of Europe and
subsequently overtaken it. Another interesting comparison is the following: in the seventy-
year period 1871–1942 the population of Japan increased by 36 per cent whilst the population of India increased only [*sic.*] 54 per cent (1872–1941) (*The Modern Review*, 1948,
vol. I, pp. 79–80). Lastly, the population growth rate in modern, independent India is
considerably higher than in colonial India and continues to grow. Hence, the population
growth rate in British India was in fact considerably lower than in the independent
countries. However, whereas in such countries with higher rates of population growth than
India, the proportion of the population depending on agriculture usually declines
gradually, in colonial India exactly the opposite took place. In 1891 this proportion was
61.1 per cent, in 1901 66.5 per cent, in 1911 72.2 per cent, in 1921 73.1 per cent and in
1931 at least 75 per cent (calculated by the methods used in previous censuses. Cf. Wadia
and Merchant, *Our Economic Problem*, 1945, page 86.), Professor A. Briggs believes that
besides the British rule there were other factors involved in the growth of population in
India.

12. In the opinion of E. N. Komarov and A. K. Vafa, the author tries to raise objections
against Indian critics for not accepting the necessity of the so-called Indian debt. He chides
them for not distinguishing the 'productive role' of the 'invested capital' included in the
debt. This debt grew up and increased mainly as a consequence of British military expenditure (including expenditure on suppression of the national uprising in 1857–9) and
other expenditure, which was debited to India. The cost of railway construction and
certain other works—irrigation, etc.—undertaken by the colonial administration was
later included. It is this part of the debt which the author calls 'productive' and considers
justifiable.

Throughout the whole nineteenth century and until 1914, with the exception of the
seven years 1856–62, India's exports always exceeded her imports. In 1856–62, imports
exceeded exports by a total of £22,500,000. A widely accepted estimate for total British
capital investments in India up to 1914 is £500 million. In other words, the investment
of British capital was covered many times over by the flow of exports from India to Britain.
This meant that the British capital invested in India had in fact been obtained from the
exploitation of the Indian people and was then debited to India which then had to pay
interest and dividends on the debt (cf. R. P. Dutt, *India Today*, 1947, p. 136). Furthermore, about 87 per cent of British investments in India immediately before the First
World War were for Government needs or were invested in transport, plantations and
finance, but *not in industry*. In other words, these investments served to exploit India, not
only by producing colonial excess profits but also and especially by turning the country
yet further into a source of raw materials and a market for British goods, keeping the
balance of trade between Britain and India weighted against the latter.

13. Professor A. Briggs asks: was not Trevelyan's interest in balanced budgets a very limited
interest in relation to the real financial interest and investment needs of India in the
nineteenth century? Moreover he feels that British economic commitment to India has
not been sufficiently discussed here.

14. In asking this question, the author obviously believes the enfranchisement of money and
the introduction of modern means of transportation are adequate economic conditions for
profound changes in the social fabric (write E. N. Komarov and A. K. Vafa). In actual
fact, only the wide development of factory industry can ensure a reliable acceleration of
economic growth and finally render pre-capitalist social relationships obsolete. In India,
colonial rule and in particular the restraining by foreign capital of domestic industrial

development held up economic development and hindered the process of replacing the pre-capitalist order.

In his desire to find some sort of 'mystic' causes for the backwardness of India during the colonial period, the author launches into a comparison of 'Western' and 'Eastern' civilizations which is beyond the scope of the historian, and draws absolute distinctions between them. In comparing them, he fails to see that the distinctions which he draws and to which he attributes a mystical nature are in themselves the product of differences in the levels of historical development reached by the societies concerned at the beginning of the modern period and are therefore, from the historical point of view, transient.

15. E. N. Komarov and A. K. Vafa feel that at the end of the section on the impact of British rule on Indian society, the author gives his own peculiar explanation for the maintenance of the country's social and economic backwardness. To a certain extent he remarks on the conservatism of British rule but passes over the most important features of this conservatism. Thus he speaks about the preservation by the British authorities of the anachronistic institution of the Indian princedoms but fails to mention a much more wide-spread feature, the maintenance and support by the colonialists of feudal and semi-feudal landownership, a system which they adapted to their own economic and political interests and which also became in the course of time an anachronism and one of the greatest obstacles to economic progress in India.

16. E. N. Komarov and A. K. Vafa feel that there is no justification for the fact that the second section of this chapter, devoted to the history of the national organizations, to new social, political and religious thinking and to literature is only about half as long as the previous section. It is the second which deals with the activities of the Indians themselves, whilst the first section dealt almost exclusively with the activities of the British administration.

In this section the author treats the appearance of new features in the social, political and cultural life of India almost exclusively as being the result of Western influence. (cf. page 235). However, many of the ideas which the author considers reached India through her 'contact' with the West had existed there for many centuries before the colonial conquest, though naturally in *characteristic ancient or medieval forms*. Surely India had a secular literature going back to the most ancient times ? Surely Hindu religious philosophy was acquainted with the concept of one God, the Brahman, not to mention the mono-theism of Islam ? Did anarchy really reign in India and in other countries throughout the Middle Ages and was there no conception of law and order ? Of course, India's 'contact' with the West—i.e. between the rising Indian intelligentsia and the bourgeois ideas and con-ceptions which already existed in the West—stimulated the spread of these ideas in the country and in the course of this process they took on their own characteristic forms and features. It would, however, be a great mistake to regard the rich spiritual culture of nineteenth-century India as the product of Western influences and borrowings.

17. E. N. Komarov and A. K. Vafa claim that the author again compares the two civilizations when dealing with the history of the Indian national movement. In fact, Indian move-ments were increasingly directed against colonialism and subsequently against capitalism. The leaders of the Indian liberation movement, from Ram Mohan Roy to Jawaharlal Nehru, always emphasized that they were acting in opposition to the colonial system which had been imposed on India and not to the West as such.

18. In E. N. Komarov's and A. K. Vafa's opinion the author's treatment of Bal Gangadhar Tilak is extremely one-sided. Furthermore, he speaks slightlingly about one of the major leaders of the Indian national liberation movement, whose name is indissolubly linked with an important stage in its history, with references to 'sowing hatred in prejudice' and 'the most obtuse fanaticism', etc. The author sees Tilak as merely playing on the religious sentiments of the Hindus and defending medieval customs. In fact the historical impor-tance of the work of Tilak and other radical nationalists at the turn of the century was not their appeal to religion but their attempt to wage a resolute struggle for national freedom, to involve the masses of the people in this struggle and to create a strong, organized and widely supported national liberation movement. This was the important new contribution made by the radical nationalists ('extremists') as compared with their predecessors and opponents in the national movement, its liberal leaders ('moderates'). Under the leader-ship of the latter, the national organizations remained representative of the upper classes and could therefore only act by appealing to British public opinion and the colonial

authorities, which could easily ignore them. Tilak called this a policy of 'requests, petitions and protests'. In rejecting this policy, he urged the nationalists to take the masses in hand, to give the rural population the best possible political education, meeting them on an equal footing and showing them how to use their rights and to wage the struggle by constitutional means. Only then, according to Tilak, would the Government understand that to scorn the Congress meant to scorn the Indian nation. This work, Tilak said, required a large group of well-informed and dedicated workers for whom politics would not merely be a leisure activity but a daily duty performed with the most precise regularity and extreme intensity (*Kesari*, January 1896; Vile J. L. Shay *The Legacy of Lokamanya* [Bombay, 1956] p. 79). In their basic programme, Tilak and his supporters were the democrats and republicans; they tried to awaken the masses to political awareness and spoke in favour of a democratic republic in India.

19. In this third and final section, for E. N. Komarov and A. K. Vafa, the author writes mainly about the discovery and appreciation of Indian civilizations in the West from the end of the eighteenth to the first half of the nineteenth centuries. In our opinion, he should have noted the fresh wave of interest shown by the West in India towards the end of the nineteenth century, in particular the interest in neo-Hindu moral philosophy aroused partly by the appearance of Swami Vivekananda in the West in the 1890s. The section could be extended to include mention of the development of Indian and Buddhist studies in Russia in the nineteenth century (O. N. Betling, K. A. Kosovich, I. P. Minaev and others) which made a considerable contribution to Indian studies as a whole. Some mention should also have been made of Tolstoy's interest in Indian civilization; this subsequently had a certain significance for India itself as a result of the relationships which grew up between Tolstoy and Indians, especially Gandhi.

In addition the late nineteenth century gets short shrift in this section and surely there should be a reference to Kipling, after mention of the increasing specialization of Indian scholarship in the West. The section relies too much on Schwab.

CHAPTER XXV

CULTURE CONFLICTS IN SOUTH-EAST ASIA

I. TRADITIONAL CIVILIZATIONS

Economy and ways of life

SOUTH-EAST ASIA, bounded by the great land-masses of India and China, is distinguished by the variety of its peoples, languages and civilizations. From the coastal plains to the tablelands and the mountains of the interior, it displays a succession of cultures, their individual stage of development closely related, in many cases, to the nature of their agricultural methods and the density of the population concerned.

The most 'primitive' tribes simply live by gathering wild fruits, hunting and fishing. Few in number, they appear to be all that remains of the earliest inhabitants; they include the Negritos of the Andaman Islands, the Semang and Sakai of the Malay peninsula, the Aëta of Luzon and the Toala of Celebes. Their tools are made of wood and bamboo, not stone. They roam about a well-defined territory, hunting with the bow or the blowpipe and digging up the sprouts and roots of plants with the long sticks they carry for that purpose.

At a higher stage of evolution we find itinerant cultivation based on the system of burnt land, which is practised by many mountain tribes and is known as *ray* in eastern Indo-China, *taungya* in Burma, *ladang* in Indonesia and *caingin* in the Philippines. A fertile patch of forest is chosen, the trees are cut down at less than 3 feet from the ground, and as soon as the stumps have dried out they are set on fire. The ash enriches the soil, and sowing takes place after the rainy season. No other type of fertilizer being available, the plot has to be left fallow after two or three years, and a fresh start made elsewhere: such is the life of the Man and Meo tribes of Tonkin, the Moi of the Annam mountains, the Chin and Kachin of Burma. This system, which requires neither ploughs nor irrigation, is well adapted to the natural environment. It produces not only rice but maize, manioc, sweet potatoes and yams. But the crops are very small, so that the people lack vigour and the land is thinly populated. The constant change of ground makes a permanent, progressive organization impossible, so that in these areas the village is the only political unit.

Only the irrigated ricefields yield a surplus large enough to support a large population and a complex administrative system, the necessary bases of any powerful civilization. They are not confined to the plains: the mountain slopes, too, are terraced with ricefields, the most remarkable of which are to be found in northern Luzon. In this region the fields of the Ifugao and Bontoc peoples climb from the depths of the valleys to a height of over 6,000 feet, and have been cultivated with methodical care for centuries. The soil is hoed and manured, and is irrigated by trenches dug in the ground, or through bamboo pipes; the birds are frightened away from the crop by scarecrows which flutter perpetually, for the trickling water drives them, thanks to a simple but ingenious mechanism. In Bali, too, the *sawah* terraces follow the steep contours of the hills and are watered by a remarkable system of irrigation. But even rice cultivation, however skilfully organized, cannot give rise to enduring states unless fairly extensive plains provide its main basis. The Balinese, the Minangkabau, the Lao of the Middle Mekong, the Thai of Upper Tonkin and the Shan who live along the Salween formed kingdoms and principalities which were always ephemeral (I am not referring here to their civilizations, for that is quite a different matter) because their only available territory was broken up and their rivers were turbulent and interrupted by rapids, giving no access to the sea.

The great states grew up in the river deltas, where the ricefields had the benefit of alluvial soil and could produce large crops without becoming exhausted or needing to lie fallow, and where the coast was visited by the tide of all the world's civilizations. The people of Vietnam were served in this way by the Red River, the Siamese by the Menam Chao Phaya, the Burmese by the Irrawaddy and the Khmers by the Mekong. There are no such deltas in Java or Sumatra, but the fertility of their volcanic soil, the abundant rainfall, and a strategic position on the international sea-routes brought prosperity to the empires of Çrivijaya, Mojopahit and Mataram.

This rice cultivation, which constitutes the people's chief occupation, has set its mark on the landscape. The plough, which originally came from China or India, is drawn by one or two buffaloes. The ploughman first breaks up the soil, without making furrows, and then harrows it, while the women prick out, by hand, the rice seedlings which were sown a while before in heavily manured seed-beds. From now until the harvest, a certain level of water must be maintained in the ricefields, so that the plants can grow. Irrigation is unnecessary in countries such as Cambodia, where the rivers swell and flood the fields; but elsewhere it is carried out in a number of different ways—the water may be led from the nearest river through trenches, carried in baskets which two people manipulate by ropes, or in dippers slung from a pole that rests on a tripod; while in some places there are *norias*, the most powerful of which, at Kwang-ngai (Annam), have as many as ten wheels, 12 m in diameter. The harvest depends on the incidence of the rains. There may be two in thickly populated areas, such as northern Vietnam and Java, where subsistence is a problem. Where the population level is not alarmingly high, cultivation is less intensive and one annual harvest is felt to be sufficient; this is the case in Cambodia, Laos, Siam and Burma.

These differences are reflected in social organization and habitat.[1] The demands of irrigation and the struggle to cope with a shortage or excess of water call for large-scale collective effort. One outstanding testimony to this may be seen in the dykes which protect the countryside in Tonkin against flooding by the Red River: the system was begun in the year 1108, and by the end of the nineteenth century it extended for nearly 1,500 miles. Whether the effort was spontaneous or co-ordinated by the monarchy, which existed largely for that purpose, this collective undertaking, to which all the inhabitants contributed, gave them a sense of community and a political structure that proved extremely durable. The people of Vietnam and Java live in big villages that straggle along the roads or rivers, backing up against the hills in order to escape flooding or to leave as much space as possible for cultivation. Every village is completely protected from the outer world by a bamboo hedge with only one gate in it, and sentinels on their perches blow on conch shells to warn against approaching danger. In Vietnam village life centres on the *dinh*, or community house, where the tutelary diety is worshipped and public meetings are held; every inhabitant has his allotted place there, according to age and rank. Despite this strict hierarchy and the domination of the village notables, there is a strong communal feeling, evidenced by numerous welfare and mutual assistance organizations.

On the other side of the Annamite mountains, social life is not nearly so close-knit. The reason seems to be that existence is easier here, the population smaller, and Confucianism, with its influences and the political institutions to which it gives rise, is not present. In Cambodia, Laos, Siam and Burma the huts are surrounded by gardens and, instead of huddling together as they do in Vietnam, lie scattered along river-banks or out in ricefields. The centre of village life is not the community house but the pagoda. Buddhism plays a much more important part here than in Vietnam: the bonzes are the purveyors of education, and every young man spends a certain time in a monastery, to acquire merit, before going out into the world. Buddhism is not so conducive to communal life as Confucianism. Houses, too, are influenced in their shape and structure by natural surroundings and by the whole range of social and religious factors.

In Vietnam and Java, houses are built on the ground, whereas in the rest of South-East Asia they are raised on piles. This seems to have been a fairly recent divergence, for the *dinh*, the most characteristic architectural structure of Vietnam, is built on piles. These piles, which are usually between 1 and 2 m in height, give protection from damp, from enemies and from dangerous animals, provide storage space for agricultural implements, for the pestle and mortar used for crushing rice, for the loom, the cart or canoe, and at night for the domestic animals. The roof, of banana or palm leaves, rests on wooden beams or lengths of bamboo. Size and interior arrangement reflect the development of the large family—matriarchal, patriarchal, or jointly governed by the individual couple. Among the Dayaks of Borneo and some of the Moi of southern Annam, the whole village consists of a single immense hut, 'long as a sound-wave', where several hundred people live under one roof. Elsewhere, a house may be shared by several families, as among the Minangkabau or the Karo-Batak of Sumatra; or it may be reserved for one couple and their children, as in Vietnam, Laos, Cambodia, Siam, Burma and Java. These differences also illustrate the transition from collective to individual ownership; in many cases the communal dwelling-place denotes a collective agricultural system, whereas the one-family house is found in more heavily populated areas, where individual ownership has developed.

But all these forms of economic and social organization have one feature in common—the great freedom enjoyed by the women. Although Chinese women did not achieve emancipation until halfway through the twentieth century, women in South-East Asia have always been the equals of men in nearly every respect. This may be a vestige of a long-ago matriarchy, but economic conditions are sufficient to account for it. Women help men in all their work—they prick out the rice plants, harvest the crop, dry and husk the rice; they weave and dye, they make baskets, they go to market to sell what they have grown and what they have made. Even in Vietnam, which has been influenced for centuries by Confucianism, a daughter shares with her brothers in the heritage from their parents, and where there are no brothers she may even celebrate ancestor-worship (Code of the Lê). Although the country of the Minangkabau is deeply permeated by Islam, their women play an active part in the family council and in politics. Everywhere except in Vietnam a woman can apply for divorce; in Burma her property is always kept separate from that of her husband, which makes her more independent than many European women. She usually chooses her husband herself, for young people have plentiful opportunities of meeting—at work in the fields, or at the pagoda ceremonies and village festivities, where groups of boys and girls sing in alternate chorus.

Rice is the principal food crop and, cooked in a variety of ways, serves as the staple diet. It may be boiled in water, crushed into vermicelli, served 'green', or mixed with oil as a sacrificial offering; in the languages of Malaya and in that of Vietnam, the same word denotes 'boiled rice' and 'food'. The rice is supplemented by many other products—maize, which is almost equally important, sweet potatoes, manioc, soya, yams, taro, coconut, groundnuts, sesame, tea, tobacco (extensively grown in the Philippines and in Burma) and various fruits, more especially bananas and sugar-cane, a source of exports. The betel and the areca palm are also cultivated, and provide the famous 'chew' which is popular throughout South-East Asia: for two thousand years the areca nut, wrapped in a betel leaf together with a little lime, has been a ritual offering at every ceremony and festival, whether public or private, and has served as 'the beginning of every conversation', to quote a saying common in Vietnam:

> At this meeting, take a betel chew,
> Just a memory to greet us later,
> A betel chew, light as a feather,
> Yet linking the willow and the fisherman . . .

Immediately after agriculture comes fishing. The length of the coastline, the number of rivers and lakes, even the existence of the flooded ricefields, all encourage that activity in the most varied forms. The peasants search every tiny pool for frogs, small fish and crabs, catching them with line, eel-pot, or even by hand. On a larger scale, the fishers' villages specialize in fishing with nets—large ones or the small, square dipping-net—or with cormorants, often working at night by torchlight and using their boats and rafts as floating houses. In Cambodia a natural phenomenon transforms the Great Lake into a unique fishpond: in the rainy season (July–October), the Mekong floods down into it through the Tonle-Sap, expanding its surface from the normal 3,000 sq. km to 10,000 sq. km; the surrounding forest is flooded and the fish feed there; when the water falls again the fishermen build dams or *samras*—piles of branches—and thousands of fish are caught in these. Sea-fishing is carried out from junks, sampans, rafts, and boats made of twisted bamboo shoots and caulked. Few of these vessels venture to sail very far out to sea; many of them have eyes painted in red and white on their prows, to guide them.

In addition to the fish which is eaten as such—fresh, dried, salted or smoked—fishing provides the national condiment to be eaten with rice; the *nuoc mam* of Vietnam, the *prahoc* of Cambodia and Siam, the *padec* of Laos and the *ngapi* of Burma. These are highly valuable food products, for they contain salt, nitrates, mineral and organic phosphorus, and vitamins. *Nuoc mam* is a liquid obtained by leaving fish to lie, whole, in salt, in wooden vats: it is an industry in its own right, carried on principally at Pham-thiêt and on the island of Phu-quôc. *Prahoc, padec and ngapi* are prepared by cleaning and salting the fish, pounding them up and drying the resultant product in the sun; but the juice that rises to the top of the big jars in which it is placed is poured off and used as well, as the equivalent of *nuoc mam*.

Generally speaking, conditions are not propitious to stock-breeding, owing to the climate, which is hot and humid, and the type of soil and vegetation. Cattle-breeding is carried on principally by mountain-dwellers such as the Meo and the Muong of Tonkin, or on such parts of the plains as are not entirely given over to the cultivation of food-crops. Vietnam is so densely populated that the lowlands are intensively cultivated and no animals are bred except pigs and poultry on a domestic scale, and the bullocks and buffalo required for farm work, which can subsist on the grass which grows on the low dykes. In neighbouring countries, where the shortage of land is less acute, grazing ground can be set aside and large cattle bred, more especially bullocks and zebu.

Mining, particularly of precious metals, has been practised for a very long time in South-East Asia; Ptolemy's *Geographia* mentions the golden Chersonese. By the nineteenth century these ancient mines were becoming exhausted, but deposits of other kinds began to be worked: tin in Malaya, Siam and Tenasserim, zinc, copper and lead in Burma and Vietnam, rubies and sapphires at Mogôk (Burma), salt in many regions, coal in Vietnam, iron in Vietnam, Siam and Cambodia (Phnom Dek), marble in Pursat—used for statues of the Buddha—and petroleum found in open wells at Yenangyaung (Burma) and used not only for lamps and torches, but for preserving wood, mats and the manuscripts which were written on palm-leaves. These mines were royal monopolies and were generally leased to Chinese; for centuries the latter had been working the tin-mines, for instance: they refined the tin themselves, but by primitive methods which gave a very low output.

A peasant wishing to make a little extra money would turn to craftsmanship rather than to cattle-breeding or mining. There were a number of simple industries (requiring practically no outlay) which he could take up in the slack periods between work in the fields—such as making fishing-nets and hammocks, making all kinds of baskets (these are very varied, baskets being woven of bamboo, rushes or cane and used for many different purposes, in the kitchen, for transport and in irrigation), mats, awnings and raincoats. The articles produced in the Philippines were particularly celebrated for their delicacy and beauty; owing to the fragility of the raw material, the greatest care had to be taken during the work. Mallat, in his description of the Philippines (1846) says that the weavers of a material called *pina* had to be protected from the slightest breath of air by working under mosquito-nets. Cotton and silk were woven in all parts of South-East Asia: with the help of the simplest implements, made of cane or bamboo, silk was transformed into the luxurious fabric, worked with gold or silver thread, for which the Khmers, the Laotians, the Siamese and the Trengganu Malayans were renowned. Turning to dyeing and textile printing, we find batik, an art which flourished chiefly in Java. The existence of magnificent teak forests in Siam and Burma produced excellent carpenters and joiners, who showed their skill in building pagodas and houses. Vietnam was famous for its bronzes (its bells, and the dynastic urns of Hué), its Thô-hà pottery, its Bat-trang porcelain, and its articles of furniture, lacquered or inlaid with mother-of-pearl. The most 'primitive' races worked in iron, including the Kouy of Cambodia, whose mud 'blast furnaces', described by Father Bouillevaux in 1850, have survived unchanged to the present day. Goldsmiths used only sheets of pure, unalloyed gold and silver, and the jewellery, especially the filigree work, produced in Bangkok, Brunei and Manangkabau was the admiration of all visitors.

The sites of these industries were not always determined by logical reasoning. Some of them were situated in the vicinity of their raw material (*nuoc mam*), but other villages of craftsmen were created by historical events. For instance, Bat-trang owed its prosperity to the fact that Chinese ceramists established themselves there in the sixteenth century, though all the materials for their work had to be brought from a distance: and Liêu-trang had a monopoly of wood-engraving for a long-time, simply because Luong Nhu Hôc, who was born there, introduced that art to his native place in the middle of the fifteenth century. Hanoi even had special streets for the different crafts—Cotton Street, Silk Street, Copper Street and so forth—as recalled in a folk-song which says that:

Hanoi has thirty-six streets for its guilds . . .

For as in medieval Europe, these craftsmen all had their *phuong*, or guilds, usually under the patronage of a protective genie. Each guild had its rules and traditions, and it was the duty of the *tho ca*, or head worker, assisted by the *tho po*, or second worker, to see that these were respected by the members. The guilds and the craftsmen's villages guarded their professional secrets jealously, so that technical methods were not handed round. The best workers were chosen by the Court to decorate the royal palaces, but they were sometimes taxed so heavily that they preferred to break up their looms or lacquering spindles.

The expansion of trade, too, was impeded by regulations and feudal taxes. In the old communities the prevailing ideology was not favourable to commerce: Confucianism and Buddhism despised profit-seeking and taught that the purpose of life should be to attain moral perfection or overcome desire. In the traditional order of rank in Vietnam, the merchant (*thuong*) occupied the lowest rung of the social ladder, below the scholar (*si*), the peasant (*nông*) and the craftsman (*công*). But trade was also weakened by the preponderance of community life, low purchasing power, small needs, abundant labour and bad communications.

Transport was slow, and took place chiefly by water, along the rivers and canals of which South-East Asia has such an abundance. Roads were little used except by government officials, who travelled in palanquins, and the royal messengers, who rode or went on foot. The famous Mandarin Road, built by the Nguyên in the early nineteenth century to symbolize the unification of Vietnam, never goes round obstacles, but runs in a straight line, cut into steps, up and through the passes of the Annam Gate, Cu-mông and Varella. This is because in Vietnam, as in Cambodia, Siam, Burma and Indonesia, a road was not an economic thoroughfare, but a manifestation of royal authority carrying order into the provinces. Transport was not rapid on the paths and lanes either; small carts were drawn by buffaloes or bullocks, or goods were carried in baskets hung at either end of a bamboo rod which rested on the bearer's shoulder.

The villages were practically self-sufficient, in time of peace or in time of war. Trade was confined to a few basic foodstuffs (rice, salt), to produce grown in geographically restricted areas (sugar, cotton), and to the products (*nuoc mam*) of the specialized craftsmen's villages. But in the early nineteenth century, when Siam, Vietnam and Burma were unified and politically consolidated, domestic and foreign trade began to expand. It was helped by advances in navigation as well. Crawford, who went to Bangkok and Hué as the envoy of the Government of India, described the 'Cochin-Chinese' in 1822 as being known as the best sailors in the Far East for endurance, activity, and good humour in obeying orders. Experts, he said, declared their boats to be the best that could be found among the native vessels of India; they could safely face the stormiest weather. John White, an American sea-captain who visited Saigon in 1820, was of the same opinion. Trade was further stimulated by the issue of gold and silver bars and the standardization of weights and measures by the Nguyêns.

Trade between north and south Vietnam was conducted by coasting-vessels and boats that sailed inland up the waterways; the principal products dealt in were rice, salt, fish, areca nuts and *nuoc mam*. China was the chief foreign customer, buying salt, sugar, precious woods and cinnamon and selling paper, silk, tea and medicinal drugs. Crawford estimated that the junks which sailed from Tonkin, Faifo, Hué and Saigon to China represented an annual total of some 17,000 tons. Other ships went to Singapore and Batavia to buy Indian cotton yarn to be worked up by the craftsmen. From Europe the Government bought little except armaments.

Siamese trade was on a larger scale; Crawford estimates it at 28,000 tons, 24,500 of which went to China. Thanks to its central position and the activity of its Chinese minority. Bangkok served at this time as the regional warehouse, a position from which it was later ousted by Singapore. It was here that goods arrived from the Malayan peninsula, from India, Cambodia, Manila and other neighbouring markets, to be sent on to China and Japan, and vice versa. Exports included rice, sugar, coconut oil, salt, pepper, tin and cotton. Siam, unlike its neighbours, was able to export rice owing to the fertility of its soil, which provided abundant harvests for the comparatively small population; whereas in Vietnam the terrible floods of the Red River were liable to reduce entire villages to famine at a moment's notice.

Burma, too, prohibited the export of rice, in order to safeguard the country's supplies. Here the principal export was teak, a wood which never rots and was used for building houses and ships; the trees grew in Tenasserim. The timber was sent to China, to Siam and, from Rangoon and Syriam, to Calcutta; in 1795 this export was worth approximately £200,000 per annum. It is interesting to compare this figure with that of the total of British goods imported via Rangoon at the same period, which consisted of textiles, hardware and glassware to the value of £135,000.

On the whole, in fact, South-East Asia exported more than it imported. The import figure was small because of the limited purchasing power in the countries concerned. Chinese and European goods were either intended to meet the demand from a wealthy minority—the Court and the mandarins—or consisted of arms and munitions. There was thus a credit balance which was covered by sending gold and silver into the region. This position was reversed after the European conquest; as a result of colonial exploitation the markets were flooded with manufactured goods from Manchester, Lyons and Twante, capital left the country and the national craftsmen were ruined.

Trade was further hampered by the controls or monopolies imposed by the kings, which affected exports and imports alike. Finlayson asserted that in 1821 'the King and his ministers still continue to be the sole merchants (in Siam), retaining in their own hands the monopoly of all articles of consequence, and holding it contraband for any others to intermeddle'. Until about 1820, indeed, the budgets of that country were maintained chiefly by trading profits; when trade diminished, Rama II gave more freedom to private merchants, but taxed them rather heavily. The system in Vietnam and Burma was very similar.

Such were the main features of economic life. Despite hard circumstances, natural calamities, oppression from notabilities and government officials, and a despotic monarchy, the South-East Asian peasants were remarkable for persistent optimism, good humour and common sense. Writing of the Burmese in 1878, a British observer named Forbes described them in terms that applied equally to all their neighbours when he declared that:

'The Burmans are a lively people, fond of amusement. Horse and boat racing and dramatic performances are the greatest attractions. The young men and boys may often be seen of an evening playing football in the street, and elders engaged at chess on the verandah. The great national sport of the Peguans is boat racing . . . The boats belong to certain towns or villages, and are rowed, or rather paddled by the men belonging to them; and sometimes, when a match occurs between two localities that have long been rivals, the enthusiasm, wild excitement, is almost incredible and certainly indescribable . . .'

There were other popular amusements common to all countries in the region—fights between cocks, buffaloes, crickets, birds or goldfish always drew crowds and there was much betting on the results; then there were wrestling and acrobatic displays, ball games, rice-cooking competitions, swings and—in Vietnam from the third to the sixth month of the year—the flying of kites fitted with whistles.

These games were often a feature of the many festivals which broke the monotony of peasant life (a life that was monotonous, but not unhappy). The festivals were strictly seasonal, held to celebrate the beginning or end of various agricultural activities. Most important of them was the New Year, which marked the re-awakening of Nature and renewed man's pact with the world by a series of rites, including lustration, the opening of the fields, antiphonal songs, and contests of all kinds. In Vietnam, where the Têt falls in January or February, according to the lunar calendar, it has a family character as well; that is the time when all the members of a clan assemble before their ancestral shrine, to cummune with the dead. In Cambodia, Laos, Siam and Burma, New Year falls in April, at the critical moment when the wet monsoon is about to succeed the dry one: water is then the most precious of blessings, and after washing the statues of Buddha, the men and women joyfully splash one another with it.

During the period of work in the fields there are not many festivals; but they begin again at the end of that season. In Vietnam the mid-autumn festival (*Trung thu*, the fifteenth day of the eighth month) is presided over by the *âm*, or female principle, whereas the *duong*, or male principle, was dominant in the spring: by the light of a moon which now attains its greatest beauty, boys and girls sing in alternate chorus, to the accompaniment of the stringed drum; betrothals and marriages soon follow. In the Hinayana countries the rainy season (July–October) is a time of fasting, and its conclusion is celebrated by the *Kathin* ceremony, at which presents of clothing are offered to the bonzes. The pagodas and houses are illuminated, and the villagers bring thousands of little earthenware oil lamps, fastened to tiny bamboo rafts, and launch them on the water to carry away the evil spirits. This is followed by processions, with dancing and music, the offering of flowers to the Buddha, and piroga-races. In Cambodia this water festival, accompanied by moon-worship, takes place at the time when the waters of the Tonle Sap surge back into the Mekong, revealing the fertile alluvial deposits they have left on the flooded land, and giving the signal for the miraculous draughts of fishes.

These are merely the principal feasts. Almost every event gives occasion for others—birth and marriage, withdrawal into a monastery, the birthday of the Buddha, the memory of the dead, thanksgiving to the spirits for a good harvest; and even death itself, which is greeted not with mourning but with music, song and dance—for it does not signify extinction, but the beginning of a new and better life, a step towards Nirvana . . .

The blossoming of national cultures[2]

By the beginning of the nineteenth century the principal states of South-East Asia had taken permanent shape. Frontiers being now more or less stabilized, original cultures came to flower, maintaining their individuality despite foreign influences and an underlying foundation common to the whole region. Each of these nations developed, at the promoting of its particular genius, a civilization adapted to its environment, temperament, manner of life and language.

Vietnam, to the east of the peninsula, achieved political unification in 1802. Gia-long, founder of the Nguyên dynasty, was the first sovereign to exercise undivided rule from the Nam-quan Gate to the Cape of Camau. His country, a long strip between the South China Sea and the Annamite mountains, had developed in the course of seven centuries of *Nam-tiên*, or 'southward march', starting from the delta of the Red River, where the Viêt people had been established since the third century B.C. Their swing-ploughs slowly brought the coastal area under cultivation, and then the Mekong plainlands, left fallow by the thinly scattered population of Khmers. Unlike other instances of political unification, this was a single race, already long in possession of well-established institutions, gradually expanding to occupy a far greater area.

The same thing happened with the Siamese. Coming down from South-West China, they slowly infiltrated along the central valleys of the peninsula, emerging as a state in the thirteenth century. As their seaward thrust continued, the centre of their kingdom travelled with it—from Sukhôthai (mid-thirteenth century) to Ayuthya (1350) and later to Bangkok (1782), following the Menam Chao Phya as it led them towards the fertile plains to which they were to owe their prosperity. Siam was almost destroyed by disastrous war with Burma in the eighteenth century, but Phya Taksin (1767–82) re-unified the country and his successor Rama I (1782–1809), the founder of the present dynasty, consolidated peace, order and the administration.

The Lao, another Thai group, were less fortunate than their cousins in not having a good river, navigable as far as the sea; their Mekong was broken up by rapids and their land was a series of plateaux divided by rivers or mountains. Lan Chang, the 'kingdom of a Million Elephants', reached its peak of prosperity halfway through the seventeenth century and then declined into internecine conflicts as a result of which three rival states were created in 1711–13: Luang-Prabang in the north, Vientiane in the centre, and Champassak to the south. Vientiane was wiped off the map in 1827 by attacks from the Siamese, whose influence was already dominant in Champassak, while Luang Prabang, to avoid the same fate, took Vietnam as its protector. In spite of this dismemberment the Lao remained united and vigorous in their language, manners, customs, religion, literature, art and so forth, and above all in the minds of their people.

Cambodia lay to the south of Champassak, squeezed between Vietnam and Siam, and for a time provided them with a battlefield during their expansion, which was facilitated by conflicts of succession and rivalry among the mandarins. Little by little, portions of what had been the great Empire of the Khmers were severed from Cambodia—Korât, Chantaboun, Battambang and Stung-treng on the west, the Mekong delta on the east. Not until the reign of Ang Duong (1845–59) did the kingdom recover comparative peace by achieving a balance between the respective influences of its two neighbours.

Burma came into existence in the central Irrawaddy basin, between the Shan plateau and the Arakan mountains, at the meeting-point of the principal routes of communication and bordering the fertile rice plain of Kyaukse. It was the work of the Burmese people, who came down in the seventh or eighth century from the border between China and Tibet and assimilated the civilization of the Môn of Pegu, together with Buddhism in its Sinhalese form. Alaungpaya unified it once and for all in 1757, and Bodawpaya, by his conquest of Arakan (1785), Assam and Manipur (1817-22), advanced the frontiers of Burma till they met those of British India.

In the archipelago, the period of the great empires of Çrivijaya and Mojopahit was over. In Java, under the pressure of Dutch expansionism, the kingdom of Matarâm was split, from 1755 onwards, into two principalities, Surakarta and Jogjakarta. The Dutch also controlled the Moluccas—the spice islands—but most of Sumatra, Borneo and Celebes, together with the island of Bali and the sultanates of the Malay peninsula, were still independent. Here, as in Lan Chang, neither political disruption nor foreign domination could impair the underlying unity of the civilization, which was due to the predominance of the Malayan people and their language, and to the maritime traffic among the islands which enabled first Hinduism and later Islam to spread and to overlie a common foundation of *Adat* and animistic beliefs.

This animistic basis was common not only to Indonesia and Malaya, but to the whole of South-East Asia. It was continually breaking through the upper crust of foreign contributions, regardless of whether these latter took the form of Confucian culture, as in Vietnam, of Buddhist–Hinayana culture, as in Cambodia, Laos, Siam and Burma, of Moslem culture, as in Java and Sumatra, or of Hindu culture as in Bali. In Europe, all primitive beliefs had been uprooted by Christianity; but in South-East Asia they preserved their vitality, no doubt because of certain fundamental affinities.

Their chief characteristic is the worship of ancestors and of the nature-spirits known as *thân* in Vietnam, *neak ta* in Cambodia, *phi* in Laos and Siam, *nat* in Burma and *hantu* among the Malays. These spirits are present everywhere, in the air, in mountains, lakes and rivers, in stones and trees. They may be malevolent or charitable; some of them are heroes and sages who became divinities after their death, others are the wandering spirits of people who perished by accident or were left unburied, etc. They are worshipped under big trees, their little wooden altars being suspended from a branch or raised on a stake. In Laos the festival of the Phi takes place in the seventh month (May–June), when the dry season makes way for the rainy season on which the harvest depends. The Talaings and the Burmese in the Irrawaddy delta celebrate the festival of the *nats* just before the monsoon breaks. This belief in invisible powers influences every action in life. When a house is to be built, for instance, a whole series of rules must be applied, and rites performed, to discover when work should be started, on what site the house should stand and in which direction it should face. The portents are investigated before a journey or fishing expedition is undertaken, horoscopes are cast, the spirits of the dead are conjured up . . .

The interpenetration of religions is particularly marked in Vietnam, where animism is tangled up with Taoism, Confucianism and the Buddhism of the Mahayana. It is not unusual for a single temple to enshrine Confucius,

Lao-tse astride his blue buffalo, and Sakyamuni seated on his lotus blossom. To tell the truth, the people of Vietnam have no deep-seated religious principles, but cheerfully adapt themselves to circumstances—consulting Quan-âm when they wish for children or a Taoist sorcerer when they are sick, and getting married with the help of Confucian rites. This 'eclecticism', which is to be found in every country in the region, accounts for the religious tolerance, or indifference, shown there; it was not out of fanaticism, but on political grounds, that Christianity was persecuted. Under the influence of local beliefs, Taoism degenerated from the very lofty philosophy of the 'Universal Way' (Dao) into a set of magical practices. Its pantheon comprised innumerable divinities, led by Ngoc Hoàng, the 'August Emperor of Jade', but the most popular among them were the Chu vi, or 'Spirits of the Three Worlds', the Thanh Mâu or 'Holy Mothers', and the Nôi Dao or 'Inner Way', which worshipped the national hero Trân Hung Dao, who defeated the Mongols in the thirteenth century. Female mediums, the ba dông, served as channels of communication between the human and divine worlds.

The Buddhism of Vietnam was the Great Vehicle, as in China and Japan. It is based on the concept of universal suffering which can be abolished only by doing away with the life-urge itself, after which comes Nirvana. This atheistic, agnostic philosophy was rendered more subtle and more beautiful in order to increase its attraction for the masses. Every karma (individual destiny) consists of a succession of reincarnations resulting from the trans-migration of the soul and governed by the sum of all the good and bad actions committed during previous existences. The karma can be improved by acquiring merit, which is done by practising charity. In this course of action, everyone is assisted by the bodhisattvas, beings who could have become Buddhas, but who have renounced that condition so as to remain in the world and work for the salvation of mankind. The most popular among them are Quan-âm (Avalokiteçvara) and A-di-da (Amitâbha). Under the earliest dynasties of Vietnam, Ly and Trân (eleventh–thirteenth centuries), Buddhism was the State religion, but since the end of the eighteenth century it had ceased to exert any great influence at Court. Nevertheless, the people in general and the literate class in particular were deeply imbued with its con-cepts—the impermanence of earthly things, charity, respect for all forms of life—which inspired some of the finest works in the national literature.

At this later stage Confucianism was regarded as the official 'religion'. It is not, in point of fact, a religion, but a philosophy and a system of ethics—without metaphysics—aimed at consolidating social order with the help of individual morality: tu thân tê gia binh thiên ha—'mould oneself, guide one's family, bring peace to the world'—those are the three stages in the govern-ment of men. Human order must conform to natural order, harmony being maintained by the correct performance of ritual and the strict observance of rules by each individual, according to his position in the family and in the community.

This moral outlook conditioned the whole system of education. which was concerned not merely with imparting knowledge, but with forming the character. The teacher did not only teach his pupils to read and write, he shaped their minds and personalities at the same time. Education was widespread and practically free. Every village had its school, kept by a member of the literate class who in most cases was not paid either by the State or by the village, but used to receive a few small presents from the children's parents. In spring and autumn a sacrifice was offered in the temple of Confucius.

In regions where Buddhism took the form of the Lesser Vehicle (Hinayana or Theravada), religion exerted a much stronger influence than in Vietnam. It affected every aspect of life, if only because education was dispensed by the pagodas.

In theory, Hinayana kept closer than Mahayana to the original precepts of Buddhism. Whereas the latter took account of the oral tradition—the Master's teachings as received by his disciples—the former relied solely on the canon preserved in the pâli language, the *Tripitaka*, or 'Three Baskets of the Law', the Discipline, the Discourses and the Scriptures. Here there are no bodhisattvas, each individual must strive towards Nirvana by his own efforts, through study of the texts, meditation, and the suppression of desire. In practice, however, Hinayana drew closer to Mahayana, for it, too, stressed the virtues by which the individual could improve his karma and escape from the cycle of reincarnation—kindness to all living beings, an absolute ban on the taking of life, charity to the poor and to bonzes, and religious retreat to a monastery for a certain period. The most popular form of literature was the *Jatakas*, which related the earlier lives of Buddha, describing his acts of kindness to his fellow humans or to animals.

The pagoda schools were open free of charge to prince and peasant alike, so that here, as in Vietnam, education was widespread. Here too, as in Vietnam, the aim was to make known and explain religious principles, the duties of the Buddhist, rather than to impart intellectual knowledge. At about the age of fifteen, or sometimes rather later, a boy would withdraw from the world for a time and don the saffron robe. Not until then did he achieve the full dignity of his human condition; until he had subjected himself to monastic discipline he could neither reap the harvest of his previous actions nor hope for a better life in his next incarnation.

The Malayan peninsula and the archipelago were the domain of Islam, which spread throughout this region (except for Bali) and southward from Mindanao to the Philippines, at the beginning of the nineteenth century. But though in 1817, when Raffles wrote his *History of Java*, every village already had its mosque, the Moslem influence was merely superficial. The princes had been converted for political reasons—because by accepting Islam they were admitted to a far-flung community and gained the support of the Ottoman and Mongol empires against Europe. Furthermore, Islam did not come to South-East Asia direct from the Arabian countries, but by way of India, in a version already adapted and assimilated by Hinduism, which made it more widely acceptable. It led to the gradual abolition of the caste system and of polytheism, but the fundamental concepts of the State and the monarchy remained unchanged, *adat* maintained its influence in the Javanese legal system (which allowed women rights they enjoyed in no other Moslem country), the *wayang* shadow-puppets still drew their themes from the *Râmayâna* and the *Mahâbhârata*, as did the ballets performed in the villages and royal palaces to the strains of the *gamelan* orchestra.

Islam was rejected only by Bali. That little island—a place of magnificent natural beauty, protected by reefs and rough seas—had always been proudly independent. As a means of resisting the political domination of Java, it remained faithful to Hinduism and the social structure that went with it. Bali still had its four traditional castes (Brahmin, Kshatriya, Vaishya and Shudra), its Untouchables—who were usually potters, dyers or distillers of alcohol—and the custom of suttee, by which widows were burnt on their husbands' funeral pyres. But this Hinduism was inextricably mingled with primitive animism, and the combination had given birth to innumerable divinities whose existence was evidenced by a multitude of temples and altars which clung to the sides of mountains or were scattered through the markets, villages, fields and private gardens. Thanks to the fertility of the soil and to traditions of co-operation in agriculture which enabled them to live in dignity and freedom, the people of Bali had turned their everyday existence into an endless festival, a perpetual round of ceremonies, rites, sculpture, music and dance, performed in an architectural setting as harmonious as the terraced ricefields whose flooded surfaces mirrored the peaks of their volcanoes.

In Bali the popular culture and that of the aristocrats met and mingled, but in other countries they remained separate. One of the richest traditions of South-East Asia is its folk literature, handed down by word of mouth. From the Philippines to Burma it presents many common features, partly because all these peoples shared a way of life based on the cultivation of rice. Their folk-songs, fables, tales and proverbs give a faithful picture of peasant life with its labour, its sorrows, its joys and loves, its beliefs and superstitions, and its shrewd common sense, humour and wisdom. It is they, rather than the writings of the learned, which make up the real national literature of these countries.

For instance, a delicate subject could scarcely be more tactfully approached than this:

> Little sister, you are like a piece of rose-pink silk;
> Is it still complete, is it in anyone's hands?'
> 'I am like a piece of rose-pink silk
> That flutters in the market-place, not knowing into whose hands it will fall!

Anyone familiar with the Tonkin delta will appreciate the melancholy of this other song, sometimes heard among the ricefields that stretch in endless monotony to the thin line of mountains on the horizon:

> Mountain, oh mountain, why are you so high?
> You hide the sun from me, and the face of my beloved!

Some of the *cao dao* strike a note of romantic passion unknown to Confucian literature:

> The memory of whom sets all my limbs afire
> As though I were standing in the midst of flames,
> As though I were seated on glowing coals,
> The memory of whom half-closes my eyes
> And I walk with tottering steps,
> Like the bird that bears away its prey . . .

The peasant who sang thus of his love could also, on occasion, make a caustic, biting attack on the many soothsayers, charlatans and false bonzes who exploited the credulity of the people, on the insatiability of women and the boasting of men, the impudence of scribes and the cupidity of mandarins. The style of Trang Quynh in Vietnam, Thmenh Chey in Cambodia and Xieng Mieng in Lan Chang ranges from good-natured satire to merciless criticism of the feudal system. Yet for all their criticism they love their country:

> As the red cloth covers the supports of a mirror,
> So should all men of a country love one another!

The people expressed themselves in pictures, theatre and music as well as in poetry. The folk-pictures with their bright primary colours were produced by village craftsmen whose technique had been unchanged for centuries, and provided lively illustrations of the religious and moral universe around them. In Cambodia and Laos they dealt chiefly with themes drawn from Buddhist religion or the legends of the *Ramâyâna*: in Vietnam the prints which fluttered in the markets at New Year had a wider range, depicting historic heroes, comic or satirical scenes (cat and mouse, the school of frogs), work in the fields, and the emblems of traditional good wishes—a pig to symbolize abundance, a fish for long life, a pair of ducks for perfect married harmony, and so forth.

The folk theatre, also an oral tradition, was very rich. In Vietnam there was the *Hat cheo*, which drew upon history, legend, and rural life. Devised and acted by the peasants, usually for the entertainment of the *dinh*, these pieces had ordinary people as their characters and the whole audience would be drawn into the performance. Like the folk-songs and pictures it is characterized by humanity of outlook and a satirical spirit; the good are rewarded and the wicked punished, and notables, mandarins and even the king himself must submit to criticism. All this is accompanied by music played on simple instruments—gongs, rattles, strings, drums and tambourines. In contrast to the classical theatre (*Hat tuông*), gesture is stylized and reduced to a minimum, a distinction which is also to be found in the neighbouring countries. These too possess a highly popular marionette drama, known as *nang* in Siam and Cambodia, *yokthe* in Burma and *wayang* in Java. *Wayang* and *nang*, strictly speaking, are shadow plays; the figures, cut out of leather or carved from wood, are moved about behind a white linen screen on which their shadows are thrown by lights in the background, to the strains of a small orchestra. The plots are taken from national myth and legend or from the *Ramâyâna* or the *Jatakas*, duly adapted to the national taste and re-interpreted. Every performance is preceded by ceremonies intended to place the actors under the protection of the gods and ancestors.

The richest written literature grew up in Vietnam, Siam and Burma. In the second half of the eighteenth century the national languages came into their own, with a flourish of poetical and historical works.

Before the reign of Alaungpaya in Burma, Môn and Burmese had ranked equally as languages for cultural purposes, but during the Konbaung period (1752–1885) the latter established its predominance not only in lyric, epic and didactic poetry, with their great variety of forms, but also in written chronicles, prose tales taken from the *Jatakas*, Court plays and folk drama.* Written drama originated somewhere about 1785, when the first Burmese play was put on at Court. It was by U Sa, entitled *E. Naung*, and recounted the love story of a Siamese prince. This marked the theatre's emergence from oral tradition and mime to become a branch of literature. U Kyin U, who was writing from 1824 to 1837, and U Pon Nya (*c.* 1855–66) brought it out of the narrow circle of the Court and made it popular with the general public, largely thanks to two plays—*Parpahein*, by U Kyin U, whose characters are particularly lifelike, and *Yethè* (*The Water-Carrier*), by U Pon Nya, which has a classical plot comprised in a single day. The following is the climax of this latter play: the King has fallen asleep in the arms of his new favourite, the Water-Carrier, who utters the following soliloquy:

'My wish has been fulfilled and the hour of my fortune strikes. Now I might seize the throne for myself alone. My royal lord, full of trust in me, has dismissed his suite and fallen asleep in my arms, smiling as he dreams. It is not easy or satisfactory for two people to rule one kingdom, and I have a means of escaping from that situation: the King is now in my power, though I did nothing to bring this about. I will grasp his top-knot, hold it tight, and cut his throat. Yes, if I do that I shall have no further rival, no further danger,

* The following passages, dealing with Burmese literature, are based on a work by Mrs Denise Bernot, who has been kind enough to allow me to consult her manuscript, and to whom I take this opportunity of offering my thanks.

the city, the palace and the law courts will be mine. Yes, I will do it—courage, my boy, and draw your sword.

'No my mind has planned a fine journey, calculated to lead me along a charming road to final success; but it also leads me to a barbarous, horrible deed . . . No, I cannot do it, it would be a disgusting crime . . .

'And . . . You are a man, and if you begin to worry about morality and try to remain pure, you will never succeed in life—fortune is flying past, seize it at once . . . But no—reflect, Prince, you cannot kill your best friend . . .

'All that is idle talk. Come, get on with it! When one means to eat a monkey one cannot stop to look into his pathetic face. You have no choice: you have to do it, you have to triumph, just as a valiant cock must fight until he wins, when he is attacked. In this world a man who does not attack will be attacked. Come, abase yourself, for your own sake. Just one little, trifling sin, then power for the rest of your life! If you would be powerful, kill him, at once, and quickly, for your own safety, for if he awakens and sees you draw your sword, you are lost.

'Stop! What horrible deed were you about to perpetrate against your blameless Prince, so glorious and good, so spotlessly pure! He is your master, deserving of all your gratitude. Control yourself, that your heart may not obey your mind. Enough! you were about to commit the vilest action of your life.'*

With the introduction of the printing-press in the latter half of the nineteenth century, plays were able to circulate more widely and the theatre became more popular than ever. The best playwright of this period was U Pok Ni, whose masterpiece, *Konmara pyazat* (the name of one of its heroes) appeared in 1875. The action is divided between a village and the royal Court, and the characters are full of life—avaricious farmers, gallant farmhands, coquettish, determined girls, a cynical procuress and some sycophantic, affected Ministers and courtiers.

Writers and poets were very numerous; they were usually either monks who drew their inspiration from the *Jatakas*, or noblemen who sang the praises of the monarchs and their irrigation works, but who could also compose lullabies and other simple, graceful lyrics, such as the following poem in which U Sa (1819–51) compares his lady-love to the mythical flower named *pizu*.

'On Mount Gaudhama, in its chasms and caves, your perfume scents the air; *pizu* flower, flower wrought by the fairies, I long to pluck you and wear you in the hair, but I may only gaze at you . . .'

Several women poets produced 'plaints', lyric poems and dramas; the most celebrated of them was Princess Ma Pwa Gyi (1833–75).

The great prose chronicles, too, date from this period: *Hman Nan Yazawin*

* From the French translation by Denise Bernot.

(the Chronicle of the Palace of Mirrors) was compiled between 1829 and 1833 and followed by the *Dutiya Mahâ Yazawin* (Second Chronicle), begun in 1867, during the reign of Mindon, and resumed in 1905 to cover the whole period of the Konbaung dynasty, the title of the entire work being *Konbaung Set Yazawin*. These records have the same defect as those of the neighbouring countries—they deal only with kings and political events, without touching on the economic and social life of the nation; but by recalling past achievements and glories they contributed to the subsequent national revival.

Siamese literature (like that of Cambodia and Laos) had much in common with Burmese, because of the Buddhist influence. Royal patronage for artists was even more generous here than in Burma. Many sovereigns were cultivated men of letters, who not only commissioned official chronicles and ordered laws to be codified, but summoned writers to Court and wrote poems or plays themselves. Phya Taksin, Rama I and Rama II (1809-24) wrote dramas based on the *Ramakien*, which is the Siamese version of the *Ramâyâna*. Rama II, one of Siam's finest poets, was the first monarch to be perceptibly influenced by the oral folk-literature in the plays he wrote for the 'outside theatre' (*lak hon nok*), so called in contrast to the 'inside theatre' which was reserved for the Court. Rama III (1824-51) turned the Wat P'ho into a kind of living encyclopaedia of his time: every plant found in the country was cultivated within the monastery walls, and the basic elements of all that was then known about astrology, medicine, history, literature, etc. were engraved on slabs of marble and set up on its walls and pillars.

The celebrated *Khun Chang Khun P'hen* dates from the beginning of the nineteenth century. This is the collective work of a committee of poets set up by Rama II to give literary form to a popular rhapsody (*sep'ha*) which had hitherto been handed down by word of mouth, rearranged or embellished at the narrator's pleasure. It has a genuinely Thai plot; its heroes, Khun Chang and Khun P'hen, are thought to have lived at the end of the fifteenth century, and their deeds to have been chanted at that early period. The poem differs from many Siamese works inasmuch as its leading figures are not kings and princes, but humble people and officers. It is to be regarded as a national masterpiece owing to its homely style, its language, which retains the folk touch, and its subject—daily life and its incidents, which it describes with no trace of foreign influence.

Among the poets who helped to edit it was Sunthon P'hu (1786-1855), one of Siam's finest writers. He led an adventurous life and his output was prolific, including tales, proverbs, poems and lullabies. His style is simple and natural, his verse melodious, with an occasional touch of bitterness or irony seldom found in Siamese poetry.* His *nirat* ('songs of separation') give a lively, colourful picture of his native landscape, with its floating villages and aquatic markets and its famous places of pilgrimage, and every scene prompts him to some reflection on the human condition:

* P. Schweisguth, *Etude sur la littérature siamoise*, Paris, 1951.

'The women of Pakrèt, a Môn village, used to wear their hair in a knot; such was their custom; but now they have cut it off, they pluck themselves round their topknots like dolls, they powder their faces and grease their hair like the Thai. Oh clumsy, insincere imitation! In abandoning their country, these men and women have abandoned their customs; is that not like having several hearts?

'But that man is single-hearted, we may not venture to believe.

'Here comes Bangp'hut:* to speak well is a fine thing, there are those who love the perfume of words, who delight in it; but to speak ill destroys friendship; one is loved or hated, according to the words one utters ...

'Now we come to the village of the *madeüa*; O *madeüa*, strange fruit, an insect dwells within it; like wicked people, it is sweet outwardly and bitter inside ...

'We are coming to the old town ... We must tie up the boat opposite the P'hramen temple; boats are lined up all along the bank; some go up and downstream, exchanging verses of some song; others are taking cloth to offer to the monks in the forest.

'They sing ... the xylophones chime ... there are rows of lanterns, the temple is like the Samp'hèng† ...'‡

Sunthon P'hu also wrote a brisk, fantastic adventure story, *Ap'haymani*, whose extraordinary episodes, in which pirates and European missionaries take part, were highly popular with Siamese readers.

Other outstanding poets of this period were Prince Paramanuchit (1790–1853), author of an epic (*Taleng P'hay*, 'The Defeat of the Burmese'), lyrical and religious poems, songs intended to soothe wild elephants, sermons and a chronicle of Ayuthya; and two women poets, Khun P'hum (c. 1815–80), who was subtle and witty and whose floating house became a literary *salon*, and Khun Suwan (c. 1820–80), who was celebrated for her eccentricites and for her burlesque poems, where passages of meaningless sound were used to link up phrases 'without head or tail'.§

In Vietnam, classical literature was at its zenith in the latter half of the eighteenth century and the beginning of the nineteenth. Until then the dominant language had been Chinese, but it now had to take second place to Nôm, Vietnam's own language. The great masterpieces of lyric poetry were composed at this time—*Chinh phu ngâm* (Lament of the Warrior's Wife) by Dang Trân Côn and Phan Huy Ich, *Cung oan ngâm khuc* (Song of Grief in the Harem) by Nguyên Gia Thiêu, *Hoa tiên* (Flowered Leaflets) by Nguyên Huy Tu and Nguyên Thiên, and finally, about 1800, *Truyên Thuy Kiêu* (Story of Thuy Kiêu) by Nguyên Du.

* *P'hut*: speech.
† A particularly lively and well-lit district in Bangkok.
‡ Translated by P. Schweisguth, *op. cit.* pp. 231–2.
§ P. Schweisguth, *op. cit.* p. 262.

Under the beauty of its verse, which deals with the traditional theme of the soldier's departure for war and the parting between him and his wife, the *Chinh phu* conceals some discreet social criticism, revealed in the poet's sympathy for the sufferings of the common people. For this was a time when peasant uprisings were breaking out in all parts of the Empire:

> The moon hangs above solitary Mount Ky
> The cold wind wails round the burial-mounds of Phi
> Souls of dead warriors stir of tremendous wind
> Masked faces of fighting men cold sheen of moons
> Fighting men and warriors lying stiff and silent,
> Who, who will paint your features and summon your souls?

The Nôm language reached perfection in the *Kiêu*, a long narrative poem relating the adventures of a girl who is compelled to sell herself in order to save her parents, but is ultimately rescued by Buddhist priests and restored to her family and to her former fiancé. The story is commonplace, but the *Kiêu*'s reputation is based on its matchless style and the vivid picture it gives us of life in that period. Society is depicted with all its traditional refinements, its splendour and its vices, cultivated circles with their love of poetry and music, the sacrifices exacted by the Confucian code of filial piety, the district of the 'green pavilions' with its pimps and procuresses, the corrupt or perfidious officials, the rebellious commoners, the serenity of the Buddhist pagodas. Written in a harmonious six-eight metre (an alternation of six-feet and eight-feet lines), the poem can convey in a few delicate touches a personality of striking realism, an entire scene, or the faintest tremors of the heart.

The beauty of its style, its admirable psychology and the completeness of the world it describes have made the *Kiêu* a kind of bible for the people of Vietnam. From the scholar to the humblest peasant, everyone knows at least a few verses by heart and turns its pages devoutly, seeking for an echo of his own joy or grief or a clue to the mystery of his future.

Many other poets deserve mention, including Nguyên Dinh Chiêu, who sang of the lands to the south, Nguyên Công Tru, a great mandarin who colonized the seaward districts, Cao Ba Quat, a passionate champion of justice who even took arms against the Court; and the Emperor Tu-duc himself. There were some great women poets in the same period, among them Queen Le Ngoc-Hân, wife of Quang trung, Madame de Thanh-quan, and above all the astonishing Hô Xuân Huong, stirred by disappointed love to rebel against the traditional code of ethics and express herself in a pithy style of frank imagery, its erotic allusions interspersed with bitter irony. Her work shows no trace of influence, and is undoubtedly the most original to be found in the literature of Vietnam. The following is one of her best-known poems, entitled 'The *Ba-dôi* Pass' (or 'Pass of the three bulges', a name it takes from its three successive gradients):

A pass . . . a pass . . . yet another pass . . .
Praised be the creator of this steep stretch!
Like the shell of a tortoise the ground bulges, carpeted with green grass;
A stone, red as a chicken's liver, rises from the greyish moss.
The pine branch tosses in the keen wind
Drops of dew fall from the leaves of the soaking willow.
Sages and gentlemen, which of you would not be happy,
Despite weary knees and legs, to climb this pass for ever?

Historical and geographical writings were equally abundant. The *Quôc su quan* (Record Office) of Huê compiled the *Dai Nam thuc luc* (Episodes of the History of Vietman), the *Dai Nam Liêt-truyên* (Biographies of Vietnam), the *Khâm dinh Viêt su thông giam cuong muo* (Texts and explanatory notes constituting the complete mirror of the history of Vietnam) and the *Dai Nam nhât thông chi* (general geography). In addition to these official compilations there appeared Triuh Hoai Duc's *Gia-dinh thông chi* (Description of Cochin-China), and Phan Huy Chu assembled in his *Lich triêu hiên chuong loui chi* (Monographs on the institutions of all the dynasties) an enormous amount of geographical information, biographies of famous men, descriptions of official posts, ritual, examinations, the resources of the State, the system of justice, the army, literature, and relations with China (1821).

In the field of science, mention should be made of the work of the physician Lan Ong, in the second half of the eighteenth century. He adapted Chinese medicine to the Vietnamese temperament and made a study of the country's medicinal plants, as being more suitable for use in treating his compatriot's illnesses than those of the foreign pharmacopoeia. His works fill 66 volumes and form a veritable encyclopaedia of medicine, covering practically all subjects, from acupuncture to pediatrics, obstetrics and gynaecology.

Like the literature of the South-East Asian countries, their art displays both generic features and individual characteristics, varying from one country to another: these national touches, which influence shape, design, general form, flow of line and combination of colours, it is impossible to mistake one for another the ornamentation, sculpture or painting of Cambodia, Lan Chang, Siam, Burma and Indonesia, let alone to confuse them with those of Vietnam. It is not easy to make a historical study of these works, for the artists are in most cases unknown, the artist's name being regarded as of far less importance than the work itself and the religious spirit pervading it.

For these works of art, especially in the countries of Buddhist culture, were intended first and foremost to adorn the pagodas, the palaces coming afterwards. Few examples of painting have survived the humidity of the climate and the smoke from torches and oil lamps; these few include the frescoes in the Wat Pho at Bangkok, painted in the reign of Rama III, which drew their themes not only from the Life of Buddha and the *Ramakien*, but from Siamese folk-songs as well. Sculpture, in bronze or wood, also takes as its chief subject the Buddha in his traditional positions—seated on a lotus or lying on his right side; these works can only be dated by minor details such as the shape of a topknot or the curls on the head. But a few 'secular' pieces of sculpture were produced as well, such as the magnificent imperial urns at Huê, cast in 1835–6 in token of the duration and stability of the dynasty. For ornamental purposes, stylized motives were invariably used; these were derived from the local fauna or flora—and in Vietnam, from the Chinese ideograms—combined with raised lines and arabesques: the most lavish example of Lao art is the carved and gilded doors of the Luang Prabang pagodas, on which the raised knots and flames seem as though cut out in the wood. Then there are the inlaid enamel and filigree work of Siam and Cambodia, the inlaid lacquer work of Hanoi, the enamels and blues of Huê, the carved ivories of Burma, the Lao and Khmer *sampots* and *sarongs*, the krises and batiks of Bali and Java, the designs of which vary according to whether they come from Surakarta, Jogjakarta, Cheribon, Pekalongan or Banjamas.

But the supreme art is architecture, inseparably associated with the landscape. Even the humblest dwelling fits into its setting of bamboos and palm, rain and light. The pagoda, with its curve-tipped roofs casting heavy shadows on pillars, bare walls and carved and gilded doors, gives an impression of mystery heightened by its isolated position amid banyans and mango trees. The imperial tombs at Huê offer one of the finest examples of nineteenth-century architecture. It was to the south of the capital that the Nguyên, in their own lifetime, built themselves last resting-places at the brink of the River of Perfumes. These are not mere tombs, but great groups of monuments lying amid gardens. The bodies of the emperors lie beneath an untended mound of earth, grown with pine-trees—where exactly, no one knows. The sacred area is surrounded by a wall with one bronze gate in it. Outside is an expanse of crescent-shaped pools, terraces, ritual temples, pavilions and steles, porticoes decorated with polychrome enamel work, and courtyards flanked by a double row of stone mandarins and horses. Nothing here suggests the idea of death, all testifies to the eternal beauty of Nature and the flowing course of all earthly things: the magnificence of the wild woodlands, the ancient, lustrous bronzes, the frangipani trees whose branches, with their sweet-scented flowers, line the silent paths, and the pools covered with pink lotus flowers where the Emperor used to sit in a summerhouse raised on piles to watch his wives bathing and to improvise verses . . .

The essential function of architecture, as of all other arts, is to convey the sense that all life is illusion.

Forces of conservation and forces of change

On the eve of European intervention, the Asian communities displayed a balance which was consequent upon the enduring nature of their economic systems. There were no periodical economic crises, for production was geared to meet requirements, and those were limited. Where no great range of products is on offer, there is little inducement to make money, since it would find no outlet. The dominant ideology and the sumptuary laws were there to maintain respect for tradition and for the feudal order of rank; and the small amount of currency in circulation—which in many cases included cowries—kept prices down without enabling capital to be accumulated. Land was the only form of wealth, and since rents were largely paid in kind there was nothing to stimulate technical progress. But the entire body of civil and religious institutions combined, in addition, to preserve the social order.

In Vietnam the individual was captive in a web of rites and obligations resulting from family and community life and from Confucian morality.[3]

Here, as in China, the family structure was patriarchal; it was based, theoretically, on the clan—*ho* or *tôc*—which comprised all persons of the same name (Nguyên being the most common) and in which ancestor worship was celebrated by the head of the senior branch. The upkeep of tombs, and the anniversary festivals to which the clan members flocked from all sides and met under one roof, helped to preserve a link between the living and the dead and to unite them in a common attitude towards honours and sorrows. The great virtue was filial piety, which made it impossible to leave the parental home. Even marriage was a collective act, arranged by the two families with an eye to their own interests, not to the happiness of the couple concerned.

In actual fact, though the large patriarchal families were still very strong in China, they were no longer so firmly established in Vietnam. By the end of the eighteenth century a father no longer had the power of life and death over his children, and among the common people, as we have already seen, women were practically the equals of men. The Confucian influence was strongest in the upper classes, but even there Vietnam's gradual southward expansion, which continued for a thousand years, would have been impossible without some slackening of family bonds.

Similarly, attachment to their villages did not prevent the peasants who lived along the Red River from pushing their ploughs across the coastal plains till they reached the Mekong delta. Yet the village—*xa* or *làng*—also had a strong hold on its members. This particular institution took a very original form in Vietnam. It formed a religious, political, economic and social unit, grouped around the *dinh*, where stood the altar of the tutelary spirit. Since the villages had won their independence, in the eighteenth century, 'the king's laws give way to their customs', as a famous saying declared with pride. The State dealt with them, not with their inhabitants. These local freedoms had, by repercussion, a weakening effect on national sentiment; the horizon was bounded for many people by the bamboo hedge that enclosed their village.

There were both sentimental and material reasons to keep a man at home —the communal spirit expressed in mutual help in agricultural work and in the numerous mutual welfare associations (*giap*, *phuong*, *hoi*); the local political life, which dispensed honours and benefits; the periodical division of the communal ricefields (*công điên*), which enabled even the very poor to make a living. This last factor was of paramount importance to the balance of society; so as soon as a district began to be developed and a village to be built, the law required that ownership should be collective or, if private, untransferable.

In practice the village was not, as some writers have asserted, a democracy; it was an oligarchy, where the effective power rested with the notables— mandarins of various classes, the literate, and the old. The Council of notables was, indeed, an elected body, but, as elsewhere, the pressure of influence and money made itself felt in elections. This Council collected the State tax, organized the local finances, tried small lawsuits and, as its most important function, distributed the *công điên* every three or six years, managing all this business in the best interests of its members. Thus, although the fields were supposed to be divided equally among all the inhabitants, the notables would reserve the best lands for themselves, and even usurp them by fraudulently manipulating the real-estate registers. The law was frequently obliged to issue reminders that the *công điên* were untransferable, and to recall the principles of their tenure, which is a sign that corrupt practices were common.

Thus it is that during this period, from the end of the eighteenth century, we find private property expanding at the expense of communal ownership. This led to the most serious consequences, for it caused a perpetual increase in the number of landless peasants, the number of malcontents and vagabonds who roamed from place to place, and of whom the State made use as best it could, to populate the south of the country or bring fresh land under cultivation. This situation was one factor in the number of peasant uprisings which disturbed Vietnam under the Nguyên (1802–84) and led to their downfall.

The highest factor in the social trilogy was the State, which stood above the family and the village. The village ancestor-worship and worship of the local tutelary spirit was paralleled at this upper level by the worship of Heaven and Earth, at which the sovereign officiated. Its supreme rite was the sacrifice of *Nam-giao*, celebrated by the Emperor every three years in a majestic setting of hills and pine trees in the southern outskirts of Huê. No words can describe the majesty of this ceremony, the more impressive because it took place in the middle of the night, by the light of archaic torches. Amid orders shouted by the heralds and to the accompaniment of songs and dances which had been handed down for many centuries, the monarch, followed by his Court dignitaries, prostrated himself before the altars on the Round Mound and the Square Mound, to invoke for his people the benevolence of the invisible powers. For the Emperor was the 'son of Heaven', which had entrusted him with the 'mission' (*Thiên mênh*) of maintaining order in the cosmos and among mankind. As the arbiter of all lives and all property within the territory, his authority extended to the spirit world as well as to his human subjects. But the Emperor ruled only to ensure his people's happiness. If he fell short of his mission and, by injustice or tyranny, caused misery and disorder, he lost his celestial mission and the people regarded themselves as entitled to rebel. In point of fact the chief function of the monarchy, in Vietnam as in all the other traditional communities of South-East Asia, was to ensure the prosperity of agriculture by providing for irrigation and taking steps to remedy natural calamities. But the need for large-scale hydraulic works, by concentrating power in the hands of the monarchy, gradually turned it into a despotism.

Gia-long (1802–20), Ming-mang (1820–41) and Tu-duc (1847–84) pursued the work of the previous dynasties by strengthening the system of dykes and establishing settlements to exploit the foreshore in the Middle Region and in Western Cochin-China. Meanwhile they were developing the most centralized form of government known in South-East Asia at that period, by unifying the political institutions and abolishing the last vestiges of the feudal system, which still survived in neighbouring countries.

There was no aristocracy of privileged birth to interpose between the sovereign and his people. The nobility did not form a closed group, and titles were not even automatically inherited. They were, it is true, passed on from one generation to the next, but declined by one step on each occasion; and even so the heir must show himself worthy of his rank and secure a new patent of nobility for himself. Another remarkable feature of the nobility at this period was that its members no longer enjoyed any political or economic privileges. To prevent the formation of vast estates, the rulers of Vietnam steadily reduced the size of the fiefs formerly conferred upon nobles, which were hereditary, entailed and free from taxation. In the reign of Thiêu-tri this landed property served no more than the cultural purpose of providing for the upkeep of the family tombs; for this, a duke received ten *mâu* (3·6 hectares) a baron three, etc. Moreover, Tu-duc, towards the end of his reign (1883), decided that a rental of 140 (strings) per *mâu* should henceforth replace these holdings, which were made over to the villages to be divided among the population.

The central Government comprised six ministries—Interior, Finance, Ritual, Army, Justice and Public Works; significantly enough, there was no ministry for industry, foreign or domestic trade, or foreign affairs. Each ministry had a president, two vice-presidents and two assessors; decisions were taken by this council, not by the minister himself; if even one member was of a contrary opinion, the matter had to be referred to the sovereign. In the reign of Ming-mang the imperial Cabinet (*Nôi cac*) began to wield greater powers, while the authority of the *Cô mât viên* increased to a still greater extent, for it not only dealt with international affairs, but took over the responsibility for the principal political and military decisions. In addition to these essential bodies there was a tribunal of censors whose duty was to supervise the working of the administration and to criticize the sovereign himself; some of these censors paid with their lives for their professional conscientiousness. On the provincial level the country was divided into 31 *tinh,* each placed under the authority of a governor who controlled all military and civil activities with the assistance of an administrator, a judge, a military commander and an inspector of education.

This bureaucracy of mandarins had a fixed order of rank. It was divided into two branches, civil and military (the former having precedence); each branch comprised nine grades, and each grade consisted of two classes. Just as they did with the nobility, the Nguyêns swept away the last vestiges of feudalism here. Until 1839 the nobles and dignitaries had lands bestowed on them by the sovereign, either in perpetuity or for life, and were even allotted a certain number of villages or families whose taxes went into their pockets. This practice had perpetuated a semi-feudal system and encouraged the building up of latifundia, the cause of so many economic crises and peasant uprisings in the course of centuries. After 1839 members of the imperial family and government officials received only a pension or a salary paid partly in cash and partly in rice. The low level of salaries frequently led to corruption, and this laid a further burden on revenue from taxation and on the forced-labour (*corvée*) system, the whole weight of which already lay on the shoulders of the common people.

The mandarins might be chosen from the ancient families, but were usually recruited by competitive examination. There was a national college at Huê (*Quôc tu giam*), and even the smallest village had its school; the whole public educational system was completely free. The Nguyêns took pains to promote education, for as Ming-mang pointed out, a country cannot be governed without an educated class. Regional and central competitive examinations were open to all, irrespective of rank—a democratic innovation which was introduced by the Nguyêns and distinguished them from their predecessors; but the difficulty and duration of studies was such that few children from poor families could benefit by them.

Confucian education was second to none as a means of forming the mind and the heart: it invariably produced highly cultivated men, upright magistrates and skilled administrators, imbued with a profound love of their country and ready to accept an honourable death rather than submit to foreign domination. But as centralization increased and officialdom spread its tentacles further afield, education dwindled till it was no more than a means of access to the civil service. The examination system was the best guarantee of the candidates' quality, for it brought into the public service recruits of recognized orthodoxy and loyalty. The ambition of every student, from young lads to old men, was to occupy a public post and thus rank among the mandarins, enjoying their centuries-old prestige.

But the system proved to be disastrous, largely because it was utterly divorced from ordinary life and its realities: the examinations still consisted mainly of dissertations on the Confucian classics, compositions in verse and stylized prose, and the drafting of proclamations and statutes. Physical and natural science had no place in the curriculum. And if a history subject were set, it was invariably an essay on some Chinese dynasty of the most remote antiquity, which was regarded as the golden age of the human race. Students had to devote most of their energies to memorizing the Four Classics and the Five Canonical Books, together with the official commentaries on them, and then expatiating on these in purely rhetorical exercises or scholastic glosses. In the long run their minds were all forced into the same mould by this formalism and most of them became incapable of thinking for themselves. Vietnam, like China, was gradually desiccated and benumbed as a result.

Ming-mang was not without some inkling of the trouble. He deplored these ill-directed studies, pursued only for the sake of official position.

'For a long time,' he observed to his familiars, 'education has been warped by the competitive system. Nothing is esteemed in the written compositions except old-fashioned tags and empty phrases; the display of useless erudition is the only distinction aimed at. With such methods, is it surprising that real talent should become increasingly rare? But the examinations have become an established habit, which is difficult to change at one stroke.'

Although he thus showed his uneasiness, Ming-mang had not sufficient will-power to make any radical reforms, nor, perhaps, was he very clear as to what changes he could effect in the curriculum.

Despite the alarm caused by the Opium War and the increasing Western pressure along the frontiers, the Court at Huê set its face against any modernization of political institutions or economic life. Vietnam, being an agricultural country, differed from Japan, which had already passed to the monetary stage of economy, in having no emergent middle class, enriched by trade, to urge the 'opening' of the country for international relations. The common people had no say in public business, and the leading class consisted of scholars who were convinced that traditional intellectual and moral concepts were far more important than technical progress, and generally speaking disliked innovations.

The Buddhist countries on the far side of the Annamite mountain range had a much less rigid social and political structure than Vietnam. Family and village life was not so firmly established, nor was the monarchy so centralized. Religion, however, played a far more important part. It is probably to the influence of this doctrine of self-denial and compassion, combined with easier conditions of existence and a more scattered population, that we may attribute the more relaxed social structure and the greater freedom of the individual.

The Cambodian, Thai or Burmese family was based on the couple, not on the clan. There were, in fact, no clans; people had only their own individual names, hereditary surnames being unknown until the twentieth century. Confucianism gave the father unlimited rights; in the Buddhist system he had duties as well, decreed by morality and sanctioned by custom. Women could apply for divorce (a right denied them in Vietnam), and in a marriage the consent of the young couple was more important than that of their parents. The village was less closely knit, too, because there was no collective worship. The headman might be elected or hereditary, but he was there not so much to represent the village as to carry out government orders, his chief task being to see to the administration and collect taxes. In some cases his authority was not territorial but personal, extending not only to the population of his own village, but to those of another as well.

In these countries it was religion, rather than the bond of family or village, that held the community together. The pagoda was the centre of village life; it was there that the children learnt to read and write, and every young man, be he prince or peasant, lived there for a period at the age of about twenty. While there he spent his days in study, living on the rice put into his bowl by the villagers each morning. The priests formed a community (*Sangha*) with its own organization and order of rank, but without the powerful structure of the Catholic church. The high dignitaries of the priesthood were appointed by the king, but the bonzes were genuinely independent for all that. Burmese history keeps alive the memory of courageous monks who protested against the oppression of the Court or the local governors, and even led the people in rebellion against some unworthy monarch, as happened in the reign of King Bagyidaw (1831). It was from a monastery that Mindon emerged in 1852 to take the throne from his brother Pagan Min, who had disgraced himself by loose living; he appointed a *pongyi* from his pagoda as one of his ministers; and many bonzes led the national resistance to the British conquest, in the delta in 1852 and in Upper Burma in 1885.

In ordinary life the bonzes usually kept well away from politics. The contemplative morality of Buddha discouraged action, ambition and the desire for riches. But the high regard felt for the bonzes as symbols of moral order and guardians of the sacred books, and the privileges they enjoyed, resulted in their becoming far too numerous. Gervaise, in his description of Siam at the end of the seventeenth century, already noted that 'they are dispensed from all manner of tributes and charges, and this is what produces so great a multitude of them'. By about 1850, according to Pallegoix, Siam had 10,000 bonzes at Bangkok alone, and 100,000 in the rest of the country. In Burma at the beginning of the nineteenth century the capital had about 20,000 monks, who made up approximately one-fifth of its citizens. This withdrew a large labour force from work in the fields, and aggravated the extensive character of agriculture in the countries concerned. Moreover, since the building of pagodas was reputed to acquire great merit for the *karma*, there was a waste of capital, wealth being used to erect and embellish such temples instead of being invested in productive activities. Khmer, Burmese and Siamese histories all mention these magnificent structures, on which the nations' gold was squandered. King Bodawpaya, for example, neglected the government of his domains in order to build a huge pagoda at Mingun. The work was finally abandoned, unfinished, but only after seven years of forced labour, toil and distress for the humble people of Burma. 'The temple is built and the country ruined' was a prediction murmured long before, with reference to a similar project undertaken during a reign which came to an end with the Mongol invasion of 1287; and this time, again, it was fulfilled.

The consequences of despotic monarchy made themselves felt here, just as in Vietnam. There was no fundamental difference between the Chinese and Indian conceptions of royalty. Whether derived from the Confucian theory of the 'celestial mission' or the precepts of Manu and the Hindu cosmology, it regarded the sovereign as a god upon earth, provided he followed the *dharma*. Just as the Forbidden City of Huê was built along a N.W.–S.E. axis, so that everything should converge towards the throne room, the centre of the universe, so the palaces at Ava, Bangkok and Phnom Penh symbolized Mount Meru, round the sun, moon and stars. In all these countries the king was the high priest of the national religion, and the correct performance of the proper ceremonies was expected to bring material and spiritual welfare to the people—one of these being the annual ritual of the first ploughing, also found in Vietnam. But while absolute monarchy found its justification in the need to maintain the harmony of Nature, the king assumed personal responsibility for all the calamities that smote his country—floods, famines, epidemics or military defeat. The majority of Court ceremonies were based on the tenets of Hinduism, and the Brahmins who officiated at them were at the same time astrologers and soothsayers. This was the only surviving trace of Hindu influence in these countries, where the national religion was now Buddhism of the Lesser Vehicle.

Government was not as centralized as in Vietnam. There was no definite system of succession to the throne. No specific rules determined the choice of its heir, there was no order of primogeniture, sex or kinship; the principle was, in fact, that of an elective monarchy in which, when the sovereign died, his successor was chosen by the chief dignitaries. This led to serious disturbances within the country and even to civil war between rival princes, each of whom would enlist the aid of some foreign power which afterwards demanded payment in the form of territorial concessions. It was troubles of this kind that cost Cambodia certain eastern and western provinces, forfeited to Vietnam and Siam; and Burmese history is full of the palace massacres which so often marked the accession of a new ruler. As a result, every sovereign was at pains to nominate and consolidate the position of his heir during his own lifetime; but Chakri was the only heir-apparent who came peacefully to the throne at Bangkok.

The king had absolute authority. He was assisted by ministers who were directly answerable to him. Specialization of functions was not yet carried very far, however. In Siam, until the end of the nineteenth century, no ministerial department had sole charge of any branch of the administration— not even of finance, the army, or justice; all had to share their authority with certain territorial ministers, who were apt to assume full administrative powers in their respective districts. This led to duplication of responsibilities and to confused government. Confusion was at its worst in Burma, where the Supreme Council (*Hlutdaw*) met in plenary session to discuss every conceivable subject, from foreign affairs to civil and criminal cases.

The provincial administration was still feudal in character. The governors controlled all its branches—military, civil, judicial and fiscal. In provinces that lay far from the capital they enjoyed considerable independence. In Burma the king granted to queens, princes and high dignitaries an income— usually in the form of half the revenue from taxation—derived from a specific district: this system of *myosas* ('devourers of provinces') led to such abuses that Mindon set himself to replace it by regular allowances, paid in currency.

How were government officials recruited? There were no rules on this subject, everything depended on the king's pleasure. Nobility, rank and dignity were not hereditary, but derived solely from office; in Siam even the royal princes declined in rank by one degree in each generation, so that after five generations they became commoners. In theory any free man could become a mandarin, though in practice, just as in Vietnam, very few had the right education or connections to enable them to do so. Though there were no castes, in the Indian sense of the word, the structure of society was extremely rigid: the sumptuary laws and the rules of etiquette laid down for every individual what clothing and type of umbrella his rank permitted him, what furniture he might have, what speech he might use and how much land he might own; in the Sakdi Na system in Siam the scale went from 25 *rai* (4 hectares) for an ordinary peasant to 10,000 *rai* (1,600 hectares) for a Chao Phya of the first degree.

Below the free men came the slaves. By the nineteenth century they had practically disappeared from Vietnam, where workers were free; but they were still a feature of the neighbouring countries. Prisoners of war or enslaved by debt, they provided most of the labour for public works, on the estates of the nobles, and in the temples. Their circumstances were by no means harsh ('they are treated like children of the household', writes Pallegoix) and differed little from those of the free men; but they were so numerous— amounting in Siam to a quarter or even a third of the population—that their very number kept technical processes and productivity at an extremely low level.

Thus it was that, generally speaking, economic and religious factors and the nature of the national institutions all concurred to prevent any fundamental change in the structure of the Asian communities. These were by no means static, however. Evolutionary and even revolutionary forces were stirring, the premonitory signs of transition to the modern age.

Chief among these forces were the peasant uprisings. Though they varied in gravity and frequency, not one country in the region was exempt from them. Their contributory causes were the spoliation of the humble peasants by the great landowners or the Church, the burden of taxation, the despotism of the monarch and the abuse of authority by the State officials. In the lower Irrawaddy the Burmese and the Môn rebelled many times against the policy of foreign conquest pursued by their kings, which decimated the population by conscripting the able-bodied men at frequent intervals. In the Philippines, the three centuries of Spanish occupation witnessed more than a hundred uprisings—an average of one every three years—directed against the Government and the monastic Orders. And in the overcrowded delta of the Red River, whenever the oppression of the mandarins was aggravated by floods, drought or swarms of insects which destroyed the crops and caused famine, the people rebelled because they had nothing left to hope for.

True, these peasant insurrections were usually put down; true, even if they succeeded—as in Vietnam at the close of the eighteenth century—their sole result was to place another dynasty on the throne; but all the same they shook the feudal structure and thus tended to change and even to renovate it. In this connection it is interesting to study the experience of the Tây-son, which, though brief, stands as a milestone in the development of Vietnam.

Since the early seventeenth century, that country had been divided between two factions, the Trinh and Nguyên, under the nominal authority of the Lê emperors. Peace was finally concluded between them, but since neither had managed to gain the upper hand, the only result for the population was to increase the burden of taxation and forced labour, so as to satisfy the pride of these great lords and their schemes for extending their domains towards the Muong Lao or the Mekong delta. In the eighteenth century a new element was added to the long-standing sources of disturbance by the emergence of a group of merchants as a result of the expansion of trade at home and abroad. They were not strong enough to foment a revolution, as the Japanese Chonin did later; but they supported the peasants. Rebellion flared up in the north before 1760; but it was not until 1771 that the south experienced the insurrection led by the Tây-son brothers and backed by certain tradespeople of Qui-nhon. The most brilliant of the three brothers, Nguyên Huê, defeated the Nguyên and the Trinh, routed a Chinese expeditionary force sent to intervene, and came to the throne under the name of Quang-trung (1788–92).

The new King proved to be intelligent and realistic. He opened markets on the frontier between China and Tonkin, tolerated the Catholic missions, and tried to raise the intellectual level of the bonzes. His most important reform was a cultural one. In order to build up a national spirit, freed from Chinese influence, he decreed that all public announcements, prayers repeated at sacrifices, and military decrees, were to be written in nôm, and that the literary examinations, too, must include compositions in the language of the country. Until then, Chinese had been the official language of Vietnam; its supremacy was due to the leaders' desire to keep a monopoly of culture, and to their fear of the possible effect on the masses, so far as their own authority was concerned, of works written in the 'vulgar tongue'. A national script, nôm, derived from the Chinese characters, had existed since the thirteenth century, and the first attempt to generalize its use had been made by King Hô Qui Ly at the end of the fourteenth century. Unfortunately, neither Hô Qui Ly nor Quang-trung reigned long enough for his ideas to be firmly established.

The reign of Gia-long marked the beginning of a period of reactionary Confucianism. Yet the founder of the Nguyên dynasty showed an interest in Western technology. Before he succeeded in unifying the country he had a long, hard struggle against the Tây-son. He owed his success partly to the support of French volunteers, led by Pigneau de Béhaine, Bishop of Adran, who helped him to train his troops in the European manner, cast cannon, build ships of the European type, and fortify Saigon. After this, the Nguyên built all their citadels in the style of Vauban. The largest of them, with a circumference of 6 miles, is that of Huê, built between 1804 and 1819. The outer wall, which is in point of fact a fortress, aroused the admiration of European travellers, who declared it to be the most remarkable in all east Asia. An Englishman who saw it in 1819 described it as follows:

It is a square, five or six miles in girth . . . It has twenty-four bastions, each with thirty-six guns of 18 to 68 pounds, all cast in his [Gia-long's] own foundries. The ramparts are about 50 feet tall and very thick, with bomb-proof casemates, magazines, etc. . . . The gates, made of heavy slabs of freestone, are at least 60 feet high. The moats, which are faced with brick, are at least 100 feet wide and deep in proportion: the glacis and covered passages are faced and roofed with hewn stone, so is the esplanade that slopes down to the river. Above each gate is a two-storey structure, well roofed with tiles, and the turret-roofs are of polished copper . . . At equal distances there are stairways for the troops and inclined planes for the guns. In short, the whole thing is a splendid work; its design, finish, massive solidity and scientific regularity are truly astonishing . . . I have seen other fortifications, at Madras and Manila, but they are far from presenting the imposing appearance of those at Huê.

While these citadels followed a French plan, they had a number of features indicating their Vietnamese character, such as the tiered pavilions, built of brick or stone, which surmounted the main gates and served as guard-houses, and the miradors—a kind of quadrilateral tower—on the central terrace, from which the imperial standard flew. The principal alterations to the plan were made in accordance with the precepts of geomancy, in order to harness the subtle forces emanating from the geographical structure of the land; the citadel of Hanoi (1805) was built, for instance, on a site where a concentration of magical influences would reinforce its military strength.

Unfortunately the Nguyên borrowed nothing from the West except its military methods, and even those were used to consolidate their own power by crushing the peasant insurrections. They took no interest in the industrial innovations which alone contained the seeds of future developments, because they were still imbued with the tenets of Confucianism and convinced that their traditional code of ethics was more important than economic progress.

Other countries, however, were striving—some more, some less vigorously —for spiritual renovation. In Siam the Thammayut Order was established, and in Indonesia Islam was beginning to supersede *Adat*.

Catholic missionaries had been coming to South-East Asia ever since the sixteenth century, following or accompanying the Western merchants and, like them, working simultaneously for 'the glory of God' and for the profits of trade. At first they had been greeted without hostility, Asians being habitually tolerant in religious matters. Indeed, they had even been accepted as Court physicians, astronomers, mathematicians or naturalists by certain rulers, who wished to increase their military strength or who were curious about Western techniques. The Jesuit Fathers Köffler, Siebert, Monteiro and Loureiro were advisers at the Court at Huê in the eighteenth century, and during the reign of Rama III of Siam (1824–51), that country was eager to receive 'missionaries who were experienced botanists, chemists or mineralogists'. The Catholics were chiefly concerned with the conversion of souls, but the Protestant missions which arrived later added to their proselytizing efforts in the nineteenth century the establishment of schools, printing-presses and workshops and spread the knowledge of Western medicine.[4]

The propagation of the new doctrine, however, aroused the implacable hostility of the traditional religions. Buddhism, Hinduism, Confucianism and even Islam had made their way by absorbing or tolerating the ancient animistic background, the worship of spirits and ancestors, that characterized the whole region. Whereas Christianity claimed to be an exclusive faith, spurned all forms of 'pagan' belief, and placed duty to God before duty to the king. In so doing it sapped the whole social structure and wrenched its converts completely out of their environment. In Vietnam, as early as the seventeenth century, the missionaries invented a script, *quôc ngu*, based on the Latin alphabet, and used it for printing their books. That in itself threatened to disrupt the existing system of education, by isolating the Christians from the rest of the nation. All these factors contributed to the comparative failure of Christian preaching and account in part for the decrees issued to prohibit it. The latter were also prompted, however, by an important political motive—the fear that the missionaries might prove to be the advance guard of a Western invasion, as had been the case with Portuguese and Spanish expansion. The result was that Christianity, even with the support of the colonizing powers, had no success except in communities which were still at the clan or tribal stage of development, with no central government or elaborate civilization—in the Philippines, for instance, where the Spaniards arrived to find nothing but *barangay* chiefs, quarrelling among themselves; in some of the Molucca islands (Amboine); and among the Toba-Bataks of Sumatra and the Karen of Burma.

But the presence of an aggressive, intolerant religion was sufficient in itself to call forth a reaction among upholders of the traditional faiths. This was particularly evident in Siam, where the Thammayut reformation took place. It was launched by Prince Mongkut, who was then following the established custom by spending his youthful years in a pagoda. Mongkut was intelligent and broadminded, and in order to widen his horizon he had gone to the missionaries to study Latin, English, the Christian religion, mathematics and astronomy. In 1837, when he had become Superior of the Bowonniwet wat, he launched the movement which was to give birth to the Order of the Thammayut, 'those who abide by the law'. The aim was to purge Siamese Buddhism of everything that did not conform to the canon, by eliminating superstition, overhauling discipline, and reverting to the authentic texts. At the same time, faith must be rationalized by explaining the tenets of religion instead of trying to impose them as preconceived ideas. Finally, this return to the sources laid emphasis on lay preaching and popular education, in conformity with the ideas of the Buddha, rather than upon monastic life. The Thammayut were to be active missionaries, visiting even the smallest villages and preaching in simple words that all could understand. Mongkut set up the first printing-press, which produced prayer-books, formularies and religious manuals. By the time he came to the throne, in 1851, the Order was well consolidated. Its character was such that it made its chief appeal to the best elements among the aristocracy, but the very quality of this membership gave it considerable influence among the other bonzes and enabled it to spread in due course to Cambodia.

On the continent it was Buddhism and Confucianism which successfully resisted the Christianity brought in by the Western invaders; in the archipelago it was Islam. But Islam, in this area, was equally opposed to the ancient *Adat*, which was held responsible for Indonesian decadence. As the eighteenth century progressed, pilgrimages to Mecca became more and more numerous, connections with the Arab world were strengthened, Arab theologians arrived on the scene, and all this gradually developed into a movement of moral reform which came into conflict with the luxury and idleness of life in the princely Courts. The spread of the Moslem religion among the great mass of peasants considerably strengthened the hand of the *kyahis* who supported the movement. It was a form of spiritual resistance to the aristocracy on the part of the common people (similar to that of the earliest Christians in Rome), and it also heralded the birth of a new style of 'bourgeois' life, marked by economy and frugality (like that of the Javanese merchants who lived on the north coast).

In Sumatra this clash between the forces of preservation and the forces of change, between Islam and *Adat*, took a violent form and indeed developed, owing to foreign intervention, into civil war. In that country, in the early nineteenth century, the Padri, who had witnessed the Wahabi reforms at Mecca, began to preach the simple, pure life and to denounce corruption, heresy, and the laxity of the princely Courts (*kratons*). They wished to abolish all rules and customs connected with *Adat* which were incompatible with Islam. They were prepared, if necessary, to carry through their reforms by force, and were soon at war with the traditional chiefs. Hostilities broke out in central Minangkabau in 1803, and spread northwards. After a time the princes appealed for help, first to the English and then to the Dutch, who were only too glad to intervene (1821), whereupon guerrilla warfare continued, as a form of popular resistance, until 1837, when the military superiority of the Dutch brought them victory with the capture of the heroic Imam Bondjol. Not for the first time, nor for the last, a colonial power had intervened to assist the representatives of feudalism in their suppression of a national attempt at revival.

As it proved, however, this coalition was powerless to arrest the progress of Islam, which continued to advance because it satisfied the aspirations of the mass of the people. In the ancient *Adat*-Hindu system, the common people were regarded as inferiors, eternally subordinate to the higher castes. Islam gave them equality, personal dignity, and the feeling that they belonged to a wider community. Islam generated a sense of fellowship which united the Indonesians despite their regional and ethnic differences, and to that extent it promoted national unification as well as social democracy.

Thus it was that in all parts of South-East Asia the seeds of change—technical, spiritual, social and political—began to sprout; only the most striking examples have been mentioned here. But it was in the economic sphere that the most powerful forces made themselves felt, and it was they which heralded the transition to the modern age.

2. THE TRANSITION TO THE MODERN AGE[5]

The emergence of new economic trends

We have seen that despite the barriers to trade inherent in the feudal system, the steady though slow development of economic forces, in which the ferments of an Asian form of capital were latent, was beginning to make itself felt by the end of the eighteenth century. In the second half of the nineteenth century this development was accelerated by the influence of factors such as the rise in the population, the expansion of the domestic market, the increased monetary circulation and, more important still, the opening up of the countries concerned to international trade, with the consequent growth of foreign demand and the creation of fresh needs at home as a result of contact with Europe.

There could be no better illustration of this spontaneous expansion of Asian trade than the example of Singapore. It must be realized that the place owed its prosperity not to the British occupation as such, but to the liberal policy pursued there by the British. But such liberalism was no new thing in South-East Asia in 1819, nor was Singapore created *ex nihilo*.[6] Known in the time of Çrivijaya by the name of Tumasik, the island was even then one of the busiest seaports of the whole region, thanks to its position halfway between India and China: the merchants of those two great countries used to meet there, as did those of Sumatra and Java, Siam and Champa. Foreign aggression and internal disturbances put an end to its prosperity early in the fifteenth century, and Tumasik yielded the palm to Malacca. The rapid rise of the latter port was no doubt due to its strategic position in the narrowest part of the straits, far removed from the areas of expansion of the Siamese and of Mojopahit, and to the fact that its rulers were shrewd enough to follow the example of Tumasik by making Malacca a practically free port. After the Portuguese occupied it in 1611, however, Malacca sank into decline because of their brutal policy of trade monopolies and religious intolerance. British liberalism in due course brought about the revival of Tumasik, now known as Singapore.

When Raffles took possession of the island in 1819, he found only a tiny population of Chinese and Malayans. By June of that year the figure had risen to 5,000 inhabitants, and a year later it stood at 10,000. The port, which was open to all comers, attracted Chinese, Arabs, Bugis, Malayans and Indo-Chinese. Colonel Farquhar, visiting the island on 31 March 1820, wrote that:

'Nothing can possibly exceed the rising trade and general prosperity of the infant colony, indeed to look at our harbour just now, where upwards of 20 junks, 3 of which are from China and 2 from Cochinchina, the rest from Siam and other quarters, are at anchor, besides ships, brigs, prows, etc. etc. a person would naturally exclaim: "Surely that cannot be an establishment of only 20 months' standing!" ... Merchants of all descriptions are collecting here so fast that nothing is heard in the shape of complaint but the want of more ground to build on ... In short, this settlement bids fair to become the emporium of East trade, and in time may surpass even Batavia itself.'

While the case of Singapore was the most spectacular, similar developments, though on a smaller scale, were taking place in the neighbouring countries.

In Vietnam, domestic and foreign trade were playing an increasing part. Many merchants were visiting Hanoi, bringing silks from Hàdong, porcelain from Bat-trang, mats from Ninh-binh and pitchers from Thanh-hoa, while others travelled through the provinces, even penetrating to the Middle and Upper regions, to sell town-made goods. The centre of this trade was at Hanoi, where traffic-jams were a commonplace on market days, between 7 a.m. and 2 p.m. In the south it was to Cholon that the produce of the surrounding areas made its way: in 1859 a visitor compared the Saigon river to a floating city, because of the thousands of sampans that crowded its surface. Big junks carried rice from south to north and sugar and cotton from Vietnam to Kwang-si and Malaya. (Pl. 77b.) In the industrial sphere, workshops employing paid workers began to come into existence for silk-weaving, the manufacture of procelain and bricks, and shipbuilding—though few of them employed more than ten or a dozen people.

In Burma too the capital was a busy centre for trade from many directions. Hundreds of sampans arrived daily from Lower Burma with cargoes of paddy, fish-paste (*ngapi*), dried fish, salt, and manufactured goods from Europe, and sailed back to the delta with sugar, edible oils and petroleum. Caravans from the Shan countries brought stick-lacquer, sugar, bulls, horses, parasols, cotton goods, lead, gold and silver from the Bawdin mines. Via Bhamo came paper, silk, ropes, tea, liqueurs and coins from China, to which Burma in return sold cotton, amber, ivory, precious stones and, after 1835, opium from Bengal.

But it was rice production that showed the most amazing economic expansion. Until this period it had been gauged to satisfy domestic consumption, with little thought of exportation—which, even when not prohibited by the Government to offset bad harvests, fluctuated considerably in accordance with atmospheric conditions and the state of the harvest in the neighbouring countries. In the middle of the nineteenth century foreign demand became *regular* and increasing, owing to the rising birth-rate in India, China and Malaya, the growth of sea traffic, and the opening of the Suez Canal which shortened the voyage to Europe at a time when that continent, having sacrificed its agriculture to industry, was being compelled to import greater quantities of food. The result was a rise in prices which naturally stimulated the production of rice.

In Burma the price of rice rose from 35 rupees per 100 baskets in 1852 to 53 rupees in 1856; it then remained more or less stationary until 1890, when it began to rise again and continued to do so until the beginning of the twentieth century. Exports increased from 470,000 tons in 1865 to 720,000 tons in 1873 and over 2 million tons in 1900. This expansion was entirely due to the Burmese themselves who, usually coming down from the highlands, cleared marshes and jungle and transformed them into fertile ricefields. Between 1875 and 1900, land under cultivation in Lower Burma increased by 1,650,000 hectares, chiefly in the Irrawaddy delta and the lower Sittang and Salween valleys; during the five-year period from 1895 to 1900 alone, the increase amounted to 600,000 hectares.

The picture was the same in Cochin-China, where thousands of small peasants climbed into light sampans with their families, their dogs and poultry, and travelled along the rivers, further and further westward, to bring the virgin lands under cultivation. Here the area under rice increased from 520,000 hectares in 1880 to 1,175,000 hectares in 1900, output rising from 650,000 to 1,500,000 tons, and exports from 300,000 to 800,000 tons.

The fact that this progress was not due to the colonial occupation but to a *national* reaction to the new monetary economic system, is made clear by the parallel example of Siam. Mongkut (1851–68), an enlightened King, was brought by the Opium War to the realization that it was a matter of life and death for his country to establish a *modus vivendi* with the West. As soon as he came to the throne he took steps to intensify international relations, by reducing customs tariffs at Bangkok and abolishing a number of government monopolies. (Pl. 80a.) In 1855 he signed a treaty with the English representative, Bowring, which served as a model for subsequent agreements with other Powers: it gave extra-territorial rights to foreigners and allowed them freedom of trade, while restricting import and export duties (3 per cent in the former case). True, Siam was thus obliged by the pressure of circumstances to renounce part of its sovereignty and its public revenue, but it at least preserved its formal independence. The following half-century witnessed an increase in production and population, in exports and imports. Rice exports rose from an average of 60,000 tons per annum in 1857–9 to 680,000 tons in 1900–4, and its proportion to total production increased from 5 per cent to nearly 50 per cent. Here as in the neighbouring countries, the increase was due entirely to the initiative of the Thai themselves, and was fostered by the gradual elimination of slavery and of the forced labour system (*corvée*). In the second half of the nineteenth century the chief expansion took place on the central plain, where a dense network of waterways enabled the rice to be conveyed at little cost to the port of Bangkok.

Burma and Vietnam, less fortunate than Siam, lacked the wisdom or the opportunity to adapt themselves to changing international conditions with the rapidity required for survival. This despite the fact that after the loss of their southern territories both governments made some attempt to modernize their institutions.

As a result of the British occupation of Arakan and Tenasserim (1826) and ultimately of the whole of Lower Burma (1852), the kingdom of Ava was cut off from the sea. (Pl. 78b.) King Mindon (1853–78), the best representative of his dynasty, realized that reforms were necessary. He therefore set about consolidating the State and developing the country's economy. In 1861 he got rid of the last vestiges of feudalism by abolishing the fief system of the *myosas* and substituting fixed salaries financed by a tax on non-agricultural revenue which provided two-thirds of the public funds during the period from 1860 to 1880. To offset British pressure he established direct diplomatic relations with the United States, Italy and France, sent students to Europe, allowed the French *Société des Missions Etrangères* to set up at Bhamo, and enlisted the services of French and Italian engineers and manufacturers. Nor did Mindon neglect the spiritual unity of the nation; in 1871 he convened the fifth great Buddhist Synod at Mandalay; the corrected versions of the Pali texts of the *Tripitaka* were recited during the proceedings, and were then engraved in full on 729 marble steles, to form the *Kûthodaw*, or 'meritorious royal work'. The Court became the centre of Burmese literary activity, and Mandalay was known as *Shwemyo*, the Golden City.

In the sphere of practical matters, Mindon introduced a monetary system, launched a flotilla of steamboats on the Irrawaddy and set up European-style factories for the production of lacquer, sugar, cotton piece-goods and silks, and successfully encouraged the cultivation of rice in order to make his kingdom less dependent upon British Burma. Mindon instituted a State monopoly of foreign trade, buying cotton, wheat and palm-sugar from Upper Burma to exchange for rice and British cotton goods. The increasing prosperity of Ava can be seen from the expansion of trade with Lower Burma, for between 1858-9 and 1877-8 exports to the south rose from 32 lakhs of rupees (1 lakh = 100,000) to 200 lakhs, and imports from 40 lakhs to 178 lakhs. So that by the time Mindon died, the trade deficit had been turned into a surplus.

But this progress only served to whet the appetite of the English merchants and manufacturers, who regarded the royal monopoly of trade as detrimental to their interests. Moreover, they were also looking beyond Upper Burma to the immense Chinese market. So when Mindon's successor, Theebaw, on being refused permission to import arms through Rangoon, signed a treaty of co-operation with France, the English took the initative and invaded Upper Burma. They annexed the territory after a four-week campaign, on 1 January 1886. Pacification, however, was to require several years.

Just as in Burma, plans for modernization in Vietnam were brought to an abrupt end by imperialist aggression. In the middle of the nineteenth century, while the great majority of the educated class was still steeped in the traditional concepts of Confucianism and hostile to the thought of change, a few men had begun to travel outside their country and to see what was taking place in the rest of the world. Prompted by the example of Japan and Siam, they submitted many proposals for reform to Tu-duc (1848-83).

The most celebrated of these innovators was Nguyên Truong Tô. A Catholic from Nghê-an, born in 1828, he had travelled with some French priests to Italy and France, visiting Hong Kong and Canton on the way back. Between 1863 and his death in 1871 he addressed no fewer than fifteen petitions to the Court, calling for radical changes in the policy of Vietnam. The principal measures he advocated were: abroad, a policy of co-operation with all the Western powers, so as to balance their respective influences; at home, separation of the administration from the judicial authority, reduction of the number of civil servants and increased salaries for the remainder, to discourage corruption; in education, introduction of the study of the natural sciences, substitution of Nôm for Chinese characters, publication of newspapers, translation of European books, students to be sent to foreign countries. With the help of European technicians, the State would proceed to modernize agriculture, develop industry, trade and mining, reorganize the army, manufacture modern arms and ammunition, and make strategic roads. Tô proposed to cover all this expenditure by reforming the nation's finances, distributing taxation more fairly and introducing protectionism: no one would be exempt from taxation, there would be censuses and landownership surveys at regular intervals, income-tax on large fortunes, taxes on gambling, duties on drink, tobacco and opium, increased customs duty on luxury goods, and a protective system to promote industrialization.

The ideas of Nguyên Truong Tô were prompted by enlightened patriotism and an intelligence which was in advance of its time. At first Tu-duc was attracted by them. In 1866 he sent Tô to prospect for minerals in Nghê-tinh and dispatched him to France in the same year, to buy machinery and recruit technicians. But his journey was brought to an end by the French occupation of western Cochin-China (1867). Moreover, the narrow conservatism of Court circles led to sharp criticism of his schemes and finally induced the vacillating, hidebound monarch to reject them.

In any case it was already too late. The opening of the Suez Canal (1869) and the progress made in steam navigation had considerably shortened the distance between Asia and Europe. The expanding European industries were demanding larger and larger quantities of raw materials and tropical goods, and colonial policy was taking firmer shape. Henceforth its aim was to occupy territory not merely for the sake of its commercial or strategic value, but for the riches of the soil and subsoil, which were to be 'developed'. After 1880, when capitalism passed from the competitive to the monopolistic phase, the struggle for the partition of Asia, the drive for colonial conquests, was intensified. The concentration of production led to the formation of powerful groups, dominated by big business, which brought influence to bear on the authorities and encouraged colonial expansion. Towards the end of the century the maturity of Western European capitalism, expressed by a great abundance of money and a lowering of interest-rates, brought about the export of capital as well as of goods.

To find a route of access to the Chinese 'Eldorado', France and England completed their conquest of the eastern and western portions of the Indo-Chinese peninsula; while England, as we have already seen, annexed Upper Burma, France occupied Chochin-China (1866) and Cambodia (1867) and established protectorates in Annam and Tonkin (1884) and subsequently in Laos (1893). (Pl. 82.) Siam maintained a precarious independence thanks to its position as a buffer state between the two rival Powers. King Chulalong-korn (1868–1910), like his contemporary Mutsu-Hito, tried to modernize the country by adopting Western techniques and reforming the civil service and the educational system. But he was compelled to hand over Battambang and Angkor to France in 1907, and to surrender his overlordship of the Malay States to Britain in 1909.

The British influence spread from Singapore throughout the peninsula. The first of the Malay States to submit to its protectorate was Perak. In 1895 Perak, Selangor, Negri Sembilan and Pahang were formed into a federation which was purely nominal—for nothing was done to define the respective powers of the federal government and the member States—but which enabled their general policy to be co-ordinated by a resident-general whose headquarters was at Kuala Lumpur. After the Anglo-Siamese agreement of 1909, the British protectorate was extended to the four sultanates of Kelantan, Trengganu, Kedah and Perlis, which, with Johore (1914) made up the non-federated States.

North Borneo, with the territory of Sarawak and the Sultanate of Brunei, was attached to Malaya. South Borneo had been a Dutch possession since the latter half of the nineteenth century.

Looking for sources of raw materials, more especially coal, tin and oil, and wishing to forestall British or American intervention, Holland, which had hitherto concentrated on Java, now turned its attention to the outlying provinces. The Dutch moved along the east coast of Sumatra, the importance of which had been considerably enhanced by the opening of the Suez Canal. Achin, the northern kingdom, which maintained a flourishing trade with Penang and Singapore, put up a determined resistance, and guerrilla warfare continued for thirty years, until 1903. Nor did the occupation of Bali (1908) and the western half of New Guinea (about the same time) take place without a struggle.

The end of the nineteenth century had witnessed the emergence of a new imperialist Power—the United States. Until the Far West had been completely occupied, American energies had concentrated on economic development. But so soon as there were no more lands to be colonized within its own boundaries, and the frontier stretched to the Pacific, Washington began to look overseas for markets to absorb its surplus production. Expansion was favoured by the big industrial and financial trusts which controlled political life. The Republican victory in the 1896 elections was the triumph of the 'imperialist party', and it was reflected two years later by the war against Spain and the annexation of the Hawaiian Islands, the Philippines and Guam.

Nineteenth-century imperialism, unlike that of earlier periods, had profound repercussions on the economic system and social structure of the Orient.

In point of fact the upheaval had been foreshadowed right at the beginning of the century by the policy adopted by Raffles in Java, during the short-lived British occupation from 1811 to 1816. Here we must take a backward glance at the early period of Western economic colonization.

Raffles had proclaimed freedom of crop-raising and trade and abolished the tribute system, replacing it by a land-tax payable in money. The idea was to release the peasants from the shackles of feudalism, increase their productive capacity and, by establishing an economic system based on currency, promote the sale of British goods. The experiment proved to be premature and the immediate financial results 'embarrassing'. Indonesia was ceded back to the Netherlands which in 1830, threatened with a fresh collapse, introduced, under Van den Bosch, the system of forced crop-raising (*Cultuurstelsel*).

This was merely an improved form of the old system of tribute, with the State taking the place of the company. There was a precedent for it in the Philippines. A tobacco monopoly had been set up there in 1782, to balance the budget and make the islands independent of Mexico. Tobacco-growing was restricted to certain areas, and output rigorously controlled even there. Thanks to this forced labour by the Philippine peasants, the State soon accumulated a large surplus. The monopoly lasted for a century, being abolished in 1882 as the result of serious disturbances.

The Dutch spread this process far and wide. In Java the Government reserved for itself a fifth of the land, on which every Javanese was obliged to work in theory for 66 days a year (but in fact, for as much as 240 days). Forced crops included coffee, sugar and jute, and to a lesser extent tea, tobacco, cotton and pepper. The system required no capital investment, but relied on the co-operation of the native chiefs, who received a share of the profits. It turned Java into one vast State plantation, the produce of which could be exported only by the Dutch Trading Company. From 1831 to 1877 Holland drew a total of 832 million guilders out of Java by this method—a sum which enabled her to pay off the debts of the former India Company, reduce the national debt, make cuts in taxation, build its railways, and raise its navy to third place in the world. In Java, however, the reduction of the ricefields to make more room for commercial crops led to famine, and the small peasants, crushed by forced labour and feudal oppression, had no resource but to rebel. The system was gradually abolished after 1860, not so much in order to alleviate the wretched lot of the Javanese as in response to pressure from Dutch firms whose profits were diminished by competition from the State. Coffee, the last forced crop, survived until 1910.

The establishment of European interests in South-East Asia, which marked the last quarter of the nineteenth century, was bound up with the growing Western demand for raw materials. That demand, fostered by the creation of a modern network of communications, related chiefly to two sectors, plantations and mines.

Roads and railways formed the great routes of strategic penetration and commercial and economic development laid down by the colonial Powers immediately after each conquest. The first railway was built by the British, in 1869, from Rangoon to Prome; a few years later Rangoon was linked to Tungoo, this line being extended as far as Mandalay in 1889; the year 1895 saw the beginning of the Mandalay–Lashio line to the Shan States in the north. In Malaya, too, railways kept pace with British expansion and with the development, first of tin-mines and later of rubber plantations. The first lines built in Vietnam ran from Saigon to Mytho (1881–5) and from Phu-lang-thuong to Langson (1890–4—extended to Hanoi in 1902 and to Vinhlong in 1905); next came the Haiphong–Vietri line (1903), extended to Lao-kay in 1906, the route of penetration into Yunnan. In Java a great military road linked the chief towns in the island by the early years of the nineteenth century, and was lengthened after the introduction of the forced-crop system, while links between the different islands grew closer in the 1880s, after the foundation of the Paketvaartmaatschappij.

Once 'pacification' was completed, the colonial governments opened up these countries for private investment by making generous 'concessions' of land and mines. This had the gravest repercussions on agriculture, for the laws passed in Burma in 1852, in Vietnam from 1865 onwards, in Indonesia in 1870 and in the Philippines right back in the seventeenth century resulted in the spoliation of the peasant masses. Those laws declared that land formerly under cultivation, but abandoned by its owners at the time of the conquest, was to be regarded as 'fallow' and as common land. Its owners were thus expropriated and, on their return, had no choice but to become tenants of the new masters for their own fields. Even where, as in Indonesia, the law prohibited the transfer of land to foreigners, whether Europeans or Chinese, the peasant became merely the nominal owner, for the operation of the capitalist system was such that, as we shall see later, he was frequently reduced to farming for the sole benefit of his creditors.

The largest plantations were in Indonesia; on the continent they did not come into existence until rubber began to boom. Until 1905 the principal crops were tobacco, coffee, sugar-cane, tea, pepper, jute, coconuts and quinine. The last of these (*cinchona ledgeriana*) came to Java from Bolivia about 1870, and by 1885 had captured the market from the quinine produced in Ceylon and India, accounting for 90 per cent of total world output. The first plants of *hevea brasiliensis* reached Singapore and Buitenzorg in 1877; small plantations had begun to come into existence by 1890, and seven years later they were beginning to yield crops: by 1905 there were 20,000 hectares of rubber plantations in Malaya, with an export figure of 200 tons. The oil-palm (*eloesis*) made its way more slowly; it arrived in Java from the Reunion Islands towards 1848, but did not become an important item until after 1910. Before the nineteenth century had completed a third of its course, a succession of economic crises had begun, its long-term effect being to do away with individual holdings, which were swallowed up by large companies. In Java, for instance, 44 per cent of the total production of sugar was controlled, about 1884-5, by five 'crop banks', and this proportion had risen to 57 per cent by 1904, while the Nederlandsche Handelsmaatschappij reigned supreme in the matter of tobacco-growing (the Deli Company) and tea plantations, in which it invested nearly 10 million guilders in 1875.

Mining, which began to expand during this period, was dominated by combines from the very first. The real or supposed mineral wealth of South-East Asia had been one of the causes for the imperialist drive in the 1880s. Companies were floated after the conquest (or in many cases before!), to seize these riches. Tin was abundant in Indonesia: Bangka produced 2,200 tons of it in 1870, 10,000 tons in 1900. The near-by island of Billiton had even more: the Billiton Company was formed in 1860 with a capital of 5 million guilders; at the end of 32 years it had already made a profit of 54 million! Sumatra had petroleum, which the Indonesians already knew and used; the Royal Dutch Co., formed in 1890, competed victoriously with its rival, Standard Oil, thanks to lower transport costs, especially after its merger with British Shell. In Burma, oil was monopolized by the Burmah Oil Co. (1886), a subsidary of Anglo-Iranian, which produced over 20 million gallons in 1898; another big company, the Burma Corporation (1890) took the Bawdin silver, zinc and lead mines. In Vietnam the foreign companies were concentrated in Tonkin, where mines and labour were plentiful; they included the Hong-gai coal-mines (1888) and the tin-mines (1901–2). In the case of Malaya, too, it was tin—found in the Kinta district—which formed the largest export item: 26,000 tons in 1889, 52,000 tons in 1904.

Processing industries were few and far between during this period, for they could come into existence only providing they did not compete with imports from the colonial countries—i.e. that they produced simple articles for purely local consumption—and in towns of a certain size where the necessary raw materials were available. They included cotton-spinning mills, distilleries and breweries, tobacco manufacture, match factories and cement works. Many of these undertakings, as also certain commercial firms, came under the control of large commercial banks, some of which had the right to issue loans, such as the Banque d'Indochine, founded in 1875.

All these economic changes took place in the new political framework established by the colonial Powers in order to promote them. Whether the administration was 'direct', as in Burma and Cochin-China, or 'indirect', as in Indonesia, Tonkin and Annam, its effect was much the same: strict control by the occupying authorities led to the decline of the local institutions, robbed of their traditional meaning, and the substitution of impersonal, mechanical laws for custom and morality. The twofold shock completely destroyed the balance of Asian society. It remains for us to look beyond the evidence of material expansion as expressed in figures of production and foreign trade, and discover the facts of the new situation.

The destruction of the social balance

The irruption of capitalism and the imposition of a European administration led to tremendous upheavals in South-East Asia. The changes not only affected the social structure, introducing new elements alongside the traditional classes; they also influenced the political and religious ideology and the psychology of the people themselves, in which individualism began to drive out the community spirit of earlier generations.

It was in the life of the peasants that disruption became most seriously apparent. Until this time they had worked almost entirely to meet their own needs, not to grow produce to sell in the market. Though trade was expanding, it dealt only with a small number of products, and always on a small scale. Most of the taxes levied by the rulers were paid in kind, or in the form of labour (corvée). But European colonization led to an increased use of currency in the economic system, a greater volume of imports and exports, the imposition of taxes payable in money, and the formation of large estates exploited by capitalist companies, colonists or native landlords. The result was a steady deterioration in the condition of the peasants. It is important to show how this came about.

As we know, the aim of imperialism is not only to capture sources of raw materials, but to seize markets as well.[7] In order to encourage trade and to cover the expenses of an administrative system far more complex and costly than the earlier forms of government, the existing taxes were increased and made payable in cash only. In addition to the poll-tax and the land-tax there were indirect taxes, imposed not so much on goods imported from Europe as upon locally produced consumer goods. These taxes, which accounted for between half and two-thirds of the total revenue from taxation, thus weighed most heavily on the class with the lowest income, i.e. the mass of the peasant population. The province of Pegu, for example, paid only 1,469,000 rupees in taxes under its Burmese sovereigns; but under British occupation it was paying 2,978,000 rupees even by 1852–3, and 5,700,000 rupees by 1861–2. Taxes in Cochin-China, which did not exceed 2 million gold francs before the French conquest, had risen to 5,375,000 gold francs by 1867, to 10,174,000 by 1871, and to over 19 million by 1879.

In order to meet these demands, the peasants were compelled to begin raising commercial crops, usually to the detriment of what they cultivated for their own subsistence. This situation developed gradually in every country as the capitalist economy gained ground. Sometimes it took the form of increased cultivation of the traditional food-crops (rice, maize, coconuts, sugar-cane); in other cases plants introduced by the Europeans, such as *hevea*, were adopted. The result was the same everywhere—to link the traditional economy to the fluctuations of international prices.

In boom periods the result might seem satisfactory. But in practice the small farmer, even if a free man, was dependent upon the Chinese middleman or the European firm which had advanced money to him or provided him with seed, or which owned the plant through which his paddy had to pass to be husked and transformed into rice of export quality. The greater the distance from the place of production to the market, the greater the concentration of trade in foreign hands and the subordination of the farmer to foreign authority. Moreover, the European or Chinese firms would often resort to collusion to keep down the price paid to the producer. For instance, the British rice combine at Rangoon managed to force down the price of rice from 127 rupees per hundred baskets in 1882, to 77 rupees in 1894. A boom brought little profit to the peasants. Whereas they bore the full brunt of a slump—which meant an abrupt drop in their income, the seizure of their crops, and their expropriation for the benefit of their creditors.

For a new and alarming phenomenon had made its appearance—usury. This had had little chance of developing under the earlier social system, being checked by the general standard of morality, the strict order of feudal rank, and the fact that most land tenure was untransferable. The traditional system was now to be disrupted by the introduction of Western legislation, which operated impersonally and mechanically and was intended to encourage capitalism—in other words, free enteprise, freedom of contracts, and dealings in movable property and real estate. This legislation gave opportunities of enrichment to those who knew how to grasp them, and it also became possible to spend money, without restriction, on clothes, houses and other external signs of the wealth which, in this changed environment, was used to demonstrate social status.[8]

But the small farmer, being short of funds, was perpetually forced into borrowing—to 'make ends meet' between one harvest and the next, to pay his taxes, or to cover the cost of some special event such as an anniversary, a marriage, a funeral or a New Year celebration. Worse still, he also had to borrow for current expenses, to buy tools or seed. The lender would be either a Chinese, with his shrewd sense of a bargain, an Indian Chetty with centuries of money-lending tradition behind him, a local landowner, or even, in rare cases, a European. Interest ranged between 15 and 36 per cent, or even more, and compound interest increased the debt with every passing year. In these circumstances, how could the peasant-farmer hope to extricate himself? He would be forced to pledge his harvest and his personal possessions—and set foot on the slippery slope leading to expropriation. Thus, although a British law of 1876 declared that newly cultivated land should become the property of the farmer after he had paid tax on it for twelve consecutive years, a Burmese peasant could hardly ever satisfy this demand for continuity: hounded out by debt, he would have to surrender his right of occupation before it matured and go elsewhere to bring some fresh plot under cultivation, or sink to becoming the tenant or share-crop farmer of his creditor. Even where—as in Indonesia from 1870 onwards—the transfer of land to foreigners, whether Dutch or Chinese, was forbidden by law, the peasant was only the nominal owner of his land, for it was mortgaged in perpetuity to his creditor, who allowed him a mere pittance for working it.

This was the most frequent reason for eviction in agricultural areas. Another was an outcome of the policy of the colonial authorites. In the seventeenth and eighteenth centuries the Dutch Indies Company had seized a great deal of land in Java at the expense of the population—thus creating, for the Europeans, large private estates (*particuliere landerijen*) on which the original owners lived no better than serfs. In the nineteenth century the famous law of 1870 was aimed far less at protecting the local population—as was asserted—than at paving the way for European plantations, which were encouraged by the 'Liberal System' (1870–1900). It authorized private firms to rent uncultivated land from the State on a seventy-five-year lease, or to rent cultivated land from the inhabitants for shorter periods. In actual fact, however, the land declared by the Government to be fallow, and therefore public property, belonged, according to the *Adat*, to the local communities, which were thus robbed of their traditional rights.

In the Philippines, Spain claimed the sovereign right to allocate vast estates to the Catholic church, the nobility and the local *caciques*. During the century that followed the conquest, government was carried on by means of the *encomienda*, the king's delegation of authority to the *conquistadores*. The *encomienderos* were supposed to supervise the local government of the caciques and make sure that the people were receiving religious instruction; but most of them were content to exact vast sums in tribute and to exploit cruelly the men sent to work in the mines. The large modern estates began to be formed towards the end of the nineteenth century, when legislation about land tenure was introduced. Any wealthy Spaniards, Philippines or religious bodies who knew how to interpret the law to their own advantage were thus able to grasp huge estates at the expense of the small farmers, who were illiterate: by the beginning of the twentieth century the Catholic Orders possessed more than 165,000 hectares, with a population of 60,000 smallholders.

France in Vietnam and England in Burma similarly encouraged, by direct or indirect methods, the formation of latifundia for the benefit of the colonists and their political hangers-on. The French concessions theoretically consisted of 'free lands', but were in reality made up of villages and ricefields from which their owners had fled at the time of the conquest—and to which they later returned, only to find themselves compelled to become tenant or share-crop farmers under the new masters. These estates were sold for a song to colonists or collaborating notables, and paid no tax for the first three or five years; some of them covered more than 10,000 hectares: in 1900 the area of French concessions totalled 301,000 hectares—198,000 in Tonkin, 25,000 in Annam and 78,000 in Cochin-China; but many of these estates were not fully cultivated, whereas the near-by villagers had not enough land to meet their most elementary needs.

Not only were the peasants ousted from their land, but their earnings from handicrafts dwindled as well, either owing to competition from manufactured goods imported or produced locally in up-to-date factories, or as a result of fiscal policy. In the former case it was the weavers who suffered most, from the flood of cotton goods that poured in from Manchester, Twante, the Vosges and northern France.[9] The latter case is illustrated by the government monopolies of opium, alcohol and salt, which were set up between 1898 and 1903. The administration held a monopoly in the purchase and sale of opium; it would be superfluous to dwell on the moral, social and political implications of this monstrous tax. The right to distil alcohol, hitherto exercised by the whole population, was withdrawn so that a monopoly might be granted to the Société des Distilleries de l'Indochine, with severe penalties to safeguard it. As for the salt monopoly, it resembled the *gabelle* of medieval Europe. The small salt-maker had to sell all his salt to the Government and buy back at five or ten times the price he received. The last two of these monopolies, while they fostered the growth of big firms and built up huge budget surpluses, spelt ruin to the traditional occupations of whole villages and made trouble where there had always been harmony, by encouraging informers and leading to penalization.

Political and religious changes also did much to destroy the communal spirit in the villages. The introduction of a Western-style administration, much more centralized than the former system, led to strict supervision of the local authorities, who were no longer allowed the slightest initiative; they gradually ceased to be the accredited representatives of local interests and became mere government employees, responsible for maintaining order and collecting taxes. This went side by side with a loosening of spiritual bonds— a decline in the worship of the tutelary spirits in Vietnam and in the influence of the pagoda in the Buddhist countries. The latter development was particularly marked in Burma, because of the abolition of the monarchy, the patron and supporter of the Theravada, and the institution by the British of secularized government. When Lower Burma was conquered many of the inhabitants, with their village bonzes, fled up-country and the pagodas, being built of wood, soon fell into ruins. When in 1875 the villagers began to return, most of the bonzes stayed on in Upper Burma, so Pegu never recovered the spiritual atmosphere of the old days: instead of a pagoda in every village, there was now only one for three or four villages. Moreover, the bonzes in the occupied territories were no longer obedient to the religious leaders who had their seat in Ava, and to whose status and authority the British refused official recognition, even after annexing the whole country. That authority came virtually to an end in 1891, when a ruling by the *Sangha* in a matter of discipline was reversed by a secular judge: moral standards and discipline continued to decline. After 1900 the educational role of the pagoda was also reduced, owing to competition from the State schools which alone gave access to the modern branches of employment, for which a knowledge of English was required. Moral teaching now ceased, leaving only a completely utilitarian form of education. In all the countries of South-East Asia these economic, political, social and religious circumstances brought about the rapid disintegration of the rural communities.

The peasants were driven by their dire poverty to leave their villages and seek employment on the plantations, in the mines and in the first processing industries. The proletariat which thus began to form could not yet be described as a class. It was small in number, widely scattered, politically uneducated, and strained by internal tensions owing to the racial antagonism between the local people and the Chinese and Indian immigrants.

In the early stages, and for a lengthy period, the governments resorted to forced labour to open up the country and bring the jungle under cultivation. The *corvée* had existed under the monarchy, but had been used in moderation, owing to the fact that the royal houses took little interest in economic development. In practice, when a local road was to be built or a canal cut, the villagers had no need to leave their homes. But the capitalist system was to make use of forced labour on an unprecedented scale, in order to create the technical infrastructure required to transport men and goods and to penetrate the interior. The Javanese still have tragic memories of the dredging of Batavia harbour in the eighteenth century, the building, under Daendels (1808–10) of the military highway which crosses Java from West to East, and the system of cultivation introduced by Van den Bosch. Even the Dutch themselves were made aware of the excesses of this colonial exploitation when *Max Havelaar*, the famous book by Multatuli (Douwes Dekker) was published in 1860. Similarly, the British in Burma and the French in eastern Indo-China took thousands of peasants and compelled them to work, often for months at a time and sometimes far from their homes, building the roads and railways which were to open up the country for the mining companies and plantation-owners. Not until 1930 was a convention on forced labour adopted at Geneva and applied, in part, to the colonies.

Forced labour, though it cost nothing in wages, had its drawbacks; the yield was very low and there was a limit to the supply of workers. Private enterprise was obliged to offer wages, but in the early period the working conditions imposed were tantamount to slavery; they were described, for instance, by Van den Brand in his *De millioenen uit Deli* ('The Millions from Deli'), the publication of which, at Amsterdam in 1902, caused a burst of profound indignation in the Netherlands and contributed to the establishment of a Labour Inspectorate. The majority of these workers were employed on the plantations, of which Indonesia's were then the largest. But nowhere was labour 'free' (indeed, was the destitute worker free even in Europe?). The sugar and tobacco growers called on the authority of the village headman—rewarded by a stiff commission—to provide them with land and with workers. Another method was to persuade the headman to induce his peasants to rent their fields, and then to advance money to them; the money was soon spent and the peasants were thus obliged to hire themselves out to the plantation for a wage, until the next harvest. On the plantations a paternalistic relationship prevailed, and to the tyranny of the planter were added the extortions of the foremen. Abandoned in this hostile world, for which nothing in his traditions had prepared him, the worker was liable to react by running away, setting fire to the sugar-cane fields, or killing his overseer. Very few peasants remained for long in this employment; even in the course of one year many of them would vanish for weeks or months, going home to refresh themselves with the village atmosphere, to celebrate some anniversary or the New Year. This instability, or mobility, while it increased the number of peasants subjected to 'proletarianization', delayed the formation of a separate, conscious working class.

Another factor contributed to this delay—the flood of Indians and Chinese who poured in, at the instigation of the colonial authorities, and heightened the inter-racial tension.

Indian immigration went chiefly to the British-occupied territories. The

British had been accustomed to working with Indians since they first settled in the sub-continent, and brought them in first of all to act as intermediaries between their administration and the people of the country, and later, when the economy began to expand, as workers. Thus it was that the number of Indians in Burma rose from 73,500 in 1861 to 131,000 in 1872. After that, the extension of the ricefields called for an even greater importation of man-power. The annual figure of immigration through Madras rose from 16,000 to 40,000. Transport and labour conditions were appalling and the death rate enormous; but the companies found this method cheaper than training Burmese workers on the spot. By 1901 the number of Indians had reached 613,000, or 5·8 per cent of the total population of 10·5 million. They held a monopoly of employment in public works, railways and inland waterways, and in the hospitals. In Arakan the influx of Bengalis drove the population away from the coast, into the interior; in the Irrawaddy delta numbers of small-holders were ruined, driven out or reduced to the status of tenants by the Chetty usurers. In Malaya, too, the rapid growth of the plantations—sugar, coffee, and later rubber—led to an increase in the annual immigration of Indians from an average of 20,000 for the period 1880–1900 to an average of 48,000 between 1901 and 1910. By 1911 they numbered 267,000, or nearly 10 per cent of the total population; most of them came from southern India, the majority being Tamils of very low caste. Those who did not work on the plantations were employed in government offices or by private firms (trade or transport); Chetties were also to be found in such positions.

The Chinese presented an even more important problem, owing to their great number and their economic power. The Indians were concentrated in Burma and Malaya, but the Chinese formed vigorous communities in every country in the region, and by establishing international connections among their various trading firms, and forming secret societies, they tended to build themselves into monopolies.

Like the Indians, the Chinese had been immigrating into South-East Asia for a very long time. Seventeenth-century European travellers had found colonies of merchants already established in the principal seaports of the region, such as Faifo, Manila, Bangkok and Batavia. The Chinese were prospectors as well, searching for the mineral wealth which was farmed out to them by the local rulers—tin in Siam and Malaya, gold in Borneo. Most of them came from southern China, especially Kwantung, Fukien, Kwangsi and Hainan. Poverty, civil unrest and dynastic changes lay at the origin of their emigration and settlement on the shores of the Southern Seas (*Nan Yang*); after the fall of the Ming dynasty, for example, a number of Chinese came to live in Cochin-China, where they founded Hatinh and Cholon (eighteenth century). Many of them, having decided to remain permanently in their new countries, took wives there, and after a few generations their descendants became indistinguishable from the original population. Others gathered into communities, according to their home provinces and dialect, electing a headman to take responsibility for the payment of taxes to the local authorities.

But it was the development of capitalism in the nineteenth century which produced the first enormous influx of workers and traders. In 1850 the Chinese already made up one-third of the population of Malaya. By 1911 there were 916,000 of them, as against 1,437,000 Malayans. The three British 'Settlements' were becoming Chinese cities, particularly Singapore, where their number rose from 3,000 in 1823 to 50,000 in 1860, and by 1901 they made up more than two-thirds of the population. In Java there were 150,000 Chinese in 1850 and 277,000 in 1900, with a further 250,000 in the other islands. In Siam the annual immigration rose from 7,000 in 1824 to 15,000 in 1850 and 18,000 in 1900. In Cochin-China the Chinese numbered 44,000 in 1879, 56,500 in 1889 and 120,000 in 1906: in Vietnam, Cambodia and Laos, considered jointly, there were 293,000 of them by 1912.

The great majority of these immigrants came to work in the tin-mines and plantations as a result of the discovery of the Larut tin deposits, the development of the Bangka islands, and the prosperity of the tropical crops. For a long time they were recruited by a kind of slave trade. The recruiting agents induced the unfortunate men to sign a working agreement covering their voyage, food and clothing: they were then packed into cargo-boats and taken to Malaya or Indonesia, where they were put ashore and sent straight off to clear jungle land, build roads, or work in the mines or on the plantations. No thought was given to their welfare, no medicines were available, and the consequent mortality was appalling; but the system, being profitable to the capitalist communities, continued up to the First World War, and in some countries even until a much later period.

Though the majority of them worked as manual labourers, the Chinese were ready to turn their hands to anything the local population neglected, either through distaste or from lack of capital. They were seldom to be found in the ricefields, but they worked as fishermen and craftsmen, grew pepper, copra and rubber, made noodles, ran sugar-refineries, worked as clerks or *compradores* in banks and trading firms. Some of them owned timber enterprises (teak forests) or tin-mines. But their adaptability found its best expression in trade—as retail salesmen and money-lenders in the small villages or as rice-dealers, owning their own junks and hulling plant, in towns and seaports.

They acted as middlemen between the local landowners and the European export firms, buying up the paddy with the help of specialized agents and collectors and running the whole business on a basis of cumulative credit. This took the form of successive advances from which the small producer seldom managed to extricate himself, and gradually gave them the control of a great part of the agricultural output and of the handicrafts (such as Indonesia's batik work) as well. In the middle of the nineteenth century the Chinese were already in complete control of Siam's domestic trade, and by

1889 they owned seventeen of Bangkok's twenty-three rice plantations. The situation in the neighbouring countries was no different.

This success was not only due to perseverance, economy, hard work and love of lucre, but came in part from an exceptional solidarity among people of the same geographical origin, family connections, dialect or occupation: in addition to mutual assistance organizations and trade unions there were innumerable secret societies, modelled on those of China itself. The most famous of these was the Triad, or 'Association of Heaven and Earth', which had as its emblem a triangle symbolizing the trinity of Heaven, Earth and Mankind. Brought to Malaya by immigrants from southern China in the nineteenth century, it first operated as a mutual assistance organization, but later developed into a kind of secret government of the Chinese colony. Factional rivalries led to violent battles which finally turned to the advantage of British penetration: it was the war that broke out between some 30,000 Chinese and 4,000 Malayans and Indians for the possession of the rich Larut tin deposits, discovered in the 1850s, which led the English to intervene 'to save these fertile, productive countries from the ruin that must overtake them should the present disorders continue', and to impose upon Perak the Treaty of Pang-kor (1874), the first step towards the establishment of a protectorate over the whole of the Malayan peninsula.

The combination of European colonization and Chinese and Indian immigration in South-East Asia thus gave rise to what, because of their ethnical diversity, have been called 'pluralist' communities, in which 'division of labour' followed the racial boundaries. Each group—European, Chinese, Indian and indigenous—lived its own separate life and carried out different functions. This definition should not be carried too far, however, for the individual communities were not themselves homogeneous; they comprised various social strata or classes. There was more difference between a rich Singapore merchant and a miner, both of them Chinese, than between the miner and an indigenous peasant. It is true that the language difference was an insuperable obstacle, as was religion in the Malayan world, where the Islamic precepts were radically opposed to Chinese customs (Moslems being forbidden, for instance, to eat pork, a staple item in the Chinese diet).

Although the economic situation was controlled by the European firms and the Chinese communities, the expansion of trade and the colonial custom were bound to result in the emergence of middle-class elements in the different nations. The earliest and largest middle class developed in the Philippines, the area into which Western monetary policy and Western ideas first penetrated; its development here was also favoured by the fact that there were no hostile political or religious institutions to combat it, as there were on the continent and in Indonesia. In the nineteenth century, thanks to less stringent enforcement of trading monopolies, the abandonment of the galleons' trading voyages (1811), the opening up of Manila to international trade (1834), the cutting of the Suez Canal (1869) and the progress of steam navigation, a 'bourgeois' nucleus was formed among the descendants of the Philippine *datu* and the Philippine-Spanish or Philippine-Chinese *mestizos*. At the same time they began to be imbued with liberal ideas. The only source of education up to now had been the Catholic church, which imparted a pronounced religious and medieval flavour to its teaching; it used the hospitals, the schools and the 'Royal University of Santo Tomas' as a means of dominating the souls of the population rather than of providing a modern education. It was not until 1863 that an attempt was made to set up a system of public schools, by royal order, to give teaching in the Spanish language. Even this was not completely followed up; in 1897 there were scarcely 200,000 children attending the elementary schools. The opening of the San Jose College of Medicine in the University of Santo Tomas in 1871 had greater repercussions; its graduates included Pardo de Tavera, Manuel Gomez and Rizal, who were to play such a prominent part in the nations' development. The Suez Canal, by reducing the distance between Asia and Europe, also enabled an increasing number of young Filipinos to go there to study and to absorb the new concepts of liberalism and nationalism from which the 1896 revolution was to spring.

In the other countries the middle class took longer to develop, circumstances being less propitious than in the Philippines. In the imperialist age there was a tendency for colonial capitalism to monopolize the sources of raw materials and the markets, thus preventing the industrialization of the dependent countries. On the other hand, the introduction of a monetary economy destroyed the independence of the villages, fostered the production of commercial goods, and encouraged domestic and foreign trade. As a result of these two contradictory influences a middle class did slowly emerge but it was never to become very strong. At the beginning of the nineteenth century it was not, strictly speaking, a 'class' at all, but merely a small number of shopkeepers, public works contractors and manufacturers of current consumer goods. In Vietnam, for example, there were textile mills at Ha-dông, potteries at Bat-trang and Thô-hà, mat-weaving workshops at Ninh-binh, sugar refineries at Quang-nam, and several transport firms and public utility enterprises. Some of these employed as many as fifty workers. An official report issued in Java in 1905 mentions the existence of 385,500 small independent shopkeepers (or 560,000 including those who also earned money by agriculture)—equivalent to 1 per cent of the population.

In addition to this 'capitalist' nucleus a new class of 'intellectuals' was emerging, those who had been given a European-style education for the purposes of the colonial administration. As in the Philippines, the modern education spread only very slowly, for the Government merely wanted to train subordinates for the senior officials sent out from Europe. For instance, in Indonesia in 1900 only 1,615 children were admitted to the Dutch primary schools and only 150,000 were attending village schools—this out of a total population of 35 million.

At this time, in fact, privilege still rested with the landed proprietors, who were drawn either from the old aristocracy or from among the notables who had sided with their conquerors. The colonial custom and the rise in exports contributed to their prosperity, especially in the centre of Luzon and in Cochin-China, Lower Burma and western Java. But their mentality was 'feudal' rather than enterprising; they lived in the towns, leaving their estates to be cultivated by tenants, and were less interested in improving productivity than in making a large income by farming out their rights and by usury.

The most politically alert elements of the period were members of the former intellectual élite—aristocrats, scholars, Buddhist and Moslem priests who, alive to circumstances in their own countries and to trends in the world outside, opened their minds to the new ideas and led their countries along the path of 'modernism'.

The search for a new culture

The Western invasion, the downfall of the monarchies and the introduction of foreign administration and a foreign economic system came as a profound moral shock to the Asian peoples. Their first reaction took the form of armed resistance, followed, after defeat, by withdrawal into nostalgic memories of the past; but little by little their zest for life reasserted itself, they began to ponder the reasons underlying the disaster, and sought a remedy for their situation in 'new knowledge'.

The earliest opposition took the traditional form of a struggle promoted by the aristocracy and the spiritual leaders. In Indonesia, for example, an alliance between the *Adat* authorities and the Moslems led to a general uprising of the population in the wars of Java, Banjermasin, Atjeh and Bali. In Java, Dutch economic oppression and heavy taxation provoked Diponegro, Prince of Djogjakarta, to foment an insurrection in 1825. After a period of withdrawal and meditation in the caverns, he proclaimed a Holy War against the infidels, and princes and people rallied to him. Despite the inferiority of his armaments, he carried on guerrilla warfare for five years—until, deserted by his military subordinates, he was captured by treachery and exiled to Celebes, where he died in 1855. The Atjeh war lasted longer. Atjeh commanded the Strait of Malacca, the importance of which had increased since the opening of the Suez Canal. The people—a race of mountaineers renowned for their courage, their love of independence and their devotion to the Moslem faith—held out from 1873 to 1903, in one of the most strenuous contests in the history of European colonization. The secular and religious leaders who most distinguished themselves were Teuku Umar and Panglima Polem: the former was killed in 1899 and the latter surrendered in 1903, but sporadic uprisings continued until 1908, when the principal leaders were captured and exiled to Amboine; even so, military government had to be maintained until 1918. The people of Bali, too, resisted heroically until 1914; many of them, together with their wives and children, chose to die like their besieged Rajahs, fighting the Dutch or stabbing themselves with their own krises, rather than surrender.

Even when a government gave up the struggle, the people would continue to resist. In Vietnam, after the treaty of 5 June 1862, by which the three eastern provinces of the southern territory (Bien-hoa, Gia-dinh and Dinh tuong) were ceded to France, the population of Nam-ky refused to submit to foreign domination and protested vigorously against this annexation. They formed a great movement, elected Truong Công Dinh as their leader, and refused to obey further orders from Huê. 'It is better to offend against the Court than to lose our country!' declared Dinh. He fought a relentless war against the French until his death in battle at Tân-phuoc in 1864. His son, Truong Quyên, continued the struggle, forming an alliance with Pucombo, the Cambodian bonze who was conducting operations in the area of Tay-niuh. Their movement persisted until the end of 1867.

The aloof attitude of the educated class, which refused to co-operate with the invaders, compelled the French admirals to introduce direct administration as early as 1862. But for a long time, in the words of one of their own number, only 'Christians and rascals' would collaborate with them. After establishing a protectorate over Cambodia in 1863, the French proceeded to unify the whole of south Indo-China, which commanded the lower reaches of the Mekong, then regarded as the route to southern China. In 1867 they violated their agreements by occupying the three western provinces (Vinh-long, An-giang and Ha-tinh). The Governor of the region, Phan Thanh Gian, yielding to superior force, took poison, after advising his sons to cultivate their lands henceforth, and never to take office under the foreigners. After his death, however, they took up arms at Bên-tie, while the peasant leader Nguyên Trung Truc seized Rach-gia and held it for a brief period. When finally defeated and taken prisoner, he refused to surrender, saying 'When this soil no longer bears a single blade of grass, our resistance will come to an end!' He was executed in 1868.

In the north, the first capture of Hanoi and the withdrawal of the royal household (treaty of 1874) led to the formation in Nghê-an of an Intellectual Party (*Van thân*) to combat the 'Western invaders' and the 'false doctrine' (Christianity). This rebellion was put down by the monarchy. But after the fall of Huê (1885) (Pl. 82), the Emperor Ham-nghi took refuge at Tan-so and issued a moving proclamation calling upon all classes of the population to take up arms; the intellectuals and the peasants rose as one man from northern Annam to Tonkin, attacking the French posts and burning down the Catholic villages. Forts were built in every province, and the most famous of them, Ba-dinh, defended by Dinh Cong Trang, held out stubbornly for four months, until stormed by a French corps of 2,500 men, supported by the navy and by powerful artillery (1887). Even after Ham-nghi was betrayed and deported (1888), resistance was maintained for nearly ten years, under Phan Dinh Phung and Cao Thang at Huong-khê, Nguyên Thiên Thuât at Bai-say and the Dê Tham at Yên-thê. All these movements were led by the educated class—either by village intellectuals living among the people, or by former mandarins who returned their seals of office to the Court in order to continue resistance; in some cases they were minor notables, such as Dinh Cong Trang, the great defender of Ba-dinh, who established their authority by determination, integrity and patriotism.

Events took the same course in Burma. The British occupation of Arakan and Tenasserim (1826), and subsequently of Lower Burma (1852) and Upper Burma (1886) was followed by general uprisings led by princes, *myothugyi* or monks. Writing of one of these leaders—Myat Htoon, who operated in Lower Burma—Lord Dalhousie declared that:

'A man who has 4,000 men under him, who repulses the British attacks and after a very stout defence is routed only by a Brigadier-General after a month's operations and with severe loss to us, must be regarded as a chief and a soldier—and a good one too.'

The rebellion led by a Karen claimant in 1857 spread from Martaban to the Irrawaddy delta and to Bassein, and not until 1860 could the province of Pegu be regarded as 'pacified'. The same thing happened in Upper Burma. In spite of the deportation of King Thibaw and the annexation of the territory by British India, the Burmese army refused to surrender, and waged tough guerrilla warfare against the invaders, especially in the region of Shwebo, from which the Konbaung dynasty originated. By February 1886 the insurrection had spread to Lower Burma, and considerable reinforcements soon had to be sent from India, raising the British forces to over 40,000 men. The most valiant of the chiefs were extolled in poems and folk-songs. Almost every family had one of its members in the resistance. The initial British policy of executing anyone found carrying arms merely strengthened the spirit of the nationalist struggle. The population, accepting the sacrifices imposed by the war, protected the combatants and supplied them with food. A British observer, Geary, wrote in 1886:

'No trumpet of sedition has such an infuriating effect on a population as the shrieks of the women in the villages . . . lamenting brothers and husbands slain not in battle, but as examples of the power and sternness of the conqueror.'

Though the reaction to the situation did not last so long in Cambodia or Malaya, it was evidenced none the less. Si Votha led his troops, armed with bows and flintlocks, against French-occupied Phnom Penh, Perak rose against the British when they set about establishing direct control over the State revenues, imposing new taxation, introducing their own civil and criminal legislation, and organizing their own civil service. Pahang, too, fought from 1891 to 1894 against the protectorate which had been imposed upon it.

The resistance forces consisted of peasants and were supported by the entire population, which fed them, gave them information and sheltered them. Their final collapse was due not only to the terrible inferiority of their armaments, but to internal causes as well—the lack of unified leadership, the chiefs having neglected or failed to launch a large-scale, nation-wide political campaign, and the treachery of the conservative section of the feudal class, which accepted collaboration with the invaders in order to preserve its privileges. But resistance was sufficient to demonstrate the people's resolute will to independence. When fighting had to be abandoned, other forces arose and turned the national movement in a new direction.

This was characterized by a change of attitude on the part of the nationalist leaders; instructed by their earlier setbacks, they now looked for inspiration to Japan—which, under the Meiji, had been transformed in the course of a few decades into a modern economic and military Power—and sought to meet the West with its own weapons. They had a second example before their eyes as well—that of Siam, the only one of the South-East Asian countries which had preserved its independence. Confronted by pressure from England and France, to which he was compelled to yield in a certain measure, King Chulalongkorn (1868–1910) set himself to reorganize and consolidate the monarchy by modernizing its institutions and its economic infrastructure, in pursuance of an effort his father had barely had time to begin. This modernization, like that of Japan, was limited to purely technical matters, for Chulalongkorn had no more intention than the Meiji or the Mongkut of fundamentally altering the social and political structure of his country, which thus retained its 'feudal' character.

Chulalongkorn's first reform was the gradual abolition of slavery. A decree promulgated in 1874 proclaimed that serfs born in 1868 should become free-men at the age of 21; no man born in that year was to sell himself, or be sold, into slavery once he had completed his 21st year. In 1905, slavery was entirely abolished, though it survived for a few years longer in remote areas, particularly in the north-east. The *corvée* was replaced by a poll-tax in 1899, but as in the case of slavery, it did not vanish immediately. Nevertheless, this two-fold reform had the effect of releasing a considerable labour force for agriculture and, together with the increase in the country's population, did more than anything else to extend the area under cultivation, which increased from 928,000 hectares in 1850 to 1,472,000 hectares in the period 1905-9.

Chulalongkorn then turned his attention to matters of government. In 1882 he introduced various measures aimed at reorganizing the administrative system and the nation's finances. The six traditional Ministries—of North, South, the Palace, the City, Agriculture and the Treasury—were replaced by twelve functional Departments—Interior, Defence, Foreign Affairs, Justice, Agriculture and Trade, Public Works, Religion and Education, the Royal Secretariat, Army, Treasury, Palace and City. This unification gave the central authorities a firmer control over the provinces. Hitherto the provincial governors had been practically independent, provided they sent the stipulated local tax revenue to the capital at the stated intervals; and as the taxes were farmed out, this gave rise to many abuses. In 1894–5 the kingdom was divided into eighteen *monthons*, the heads of which were responsible to the Minister of the Interior and received a fixed salary. Systematic methods of budgeting and accountancy were introduced at the same time, the king's personal expenditure being separated from the ordinary public expenditure, the system of tax collection improved and taken under the direct control of the State. These tax reforms alone increased the total receipts from 15 million *baht* in 1892 to 40 million in 1902 without the introduction of any new taxes— though the decline in the value of money and the rise in prices were further contributory factors.

The modernization of these institutions had to be paralleled by that of education. The Government undertook the improvement of primary education by adapting the monastery schools to the new requirements; in the secondary schools a dual system was introduced, the teaching being given in Siamese for pupils whose education would end there, and in English for those who were to continue further. There was as yet no university—the Chulalongkorn University was not opened until 1917—but specialized colleges were established for law and medicine, together with military academics. Until the beginning of the twentieth century there was practically no secondary or higher education except at Bangkok, and they remained the privilege of the aristocracy. Expenditure on education was also very small—it accounted for 2 per cent of the ordinary budget in 1892 and 4 per cent in 1900, whereas the royal expenditure for those years amounted to 29 and 22 per cent. Princes and nobles were also sent to study abroad.

'Chulalongkorn told them they were not going to Europe to learn to become Europeans; they must learn to be Thai knowing as much as Europeans: "Our country now needs men of wide knowledge to enter the civil service or make themselves useful in other ways, so that the kingdom may be efficiently governed and become wealthy and progressive." '*

It was also Chulalongkorn who laid the foundations of the new economic system. He caused irrigation canals to be dug, introduced a postal service (1883), and established a railway network. (The first railway line was, however, a private one, from Bangkok to Paknam, opened in 1893.) Bangkok was connected with Ayuthya in 1897, Korat in 1900, Lopburi in 1901, Petchaburi in 1903, Utaradit and Sawankalok in 1909. By the time Chulalongkorn died, the total length of track was about 560 miles. The railway had been constructed mainly for political and strategic reasons, as a means of withstanding the danger threatening from England and France. But its existence was an automatic contribution to economic and national unification, it encouraged the rice-growers in the north and facilitated foreign trade.

* P. Schweisguth, *op. cit.* p. 308.

In order to balance the different foreign influences, the Siamese Government called in advisers from a number of countries—chiefly British, but also Belgian, Danish, French and Italian. The effort to put an end to extra-territoriality made it necessary to revise the civil and criminal law of the kingdom, bringing them into line with Western law. In 1897 a Commission was set up for this purpose, and penal code was issued in 1908. In the following year Britain recognized, in principle, the surrender of extra-territorial rights; but in practice they remained in force until 1939. Nor did Siam succeed, until about that year, in shaking off the constraint imposed upon its economy and finance by the one-sided treaties signed during the nineteenth century with the Western Powers and with Japan (import duties limited to 3 per cent fixed export duties on a considerable number of products, etc.). But despite all these restrictions on its sovereignty, Siam was regarded, with Japan, as a model by the nationalists of the region, because it has preserved its independence in form, at least.

In their early stages the nationalists were fervent monarchists, the royal houses having always been identified, throughout the course of history, with State and homeland. But by the end of the nineteenth century their ideas had begun to evolve, influenced by the liberal, democratic philosophy which came to them from Europe and was vigorously expressed in the first national revolution ever to take place in South-East Asia—that of the Philippines.

Philippine nationalism came to birth about 1870. The islands had been under Spanish control for 300 years, ever since 1571, when Legaspi sailed from Mexico and seized Manila. The spiritual result of the conquest had been the spread of Christianity everywhere except in the islands of Mindanao, Sulu and Palawan, which remained Moslem and put up a fierce resistance to Catholic expansion. Spain established an authoritarian government, strongly centralized under a Governor whose absolute powers were but slightly restricted by the Court of Justice (*Audiencia*); an *alcalde mayor* was responsible for administration and justice in each of the provinces, while their component districts (*pueblos*) were headed by Philippine *gobernadorcillos* and the individual villages continued under the leadership of the traditional *datu*, now known as *cabezas de barangay*—who, though in theory elected, were in practice always chosen from the same local family. This political structure was paralleled by an ecclesiastical system which in many cases was the more powerful of the two. The Church, organized as a theocracy, sought to establish complete spiritual domination by its proselytizing and by the education it provided: the Santo Tomas College, the nucleus of a future university, was founded at Manila as early as 1611. But the haughty attitude of the Spanish Church, its land-grabbing policy and its discrimination against Philippine priests ultimately aroused violent hatred, and the Church was the target of the majority of popular uprisings. These were frequent, averaging one every three years. In spite of the cruelty with which they were suppressed, the Philippine people continued to rise up and assert their right to human dignity.

The period that opened in 1868 marks a turning-point in their history. The Spanish Revolution of 1868, the establishment of a short-lived Republic in that country (1873-4) and the opening in 1869 of the Suez Canal, which brought Asia closer to Europe, all contributed to the spread of liberal ideas, which were introduced by the new government officials sent out by Madrid, by the books and newspapers which now circulated more freely, and by the young intellectuals who visited Europe and returned with an enthusiasm for democratic concepts.

In 1872 a new insurrection broke out, at the very gates of Manila. Philippine troops at the Cavite arsenal mutinied and proclaimed the independence of the country. The rising was harshly suppressed, but the execution of its leaders, and even of three Philippine priests—Fathers Gomez, Burgos and Zamora, who were charged with complicity—did not put an end to the revolutionary movement. While the country was assembling its forces, a vigorous propaganda campaign was launched by the intellectuals who had been exiled to Europe or had taken refuge there. In 1888 Marcelo H. del Pilar, José Rizal and García Lopez-Jaena combined with a group of Spanish republicans to found the Sociedad Hispano-Filipina and published a newspaper, *La Solidaridad*, at Barcelona; their demand was not for independence, but for domestic self-government and social reform.

José Rizal is now honoured as one of the heroes of the Philippine Republic, and a monument to him has been erected at Manila, for his martyrdom did more than anything else to awaken a sense of nationalism. But he was also a poet, a novelist, a philosopher and a doctor, whose actions and writings were all imbued with love of his country and concern for the health and prosperity of its people. His first novel, *Noli me tangere*, written in Berlin in 1887, at the age of twenty-five, described the sufferings of the Philippines under the Spanish oppression. Smuggled into the islands, it had an influence on the nationalist movement comparable to that of *Uncle Tom's Cabin* on the abolition of slavery. Four years later Rizal's second novel appeared, this time at Ghent; under the title *El Filibusterismo*, it told the story of the peasant rebellions against the religious bodies. Rizal then went to Hong Kong, where he founded the Liga Filipina. Returning to the Philippines in 1892, he was arrested, despite his moderate views, and deported to Dapitan, on the coast of Mindanao, where he worked as a doctor, teaching the villagers the elementary principles of hygiene.

Several of Rizal's companions abandoned his programme, however, because of the severity displayed by the Spaniards. Peaceful methods having failed, they now resorted to more direct revolutionary action. Immediately Rizal was deported. Andrès Bonifacio formed a secret society, the Katipunan, with the aim of shaking off Spanish domination and confiscating the estates of the religious orders. Its political programme was inspired by a strong sense of justice, as may be seen from some of the principles taught to neophytes, which reveal a Masonic influence:

'All men are equal, whatever the colour of their skin.

'A life not devoted to the cause of justice is like a tree that casts no shadow, even though its roots may not be poisoned.

'A good deed done for personal profit and not from kindness is without value' . . . etc.

The fact that it was a secret society also contributed to the rapid success of the Katipunan, which recruited over two hundred members in three years. On 26 August 1896, an insurrection broke out in the province of Cavite. Spain sent reinforcements to increase its army to 30,000 men. Rizal, held to be responsible for the rebellion, was condemned to death. From his prison he sent a last message to his country—the fine poem, *Mi Ultimo Adiós*, which every Philippine schoolboy knows by heart.

Far from extinguishing the flame of revolution, Rizal's execution (30 December 1896) added fresh fuel to it. The rebellion spread into the provinces of Pangasina, Zambales and Ilocos. The Philippine troops fraternized with the rebels. As a result of Bonifacio's death in obscure circumstances, Aguinaldo took over the leadership, establishing his headquarters at Biak-na-bato, in the province of Pampanga. In 1897 General Primo de Rivera decided to negotiate. In exchange for various promises—expulsion of the monks, parliamentary representation, democratic freedoms, equality between Philippines and Spaniards, return of their lands to the spoliated peasants and the payment of an indemnity of 800,000 pesos—Aguinaldo went into voluntary exile at Hong Kong.

It was at this moment that the 'incident' of the *Maine* took place. On 15 February 1898 the American ship of that name blew up at Havana, leading to the outbreak of hostilities between the United States and Spain. Admiral Dewey destroyed the Spanish fleet in Manila Bay. In return for the Americans' promise to recognize Philippine independence, Aguinaldo resumed the struggle on their side. In September 1898 he convened at Malolos, near Manila, a legislative assembly which adopted the first Philippine constitution (1899). Drafted in a spirit of revolutionary enthusiasm by intellectuals the majority of whom had been trained in Europe, and during what were already the last days of the Republic, this reflected the national aspiration towards a democratic régime based on the sovereignty of the people, the rights of the citizen, the protection of minorities and the progress of the masses. It was a very progressive constitution, under which the best features of the European democratic parliamentary institutions were to be adapted to the special conditions prevailing in the Philippines.

But it was not to last for long. American imperialism had already thrown off the mask. Ever since reaching the shores of the Pacific the Americans had been looking to the vast markets of the Far East as an outlet for their surplus production; moreover, the Philippines would serve as excellent naval bases on the great transoceanic routes. In spite of the protests of the Philippines,

Spain ceded the archipelago to the United States by the Treaty of Paris (10 December 1898) for $20 million; goods were to enter the ports of the islands duty-free for a further ten years. Tension increased between the former allies, and on 4 February 1899 the inevitable hostilities broke out at Manila. The Philippines resumed their guerrilla tactics, but the opposing forces were too unequal. When Aguinaldo was taken prisoner in 1901, the war virtually came to an end, though 'pacification' was not really completed until 1903.

But nationalism had not been destroyed. In the bitter aftermath of defeat, arms gave place to the pen. Press, poetry and drama all served as means of expressing the persistent longing for freedom and independence. On the spiritual level this was demonstrated by the establishment of an independent church. The aim of its founders, Izabelo de los Reyes and Gregorio Aglipay —the latter a Catholic priest who had been excommunicated—was to appoint secular Philippine priests in place of the Spanish monks who had been driven off their lands by the Republican Government, and to form a church entirely independent of any foreign authority. Aglipay had formerly come from his native province of Ilocano to join Aguinaldo's army, in which he had served as a chaplain and had fought, too, side by side with the soldiers. Elected in 1902 to the office of *Obispo Maximo* of the independent church, Aglipay remained in that position until his death in 1940. His doctrines made a more rational and modern impression than those of the Spanish Church, but its success was due principally to its nationalism. Regarding patriotism as a sacred sentiment, Aglipay canonized José Rizal and the three martyred priests, Burgos, Gomez and Zamora. The Aglipayens at present number nearly 2 million, scattered throughout the islands, most of them coming from the poorer classes.

For the conservative elements had already lost interest in the struggle. Even before Aguinaldo was taken prisoner, in December 1900, the Partito Federalista had been formed with the avowed aim of restoring peace and obtaining the admission of the Philippines as a new state in the United States of America. At first the American administration found nearly all its Philippine collaborators in the ranks of this party. But in 1907 the Partito Nacionalista was formed; this was victorious in the first legislative elections, and resumed the fight for independence on that basis.

Liberal European ideas were entering Vietnam as well, but in this case they came by way of China and Japan. Early in the twentieth century the Court at Huê had lost all prestige. After the escapade of Ham-nghi, the French gave the throne to the puppet princes Dongkhanh and Thanh-thai, and tightened their political grip from north to south of the country. Cochin-China, the first territory to be occupied, became a colony under direct administration; in 1880 it was provided with an elected assembly, the *Conseil colonial*, with a French majority, which had deliberative powers in budgetary matters. After the protectorate was set up Tonkin became gradually detached from Huê, and 1887 saw the formation of the 'Indochinese Union', comprising the three parts of Vietnam together with Cambodia (Laos joined it in 1893). The general government at the head of this Union did not, however, obtain any practical means of action until 1897, when Paul Doumer organized a civil service and a general budget; schools were opened to train minor officials for local government and the *qûoc ngu* was taught in order to combat the influence of the intellectual class.

This latter still provided the élite of the nation, despite the decline of Confucian culture and the reduction, followed by the complete abolition, of the examinations for mandarins (which came to an end in Tonkin in 1915 and in Annam in 1918). A small minority of intellectuals went over to the colonial Power, but the others maintained passive resistance. Their views were gradually changing, however, in the light of events abroad and of the situation at home.

Learning from the experience of conquest, they came to realize that their country could achieve liberation only by modernizing itself. And this was something that one Asian state—Japan—had managed to do without renouncing its own traditions, earning the respect of the European nations in the process. With unprecedented rapidity, the Meiji revolution had completely transformed the country's economy, established a firm constitutional government, and laid the foundations of military and naval power. China, too, was slowly awakening. The Sino-Japanese war of 1894–5, and the consequent defeat of China, led to the movement of reform headed by K'ang Yeou-wei and Leang K'i-tch'ao, intellectuals from Canton who had lived for a time in Japan. During the 'Hundred Days' of 1898 they tried, with the support of the young Emperor, to refurbish the ancient structure of China. Though they met speedy failure at Peking, their political ideas spread to Vietnam, where the intellectuals, hitherto profoundly contemptuous of the 'barbarians', discovered with astonishment the revolutionary trends that were being evidenced in Europe. Certain forms of literature were banned by the Protectorate as 'dangerous', so the first acquaintance with the French thinkers of the 'Age of Enlightenment' and with the English-speaking economists and philosophers was made secretly, through Chinese translations. K'ang Yeu-wei's *Journey to Eleven European Countries* and Leang K'i-ch'ao's *Writings of the Drinker of Icicles* became the favourite reading of these intellectuals, who also set themselves eagerly to imbibe the 'new learning' conveyed in Rousseau's *Contrat Social*, Montesquieu's *Esprit des Lois*, and the works of Voltaire and Diderot, Thomas Huxley and Herbert Spencer, Adam Smith and John Stuart Mill.

This intellectual development went hand in hand with the social changes now introduced in the country. A middle class was coming into existence as a result of expanding foreign and domestic trade. Small and medium-sized firms were established for trading, the weaving of silk and mats, potterymaking, sugar manufacture and public works, which were allotted by tender.

Those concerned could scarcely be called a middle class as yet, but they formed a first small nucleus of one. Moreover, they sometimes included intellectuals, who founded trade associations and schools to speed up modernization in Vietnam.

While all the intellectuals agreed as to the role of education, they showed two trends of opinion about national liberation. One group, represented by Phan Bôi Châu, still advocated an armed combat, while the other, to which Phan Châu Trinh belonged, was in favour of gradual reform. Their action did not become really widespread until after 1905—after Japan defeated Russia.

Phan Bôi Châu (1867–1940), after heading the list in the triennial examinations at Vinh, refused the post offered him by the Court and, as early as 1900, began to gather together the last representatives of the *Cân vuong* loyalists. He was at that time a monarchist, for he gave the leadership of his group to Prince Cuong dê, a direct descendant of Gia-long. His *Luu câu huyêt-lê tân thu* (New Book of the Tears of Blood of Luu câu), in which he described his country's humiliation, failed to rouse the Court from its lethargy, but won him the sympathy of all patriotic intellectuals, from the north to the south of the country. In 1904 he founded the *Duy tân* (Reform) Society, the chief aim of which was to constitute an opposition force in the Protectorate with the help of Japan. And at the beginning of the following year a party left for Tokyo under the leadership of Phan Bôi Châu.

The part played by the modern-minded intellectuals in Vietnam was also played in Burma by an élite open to 'Western' trends, rather than by the traditional social forces. The latter were in any case considerably weakened by the abolition of the monarchy and of the Buddhist authority. The Buddhist religion itself still retained its hold over men's minds, however, for when the educated minority was prompted, after studying European ideas and political institutions, to bring about a revival of the national culture, it sought to create Buddhist schools run on secular lines, after the pattern of the Christian mission schools. The number of these 'lay' schools rose from 890 in 1891–2 to 2,653 in 1910–11 and 4,650 in 1917–18, while the number of monastic schools showed a corresponding decline from 4,324 to 2,208, with a recovery to 2,977 in 1917–18. In 1904 the Buddhist Association of Rangoon College began to hold meetings and publish papers calling for the reform of Burmese customs and institutions.

In Indonesia the national awakening was bound up with the inception of the feminist movement. As we have already seen, the women of Indonesia had always enjoyed the same rights as men in family and public life, but both were subordinated by *Adat* to the interests of the community. The *Fikh*, or Moslem law, on the contrary, encouraged a feeling of individuality, of existence apart from the group. The introduction of capitalist economy and European education in the early twentieth century, however, limited the facilities for such education (in 1903 there were only 1,700 elementary schools in the whole of Indonesia, attended by 190,000 pupils, together with a few score primary schools which were reserved for the children of Dutch settlers and Indonesian nobles) and undermined the foundations of the traditional society, while the Dutch policy was aimed at consolidating the authority of the princes who supported their administration. Islam was a danger for the Dutch because of its unifying influence, and to the princes because it was hostile to *Adat*, on which their power was based. These contradictions formed the background of the first uprisings which gave evidence of the national awakening. The uprisings originated in aristocratic circles in Java, where women had the least freedom and were most shackled by the ancient customs which allowed them no serious education and no choice in the matter of marriage (whereas the peasant women, though their lives were harder, had much greater independence).

The first to rebel was Princess Kartini (1879–1904), daughter of the Regent of Djapara, whose letters were published in Dutch after her death, with the title *From Darkness to Light*. She decided that only through education could women secure their own emancipation and that of their children. Criticizing the Government for its refusal to extend the educational system, she opened a small school in her own palace in 1903. Her example was soon followed by Devi Sartica, who opened a school at Bandung in 1904 and soon added nine others. Devi Sartica's schools gave particular prominence to vocational training. These two women did not have to work in isolation—both had the support of their husbands and their parents. Public interest was captured, and the national conscience began to awaken. A few years later, in 1908, the first nationalist association was founded. Known as Budi Utomo—'Noble aspiration'—it was composed of civil servants, intellectuals and members of the professions, pledged to obtain emancipation for Indonesia by means of education.

Thus, at the beginning of the twentieth century, the whole Asian community advanced from a rejection of the West and a withdrawal into nostalgia for the past, to a positive attitude of adaptation to the modern world. This 'open-mindedness' was based on reason and had a definite aim—the struggle for national liberation, the principal means to which must be education. Progress was conditioned by the changes introduced within the community itself, as a result of political and economic upheavals and the collapse of traditional values. The revival was not affected without friction between the modernists and the upholders of tradition. But the former were greatly encouraged by events elsewhere, particularly by the rise of Japanese power. Japan's victory over Russia in 1905 was a red-letter day in the history of Asia, for it demonstrated the value of technique to the dependent and semi-dependent countries and turned them definitely towards the search for new forms of culture.[10]

NOTES TO CHAPTER XXV

1. In the opinion of V. A. Tyurin, Candidate of Historical Sciences, the author rightly gives his basic attention to the irrigation societies of South-East Asia. Nevertheless, many highly developed regions of the Malayan and Indonesian world do not fit in with the description and belong to different structural types—'maritime' or 'littoral'.

2. V. A. Tyurin feels that the treatment of material concerning the different countries of South-East Asia is somewhat uneven. The author writes a great deal about Vietnam, slightly less about Burma, Siam, Laos and Cambodia and very little about Indonesia and Malaya. Far less space is given to the treatment of Islam in South-East Asia than to the analysis of particular features of Confucianism and Buddhism and their influence on societies in Indo-China. This sub-section contains very interesting material on Vietnamese, Burmese and Siamese literature, but not a word about Malayan and Indonesian historical prose, which reached a considerable level of development during this period.

3. V. A. Tyurin points out that a very detailed picture is given of the social and administrative structure of Vietnam, whilst the author has again left Indonesia and Malaya outside his field of vision. In his remarks on Burma the author fails to mention the basic unit of Burmese society, the *myo*. The social and political structure of Siam has not been very fully covered. Lastly, when speaking about the new features in the ideology of South-East Asian societies, the author should have mentioned Abdullah Abdul Kadir Munshi, the first Malayan educationalist.

4. To Professor Asa Briggs the references to missionaries on this and the following pages seem to be one-sided. There is very little evidence that most of the Catholic missionaries before the end of the eighteenth century were working simultaneously for salvation and profits of trade. The point becomes even more marked when the author makes very favourable references to Islam. But what was the difference between the Islamic and the Christian impact?

5. V. A. Tyurin believes that this section should have dealt more clearly with the question of imperialism and its impact on South-East Asia. The author writes that the features of imperialism started to become clear in the 1880s; in fact, however, the process of formation of monopoly capital began in the 1870s and continued until the beginning of the twentieth century. The distinction should have been made between the rise of imperialism and the period of its domination.

6. In Professor Asa Briggs's opinion the reference to the story of Singapore after 1819 is told too briefly in relation to what happened to Singapore before 1819. Moreover it is extremely difficult to separate out British occupation and British free-trade policy as different factors, given the nature of the nineteenth-century British economy.

7. In V. A. Tyurin's opinion the author quite rightly notes the importance of South-East Asia as a source of raw material and a market for the capitalist countries. This could have been expanded to include a description of the application of the capitalist economy, especially since the author gives some specific facts.

8. Professor Asa Briggs wonders whether the reference to usury is quite correct. If so, there is a distinction here between South-East Asian and Indian society as much as between South-East Asian and Western capitalist society.

9. Professor Asa Briggs is inclined to compare the reference to the effect on South-East Asian handworkers of industrialization with what is said about the effects of industrialization on Indian handworkers. I suspect that in both cases the story is the same.

10. V. A. Tyurin emphasizes that the author notes the importance of the Japanese victory in the Russo-Japanese War as a factor in the awakening of national consciousness in Asia, but what about the Russian Revolution of 1905–7 which exerted an enormous revolutionizing influence throughout Asia?

CHAPTER XXVI

AFRICA AND OCEANIA: CONTACTS WITH EUROPEAN CIVILIZATION[1]

I. THE SPREAD OF SCIENTIFIC CIVILIZATION TO AFRICA AND OCEANIA AND THE RESISTANCE TO IT[2]

EUROPEAN contact with these two continents, whose societies and civilizations were alike in many respects, came as a tremendous shock, not only because of the violence and conquest associated with it but also because it brought new ways of production, knowledge, behaviour and beliefs which were incompatible with the traditions of the various peoples in Africa and Oceania. The shock was at times so violent as to involve the almost total disappearance of the persons affected: in Oceania (Australia, New Zealand and Hawaii), as in central Africa, the peoples and their distinctive social and cultural ways of living were largely disturbed. Fortunately, however, most traditional societies were able to respond to the challenge of European expansion in ways which bore witness to their vitality and creative abilities.

It is necessary to stress the relatively static character of these societies as compared with the instability and the rapid changes in modern industrial civilizations. R. Montaigne reasserts this in one of his latest studies:

'In all these ancient countries, thousand-year-old civilizations—sometimes primitive, sometimes well developed—had become stabilized as if they had found in static traditions a perfect existence, free from anxiety which consumes and the striving which holds us in its grip.'

'Static' may be too strong a word to use, but it helps to underline the importance of the impact created by contact with Europe, even indirectly. P. Valéry in his *Regards sur le Monde Actuel* notes that

'Europeans have quarrelled for the right to awaken, educate and arm huge peoples enclosed in their traditions—peoples who wished only to be left as they were'.

This remark, while revealing extraordinary ethnocentrism, does sum up the dynamic role of European expansion. Valéry goes so far as to consider the diffusion of 'the European secret'—i.e. scientific and technical knowledge and economic skills—as a sort of *treason*, since the awakening of these great masses would threaten the privileged position held by Europe during the nineteenth century.

If, on the other hand, we consider the point of view of the young African intellectual today, we find his attitude to Western contact essentially critical:[3]

on the one hand, we find a (justifiable) attack on the insufficient advantages received in economic, cultural and medical matters; on the other hand, he criticizes the West for destroying his social order and traditional civilization. How can we estimate the facts objectively in face of such diverse statements ? A closer study of culture contacts and conflicts resulting from European expansion shows that the starting-point was really in the last twenty years of the eighteenth century. In 1788 the African Association of London was founded; its scientific aims were soon followed by distinctly political ambitions. This year, too, saw the first European colonization of Australia, which was to lead later to the settlement of free colonists. In the same period philanthropic organizations, aiming at the abolition of the slave trade, found, with the opening of the modern industrial era, conditions favouring their success. By the end of the eighteenth century the period of maritime discovery had ended and exploration and occupation of the interior began, opening a long period of conflict between the Powers which sought to divide the world between them. It was not till the eve of the First World War that the partition of Africa and Oceania came to a halt. European expansion had hardly reached its peak and the periods of 'pacification' and colonial development set in, when resistance began to develop among the indigenous peoples in different regions against foreign domination. The 1914–18 war had important repercussions especially in Africa. A new era was beginning—one of reaction against colonial rule, aiming at its abolition.

It was in this period (an extended nineteenth century) that the contact taking place between the West and Black Africa and Oceania became fully significant. The opposition between the two cultures was even more acute than was immediately apparent: particularly where religion was concerned; Christian missionaries were attempting to transform societies which were at one and the same time peasant and pagan.

Expansion in Africa

During the last ten years of the eighteenth century the situation was as follows. European commercial companies (rarely governments) had for a long time been setting up trading posts along the known coasts, where trade in men as well as in a limited number of costly 'exotic' products took place. The greatest number of posts was to be found round the Gulf of Guinea and in South Africa where there were already some white colonists at the Cape.* Permanent relations were established only with a few coastal tribes who controlled the termini of trade from the interior, and who had the monopoly of transactions with the Europeans. These tribes, by means of both force and magic (representing the white traders in a legendary context as dangerous spirits or cruel creatures) attempted to preserve their monopoly and its huge

* See 'Developments in South Africa from the end of the eighteenth century to the early twentieth century'.

profits. This economic advantage gave some of these tribes the chance of developing superior forms of political organization.

In eighteenth-century Africa the slave trade was still at its peak. The decline of the great commercial companies, however, and the rise of government intervention, particularly in the case of Great Britain, was to be a turning-point in history. Opposition to the work of philanthropic societies became weaker and the latter succeeded in 1807 in obtaining from European governments the abolition of the slave trade. This meant that the open trade was followed on a smaller scale by illegal trading, which was to be gradually wiped out by interested powers completing the occupation of the coast. Illicit slave trading can still be traced up to the beginning of the twentieth century. As the slave trade diminished, the trade in gold, ivory, rubber, skins, etc. progressively increased.

Despite successive prohibitions, the slave trade in East Africa did not really begin to decline until the very end of the nineteenth century. Although many European, Persian and Indian merchants and traders were active in it, the slave trade was largely a monopoly of the Arabs, the subjects first of the Oman Empire in north-east Arabia and subsequently of the Sultanate of Zanzibar, who had progressively 'colonized' the African coast of the Indian Ocean from Somalia to Mozambique. The Arabs made no effort to colonize the hinterland (Tanganyika, Kenya and Uganda), but sought only to maintain such authority as they required to carry on without hindrance the slave trade which constituted the chief source of their wealth, their power and their influence and on which, at the same time, their whole economy was based. Arab slave hunters conducted systematic raids on the tribes of the interior; the slaves were sometimes traded for merchandise directly from native kings and chiefs. The captives were then sent to the principal markets on the coast—at Kilwa, Mombasa, Malindi—but above all Zanzibar. The caravans took certain well-known trails (from Mombasa to Lake Victoria and from Kilwa to Lake Nyasa) which were specially adapted to the slave trade: protected by forts and armed troops. Of the slaves surviving the strenuous trip, some remained on the African coast to work on Arab-owned plantations, but the majority were exported to Arabia, Persia, Egypt or India.

The struggle against the Arab slave trade was a long and difficult one, and had to face numerous uprisings incited by the Arab chiefs and traders who derived such substantial profit from it. The struggle had initially been undertaken for humanitarian reasons and was at first led by Christian missionaries, but it came increasingly to serve as a moral justification for the annexation of the territories of East Africa by the European powers.

These activities profoundly affected African cultures even before the period of modern colonization.[4] The result on the population is not precisely known, and exact statistical information is not available. According to the most conservative estimates the slave trade drained the country of 100 million people. R. P. Rinchon estimates more than 13 million slaves coming from this area. It has to be remembered that although the number of slaves was extremely large, it was spread nevertheless over several centuries. It affected men, young women and children, and created demographic difficulties, particularly for the populations of central Africa, which have been hard to surmount. The loss of populations was even more serious because it happened in underpopulated regions. The slave trade and the growth of commerce also introduced an element of instability. Tribal groups in each area fought to secure a monopoly of the sale of slaves to Europeans. In certain cases annual wars were actually organized by the coastal states. Large groups uprooted themselves and scattered in order to escape the threats. Entire regions were ruined and became a no-man's-land between the coastal trading posts and populations of the interior for whom remoteness meant safety. Subsequently, energetic tribes migrated from the interior, and tried to reach the treaty posts at the mouths of rivers and on the coasts. Such were the Fangs and related groups in the South Cameroons and Gabon.

The trade had economic repercussions over a wide field: it divided the people into merchants or middlemen on the one hand, and 'population reserves' on the other. Lasting rivalries, affecting political life even today, were set up as a result of these unequal and crude economic relations. It is important however, not to underestimate the creative role of trade in transforming social and cultural life: favourable economic conditions led to centralization of power and more highly differentiated and complex political and administrative activities. We can quote the examples of the kingdoms of Dahomey and Douala on the Cameroon coast. In East Africa, one might mention the kingdom of Buganda, where the necessities of trade with the Arabs helped to extend, strengthen and stabilize the hold of the existing power structure and its officials on the population. In addition the coastal tribes, and through them certain peoples of the interior, had acquired during the period some of the features (mostly material) of Western civilization.

This Africa, profoundly shaken by the slave trade, was now to be penetrated by the explorers; starting with J. Bruce (the source of the Blue Nile) and Mungo Park (the course of the Niger) in the late eighteenth and early nineteenth centuries, up to Barth (Sahara, Sudan and Chad) Livingstone, Stanley, Burton and Speke (East and South Africa) during the third quarter of the nineteenth century, up to the Russian scientist V. V. Yunker who explored central Africa. They supplied accurate geographical information to fill in that map of Africa which Swift had ridiculed in his poems; these were the first documents to lay the foundations of African science. The use of their findings was, however, warped by difficulties of exploration and by national prejudices. Misunderstanding and errors of judgement concerning African civilization thus arose which were linked with the colonial expansion for a long while.

While discoveries were still continuing and missions widening their field of activity (in South Africa, Madagascar and West Africa), in the coastal zones trade was being replaced by annexation. Missions of a different kind were sent to the interior to demarcate the zones of influence of the various powers competing in the partition of Africa. They signed treaties of friendship or of protection with local chiefs, thereby establishing provisional 'rights' over large areas. The last decades of the nineteenth century were those of effective occupation. Diplomatic agreements were signed and frontiers traced—often right across ethnical groupings and cultural units. The African peoples were not a party to these agreements; it was the period when they were obliged to submit to the changes and pressures (economic, political and religious) involved in colonization.

During much of the nineteenth century, the European powers intervened in East Africa only to ensure their ships free access to the Indian Ocean ports. As a result, they maintained close relations with the Arabs on the coast and interfered in local affairs as their interests required. Until 1880, they showed no inclination to assume greater responsibilities in the hinterland and were content with sending missionaries and explorers. It was the appearance of Germany in East Africa which led to the annexation of these areas after 1880. The German explorer Karl Peters occupied several regions—belonging at least in theory to the Sultanate of Zanzibar—of what later became the territory of Tanganyika and, by signing a series of treaties with the native rulers, appropriated a large area. Next the English, with Lord Lugard, penetrated into the Kenya Highlands and the area around Lake Victoria. Initially placed under the control of the big companies, the Deutsche Ostafricanische Gesell-schaft, and the Imperial British East African Company, the territories of Tanganyika and Kenya, including the coastal region, were divided up by England and Germany before being annexed entirely.

Expansion in Oceania

In Oceania the historical background is slightly different. At the beginning of the nineteenth century contacts with Europeans were limited to a few ports of call, trading posts and mission stations of the coasts. (Pl. 75). American trade and colonization had just begun in Hawaii. Australia was merely a penal colony. Oceania did not know the slave trade. Practices such as the kidnapping or *blackbirding* of the Pacific Islanders for work on the plantations (Queensland) were an internal affair, a question rather of the transfer of labour migration, as from the Far East to such places as Hawaii, this being an important factor of the nineteenth century development of the area.

European occupation took place in several phases, and under different conditions in different regions. In Australia it began with the foundation of a penal settlement followed later by the arrival of free colonists*. The history of the country at once became the history of these newcomers, for natives were few, easily driven into the interior, and progressively fewer as a result of the direct or indirect action of the colonists. The European settlers were at first extremely hostile to the aboriginal people and actually succeeded in entirely

* See 'The Development of Australia in the nineteenth century'.

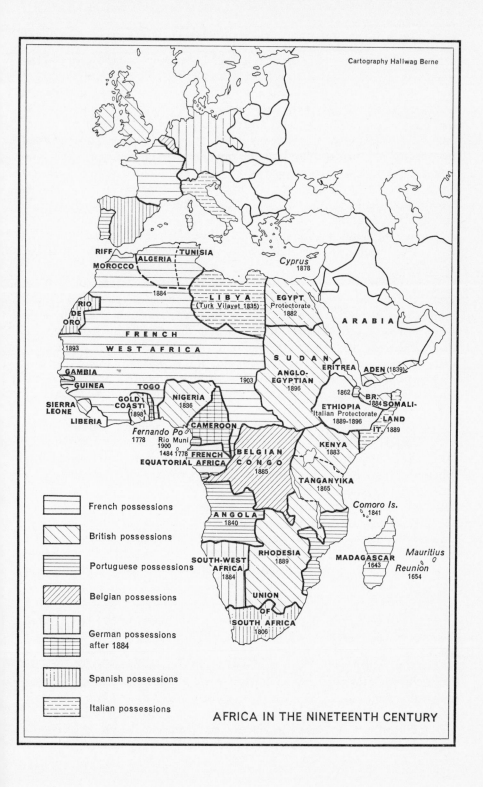

Cartography Hallwag Berne

RIFF
MOROCCO
ALGERIA
TUNISIA
Cyprus
1878

1884

L I B Y A
(Turk Vilayet 1835)

EGYPT
Protectorate
1882

A R A B I A

RIO
DE
ORO

F R E N C H

1893   W E S T   A F R I C A

S U D A N

ERITREA

ADEN (1839)

GAMBIA

GUINEA

TOGO

1903

ANGLO-
EGYPTIAN
1896

1862

BR.
1884 SOMALI-

SIERRA
LEONE

GOLD
COAST
1898

NIGERIA
1836

ETHIOPIA
Italian Protectorate
1889-1896

LAND

LIBERIA

Fernando Po
1778   Rio Muni
1900

CAMEROON

IT. 1889

1484 1778 FRENCH
EQUATORIAL AFRICA

BELGIAN
C O N G O
1885

KENYA
1883

TANGANYIKA
1865

Comoro Is.
1841

A N G O L A
1840

SOUTH-WEST
AFRICA
1884

RHODESIA
1889

MADAGASCAR
1643

Mauritius

Reunion
1654

UNION
OF
SOUTH AFRICA
1806

French possessions

British possessions

Portuguese possessions

Belgian possessions

German possessions
after 1884

Spanish possessions

Italian possessions

AFRICA IN THE NINETEENTH CENTURY

exterminating the Tasmanians in the 1870s. This reason, and the technological inferiority of the Australian natives, explains why the latter were not influenced by Western culture. Culture contacts in this period, then, were non-existent; Australia was to remain for the anthropologist a human reserve of some of the most archaic people in existence. During the same period the colonization of New Zealand began in a completely haphazard manner until the annexation by Great Britain in 1840. But here the situation was completely different: the native population was numerous and its social and political organization was able to resist external pressure. In 1853 France annexed New Caledonia, where the Kanaka population, although few in number, reacted strongly against the conquest.

The second phase of annexation occurred well before the second half of the nineteenth century. The islands which were independent underwent rapid changes.

With the improvement in communications came an increase in trade in local products (sandalwood, copra, etc.). The arrival of planters followed immediately in northern Australia, Fiji and New Caledonia. Next the need for labour on the plantations became acute. Thus, while in many parts of black Africa the slave trade was coming to an end, in the Polynesian Islands and particularly in Melanesia a new traffic in men was developing. Here, of course, its character was rather different: it included both workers recruited by force and voluntary or semi-voluntary labourers (under indirect pressures). The trade nevertheless had the same destructive effect and created an atmosphere of hostility and violence between Europeans and the islanders.

Meanwhile the work of both Catholic and Protestant missions continued successfully; entire populations were converted in New Zealand, Fiji, Micronesia and Polynesia. Religious activity cannot always be clearly distinguished from political and commercial activities. In many cases the missions assumed the leadership in public affairs and created semi-political organizations which enabled them to exercise a social control favourable to the introduction of a new moral code. Raratonga, with its strict regulations, its strong police force and its chiefs associated with the work of the Protestant missions is not an isolated example. In Micronesia, a Spanish colony, the Catholic church sometimes replaced the native authorities. Political compulsion, backed by religious and moral pressure, often provoked violent reactions. Moreover, there were often conflicts between Protestants and Catholics which, together with the excesses of the slave trade, led to the intervention of European powers and to the annexation of most of the unoccupied land.

The last twenty years of the nineteenth century are the zenith of Western imperialism. At the same time as the partition of Africa was occurring, German intervention led to a hasty division of Oceania. The procedure used in negotiation with native populations varied from one place to another. In New Zealand great care was taken to give the acceptance of British sovereignty a legal character. In many parts of the Pacific local populations presented petitions (often inspired by missionaries and established colonists), begging one or more powers for protection. Some naval expeditions among the islands became police operations. But the recognition of local sovereigns proved to be fairly illusory, especially where there was no strong native political organization. A series of agreements were signed, defining spheres of influence and demarcating territorial divisions. The indigenous peoples, exhausted and weakened by the shocks of an earlier period and often rapidly declining in numbers, offered only weak resistance to colonial rule, which in any case seemed like a return to order after a period of anarchy. Pacification was thus more rapidly achieved than in Africa, and the First World War caused less of an upheaval.

It is now necessary to consider the *capacity for resistance* of native societies and cultures towards external influences and foreign rule, taking into account both the will to resist and, at the same time, the desire of some individuals to assimilate foreign advantages. While a detailed study of each different case in its historical and sociological context would be desirable, it is still possible within the limits of a general essay to bring together some significant facts.

Resistance in Oceania

Known resistance movements operating during the nineteenth century can be classified into four categories: (*a*) organized military rebellion, as in the case of the Maori wars, (*b*) raids on the coastal settlements of Melanesia and Micronesia, (*c*) the skilful use of a complex international situation either to maintain independence or to obtain a liberal protector (as in Hawaii, Fiji, Samoa and Tonga), (*d*) unorganized outbursts of cultural conservatism. These movements were very different from those to follow in the twentieth century, which took the form of prophetic outbursts, nationalist claims and cultural action within the framework of new associations. By that time use was to be made of the teachings and techniques of the West; it was believed that the best form of resistance against Western rule was to use the very instruments (material and spiritual) which made up its strength. Although in many cases raids, looting and murders do not appear to be directed to any definite political end, we cannot be sure whether or not they sprang from conscious cultural resistance. The causes are often more accidental: for example, the case of one missionary murdered because he ventured into a region already disturbed by local intertribal feuds (Mgr Epalle at San Cristobal), another as a reprisal against abuses by Europeans (at Santa Cruz), others because they possessed food during a famine (Catholic missionaries in New Caledonia), still others, because their presence was believed to spread epidemics (Presbyterian missions in the New Hebrides). In some regions, particularly in the New Hebrides and in Australia, native outrages were provoked by similar acts on the part of Europeans either personally or in the name of authority. It was thus that the last Tasmanian tribes had to flee like haunted animals.

Some of the Polynesian peoples, thanks to their efficient social hierarchies and their ability to choose competent chiefs, seemed at first glance to be better equipped to maintain their independence and to resist cultural domination than the Melanesian peoples with their weak social organization. But this did not prove to be the case. A social system with a centralized power is in some respects easier to transform than one where power is diffused; once an authority consisting of a restricted number of people is won over, it leads almost immediately to the adhesion of whole groups of people. This explains some rapid successes of the colonists. Missionaries, as well as merchants and colonists, helped the Polynesian chiefs to form governments with a council of ministers, an army, a police force, laws, ambassadors and flags. The kingdoms of Hawaii, Tahiti and Tonga were modernized in this manner; their consolidation, however temporary, was a mixture of Western ideas and institutions with traditional practices.

These apparently centralized political systems, however, harboured quite different forces: in all Polynesian societies, except Hawaii and Tonga, the chief was only *primus inter pares*. Although heredity played a role, the chief had to win his title by individual valour, by the support of public opinion and by military or marital alliances. Competitors might arise, and it was always possible to keep the chief in check by challenging his efficiency or the legality of his power. The kingdom of Tahiti was ruined by feuds between rival factions reinforced by religious division. In Hawaii, religious deviations played a considerable role at the critical time when the survival of native peoples was at stake. In Samoa and on the Cook Islands, rival groups prevented centralization—in the latter they were enshrined in permanent institutions. Only the kindgom of Tonga survived into the twentieth century; owing to weak international competition, and the influence of the missions and the British authorities on the royal family, an efficient government was able to be evolved.

Melanesia displayed the strongest cultural resistance to Western influence; this was partly due to the fact that European expansion occurred rather late in the second half of the nineteenth century. Even today the cultural conservatism of Melanesia is incontestable: it contains the largest proportion of non-Christians in Oceania and little political organization. This cannot be explained solely by a reluctance to change; recent researches show that the impulse towards innovation was hampered by a lack of knowledge, poverty, rudimentary social organization and, above all, a lack of confidence in Europeans. The cause lies in fact in the very nature of Melanesian society: cultural units on a very small scale—the slow diffusion of change is explained by a necessity to 'reach', in some sort, every individual. During the nineteenth century effective communication was limited to individuals and groups of villages; only in the twentieth century were organizations able to act on a larger scale. Nevertheless, the effect of Westernization during the period of study was, although diffused, quite remarkable.

Resistance in Black Africa

The situation was not essentially different from that in Oceania. Most of the peoples, especially those of a clan-type organization without centralized power, barely struggled to retain their independence.[5] Even before the period of modern colonization some large areas (like the realm of the Congo) had had their populations drained by the slave trade, and were politically degraded by internal dissensions and economic competition.

Cases of organized and lasting resistance conducted by stable kingdoms are rare. The kingdom of Dahomey, with an efficient army, and politically and economically competent, reached its apogee during the first half of the nineteenth century. It fought against French invasion, but was conquered in 1894 and split up into several districts. The Ashantis, who today occupy the middle part of Ghana with a population of half a million inhabitants, were at the beginning of the eighteenth century a powerful confederation with a common defence. During the entire nineteenth century the Ashantis fought severe wars against the English who had settled in the coastal regions. Between 1890 and 1900 frequent and fierce battles led to the exile of King Prempeh, chief of the Confederation, and then to the establishment of a protectorate. In west and central Sudan, the kingdom of Wolofs (in the present Senegal) disappeared at the time of the conquest.[6] The 'empires' of Ahmadou, son of El Hadj Omar, of Samory and of Rabah, based on recent conquests and without racial or historical roots, crumbled at the touch of the colonizers, and the peoples who had composed them returned to their small scattered domains.[7] In south and east Africa, from the end of the seventeenth to the end of the nineteenth century, it was mainly the Arabs who erected a strong barrier against European penetration. At the end of the nineteenth century and the very beginning of the twentieth several Arab rebellions broke out in Kenya and Tanganyika, particularly in the latter where the Germans ruled with merciless severity. The Arabs fought fiercely and inflicted some heavy defeats on the mercenary troops recruited by the colonizers. They fought as much to preserve an Islam threatened by Catholic and Protestant missionaries as to protect the slave trade on which their whole hegemony was based. In some instances the leaders of the rebellion managed to carry some of the native uprisings in Tanganyika between 1889 and 1907. Whole tribes, such as the Wahehe between 1894 and 1898, rebelled against forced labour and taxation; the so-called 'Maji-Maji'. Between 1905 and 1907, uprisings spread throughout the whole territory. Each one of these revolts was mercilessly suppressed (the repressive campaigns of Wissmann); entire populations were wiped out and whole areas laid waste. Here again great national blocs crumbled at the time of the conquest: the kingdom of the Matabele in Rhodesia, the military kingdom of the Zulus founded by the conqueror Chaka. Similarly, the overlordships and sultanates of the central Sudan (especially the Hausa), and the states set up by the Peuls in the Sudan and in the Adamawa barely resisted the conquest. All were reduced to protectorates by the turn of the century.

The political, cultural, economic and religious plans of colonization visualized a rapid transformation of native societies—by modernizing and christianizing them wherever Islam was not strongly entrenched.[8] In opposition to this multifarious activity, the various societies reacted more or less directly, thus proving that their submission was by no means passive.

Once the period of conquest was ended, the violent opposition of any large groups was exceptional. Nevertheless cases of ephemeral revolts did occur, although limited in extent. These were rather in protest against the loss of commercial privileges associated with the old trading system or reaction provoked by a prophet or religious reformer.[9] Because of the power of the European minority, most of the opposition was clandestine or emerged only indirectly. The piecemeal occupation of territories and the incomprehensible character of African culture made it easy to keep secrets from the colonists and screened those who were in real authority. In French Africa government reports at a very early stage stressed the difficulty of rebuilding any effective power. The legitimate chiefs, anxious to preserve their prestige, remained in the background hidden behind puppets, who were often slaves or persons of inferior status. The true social structure was concealed behind a façade.

It was, in fact, under the guise of secret religious groups which aimed at preserving their indigenous culture that resistance was most effectively organized—groups both numerous and efficient, operating in a field where interference by the colonists was very difficult. Their importance was so great that they were able to act as a basis for twentieth-century nationalism in south, east and central Africa.

2. THE ECONOMIC AND SOCIAL CONSEQUENCES OF EUROPEAN EXPANSION

It was the technical inferiority of Africa and Oceania which handicapped their resistance to the foreigner. They were forced into contact—partially at first, then more completely—in the way which is typical of modern colonization. This extensive contact, together with the rule of the foreigner, produced in African and Oceanian societies a state of crisis, affecting their entire cultural patterns. The result was either an effort of reorganization or total disappearance.

It is in Oceania, where the population was already precarious, that physical decline has been most frequently studied. Every group of islands from Yap to Tahiti and New Zealand was affected, the average loss of population during the nineteenth century being 50 per cent. The Tasmanians were wiped out entirely and a number of other peoples remain only in small tragic groups. The spread of war, more deadly since the introduction of firearms, the diffusion of new infectious diseases and drunkenness, mass movements of workers leading to a high death rate—and in some cases systematic slaughter—were the main causes. It is difficult to assess the part played by the loss of will to live which some observers mention. In fact, de-population was at the same time cause and effect of the social crisis resulting from European interference. Some peoples, who suffered simultaneously from a declining population and cultural degradation, changed so radically that they appeared by the end of the century to be completely new groups. This was the case in Hawaii, where the original natives became a small minority, while half-castes increased, and it grew to be the meeting place of immigrants both from the Far East and the West; similarly with the Marquesas Islands and Tahiti.

In Africa the population problem was not so serious. Most of the native peoples survived the drain of the slave trade,[10] and populations took a normal upward curve, although the wars in the interior resulting from the slave trade seriously affected some of the Sudanese peoples. Colonial consolidation had two quite opposite results: on the one hand, pacification and health measures led to an increase in population (almost 20 per cent, per annum, in French Guinea in the mid-twentieth century); on the other hand, the recruitment of labour for modern enterprises seriously disturbed the population balance in native reserves by emptying villages of their young men, as in central Africa and the Union of South Africa where the existing system of recruitment and semi-forced labour has gravely affected the demographic and social structures.

Economic results

During the nineteenth century economic changes took place with great rapidity. In Oceania the foundations of a modern economy were laid. Immigrants from Asia soon played an important role both in agriculture and in internal commerce. As a result, the natives were soon confined to village trading and to seasonal work. Very few succeeded in founding commercial enterprises of any size. An interesting exception is, however, that of the Maoris. In the early period of colonization the Maoris were responsible for some public works and for supplying food by boat to the growing towns. But as soon as trade became more complex and Europeans began to compete, decline and apathy followed.

This general stagnation of native economies was due to their unpreparedness for the specialized activities of a money economy and by the energy of the 'pioneers' who, with their large resources, soon took the lead. It is no reflection on the ability or adaptability of the natives. Two facts should be stressed: the local demand, at first at a very low level, was rapidly satisfied by the goods brought by merchants; the cost of taking an active part in the economic field seemed out of all proportion to the advantages obtainable: it would involve a break with the old way of existence which continued to be valued. Villagers used their initiative, however, to plant cocoa and orange trees where this could be done with a small amount of capital and without upsetting their normal pattern of work. This enterprise was limited by cost, by difficulties of transport and by the marginal character of production, as well as by the small financial needs of the villagers.

These changes, although on a small scale, were revolutionary in traditional economies. Consumption changed its character: products introduced by the circulation of trade did not completely oust local goods, but supplemented them. During the nineteenth century towns only influenced the traditional way of life in a few areas, but consumption based on a monetary system began to replace the habits associated with the old subsistence economy. Only a few individuals who had the benefit of modern education and experience, and were thus more sensitive to the European example, reached the stage of conspicuous consumption. Occasionally, as in the case of the royal family of Hawaii, an attempt was made to give a Westernized flavour to the material display associated with a superior status. But on the whole, the organization of village production and the distribution of goods remained traditional: it was still undertaken by social groups, generally families who were at the same time economic units, and was as yet hardly threatened by individual initiative. Some chiefs, however, were beginning to change their ways—using the support of foreign authorities to secure greater wealth by taxing the output of their dependants.

The positive results both in Oceania and in Africa of the new economic developments may be considered under two heads:

(1) The introduction of new plants.

In Africa this started well before the nineteenth century: maize, which became the basic food product in many coastal regions, dates from the sixteenth century, and cassava probably from the seventeenth century. During our period it is a question mainly of the importation and spread of 'luxury' or 'commercial' crops, particularly groundnuts, first produced in Senegal in the 1840s, and cocoa, which was planted in the Gold Coast around 1880. At the same time plantations of coffee and cotton, until then purely local, were spreading throughout the continent, and the relative importance of basic foodstuffs became gradually modified by the spread of cassava, rice and yams. In Oceania, by the end of the eighteenth century, there was a dual development: on the one hand, explorers, merchants and colonists were introducing citrus fruits, pineapples, beans, tobacco, pig-breading, etc.; on the other hand, both imported and native products previously cultivated only in certain areas were spreading through the movement of labour. This produced a great many further changes, for example, disequilibrium in agriculture and general economic life, owing to the spread of export crops at the expense of basic foodstuffs; an apparent rise in the standard of living accompanied by the increased insecurity of an economy dependent on the fluctuations of the world market; changes in the division of labour as between sex and age groups. Thus the major social changes of the twentieth century take their rise from a small revolution in the field of agricultural production due to the introduction 'and spread of new crops mainly grown for export.

(2) The effect of tools and expanding demand.

The import of manufactured goods, although sometimes important, was very restricted in quantity. In Oceania the introduction of iron tools had a great effect; without any appreciable change in the technique of agriculture, efficiency was increased and considerable time was saved. Nothing of this kind happened in Africa, where tools continued to be produced locally well on into the twentieth century. The list of merchandise or manufactured articles which the natives were able to buy for their own use remained very short: it included firearms, which revolutionized war and hunting (for the benefit of external traders), stimulants such as alcohol, which played an increasing part in social and ritual life, and tobacco in the case of Oceania; materials and garments, which were the basis of the early import trade, kitchenware which led to a sharp decline in local craftsmanship (particularly in pottery and calabashes), and in 'pearls' and cheap jewellery. Lamps and lighting equipment came later, with the tools which were necessary for the modern manufacture which replaced the ancient crafts. New demands arose from contact with Europeans by the 'contagion' well known to economists, particularly for clothes, housing and furniture and, later, for foodstuffs.

The impact of Western economy on African societies varied considerably from region to region owing to the different policies adopted by the colonists and the varying speeds of development. In South Africa the establishment of native reservations, where over-population soon became pronounced, together with the growth of mining and industry, led to profound changes. The Bantu were forced to leave their villages and work for pay, while detribilization occurred with alarming speed. By the middle of the twentieth century 60 per cent of the Africans were living outside reservations and 55 per cent of African wage earners were employed in industry. The same process with certain reservations occurred in Rhodesia and the Belgian Congo. The pattern of change can be easily traced. In tribal life economics, which depended on limited land and almost no external trade, aimed mainly at the subsistence of the group; a kind of primitive state control existed over production and distribution. Under modern conditions an economy subject to the vicissitudes of an external market made possible an accumulation and circulation of capital formerly inconceivable. Furthermore, the introduction of industry and of modern economic concentrations led to large migrations and a rural exodus which had begun by the end of the nineteenth century. At the same time communications developed and became more rapid; in the first decades of the twentieth century the improved roads led to a redistribution of population and lorry transport revolutionized social life.

Money wages in the hands of young people became a weapon of emancipation from the restraining influence of the older generations. The development of commerce and of a plantation economy among the natives themselves profoundly modified the concepts of wealth and of power. Power and prestige based on economics no longer coincided with the social prestige of tradition, based on seniority, age, alliances, caste, etc. Rank and power cease to coincide. Among the egalitarian societies such as the Fangs in Gabon and the Ba-Amba of Uganda, threats of witchcraft multiplied with the growth of material inequality. It should be added, however, that the new economic conditions which provided the basis for new differentiations were not always followed by changes in the old social and political structure. Thus in several tribes of Uganda, the introduction of the cotton and coffee crops at the beginning of the century created possibilities for monetary revenues, but the chief beneficiaries were precisely those who already occupied an important position in the traditional hierarchy.

Social results

European influence either indirectly or directly at once disturbed the traditional social balance, with a consequent weakening of the whole social structure. The most important element was the groups and connections based on kinship. These were seldom able to maintain their ancient strength, and inner tensions forced them apart. Research shows a tendency to dispersion and to a reduction in the size of these groups, once the source of economic, legal and spiritual activities; they began to lose one by one their various functions, while conflicts between generations grew up. These changes did not reach their climax till well on in the twentieth century. On the other hand, the economic, cultural and religious influence of the settlers led to new social distinctions, a new relationship between men and women, and also between young men and their elders. Social classes were in their infancy at the beginning of the twentieth century and the modern élites temporarily co-existed with traditional authorities before challenging them. Women were learning new ideas, which were to lead to changes in the ancient ways of life and in their inferior status. Thus the impact of colonization had revolutionary consequences in many different fields.[11]

Political organizations were soon in decline: some were completely suppressed or broken up; others were ignored by the new authorities and lingered on with diminished powers beside the colonial Government. With the loss of their independence—an essential condition of their functioning— political organizations could not operate in the traditional manner. They decayed rapidly and with them the solidarity of their tribes also weakened.

Some societies, however, gave proof of great political vitality; they were to some extent able to resist the process of disintegrating and managed, by transforming themselves, to adapt to new conditions without giving up either their values or their power structure. This was particularly evident in some of the societies located around the great lakes of East Africa, especially the kingdom of Buganda, the elaborateness of whose structure and organization had impressed even the first explorers. When the Europeans arrived, this kingdom seemed firmly established and was even undergoing full expansion. New social and economic conditions and the reforms which were introduced did not have the disintegrating effect they had elsewhere and the changes were partially absorbed by the existing society.

During the nineteenth century the progress of law and order in Oceania took place mainly in ways foreign to custom and apart from it. Changes in the Polynesian kingdoms reflect ideas on government derived from the Christian missions or European advisers. In Australia and New Zealand, the natives became subject to the State Laws. In other parts of Oceania, written law in the form of command was drawn up without consultation with native authorities. Attempts were, however, made to take account of customs in certain matters. At a conference in 1893 the Pacific Order commands all officials within its jurisdiction to respect local customs not contradictory to English legal practice. The same thing happened in New Caledonia, where the government consulted its traditional usage. Criminal codes based on Western principles were introduced in most territories, but differences between natives in civil cases were judged according to local custom. Thus change in legal concepts were slow. Confusion occurred, especially concerning the idea of *property*, where the Europeans were quite unable to grasp the local concepts.

In Africa the situation was similar; custom was not considered until very late, when anthropologists finally drew attention to the seriousness of the problem. But it was too late. The growth of towns also contributed to the problem: the coexistence of different tribes with at times contradictory customs led to a complete 'legal vacuum' before the new law could be introduced.

It would not be true, however, to take a completely black view: customary societies, particularly in black Africa, often recovered the initiative and adapted themselves. Social reconstruction and reorganization followed sooner or later according to conditions and the peoples themselves. This emerges very clearly during the twentieth century with the movement of nationalism. New associations of a modern type with professional and cultural aims attempted to establish grounds for solidarity and to organize leisure. These began to replace the ancient tribal and kinship groups which could not adapt themselves to the new conditions.[12] On this type of association the new political parties were to be based, in Nigeria and on the Ivory Coast.[13]

3. ARTISTIC IMPACT

Changes in the social, economic and religious framework with the introduction of new values and new objects killed the best native art. Europe 'discovered' African and Oceanian art at the beginning of the twentieth century when they were already in decline.

In states with an elaborate organization art was often linked with the royal families or aristocracies; more often it was linked with religion, or was itself a form of religious technique. A good example is the kingdom of Dahomey. Its artistic output was very varied: there were moulded wax statuettes cast in copper, wood-carvings, stools and statues plated with copper or silver; bas-reliefs in clay on the walls of the palaces; appliqué work on woven tapestries. All these works were mainly designed for an aristocracy, whom the colonists had deprived of their dues and privileges; the best works went to families who were guardians of artistic traditions. Conditions have now changed radically: craftsmen, deprived of patronage, now work for the local market and for export. They multiply their works which have the best sale, and their art becomes a formula.

With no thought of profit, some centres of African art have still preserved their vitality up to the present time—proving that artistic expression is one of the best signs of a healthy civilization. These centres include southern Nigeria and the country of Bamileke in the Cameroon. The Bamilekean art, although clearly homogeneous in concept, varies according to the material (wood, ivory, copper, terracotta, pearls, fibres or paint) and according to the purpose (architecture, furniture, sculpture or utensils). Its works have a double purpose: they exalt and support the power of the chiefs; they bear witness to a soil hard to master, which they dominate by tools and through rites. Up to the present day their art has remained in full force. The vitality of the chieftaincy and the power of popular feeling supported them. Another reason is that Bamilekean society with its diffused power was not so easily dominated as more highly centralized state organizations. Again by steady expansion of its economy it has to some extent overcome the handicap of its colonial status. Confident of maintaining its vitality, Bamileke did not accept complete defeat. From this example one can guess that the areas on the map of Africa showing most artistic vitality will also be those which resisted most successfully all colonizing pressures. In Oceania this may be illustrated with the example of New Zealand. The Maoris, who had fought for their independence for decades, tried to preserve their highly developed fine and ornamental art in sculpture, wood and stone carving, and in jewellery. This folk art was one of the consequential factors behind the revival of national culture in the 1920s and 1930s. It led to a rise of the native powers of the people and promoted the growth of national self-consciousness.

But even in Africa, which was less affected than Oceania, there are but few areas where the old arts survive. In general their decline followed that of the state or cult with which they were connected: they existed as a function of a certain social organization and certain beliefs to which they conformed. Art was seldom inventive or existing for its own sake—hence it was not capable of evolution. Either it disappeared abruptly, or it continued for a while to produce lifeless formulae. It had no power of resistance to the cultural and social upheavals of colonization.

The great religions which were introduced into the African Negro societies were also destructive of art: Islam drove away the representations of the deities and spirits previously worshipped; missionary Christianity could not help also being iconoclastic. The example was infectious: founders of the Negro 'dissenting' churches took up on their own account campaigns against fetishes. We can find an example in the history of a movement justly called *Ki-yoka* (from *Yoka*, to burn—the products of the sacred traditional art!)

which sprung up in Angola after 1870. Similar cases occurred at the end of the nineteenth century in South Africa and from the first twenty years of this century in central Africa. In their struggle against 'idols', the Negro leaders were as zealous as the first missionaries, some even justifying themselves by reference to Leviticus.

Since the ancient art was mainly inspired by ancient religions, this obliteration is hardly surprising. Traditional beliefs had to go underground and to use new and less vulnerable symbols. Christian art inspired by the missionaries has not yet produced much or good art. Christianity, in fact, has not yet perhaps had time to take deep root in Africa or Oceania. The quality of this art is so mediocre that the Africanist, M. Griaule, did not hesitate to describe it as 'a camouflaged disappearance' of creative art. And yet in certain parts of the country, such as the Congo, attempts to portray Christian teachings go back to the sixteenth and seventeenth centuries!

Signs of an artistic revival appear only in the mid-twentieth century—apart from 'exercises' in craft schools and works 'adapted' for the European market. The art of fresco is spreading—for instance among the Bamoons of the Cameroon. The need to cover large surfaces leads to a wealth of detail and ornamental motifs, while the exigencies of transposition to two dimensions result in drawing of extreme interest. The art of painting is becoming more widespread and is leading to the foundation of schools—e.g. that of Poto-Poto (the Congo) and of Katanga (Zaire), etc. A new type of sculpture has been invented in Dahomey, where an artist has begun to create masks free from the old conventions and dissociated from ritual purposes: his faces are strange, with tormented or deformed features. In Ghana, sculptors like Okm Ampofo and artists like Orsey Ochera are joining with their brothers in art in their creative quests. In the Congo region cement is used to create works of art associated with the renewal of the ancestor cults but inspired by European cemeteries. The appearance of this art from aiming at *permanence* occurs in connection with something on which the social life of the Congo and Zaire depends—that vital link between the lineage, its classic line, and the ancestors actually present in their tombs.

This growing art can only express the present state of Negro societies and their cultures; it follows their vicissitudes and bears the stamp of their weakness and their promise. Half a century had to pass before there were any sings of it at all.

4. RELIGIOUS DEVELOPMENTS

In Africa, as in Oceania, traditional animist religions functioned only within the limited framework of the ethnic group or tribe. They reflected minutely the living conditions, the social structure and the fundamental social values of a limited group. Their cults illustrated this very clearly—some being associated with tillage, others with ancestors, royal houses, etc.; religious and tribal loyalties were not easily distinguished. The concept of 'conversion' in this context was clearly meaningless; on the contrary, complete tolerance prevailed. It is significant that in some parts of Africa religious beliefs and practices, and also the ensemble of customs, should be both described by the same word, meaning the nation or ethnic group—so closely linked were the three, with the people participating directly in each of them.

Missionaries of the world religions had reached Africa well before the nineteenth century, but only a small number of the people were affected: now it was to be whole continents. One must consider separately the activity of the Christian missions and that of Islam, which was confined to Africa.

The arrival of European missions, whether before any other form of intervention, or at the same time as the growth of the slave or normal trades, or in the wake of colonization in Africa and Oceania, had the same significance in the eyes of the natives. The adoption of the new religion was at first partly due to a desire to share the wealth and power of the foreigners through the rituals on which they seemed to depend. The conquering civilizations was at one and the same time Christian and materially successful: the two were thought to be connected. In many cases, education was a powerful incentive in evangelism. Particularly in the early stages of colonization, the principal opportunity to obtain education was by attending a mission school.

In the colonial period proper this movement became intensified, since among the subjected nations one way to regain part of their lost power was to assimilate the foreign civilization, at least in its more formal aspects: this included religious conversions. When the missionaries attempted to make the conversion go deeper, to overthrow morals, customs and beliefs which they thought incompatible with Christianity, they began to threaten the entire social equilibrium. Sooner or later various defensive reactions occurred: sometimes a straightforward rejection of the new faith, sometimes the co-existence of different religious values or the growth of mixed religious movements. It was only in the twentieth century that Christianity was to take deep root in some areas so that the growth of a native church became assured.

Christianity in Oceania

During the mission period, religious rivalries sometimes led to political and military strife, with battles among the adherents. The new churches sometimes brought separated tribal groups into harmony, or, on the contrary, were unable to expand because of tribal differences and rivalry. No doubt many people accepted Christianity for other than religious reasons, particularly in the hope of political or economic advantages. The organization of the churches was a sort of 'model' which gave the natives an opportunity to practise modern methods in public affairs.

A number of converts, if not most of them, still continued for a time to believe in spirits, magic, witchcraft and the fundamentals of traditional religion. They showed, in fact, surprising flexibility and a great capacity for harmonizing different beliefs. Christianity became involved with the concept of power brought by Western colonists. The first native religious movements, later so numerous and widespread, can be interpreted both as an attempt to capture that power and as a reaction against it.

The ethical side of Christianity, particularly in regard to conjugal and sexual morality, could not be so easily assimilated; thus, in spite of the strict regulations of the churches, many Christian communities were extremely lax. But polygamy was successfully put down in the Christian areas, and many outward manifestations of Victorian morality were accepted by the natives. Even today the Christian communities of Oceania have kept some nineteenth-century habits which reflect the austerity and strictness of the early missionaries. As a consequence the native clergy are sometimes less tolerant than their European advisers.

It is important to remember that the Oceanians themselves sometimes became active and influential missionaries. Traces can still be found of Samoan missionaries who were abandoned in the Melanesian islands which were thought unfit for European settlement. They represent one of the most remarkable achievements of the Protestant missions. Many such men died in the service of their faith.

The great religions in Africa

In black Africa Christian missions were of long standing but no major results were achieved until the period of modern colonization. In the fifteenth century the Spanish and Portuguese kings attempted to develop trade with the Guinea coast and at the same time to convert its inhabitants. But the experiment was not successful. Missionary activity on the African coast was not effectively resumed until the seventeenth century, when the Capuchins of the Norman province settled in Senegal, Cape Verde and Sierre Leone in 1635. After ten years they were replaced by Spanish Capuchins from Andalusia. At about the same time Breton Capuchins settled further east. These seventeenth-century missions met with great difficulties and were finally forced to give up. However, their teaching spread and did not completely disappear; it led to the publication of the first Christian texts in the native tongue, including the *Doctrina Christiana*. During the eighteenth century the Jesuits also resumed their efforts along the Guinea coast.

In the Congo Basin Jesuits, Franciscans and Capuchin missionaries were active from the fifteenth until the eighteenth century. They were largely responsible for the foundation of the kingdom of Salvador (now Angola); they fostered a Christian art, examples of which were found in the nineteenth century at the time of colonial expansion; they were very tolerant of local adaptatons of European art, ritual, etc. A harmony of Christian elements with traditional religions occurred—against which the Catholic missions of the late nineteenth century reacted strongly, destroying as 'fetishes' much of the material evidence (crucifixes, statuettes, etc.) of the earlier conversions.

By the late nineteenth century there was a network of Christian missions stretching over a good deal of 'animist' Africa. The new religion was already strong in some areas where it had its martyrs among the natives: for example, the Uganda martyrs (1886), beatified in 1920, who were the heart of a great Catholic area around the Great Lakes, which today holds more than 1·5 million Catholics.

From its beginning in the first twenty years of the seventeenth century right up to the era of European colonization, Islam was mainly imposed by force. It entered Africa by two main routes: the Mediterranean plains and the east coast. An important change took place after pacification: the old defence barriers crumbled, and Islam penetrated slowly southward from the Sudan and from the east coast towards the interior. In the Sudan, relying partly on the modern prestige of commercial wealth, Islam's spread can be explained, at least in the beginning, in the same way as that of Christianity. During the nineteenth century it seldom demanded any change in the traditional order: orthodoxy and puritanism appeared much later. However, since it was brought to Africans by Africans and was unconnected with colonialism, it became a rallying ground for movements against the colonial order. Thus Islam was a consolidating as well as a destructive force. Most Negro Moslems remained attached to local Moslem brotherhoods and to local particularism. They showed no interest in any 'Wahabite' puritanism. They remained tolerant, which explains the progress of their faith in the twentieth century.

More complex reactions: native religions and messianic movements

The new religions had more than religious implications: they were weapons against the sense of insecurity and of cultural dispossession, against the policies of racial discrimination.

An interesting example of a reaction to the presence of the foreigner, and to foreign rule, can be found in the 'cargo cults' of the south-eastern Pacific. These had a dual origin, at once mythical and modern. Spirits of the dead (somehow identified with the white men) were thought to be the source of all wealth: ships and aeroplanes loaded with imports seemed also to come from the land of the dead. The natives thus felt that goods intended for them had been diverted by the colonists, and they cherished the hope that one day a ship laden with treasure would bring both the material goods and the secret of power so long awaited. On the basis of these expectations a cult of a messianic type developed, complete with ritual, prayers and holy possession. In some areas the belief in this golden age was so strong and the feeling of frustration vis-à-vis the Europeans so acute that the natives chose to break all contacts with them; they ate up all their food reserves, killed their pigs, threw away their European money and began to organize their lives independently. Prophets of the new cult frequently foretold an age of natural catastrophes which would wipe out whites and unco-operative natives alike. Measures taken to repress this movement only helped to strengthen it and to reinforce the violence of anti-European demonstrations. These reactions are, of course, ambivalent: on the one hand, they reveal racial consciousness, xenophobia and anti-Western feeling combined with an ostentatious return to traditional beliefs and customs. But on the other hand they express a desire for improvement and material wealth, and the need to reorganize the social structure. Whenever an able and convincing leader emerged, the more constructive side of the movement prevailed. This occurred among the Manus of the Admiralty Islands, north of New Guinea, where a man named Paliau succeeded in leading the villagers into a *New Way*. Margaret Mead relates this incident, which led to a true cultural mutation, in her book *New Lives for Old* (1956).

Similar developments emerged from many of the communities of Christianized black Africa, but these 'messianic' movements resulted in the rise of more or less ephemeral Negro churches. This apparently religious trend rapidly became counter-racial and acquired a political significance; it was in fact the basis of a crude but unmistakable *nationalism*. The Zulu revolt in South Africa in 1906 showed the link between Bantu prophecy and awakening nationalism.

The Negro churches, despite differences or attempts at variety, all have certain common characteristics. They are all religious sects which split off from the Christian missions (hence the title 'Separatist Churches' sometimes given them). They are organized in imitation of the missions, but centre on a prophet, whose teaching foretells the end of all foreign domination. Such groups have a great power of attraction, but appear essentially unstable as organized churches. Yet they provide a lasting satisfaction for the needs of the people because of their aims: churches rise and fall, but the messianic movement itself has lasted already for several decades. Its *raison d'être* is cultural and sociological: it is always either an attempt to adapt the message of Christian missions to the African context, or a renewal of the still active elements in traditional religions within the framework of Christianity. Its character is syncretic, since on the one hand it stands for a return to authentic black African values, while on the other it is a protest against the domination of the European minority. It has rediscovered the vigour of the Old Testament prophets.

Dr Sundkler, in his book *Bantu Prophets in South Africa*, distinguishes two types of Negro church, both widespread and representing the two different reactions in religious affairs. The *Ethiopian* church adheres strongly to the organization and teaching of the missions from which it seceded; it restricts contacts with traditional sources as far as possible. Its aim is to show that a Negro church does not depend for its vitality on the Europeans, and in its teaching it helps to educate Bantu nationalism. But it is associated with the traditional social structure and is rather aristocratic than popular in character. The *Zionist* church, more unstable and always threatened with secessions, arouses more fervour. It attracts by its very eclecticism and by the liberty it allows its adherents. The priest is more like a prophet; he prefers to return to African methods of praying with intense fervour. Religious practice here re-affirms the efficiency of the ancient methods of social healing, leading to the abandonment of all modern medicine. In a way this re-establishes an atmo-sphere of confidence, and with confidence comes the courage to oppose white ascendancy. In the heart of the Negro churches has grown up a confused religious nationalism—which develops into one of the most characteristic phenomena of the twentieth century: the general movement towards self-government and emancipation.[14]

NOTES TO CHAPTER XXVI

1. Candidate of Historical Sciences V. A. Subbotin writes: 'The author does not devote enough attention to describing the material and spiritual cultures. Subjects such as the development of agricultural implements and systems of agriculture, of handicrafts and architecture, music and literature, particularly folklore, are completely passed over. Among such sections are those on art (which for some reason deals to a large extent with modern art) and religion.'

   Candidate of Historical Sciences E. A. Tarvedova writes: 'Reading through this chapter, one doubts, first of all, whether it was necessary to prevent the history of Africa and Oceania together. In spite of the common characteristics of their historical processes, the two regions have their own individual histories, which should have been covered in greater detail. A major fault in this work is the lack of chronological sequence; as a result of the mixing-up of periods it is difficult to follow the main social, economic, cultural and political questions with which the author tries to deal.'

2. V. A. Subbotin writes: 'The stated aim of the author in the first section of the chapter is to illustrate "the spread of scientific civilization to Africa and Asia . . ."' But, in the first place, nineteenth-century colonialism brought with it war, the intensification of the slave trade (particularly after it had been officially prohibited) and the depopulation of many parts of the continent south of the Sahara. Naturally enough, such factors hindered the spread of civilization. Secondly, the author writes about civilization imported from Europe but fails to take into account the fact that the civilizations of nineteenth-century Africa was primarily a native one. As to foreign influences in tropical Africa in this period, the primary influences were those of the Maghreb, Egypt and the Middle East. Thirdly, there is much evidence—today's educational statistics in particular—to show that the great upsurge in civilization south of the Sahara took place in the middle of the twentieth century, i.e. in the years of transition to political independence. Thus independence, not the loss of independence, has been the major conditioning factor in the development of civilization.

3. V. A. Subbotin draws attention to the fact that the term intellectual is ambiguous, and 'Western contact' takes various forms; few Africans would be opposed to genuine scientific and cultural contacts between nations, but it should be remembered that for centuries 'Western contact' meant foreign domination.

4. V. A. Subbotin remarks: 'It is a well-known fact that in the first half of the nineteenth century, European slave trading increased sharply whilst, as a result of this competition, Arab slave trading declined. The impact of these factors on African cultures is shown by the example of the Congo Free State where Belgium, after squeezing out the Arabs, pursued a policy of virtual annihilation of the population.'

5. E. A. Tarvedova considers that it should be pointed out that some of the major African states—Dahomey, Ashanti and the states of the Tukulors, Mandingos, Wolofs among others—fought for national sovereignty and independence in the nineteenth century.

6. V. A. Subbotin points out that there were several Wolof states, so it is difficult to see what the author means.

7. Each of the states resisted the Europeans for a few years at least. The question of their 'racial or historical roots' is not something which can be decided at the stroke of a pen. If by historical roots the author means traditions of statehood, then it should be pointed out that they had existed for several centuries. The state of Samory had quite distinct 'racial roots', with its largely Mandingo population.

8. In the nineteenth century colonization to the African meant primarily suppression by force of arms which could lead only to the general brutalization, not modernization of society.

9. V. A. Subbotin stresses that the author is wrong in this assertion. The major revolts at the end of the nineteenth and beginning of the twentieth centuries, those of the Zulus, Matabele, Herero, Bakusu and Batetela, Marka, etc., were in protest against colonial oppression, though they were sometimes concealed behind a mask of religion.

10. E. A. Tarvedova emphasizes that in examining the part played by the slave trade in the history of tropical Africa the author fails to point out that it considerably reduced the ranks of the able-bodied African population. This was a very serious problem for Africa.

   V. A. Subbotin agrees wholeheartedly with this and comments that the author says nothing about the reduction of the population throughout the nineteenth century as a result of the slave trade and at the beginning of this century as a result of colonization. Nothing is mentioned about the great famines which undermined the health of the population, favouring the spread of sleeping sickness, tuberculosis, etc. Furthermore, the author writes that 'pacification and health measures led to an increase in population' and as an example cites only French Guinea in the mid-twentieth century.

11. V. A. Subbotin remarks that the author speaks of the 'revolutionary' significance of colonization, but fails to back up his words with any concrete facts. Europeans first appeared in tropical Africa in the fifteenth century. Five centuries of intercourse is too long a period for one to be able to speak about revolution, which signifies radical changes occurring in a relatively short space of time. Moreover, in the fifteenth to nineteenth centuries, whilst elsewhere there was a tendency to increase international cultural contacts, the development of Africa was slow, and extremely painful for her population.

12. E. A. Tarvedova notes that one of the particular features of land relationships in tropical Africa was the existence of communal landownership. Even in the pre-colonial period, feudal class relationships and feudal state landownership had grown up in some countries of tropical Africa. Under the colonial régime, the ruling classes of the existing states and principalities maintained their hold over the land and the chiefs of some tribes and the elders of certain clans were invested with similar powers. This promoted the process of class differentiation in Africa. The feudal and tribal aristocracy provided the social bulwarks of colonialism. Professor Tarvedova feels, in addition, that it should be pointed out that in the mid-nineteenth century the activities of Christian missionaries in Africa were stepped up as a prelude to imperialist aggression. The methods employed to impose Christianity by force aroused opposition from the native population.

13. V. A. Subbotin writes: 'The author asserts that the political parties of Nigeria and the Ivory Coast are not based on tribal and kinship groups. But, in the first place, discussion of the modern political parties of Africa is outside the chronological frame of reference of this chapter and would better be left out. Secondly, the events of 1966 in Nigeria showed a struggle caused by the alienation of different groups involving parties representing those groups. Thirdly, in the Ivory Coast, although there is one-party rule, the party itself contains cells based mainly on an ethnic principle.'

   Cf. A. R. Zolberg, 'Effets de la structure d'un parti politique sur l'intégration nationale', Cahiers d'études africaines, no. 3 (1960).

14. E. A. Tarvedova emphasizes that there is not a special section devoted to the part played by Islam in the history of tropical Africa. It is a well-known fact that while the imperialist powers were grabbing and dismembering Africa, Islam continued to spread among the local populations. The colonial authorities, despite their different forms and methods of administration, all tried by means of various concessions and incentives to win over the local feudal rulers, sheikhs, ulemas and heads of the religious orders of dervishes. In the eighteenth and nineteenth centuries and the beginning of the twentieth, the religious orders and brotherhoods (Qadiriya, Tidjaniya) played a big part in spreading Islam in Africa. The leaders of the Dervish orders exploited the mass of the Moslem believers.

The Moslem sheikhs and the heads of the zawiyas and ribats, which were the centres of dervish activities and frequently also the political and administrative centres of the African countries, possessed vast estates. They had enormous influence in the economic and political life of the Moslem countries of Africa.

CHAPTER XXVII

THE EVOLUTION OF CHINA

I. CONSERVATIVE TENDENCIES AND CHANGING TRENDS

The imperial institutions and their development

THE Ch'ing dynasty, last of China, was in power throughout the period from 1775 to 1905. In contrast to the national dynasties (Han, T'ang, Ming) and to those which 'infiltrated' into the country, it was a foreign rule, imposed by conquest. The Manchus, who were descended from the Ju-chen, were by no means complete barbarians. They had a long experience of Chinese civilization, their own national structure was partly nomadic and partly sedentary and agricultural, and they had been waiting for a favourable opportunity to invade the Empire. They came into it with the unconcealed desire to become Chinese, and set themselves to bring about a symbiosis with the conquered nation, for which the circumstances were propitious. They were so much so, that before long the dynasty felt compelled to devise methods of protecting its tribal and feudal-military structure from the danger of being swamped by Chinese bureaucracy. In order to wrest control from the bureaucrats and keep them in a subordinate position, a dual system was set up, with two official languages, even for scientific translations. And the central Chinese Government at Peking was counterbalanced by the eight banners and six ministries of the Manchu Government, which functioned at Mukden until 1907.

Intermarriage was forbidden. The Manchu women were not allowed to bind their feet in the Chinese manner. All Chinese were compelled, as a sign of submission, to wear Manchu dress and grow pigtails.

The Manchu nobility and the Chinese nobles also formed two separate groups. The Chinese system of nobility went by award, as a recognition of services rendered in the military or civil sphere; each title conferred carried a pension and a grant of land. Titles were not always hereditary, and even if they were it was only for two or three generations. So the Chinese nobles did not form an organized class, with a definite role in political or social life. Manchu titles, however, were hereditary, the nobility being composed of all the male descendants of the dynasty, who constituted the imperial clan. In 1830 there were about 700 of them, divided into twelve 'ranks'. They received free housing and drew pensions, but prior to 1840 they held no important posts. Their titles passed to their descendants, but with a gradual decline in rank.

The whole imperial structure rested on the dynasty. Apart from the Emperor, the State was nothing. Yet the Emperor governed as little as possible, the legislature never having been able to impose the concepts of a strong, authoritative government. The ability to dispense with government seems odd in a country whose writers had a passion for the abstract discussion of constitutional problems. The Government comprised the following bodies:

The Grand Secretariat. This had been very important during the Ming period, but was now reduced to keeping the governmental records, assembling information from all parts of the Empire, and dispatching current business.

The Grand Council, set up in 1729. This consisted of from 4 to 10 members, half of whom were Chinese and half Manchu, assisted by a secretariat (in the middle of the nineteenth century there were 32 secretaries) which acted as a 'nursery' for the senior ranks of the government service; the most absolute secrecy was enjoined upon its members.

The members of the Grand Council, who were the chairmen or vice-chairmen of ministries, considered all important political, financial and military questions. They drafted edicts and appointed civil servants. But they had a purely advisory function, the Emperor being free to act against their advice or to deal personally with matters on which he did not choose to consult them.

The Ministries. They were directly responsible to the Emperor and were headed by two chairmen and two vice-chairmen, one Manchu and the other Chinese. In 1840 there were six of them—the Civil Ministry (which appointed civil servants), the Finance Ministry, the War Ministry, the Ministry of Religious Worship and Examinations, and the Ministry of Public Works.

Under the Ministry of Religious Worship (or Rites) there was the Tribunal of Mathematics, in charge of the calendar and of music; this was a State institution which had its own office until 1909.

The Censorship. This was an office with a staff of 98, half Chinese and half Manchu; two of its members bore the title of 'General Censors'. This office was responsible for reporting offences committed by princes, ministers, and civil servants in general. Only the Emperor and the members of the Grand Council were free from this supervision, though the censors could only denounce offenders and were not entitled to impose penalties. A censor could not be accused, even for making untrue allegations, unless he acted from personal enmity. Only about thirty instances of serious punishment of censors are known to have occurred between 1667 and 1840. Some of these were brave men, whose names deserve to be remembered; among these were Ts'ien Fung (1740–95) and Wu K'o-tu (1812–79).

These institutions are known thanks to Wang Huei-tsu (1731–1807), author of the *Tso-che yo-yen* (1785) and the *Hiue-che yi-shou* (1793), two basic works used as official guides by the civil servants until 1912.

The system was considerably altered during the second half of the nineteenth century. After the Peking Convention (1860), the exceptional circumstances resulted in the control of the Grand Council by four general assistants. In the following year, after the death of Emperor Hien-Fung, there came a regency, exercised jointly by the Empress-Mother, Huang T'ai-heu and the Empress Tseu-hi (1835–1908), with eight co-regents or 'imperial assistants in national affairs'. In actual fact, Tseu-hi dominated the political scene from 1860 to 1908, first as the concubine of Wen-tsung and then as Dowager Empress. For the last 37 years of her life she had virtually unlimited power.

Until 1860 there was no Department of Foreign Affairs and there were no embassies. Like all political leaders, whatever their country, the Ch'ing rulers dreamt of a general organization within the compass of which all men could pursue the same ideals. But they went further by taking this philosophical concept as the foundation of their Government, in the firm conviction that the Middle Empire was a universal empire, outside which were only Barbarians (land-dwelling or seafaring) and tributary peoples who were dealt with by a Bureau of Vassal States (Li-fan yuan).

In 1818 these tributary states included Korea, the Liu-hieu Islands, Vietnam, Siam, the Philippines, Burma, Portugal, Italy and England.

Sovereigns of countries bordering on China received from the Emperor their State seal, their investiture and their calendar. In exchange they sent him presents which were offered for his acceptance in the Hall of Vassals by delegates who were required to make the kowtow, the Chinese equivalent of the Irano-Byzantine proskynesis.

This etiquette, which also applied to Western visitors, was enforced by a special body of officials who received foreign delegates with the greatest hospitality, watched over them with the greatest vigilance and took leave of them with the greatest courtesy, never allowing them to regard themselves as real ambassadors, never leading them to hope for more than a spectacular exchange of presents and credentials. (Pl. 83a).

Russia was the only state to have secured (by the Treaty of Kiakhta, 1727) the right to maintain a permanent representative at Peking and to trade regularly with China.

It was in order to regularize relations with the Western Powers that, at the suggestion of Prince Kung (Yi-sin, 1832–98), the Li-fan yuan (Bureau of Vassal States) was closed down and replaced by a bureau responsible for dealings with foreign countries in general (the Tsung-li kuo she-wu ya-men, 1861, usually abbreviated to Tsung-li ya-men.) This was managed by Prince Kung himself, the Grand Secretary Kuei-liang (1785–1862) and the Vice-Minister for Revenue, Wen-Hiang (1818–76). Not until 1901 was the Tsung-li ya-men transformed into the Ministry of Foreign Affairs (Wai-wu pu).

It was only in 1860 that foreign ambassadors were first allowed to live at Peking, (Pl. 84), and they had to wait for their first audience (at which the kowtow was symbolically abolished) until 29 June 1873. It was not until 12 November 1894 that they were admitted into the Forbidden City.

China's representation in foreign countries gave rise to many psychological and technical problems. As a stopgap, foreigners were employed for the purpose. Afterwards, in 1862, a school with foreign professors was opened to train diplomats. This was called T'ung-wen kuan. At first the students, who numbered about a hundred, were all Manchus; later, half were Manchu and half Chinese.

In connection with the creation of diplomatic services, mention should be made of the appointment of the San-k'ow t'ong-shang ta-ch'en, or Minister superintending Trade in the Three Ports. These were the northern ports, Tientsin, Chefu and Niow-chuang, which were opened to trade in 1858 and 1860. The Wu-k'ow t'ung-shang ta-ch'en was the Minister superintending trade in the five southern ports (Canton, Foochow, Amoy, Ning-po and Shanghai), which were opened after the treaty of Nanking (1842). There was also a Naval Department; a Bureau of Agriculture, Labour and Commerce was likewise set up in 1898, but did not outlast the hundred days of the reforms.

The provincial administration differed according to whether the inner or outer provinces were concerned. In the *inner provinces* the successive administrative units were the district, the department, the Sub-Prefecture, the Prefecture and the circle. The head of a district filled the functions of magistrate, head of police, judge of first instance in the civil and criminal courts, tax-collector, curator of the cadastre, and director of public works. Like all minor civil servants his salary—fixed in the seventeenth century—was extremely low. In order to pay his subordinates and secretaries he was compelled to levy taxes on the local people, who did not resent this if it was kept within reasonable bounds.

All civil and military powers were vested in the Governor. But his assistants (the Treasurer, the Provincial Judge and the Commissioner for Education) were appointed by the central government, to which they remained directly responsible. The governor was responsible to the Viceroy, whose authority extended over a group of two or three provinces. In 1905 there were 11 Governors and 8 Viceroys. They were appointed for three-year periods, and fairly often transferred from one province to another. The administration played little part in the affairs of the village communities or of the craftsmen's and tradesmen's guilds. Many civil cases never came before the courts, and they did not concern themselves with criminal cases unless a complaint was lodged with them. It should be noted that although the Empire had extended into central Asia as long ago as the Han period, ethnical minorities (*Miao-tseu*) still survived in the reign of K'ien Lung, living in the mountain valleys of southern China and refusing to recognize the authority of Peking. The attempt to conquer them had been conducted as though the aim were their complete extermination. The pacification thus imposed could not be permanent, and very vigorous insurrections broke out in the nineteenth century.

The *outer provinces*, or confines of China (Manchuria, Mongolia, Taiwan (Formosa) and Sinkiang (Chinese Turkestan) were recent acquisitions, conquered during the campaigns of K'ang Hi and K'ien Lung. They were administered by the 'Office for the Frontier Regions', a department of the central Government. This employed 150 officials, among whom Chinese were in the minority. Manchuria was divided into three provinces, only the most northerly of which was classified as a frontier region. In Mongolia, the Emperor was represented by a Commissioner-General with his headquarters at Urga. In Tibet political power was exercised, and the lamas protected in their religious worship, by two High Commissioners supported by a small army whose effectives fluctuated considerably (from 500 to 4,500 men). Chinese Turkestan belonged to what the Han called the western regions (*Si-yu*), centred on Sinkiang. It was inhabited by 13 different nationalities, including 74 per cent of Moslem Uighurs, and its pacification proved extremely difficult.

The recruitment of officials followed the traditional and specifically Chinese method of literary competitions, or was effected by the choice or purchase of posts.

Selection by competitive examination continued until 1905, the antiquated range of subjects remaining unchanged until 1901. If successful, a candidate for the literary examination (*Tsin-she*), the doctorate (*kiu-jen*) or the examination for selected provincial students (*kung-sheng*) had prospects of a civil service post, but no certainty. Before being definitely accepted, he had to take further examinations. Candidates who were successful in the literary examination—except the first three, who were appointed *ipso facto*—had to take a second examination, in the presence of the Emperor (*Chow-kow*). This gave admission to the *Han-lin yuan* (Academy), to the post of *Nei-ko chung-shu* (Secretary of the Imperial Council) and to such provincial posts as *Chen-hien* (Assistant Prefect) and *Fu-kyow-sheu* (Assistant Professor in the Prefecture Schools).

There were two ways of awarding a post in return for a bribe: by admitting to the public service a candidate who had failed the normal competitive examinations; by allowing an official to by-pass the ordinary cycle of promotion and 'buy' his way up to a higher post.

In 1838, the price ranged from 1,000 taels for a subordinate post to 15,000 taels for a senior one. In other words, it represented several years' salary. The official thus appointed was obliged to recoup himself for the down-payments he had made by taxing the population under his authority—the well-known method of the 'squeeze'.

In accordance with the concept of responsibility, to which we shall refer more fully in discussing the legal system, senior civil and military officials were often reduced in rank and sometimes, though more seldom, imprisoned, banished or executed. Suicide was quite frequent, either in unquestioning obedience to a suggestion from the higher authorities, or because it was the only resort for a leader who had forfeited the Emperor's confidence or failed to carry out the task allotted to him. But the dignitaries of the Kiang-su and provinces persistently demanded a parliament—an early illustration of the democratic views and desire for reform displayed by the feudal landowners, who wished to become national capitalists (Chien Po-chan).

Internal loans having invariably proved unsuccessful (the Hupu Bank), the imperial Government had no means of filling its coffers except through taxes. These were as follows:

The *property tax*, which accounted for 60 per cent of income from taxation. Its level was fixed in 1713 by a decree intended to tie the rate of taxation to the 'value', viz. the annual output, of the soil. This tax, which was applied to agricultural land and to real estate, was based until the revolution upon the rate established and the land-map (cadastre). Between 1901 and 1904 this tax brought in an estimated 450 million taels (about £150 million); but less than a quarter of the money actually went into the Treasury.

The *tribute*, or *tithe*, which accounted for 15 per cent of income from taxation. This took the form of contributions in kind (cereals, copper, furs, tea, silk, etc.) sent to Peking from the different provinces. They formed a large proportion of the traffic along the Grand Canal. The tribute was entrusted for conveyance to special officials, who sometimes had to cope with considerable difficulties. Several of them have left accounts of their experiences.

The salt-tax (*gabelle*) constituted 5 per cent of the official income from taxation. Ever since the salt-marshes were nationalized, under the Han dynasty, salt had been a lucrative State monopoly. Owing to the importance of this tax, technical treatises on the running of salt-mines and the various regulations applying to them were written and have come down to us. In one of these technical treatises, Ting Pao-chen (1820–86), Governor-General of Szechwan, notes that the salt-farmers were paying dues ten times higher than the price of the salt retailed by the Government. He abolished this supertax. By 1850 the monopoly was a thing of the past in the majority of provinces.

In 1853, La Yi Sien, a government official and leader of the militia, imposed a new tax (*Li-kin*). This was an *ad valorem* tax on goods in transit in the interior of the Empire. It was justified by the need to equip local militia to put down the Tai-king rebellion. With the approval of the central Government, the provincial authorities levied this tax and dealt with the product as they chose. From 1855 to 1864, it is said to have produced 100 million taels throughout the Empire. But its economic consequences were disastrous, for the *Li-kin* formed, as it were, a succession of dykes and locks cutting off the interior of the Empire from the seaports by means of dues which did great harm to trade. Foreigners protested against them for a long time, but then came to admit their existence, regarding them as security for the loans they themselves were making to China. After the Tai-ping war, the network of *Li-kin* was steadily tightened. Yuan Ch'ang (1846–1900) called for reforms, and more especially for the adjustment of the *Li-kin* to economic fluctuations. The private interests thus threatened turned against him, and he was assassinated by the Boxers.

Maritime customs duties (which up to 1842 were meagre) were reorganized by Sir Robert Hart and by 1905 they had become the most profitable tax (35 million taels, as against 25 million from the property-tax).

Various *other taxes*, such as the conveyancing fees payable when a property was sold meant a lawful 'cut' of between $\frac{1}{2}$ and 1 per cent, not to mention the fraudulent devices of accountancy.

Thus the system made no provision for the general budget, a forecast attempting to strike a balance between the anticipated income from taxation and the expenditure to be undertaken by the State. However, until 1840 receipts and expenses seem to have been balanced without difficulty by rule-of-thumb methods. From 1880 onwards, a budget deficit was the regular thing. Parker estimates the deficit for 1910 at over 30 million taels.

The division between East and West is nowhere more apparent than in the science and techniques of law. This is due to the fact that although in ancient times China had a school of lawgivers and one of anti-Confucianist philosophies, the attempt to settle disputes by applying the law had always been frustrated throughout the history of Chinese thought, by a paternalistic concept of justice. Thus, the theory of the existence of a natural order, to which human order must undeviatingly conform, survived unquestioned until the nineteenth century. Marcel Granet has often dealt with this point, describing the essential function of the ruler or the State as that of preserving this harmony between heaven and earth. The ruler was responsible for maintaining order throughout the world, he held a mission from heaven (*T'ien-ming*) and must thus be called to account whenever that order was disturbed, not for his technical errors, but for moral ones. A sovereign who proved incapable must be corrupt, and to rebel against him was therefore lawful.

According to classical theory, a succession of heavy rains proclaimed the sovereign to be unjust; prolonged drought was a sign of errors on his part; extreme cold, of his lack of consideration; and violent winds, of his apathy. Practical legislation was accepted only in so far as it conformed to customs which were themselves deemed to be consistent with natural law. The Government's orders were obeyed because they satisfied the public sense of what was correct, gave an impression of propriety, equity and suitability (*jen-yi*)—and only in so far as they did so.

Barbarians and uncultivated persons (*shu-jen*), being incapable of grasping the natural law, could be governed solely by means of the penalties laid down in the written legislation, which did not apply to the nobility (*ta-fu*). For the latter, tradition and precepts (*li*) were far more important than the written law (*fa*). To invoke one's 'rights' as a reason for contravening custom, or *quod decet*, even if one were indeed in the right, would be to alienate public sympathy and, so to speak, make unfair use of one's advantages. Thus, the refinement of the art of living of the *Kiun tse* was to feign unawareness of such advantages, to show moderation and a sense of equity. By thus appearing to give way on certain points where he might have gained the advantage, the nobleman who scrupulously obeyed the rules of the game was putting himself in a position where he could carry the day on other points without laying himself open to criticism.

The West is aware of rights and duties to which everyone is equally entitled to lay claim, whereas the Far East is concerned with the duties each individual must fulfil. As a result, the code reveals a constant confusion between law and ethics and a belief—which indeed is very noble—in the superiority of ethics and the natural law (*li*) over practical legislation (*fa*).

Human conduct was judged not so much by its compliance with what the law allowed or prohibited, as by the intrinsic moral value of what was done.

The contrast between the concept of *li* (prescribed conduct) and *fa* (*li* always takes precedence over *fa*) is brought out strongly by the comparatively harsh penalties inflicted on the victims of the literary inquisition set up by the Ch'in. Take, for example, the case of Wang Si-heu (1713–77), author of the dictionary entitled *Tse-kwan* (1775). He criticized the great imperial dictionary, *K'anghi tse-tien*, and gave the personal names of Confucius and the earliest Ch'in emperors (which were taboo). He was executed on 27 December 1777, twenty-one members of his family were arrested, and the Governor of his native province (Kiangsi) was dismissed. Another example of literary censorship is the case of the poet Syu Shu-K'wei; his body and that of his printer were exhumed and dismembered for insults to the dynasty (1779).

Music, laws and rewards (*shang*) were aimed at uniting the hearts of the people—who, if they departed from the prescribed conduct, were immediately punished (*ch'u-li ju-hing*).

Law was simply a means of ensuring ethical behaviour by the individual, the family and the nation. Its role was to oil the wheels of the State machinery by perfecting the individuals (*Sieu-shen*, to cultivate one's person) and tightening social bonds. The basic moral principles were not founded on religious precepts, but the legislators, with their strong ethical sense, managed to surround them with an almost religious aura by basing them on the incontrovertible tenets of filial piety and respect. Everyone was expected to be aware, in all circumstances, of what was his correct behaviour towards his inferiors, equals and superiors, and what duties he owed them. This system, with its profound practical understanding of human nature, its high ideals and its elastic yet far-reaching technical ramifications, succeeded with a minimum of expenditure in maintaining for centuries a very acceptable social system among a huge population, and spread throughout Asia.

According to Huang Chung-hi (1610–95), law should not consist in a host of rules intended to protect the ruler's personal property. To mistrust the man one employs, to have him spied upon by another man, to dread the effects of a law after promulgating it, to issue another to corroborate the first, and to call all this *fa*, is absurd. Everything under the sun is *res publica*, not the private property of the monarch. Thus, so far as the monarch is concerned, the law requires him to distribute land, to have it cultivated in order to feed and clothe his people, to open schools at which they can be taught, to institute marriage so as to prevent unlawful unions, to maintain a strong army with which to discourage unrest—in short, to regulate the lives of all his subjects and protect the common property.

Private law comprised a mere handful of insignificant precepts. The great majority of legal principles related solely to public (penal and administrative) law. The essential principles of public law were the authority of the sovereign, the responsibility of the notables, each according to his rank, and the collective responsibility of the social institutions. This objective attitude is inconsistent with the subjective concept of the offence, to which the West clings. But it inculcates a sense of danger that compels all of those who may one day be held responsible to be clearly aware of the part they are expected to play in the vast mechanism set up to ensure compliance with the order of the universe.

However, the principle of legitimate authority asserted by the Ch'ing dynasty met with opposition from the very first. Countless uprisings invoked its unlawfulness as their justification.

The law was not laid down in any jurisprudence or written doctrine, it recognized no basic concepts. It was essentially the expression of a practical, living and specific system of ethics, secular in origin. The Western lawgiver tries to draw up a general precept, applicable to the greatest possible number of possible events, which shall be clear both to the judge and to the accused—in short, an adaptable intellectual instrument, a model rigid enough to provide a recognizable comparison with the facts of a specific, limited situation and to offer what both parties will see as an adequate solution for the problem confronting them. When a similar but different case presents itself, or when the same case occurs but is placed in a different light by different attendant circumstances, a fresh solution will be found and added to the first. The Western mind must have its abstract principles, its generalizations. The Chinese mind is reluctant to make deductions even from the principles which had to be laid down in drafting a code of laws.

Throughout the Ch'ing dynasty, and even subsequently, the rulers of China invariably denied the intrinsic value of law, both for domestic and for international purposes, since they considered that *li* should always take precedence over *fa*—that a moral duty, properly fulfilled, had a much greater social effectiveness than a legislative text, with its host of irritating provisions. The law was simply a model on which the individual was expected to shape himself as exactly as possible, without being required to conform to it in all respects.

As under the Sung dynasty, there were no schools of law, no formal courses. Officials with some experience of judicial procedure could enter the Ministry of Justice and there, in their spare time, study the elements of jurisprudence, with its two precepts—simplicity, according to the system of Shensi; precision, according to that of Hunan. Their training was largely practical, and took the form of studying the legal files (*ho-k'ao*). These officials, the *Hing-pu chushe* (second-class legal writers) were eligible for appointment as judges at the autumn assizes, or might become ministers or deputy ministers. Such was the training given to Shen Kia-pen (1840–1913), one of the dynasty's most distinguished men of law, who stood at the crossroads between the old concepts and those that the new school represented. Shen Kia-pen tried to separate the judiciary from the administration, to divide civil from criminal cases, and to set up a bureau for the codification of the law, of which he was chairman. Not until 1906 did the Hing-pu (Ministry of Punishments) become a genuine Sze-fa pu (Ministry of Justice). China was acquainted with Western law by the end of the nineteenth century. Tung Syun (1807–92) translated Wheaton's *Elements of International Law* under the title of *Wan-kwo kung-fa* and published the book in 1864.

The moral and paternalistic character of the judicial system simplified legal proceedings and meant that counsel was out of the question. Offenders were divided into various categories, such as the *pa-yi*. According to the *pa-yi* (Eight Deliberations), eight categories of persons had the privilege of being dispensed from trial except by virtue of a special deliberation (*yi*) of the Emperor. These included the Emperor's relatives, former servants of the imperial family, various eminent civil or military figures, and certain senior officials and descendants of former dynasties; subordinate officials, holders of academic degrees and doctors might also lay claim to special privileges. But while the idea of rank had at least a minor importance, the racial concept seems to have been unknown to Chinese thought. In principle, the barbarians, those 'outside civilization', became the Emperor's subjects once they accepted his rule, and any offences they committed were to be tried by the ordinary laws. The letter of the Ch'ing code and the code of international law attribute great importance to territorial sovereignty, but this was not the spirit of the dynasty. Even when the code declares that foreigners entering China must submit to the country's laws, it is proclaiming a duty incumbent upon them and in which they have fallen short, rather than asserting the Emperor's right to enforce his criminal code upon all his subjects. It is thus natural for every individual to be governed by his own laws in all respects. And in China, for the reasons already given, anything that conformed to natural order was invariably accepted, in the long run, by the legal system. Consequently, barbarian offenders were judged in the light of their own customs.

All punishments had a penal character and were extremely severe, but intended chiefly for purposes of intimidation. Prison was at no time included among the 'five punishments'. Very little use was made of it as an actual penalty (perpetual banishment, banishment for a fixed period, or execution); it was principally a means of causing an accused person to regret that he had offended against the natural order and failed to reach an amicable settlement. It was also a method of keeping the plantiff, the defendant and the witnesses at the disposal of the courts. Prisoners who fell victim to justice in its arbitrary form (*ch'ai-yu*) had a very hard lot, unless they could 'buy' their gaolers. The 'Chinese tortures' do not seem to have been much crueller than those inflicted by all ancient and medieval civilizations. The penalty of *Ling-che* (drawing and quartering the living victim) appears to have been infrequently imposed, and there were various means of waiving or commuting it.

Punishment was reserved for cases where authority had been flouted and the teachings of morality ignored, and the great principle of 'Punish in order that there may be no further need to punish (*p'i-yi che-p'i*)' was always borne in mind.

Among the causes of the Tai-ping uprising, an official report includes the following: the price of silver is too high and it is difficult to pay the taxes; there are too many robbers and bandits, and it is difficult for honest men to live in peace and quiet; imprisonment without motive is not unusual, and it is difficult to secure justice.

The *Manchu or dynastic army* (the Troop of the 8 Banners, or *k'i*) was exclusively composed of Manchurians, Mongols and pro-Manchurian Chinese. After its conquest of China, the Manchu dynasty with all its partisans remained as it were 'encamped' in the country.

The *Chinese army* (Troops of the Green Standard) was not a national army, but a provincial militia under the command of the Governor. In principle, officers were recruited by examination, but there was a dearth of candidates, owing to the Chinese contempt for the military calling. Apart from the highest ranks, usually held by the Tartar princes and by the Viceroys who combined their administrative and military functions, all the officers were literary men who had passed examinations but had not been regarded as suitable for the civil service posts that were the great ambition of candidates for the mandarinate.

Ordinary soldiers were recruited for 5 years, but sometimes remained in the army until the age of 60. In theory, the strength was between a million and 600,000 men, distributed as follows: Troops of the Green Standard, which consisted almost exclusively of Chinese, Divisions of the Home Guard, War divisions (the pick of the 'Green Standard') in the nature of 'commandos', the 'Braves' (*Yung*) who were volunteers and bore the word *Yong*—bravery, courage—embroidered on the back of their jerkins.

Modernization of the army began as early as the Tai-ping period, when Chinese troops came under the command of Western officers such as the English General Gordon (1833–85). In Peking the garrison became the first Chinese army corps to receive European arms and equipment. The *Ting-wu kyum* corps was organized in 1894 by Hu Yu-fen (d. 1906) with the help of German instructors. It comprised 7,000 men, and an Officers' Training College was attached to it. (Pl. 86b).

The Chinese navy was never an independent service. It was the Governors of the maritime province who, needing to rid the coasts of pirates, were obliged to fit out warships and thus become admirals. One of the most celebrated of them was Li Ch'ung-keng (1750–1808), who was killed by a shot while at sea. He had led expeditions against the pirates of North Vietnam and

Fukien under difficult conditions, for his vessels were technically inferior to those of his adversaries. In 1879 the Chinese fleet had land bases armed with 400 Krupp guns. It possessed important arsenals at Foochow, Shanghai, Tientsin, Canton and elsewhere, where torpedo-boats could be built.

This military organization was costly and had its short-comings, as the critics were well aware. But if the leaders were reprehensible, the courage of the professional soldiers was often extraordinary. It should also be noted that total war was never the aim of Chinese military art. It was closely bound up with geomancy and cosmology—for instance, during the eclipse of 1858, which could be observed from Shanghai, archers were ordered to shoot their arrows at the dragon which was thought to be devouring the moon. The lettered classes considered war to be a necessary evil and one of mankind's more degrading obligations. Patriotism alone induced some of them, such as Cheng Kovo-fan, to take up a profession they regarded as dishonouring to them. Thus war, to these men, was a *prescribed action*, aimed at achieving success with a minimum loss of life. We need only read the account of the fall of Canton (1836) or the battle of Tientsin (1857) to see how the Chinese leaders were constantly preoccupied with 'etiquette' and 'protocol', the effect of which was to cut down the military phase of the conflict as far as possible and prolong the phase of negotiation. To their overwhelming astonishment, their adversaries did not understand this attitude, and as a result the Governor of Canton died in captivity in Bengal.

Revolutionary trends

Despite the international prestige acquired by Kang-hi and Kien-lung in the course of their reigns, the 'fusion' between the Manchu conquerors and the defeated Chinese was never by any means complete, even less in the south than in the north. The consequence of a succession of mediocre rulers, coupled with the European penetration, was the outbreak of numerous and spectacular rebellions—peasant uprisings, movements fomented by secret societies, insurrection by ethnical minorities, or acts of banditry. We shall mention only the most important of these, some of which were extensive enough to set up independent governments, confronting the imperial institutions with consistent systems that have their place in history.

Between 1820 and 1850 there were very frequent revolts by ethnical minorities, isolated actions by secret societies, outbreaks of banditry, and peasant revolts caused by poverty and high taxation.

Apart from the Tai-ping revolution, the imperial government had to deal with insurrections, the repercussions of earlier outbreaks, which took place between 1852 and 1864. (These have not yet been fully studied, but they may be divided into the following categories: the Nyen-kyun ('Torch bearers') movement, in the provinces of Honan and Shantung, which had been devastated by the flooding of the Hoang Ho (1853–61); incursions by pirates along the coasts; great Moslem rebellion in the south-west; insurrections by ethnical minorities in Hainan, on Formosa and in the south-west; insurrection fomented by the secret societies (Triands) in the ports open to European trade (Canton, Foochow, Amoy and Shanghai). The occupation of Shanghai lasted 18 months, from 1853 to 1855. Even in the 18 provinces (with the exception of Shansi and Kansu), the imperial governmental machinery was operating only in the imperial citadels in 1854 and 1855. Though no new administration had actually been set up, the Manchu Government had lost control of the provinces.

The Tai-ping rebellion was a social and political movement similar to others in the history of nineteenth-century Asia. Its characteristics are much less familiar than its chronology. It had a very broad political basis, being in the nature of a national front, supported by the secret societies and the legitimists among the lettered classes, who were traditionally opposed to the Manchus. At the outset, the ethnical minorities (Miao, Lolo, Hakka) and the anti-Western section of opinion rubbed shoulders in it, for though they disagreed on many points they were united by their approval of the slogan *Fan-Ch-ing fu-Ming* (Overthrow the Ch'ings and restore the Mings). (Pl. 86a). Typical features included the presence among the rebels of an alleged descendant of the Mings, and the banning of the pigtail (*Chang-mao-tse*, hostile to long hair).

It had also a very important social basis. It began as an *agrarian* movement, born of the agricultural crisis which, as we have already shown, was aggravated by a succession of floods and natural disasters that had occurred shortly before the revolution. The rural nucleus was in Kwang-si, and around it there clustered certain historical and ethnical minorities, together with deserters from the imperial army, pirates whose ships had been destroyed by the English fleet, beggars and outlaws.

Under the agrarian and popular uprising and the national anti-Manchu movement there ran the theme of a religious movement, partly Christian in its ideology. This gave a modernistic, anti-Confucianist and nonconformist aspect to the entire procedure, with the result that the traditional nationalists ultimately broke away from the Tai-pings.

The constructive aims of the Tai-ping rebellion differentiated it from the various other insurrections, armed rebellions and peasant uprisings against the imperial Government. Its purpose was to set up a democratic, socialist and military monarchy with a theocratic basis. The 'land law' which was the political and economic spearhead of the new régime divided up the land according to an equitable system, in proportion to the mouths to be fed, and established a collective form of agriculture. The harvests would first be used to feed the peasants, after which the surplus would go to the public stores. Labour was also compulsory and nationalized in commerce and industry, the product of which went into certain State warehouses. The administrative system was simplified. The central Government comprised the Celestial King, the King of the East (the prime minister), the King of the North and the Assistant King, together with various ministers. The provincial administration was divided into regions, circles, districts (12,500 families) and elementary social 'cells' of 25 families, headed by a *Sze-ma*. No distinction was made between the civil and military authorities, who worked in close union everywhere. Religion, administered by the priests, was compulsory. It took the form of a fusion of the ancient Chinese religions with a simplified version of Christianity. This was the very essence of the Tai-ping Government. The Tai-ping leaders felt that as a substitute for the 'devilish' Manchu system (with which they had only one thing in common, the ban on opium smoking), there could only be a dualistic concept. On the one hand, a return to the golden age that haunted the imagination of the rebellious peasants like a nostalgic vision; on the other hand, reforms inspired by the West, which had proved superior to the Manchus in ideas and in military ability. Thus it was that side by side with political and military terminology taken over from the Chow dynasty and the Book of Ritual, the Tai-ping announced the reform of the calendar, the emancipation of women, and projects for expanding the Press, the road network and industry along Western lines. But when the Celestial King Hung committed suicide, on 19 June 1864, he did not use a revolver, but swallowed a gold leaf in accordance with the most ancient tradition.

The failure of the Tai-ping movement gradually developed a left wing led by Yang, the King of the East (leader of the coolies, peasants, sampan fishermen and soldiers) and a right wing, comprising the followers of Wei, the King of the North. In 1856 tension between the two kings grew so acute that they began to fight, and were killed one after the other. The Tai-ping movement failed to absorb the various insurrectional currents that were continuing parallel to itself. The left wing thought of attempting this, but its views were rejected. It also committed grave strategic errors, such as its failure to threaten Peking and thus strike at the root of the imperial régime.

After the setback suffered by the Manchu leaders, a Chinese counter-revolution with an ideological and military basis broke out in the centre of the Empire (Honan) among the landowners, lettered class and senior officials who felt themselves threatened by the Tai-ping movement, with its agricultural reforms and anti-Confucianist attitude. A force of militia, well paid, well armed, and sometimes directed by European military advisers, succeeded where the Manchu armies had failed, and the Peking Government was reluctantly obliged to give official recognition to this disruption of the Empire's dualistic balance. European intervention should not be underestimated. The Western powers were at first neutral, or even favourable to the Tai-ping, but they ultimately grew hostile. At last they intervened, directly or indirectly, side by side with the Chinese counter-revolution, while the Tai-ping State, rapidly declining, played its last cards between 1861 and 1864.

Because it failed, the Tai-ping rebellion has been neglected by the historians of the colonial period. Today it is acknowledged as having shattered the authoritarian administrative and financial system of the Empire, which never recovered its balance. It also, temporarily and involuntarily, strengthened the hand of the Western powers. Lastly, it left behind it a tradition of agricultural and national opposition and reform which influenced the political ideas of Sun Yat-sen and Mao Tse-tung.

The need to form local bands of loyal militia independent of the regular army led to the complete elimination of the futile *lu ying* who had formed the backbone of the government troops. The leaders of these militia got rid, to some extent, of the mandarins appointed on the results of the competitive examinations that were held every three years, and of the professional officers. As a result of their success, some of them, such as Cheng Kwo-fan, became governors and governors-general without having passed through the usual channels. With the *li-kin*, the financial power passed from the central Government to the provincial authorities, who enjoyed considerable independence both in collecting the taxes and in using the sums they brought in. The effect of the *Pao-kia* system, adopted to bring the Tai-ping peasants to heel, was to make each village responsible, as a unit, to the administration. It reinforced local authority to the detriment of the central Government.

An independent military and financial system thus grew up in the provinces, leading to the establishment of autonomous regional governments and the appearance of 'War Lords'. A centrifugal Chinese system developed in opposition to the centralizing authority of the Manchus.

The considerable help the Western powers had rendered to the Chinese counter-revolution put them in a favourable position for infiltrating into the administration of the Empire. Through their military and naval missions, their financial experts and customs advisers, they gained a dominant position. The disturbances of 1853–5 were the justification for a system of 'self-defence' in the foreign concessions, accompanied by privileges for which there was no provision in the 1842 treaties. An inflow of refugees, also greater than had been supposed, gave the foreign concessions a Chinese substratum which developed into a clientele consisting of a nucleus of businessmen surrounded by a middle class, a class of craftsmen, and a proletariat of clerks and servants. This was the beginning of an extraterritorial movement similar to those in Turkey, India and Egypt and in complete contrast to the attitude of Japan and of Russia in the old days.

There is a certain geographical continuity between the Tai-ping movement, the Boxer movement, the Chinese Soviets (1928–33) and the *Nien-kyun* movement in Shantung, which was first anti-Japanese and later Communist. The agricultural movement steadily expanded in this region.

The Tai-ping rebellion left behind it a tradition of national opposition to Western political and economic penetration. The reformist tradition (emancipation of women, campaign against opium, modernization of the calendar) were to be taken up again later. The attempt to combine the tenets of Christianity with those of the ancient Chinese religions was the only thing that proved a complete failure. The historical fact of the Tai-ping rebellion, its causes and its discomfiture have been very meticulously and practically studied by the present-day political leaders of China, whose ideas have been permanently influenced by it.

2. THE ECONOMY AND ITS ORGANIZATION IN CHINA

The organization of the economy

The four classes of the population, in descending order, were mandarins, farmers, craftsmen and workers, tradesmen and merchants. China under the mandarins had little esteem for manual labour, which, though held up to honour in the *T'ien-kong k'ai-wu* (Exploitation of the Works of Nature, 1637) was regarded with disdain by the Confucian scholar with his long fingernails. China was always inclined to apply to economic problems solutions inspired by the infallible value of self-improvement or by comparison between the human and the cosmic order of things. Being intensely bureaucratic, it continually strove to put a check on anti-social tendencies by restraining the expansion of trade and by neutralizing self-interest (*sze* and *li*) and the spirit of competition (*king* and *k'o*).

For the Confucianist, too much wealth led to vulgarity. For the Taoist, too much interest in business caused a decline in the life-force. For the Buddhist, it was meaningless. These views produced conditions extremely unfavourable to the progress of those economic, scientific and technological factors from which industrialism was born.

Disdaining commercial and industrial activities, the imperial Government ignored economics except under certain paternalist and administrative aspects. It used to build up reserves of rice in the south and of grain in the north, to be distributed in time of famine either freely or as a loan. Financial advances and grants of money were also given on occasion, through the banks. It looked after the dykes and canals which controlled irrigation and consequently the use of them for farming or for military purposes. The canals, particularly the Grand Canal, were used for transporting the rice tribute. (Pl. 85a). A few highroads were maintained. But the road system under the Ch'ings was far inferior to that of the Hans, which had accommodation for travellers every ten *li* and relays of post-horses every five *li*. The imperial postal organization, which had 200,000 horses in the time of the Yuan, was also in decline. The manufacture of salt, weapons and gunpowder was State-controlled. Incidentally, it is interesting to note that all reformers, from Tseng Kwo-fan to Sun Yat-sen and Mao Tse-tung, have been hostile to the development of heavy industry in private ownership, and in favour of monopolies or State ownership. There was no very definite economic policy apart from emergency action to relieve famine or deal with natural calamities (typhoons, drought, or floods).

However, although the administration took no great interest in economic development, there was nothing to prevent an intelligent official from encouraging trade, industry or agriculture within his own district. For example, after a harsh repression, Tso Tsung-t'ang (1812–85) encouraged silkworm cultivation in Sinkiang, and had wells sunk, dykes built and coins minted, thus stimulating progress among the Moslem ethnical minorities. Similar action took place in the purely Chinese provinces as well.

The economic system thus constituted was not propitious to the formation of large cities. The typical Chinese town was small and sheltered behind walls. In time of peace it was the residence of the rich landowners; in periods of disturbance all classes of the population took refuge there; it was the administrative and economic centre from which taxation was levied on the peasants and manufactured goods distributed to them. Such towns were only to be found in districts where the peasant population was large enough to produce enough surplus food for the citizens. There were a few exceptions to this rule, the semi-industrialized riverside cities and seaports. They alone grew to any great size. In the days of Tao-kwan (1821–50), Kwangtung had 50,000 workers distributed among 2,500 textile mills and employed under 5,000 workers in the tea industry (Tsien Po-tsan).

The mandarins, like the French 'physiocrats' in the eighteenth century, despised as parasites all those (apart from themselves) who did not produce food, and were therefore systematically hostile to the development of trade and industry. This meant that rural labour had no outlet except agriculture, so surplus manpower was always available, and the landowners had no need to offer equitable wages to their farm workers in order to retain their services, as was necessary in some Western countries.

Maspero made a careful study of the system of land tenure in China and of the terminology relating to it. He found that by the end of the Ming period there were imperial estates (*huang-chuang*) and private estates (*chuang-t'eu*) where the peasants were at the mercy of the Emperor's or overlord's managers and their subordinates. The abuses were so flagrant that the abolition of the system was considered several times, but never carried out.

The State bureaucracy was responsible for these latifundia, which had passed into the hands of high officials who transformed the free peasants into serfs or tenant-farmers. This was the origin of a landowning aristocracy which had to some extent lessened the Emperor's authority. In order to recover that authority, the Ch'ing dynasty abolished the imperial latifundia and confiscated those in private hands.

This land became public property or was redistributed to the princes, to members of the royal family and to military leaders. The managers, with their police powers over the population, were swept away. The estates were leased to one principal tenant (*chuang-t'eu*), who dealt with the subtenants and paid each autumn the sums for which he had contracted to the landlord.

Any of the old estates which did not pass to new owners were broken up and, on payment of a tax (*Keng-ming-t'ien*), distributed among the peasants. Large estates were now again, as heretofore in Chinese history, the subject of mistrust and supervision, whereas small holdings were steadily extended, with uninterrupted support from the administration. Finally the farmers secured a legal right to the surface of the ground (*t'ien-mien* or *ti-shang*), while the landlords retained their rights to its actual ownership (*t'ien-ti*). The time-limit to the right of surface ownership might be set aside by legal agreement, thus making it perpetual. The earlier method of landownership by life tenancy, which was peculiar to the peasantry, and the successive types of overlordship which were reserved for princes and dignitaries, were gradually abolished, so that the system ran the whole gamut from mere precarious tenure to full and unrestricted ownership. Thus it was under the Ch'ing dynasty that the Chinese countryside took on its present social aspect. Small holdings became the rule, and any property exceeding 50 *meu* (3 hectares) was regarded as a large one. There were, however, certain regional differences.

In north China, which had a continental climate and produced great quantities of cereals (especially wheat), large estates were held until a late period by members of the army, the guilds and the religious orders. This applies particularly to the suburbs of Peking. Even there, however, small plots were made over to the share-crop farmers. The landlord took 50 per cent of the harvest, sometimes even more. He paid the land-tax, and provided draught cattle and fertilizers.

In the centre and south of the Empire half of the peasants lived on the produce of their holdings; a quarter, though they possessed plots of their own, had to make up their needs by farming other land on the share-crop principle; the final quarter formed a proletariat of agricultural labourers working for hire.

At the time when the Tai-ping rebellion broke out, however, between 40 and 80 per cent of the land in certain provinces was in the hands of big landowners who represented between 10 and 20 per cent of the population.

Nevertheless, the agrarian reform had improved the peasant's lot. It explains the vast increase in the population, which rose in three centuries from 60 to 400 million. Before 1840 the peasants made up at least 80 per cent of the population. But this tremendous increase of population had not been accompanied by any improvement or extension of agricultural techniques; the cultivated surface had remained practically unchanged (7,414,995 *k'ing* in 1741 against 7,915,251 in 1851).

The Tai-ping leaders attacked the agrarian problem. As we have already seen, they successfully altered certain of its local aspects, but they failed to discover any general solution. In several provinces the big landowners and the nobility managed to raise militia who held them in check and restored a species of feudal system to which the Empire invariably reverted when the imperial authority ceased to be obeyed.

The merchants were organized in corporations or guilds, similar to those of medieval Europe. Marco Polo mentions those of Yang-chow. One of the most famous was the Canton merchants' corporation (*Co-hung*).

Internal trade was not on a very far-reaching scale, owing to the principle of economic autonomy at provincial level; every region was self-sufficient in basic products. The diversity of climate and natural resources was conducive to international trade rather than to the circulation of goods within a particular economic region. But the transport of rice sometimes assumed amazing proportions in the event of famine. The central provinces on either bank of the Yangtse used to send their surplus to Kwangtung and Fukien. The only well-established example of specific exchange within the Empire was that of the sugar produced in the Swatow region, which was imported into Manchuria in exchange for soya cake, the latter being used as fertilizer in the sugar-cane plantations. But this was a comparatively recent development.

Thus, at the end of the Ch'ing dynasty China was in a condition of economic independence regarded by the mandarin class as a virtue, but considered by economists as a necessity. Before the mechanization of transport, the importation of large quantities of foodstuffs was a precarious process, attended by great risks. The volume of export and import was therefore small, and related chiefly to luxuries and works of art. The situation could be altered only by shaking off the influence of Confucius. This was difficult, and inevitably took a very long time.

Another factor that impeded the development of trade and industry was the dearth of highroads, which moreover were falling into worse and worse condition during the first half of the nineteenth century. Up to a point the merchants' guilds saw to the upkeep of the roads, which were completely neglected by the administration. Many roads were paralleled by a canal or navigable river (the Min, for transport to Foochow; the Yangtse-kiang, which was navigable as far as Hankow for ships of medium tonnage and up to Yichang for smaller vessels; the Grand Canal from Hangchow to Tientsin). Like the Red River in north Vietnam, the Yangtse-kiang, or Blue River, in China is the country's great river (*Ta-kiang*). It prolongs the seaboard for 4,000 km and acts, economically speaking, as an inland sea. It flows through a coalfield providing fuel for the steamboats whose arrival in its waters caused a commercial revolution of great importance.

The Blue River and the Grand Canal were the two great waterways of the Empire. In 1850 the Tai-ping cut off the traditional rice traffic along the Grand Canal, and subsequent flooding of the Yellow River added to the difficulties of water transport. While the towns along the Grand Canal found their economic activity brought to a standstill, the coastal ports, which were under foreign control, were rapidly expanding. In 1853, therefore, the Tai-ping tried to consolidate their position by seizing Shanghai and the mouth of the Blue River. Had they succeeded, they would have obtained control of the coastal traffic which supplied rice to northern China, and the Western powers were determined not to relinquish this at any price. Conflict between them and the Tai-ping thus became inevitable.

As well as trade within continental China and in the ports opened to the

Western nations, trade was carried on with south-east Asia, and some of the routes are known to us. This trade was very flourishing from the Sung to the Ming period; but after the great voyages made by the eunuch Cheng-Ho, a navigator of Hui nationality, the Ming virtually put a stop to long-distance sailing. Cheng Ho made seven voyages, which took him to south-east Asia, India, the Persian Gulf, Arabia and the African ports. Between 1405 and 1432 he raised an enormous fleet, manned by 27,000 sailors. His expeditions forged new links with the East Indies and thus established a foreign trade that was specifically Chinese. However, this was soon put into the shade by trade with the West, at first through Canton and later through the treaty ports. That trade therefore requires special study.

K'ang Hi (1684) had allotted to foreigners a 'manufactory' in the port of Canton. The foreign merchants were restricted to a narrow strip of land beside the Pearl River. Any attempt to penetrate further inland was severely punished. A celebrated guild (*Co-hong*) had the monopoly of transactions with foreigners. On the other hand, however, heavy demands were made upon its members, and bankruptcies were not infrequent. The guild often clashed with the *Hoppo*, or harbourmaster. The *Co-hong*, founded in 1720, was dissolved between 1771 and 1780. In 1780-2, the India Company paid Li She-ayo 100,000 taels to revive it, and it survived until the Treaty of Nanking (1842). Not all the members of the guild were merchants. Some members made good use of their monopoly of dealings with the West, and played a not inconsiderable part in cultural and political matters. They were succeeded by the *compradores* of the treaty ports.

China prided itself on possessing the world's choicest drink, tea; the world's finest food, rice; the choicest textiles, silk and cotton; the finest ceramics, etc., and had absolutely nothing to ask for from foreign countries, as K'ien Lung said to Lord Macartney at a famous audience in 1793. But a new phase began with the arrival of the Spanish and Portuguese and of the English, the last-named being represented at Canton by Captain Wedell (1637). It continued with the appointment of a French consul at Canton (1776), the arrival of the first North American trade mission (1784) and the embassies of Lord Macartney (1792-3), Van Braan Hougg Kgeest (1794-5) and Lord Amherst (1816). These embassies were not unconnected with the importance of British armaments for China.

In 1751 there were 9 English ships anchored off Canton. In 1789, of the 86 foreign vessels calling at the port, 61—a veritable fleet—were British-owned. Of the remainder, 15 were American, 5 Dutch, 1 French, 1 Danish and 3 Portuguese (Li Kien-nung). Throughout this period, which concluded about 1825, the balance of trade was in favour of China, which was selling more than it bought. And as the Romans had once been obliged to do in India, the English had to import a great deal of silver money into China. Despite the three-way trade transactions between London, India and Canton, there was a continual outflow of British money and capital. At the beginning of the nineteenth century these exports to Canton exceeded by £1 million the value of Chinese goods imported into India and England.

The English dealt with this alarming situation by importing Indian opium and cotton into China. According to Greenberg the average importation of cases of opium was: 1820, 9,708 cases; 1828–35, 18,712 cases; 1835–9, 34,445 cases. About 1830 there was a spectacular reversal of the trade balance, so that money began to flow towards the foreign countries. Between 1829 and 1840 goods were landed in China from Great Britain to a value of £7·5 million. And the sale of opium brought £56 million to London and Calcutta. But the flow of money from East to West began much earlier than this. It was already appreciable about 1806–9, when it amounted to £7 million. In 1838, 4,375,000 lbs of opium were imported and sold for cash, producing nearly 150 million gold francs. The imperial Government, which had already prohibited the importation of opium on pain of strangulation, banishment or imprisonment (1799) was exasperated by the extent to which smuggling had increased. Its delegate, Lin Tsu-siu (1785–1850) adopted an uncompromising attitude which resulted in war.

The hostilities ended with the Treaty of Nanking (August 1842), ratified at Hong Kong in June 1843, and the Treaty of Whampoa (1844). Conditions were then highly favourable to Western trade. They were codified in the Peking Convention (1860) and in that of Chefu (Yen-t'ai) in 1876. The Kuldja Convention was signed between Russia and China in 1851, and the Treaty of Aïgum in 1858.

During the eighteenth century the superiority of Nanking cotton goods over those of Europe had been unchallenged, but in the nineteenth century Lancashire cottons made their way into the Empire. Subsequently the Western textile industries set up branches employing Chinese labour under foreign management. Steamboat firms took much of the coastal and river trade from the junks; and the 'opening' of 5 ports as a result of the Opium War put an end to the trade monopoly hitherto enjoyed by Canton and its hinterland.

The economic situation deteriorated further after the war between China and Japan. In the 35 years from 1864 to 1899, Chinese imports rose from 51 million silver taels to 264 million and the trade balance collapsed, imports representing an adverse balance of 69 million taels. The reserves of silver were practically exhausted. The introduction of machines in the cotton-mills caused marked unrest among the workers, who were accustomed to craftsmen's methods, and led to unemployment.

Two important points should be mentioned. Once Canton ceased to be China's only Western-trading seaport, all its water and land routes into central China lost much of their traffic. The Nanking treaty took away the business of many trading firms and banks, and 100,000 boatmen were thrown out of employment; in 1852–3 it was these men who transported the Tai-ping forces to the Yangtse. Secondly the reduced circulation of silver currency caused the people's copper coins to lose half their value. Two thousand cash instead of one thousand were now required in exchange for one silver tael. This created a vicious circle affecting all three levels of the economy. The peasants, who sold their produce for cash, had to pay their taxes and feudal dues in silver; the tradespeople suffered owing to the decline in the purchasing power of the general populace; Government revenue diminished.

Nevertheless, the area controlled by the Tai-ping showed increased exports of tea and silk. Their enemies declared this to be due to a fall in the purchasing power of money, whereas they themselves regarded it as evidence of economic prosperity.

Trade transactions, whether internal or external, were extremely slow, for many reasons, including inferior methods of transporting goods and transferring money, and above all, insecure conditions. In this connection we need only mention the Opium War (1840–42), the war with England and France (1857–60), the war with Japan (1894–5), the military intervention of the eight powers and the Boxer war (1900), the Tai-ping revolt (1850–64), the revolt of the Miaos in Kweichow (1854–73), the Nien revolt in Northern China (1865–68) and the Moslem revolt in Yunnan (1855–70).

Thus the problem of security and credit was continuously to the fore in Chinese trade, which had greater need of banks than most systems. The importation of foreign goods payable in 'hard' currency increased this tendency, and the interest on money rose from a minimum of 12 per cent to 40 and even 60 per cent per annum (i.e. 5 per cent per month). This led the Indian Parsees and the British capitalists to take a considerable interest in loan transactions even in the nineteenth century. These brought wealth to the 'nabobs', but put a still worse complexion on the Chinese monetary situation. Moreover, by sending their steamers to Singapore to find out the rates quoted on the Lyons silk-market and brought by the Indian packet, and afterwards by receiving them by telegraph, these same capitalists, over a lengthy period, obtained information whose value was enhanced by being absolutely confidential.

In seeking to arrive at a general idea of the volume of trade between China and other countries, we find that the opening of the Chinese ports to Western shipping rapidly doubled this, and that it continued to increase steadily thereafter. China's largest customers, in order of importance, were Great Britain, Japan, the United States, India and Russia. We can only deal very broadly here with the nature of the trade. Roughly speaking, China's principal imports were Indian opium and Manchester cotton and wool goods, so that up to 1872 85 per cent of imports were English and arrived under the British flag.

As we have seen already, Western trade had been constantly increasing over this period, while Chinese economy was in a state of endemic crisis. For all that, however, some European merchants were ruined during these years, while some Chinese merchants grew rich. For example, the Tai-ping brought a short period of affluence to Shanghai. When peace was restored there were many bankruptcies. The establishment of branches of the great English banks destroyed the monopoly hitherto enjoyed at Shanghai by such firms as Jardine, Russell and Dent. It also involved the Western capitalists living in China with the fluctuations of the international banking situation, which were sometimes serious.

Lastly, the Chinese were determined to defend themselves. Opium from Yunnan and western China began to compete, whether in open trade or as contraband, with Indian opium. Chinese mills entered into rivalry with the cotton and wool goods produced specially at Manchester for the Far Eastern market. Insurance companies and river and coastal shipping firms managed to undercut the foreigners. In 1870 several English cotton firms went bankrupt. But the assassination of Margary, the British Consul, in 1874, gave a pretext for restoring the advantage of the Europeans by new trade agreements, signed at Chefu in 1876.

In any case, from 1842 onwards the surplus of imports over exports was so great as to create an adverse balance of $200 million by 1911. There were many reasons for this disruption of the trade balance. One was the 5 per cent *ad valorem* customs duty, arbitrarily imposed in 1843 on imports and exports alike. Foreign goods were also exempted from the *Li-kin* (transit duty), which was not abolished until 1931. Originally this was 10 per cent, but it increased inordinately and Chinese products were heavily handicapped by it. Sun Yat-sen denounced this economic oppression in 1894 in a letter to Li Hung-chang: 'It is because we are economically oppressed that we suffer such a great annual loss and the people are short of food. This economic oppression is more terrible than several million soldiers coming to slaughter us would be.'

Lastly, the foreign debt rose to $800 million thanks to the Boxer indemnity (450 million taels, 1901), the war damages payable to the Japanese (200 million taels, 1894) and loans contracted abroad. It was calculated that every middle aged Chinese producer was paying an annual tax of $45 to foreign creditors (Wu Sao-fong).

By furthering their commercial and industrial activities, the foreigners—confined to the 'treaty ports' by force and with the help of the legal fiction of extraterritoriality—contributed to the economic breakdown of the Ch'ing Empire. At the same time, the wealthy Chinese landowners were attracted by the pleasure and convenience of life in the big foreign trading centres, and the Chinese merchants were investing their profits in estates they seldom visited. The absenteeism of this new class of landowners produced the same disastrous effects as those already displayed at earlier stages of China's economic history.

Technological development

At the beginning of the Ch'ing period, Chinese superiority was still evident in a number of techniques in which the patience, dexterity and ingenuity of

Chinese craftsmen was beyond compare. But generally speaking, Chinese technology was more or less set in the mould, whereas that of Europe was rapidly developing. As a result, the gap between the military, naval and industrial potential of Western Europe and the Far East was steadily widening. By the latter half of the nineteenth century it had become so considerable that a mere handful of Europeans could force millions of Chinese to submit to a succession of 'inequitable treaties' (*pu p'ing-teng t'iao yo*), and the Chinese came to regard a familiarity with Western technology as the only means of restoring a reasonable balance between East and West. We must therefore study technology in both its aspects—the traditional techniques and those of Western origin.

Agriculture used equipment which served as a model for the West, including the winnowing machine, the threshing roller, the plough with cast-iron mould-board of regular curvature, and the sowing machine for use in unploughed fields. This last consisted of two pointed stakes connected by a cross-bar supporting a funnel from the base of which projected two slender tubes of bamboo. These tubes were so narrow that the grains in the funnel could only emerge one by one as the apparatus was tipped alternately to right and left by means of two handles. This gave a lozenge-like pattern of sowing, the seeds in each row being separated by some 16–20 inches from one another. Thus, the blades that sprouted from them were between 10 and 12 inches apart, and from the collar of each there grew some twenty stems, each provided with rootlets. The rootlets were covered with the loose soil at the bottom of the furrow, and each stem sprouted as before, so that in favourable circumstances, 300 or 400 haulms, each bearing an ear of grain, might grow from a single seed.

In this agricultural system a new plant, maize, had been cultivated for a comparatively short time, having been introduced in the sixteenth century. But Chinese agriculture was chiefly concerned with nutritious plants not then known in Europe—soya, aquatic plants, cabbage (*pe-t'sai*, or *Brassica chinensis* L.), yams, the Chinese artichoke, the *hei-tu* (a leguminous plant used as a substitute for oats), the sugar-cane, tea—and vegetable products for use in industry, such as camphor, the glandulous ailanthus, vegetable wax (*Stillingia sebifera*), grass-cloth (*Urtica nivea*), gutta-percha (*Eucommia ulmoides*), and various tinctorial plants (*Polygonum tinctorium, Sophora japonica, Rhumus*). Chinese botanical species are the subject of a careful study by Heu K'wan-Chao (Peking, 1958). Chinese agriculture even included certain varieties of sheep, hens and ducks whose acclimatization in Europe is the theme of works too numerous to be listed here.

Though they had indifferent success in the breeding of mammals (except in the case of Pekingese dogs, which were produced by selective breeding), the Chinese were remarkably expert in dealing with insects, molluscs, fish and birds. Insects interested them as an addition to the diet, as producers of raw material (bees, silkworms) and as a pretext for gambling (cricket-fights). As early as the thirteenth century, it occurred to a certain Ye Jin-Yan to insert tiny objects into pearl oysters and remove them when they had been coated with mother-of-pearl. This was the principle of cultured pearls, perfected by Kokishi Mikimoto (1858–1954).

Whereas other nations could only keep fish alive in captivity, the Chinese succeeded in artificially fertilizing them and thus obtained new varieties by selection. Chang K'ien-To, writing in 1605, describes six new varieties obtained since the tenth century by selective breeding from the goldfish (*Carassius auratus*). More than ten others were obtained during the nineteenth century. It was in the late eighteenth century that the Chinese 'goldfish' made their way into the European aquarium, in the form of many-tailed creatures of monstrous shapes. At that time the Chinese were also breeding fighting fish (*Betta splendens*), of Siamese origin. The technical level of fish-breeding and fisheries in the Ch'ing period was thoroughly studied by Dabry de Thiersant, who left an exhaustive iconography on the subject. Another and more recent monograph on the subject is that drawn up by Chang Ch'uen-Lin and others (*Academia Sinica*, 1954).

Birds were used as messengers (carrier pigeons), assistants for fishers (cormorants) and hunters (falcons), fighters (quails and cocks) or pets.

Mineral deposits were numerous and known from a very early period; they included iron, copper, gold, argentiferous galena, cinnabar, zinc, lead, tin, coal, rock-salt, salt-marshes, etc. The right to free digging was a great source of disputes, and most of the mines belonged to rich corporations which exploited a necessitous proletariat. The profits of owners and managers were reduced, however, by the imposition of annual dues and the necessity of granting shares to the Government. Prior to the Moslem insurrection, the Yunnan silver-mines were sending Peking an annual tribute of 6,000 tons of silver. One-third of all the silver extracted was stolen by excise officers, soldiers or brigands.

Mining techniques, too, were deficient. A great proportion of the hours spent underground was taken up by transport rather than by work at the face. Much of the labour force consisted of children between 8 and 15 years of age, who were drafted into the mines by compulsion. There was a high rate of mortality from poisoning (arseniferous ores), sickness (pneumonia) and accident (collapse of galleries).

The salt-marshes served a fiscal as well as an industrial purpose. Wells were sunk, sometimes to a depth of 850 metres (average 200–300 m.), the brine was pumped up and evaporated by heating in basins with the use of inflammable gases. The annual output varied between 80,000 and 120,000 tons of salt.

Throughout the seventeenth and eighteenth centuries, the Chinese exported to Europe alloys composed of several metals (zinc, tin, copper, lead) which were then highly popular under the names of *packfong*, *pewter* and *tutenag*.

These were used in the manufacture of table-ware and drinking vessels. The Chinese had also mastered the craft of bronze-casting, as evidenced by the statue, 25 metres in height, which was placed in the great Lama temple of Peking during the reign of Yung Chen (1723–35). By hammering bronze according to a special technique, they were able to produce 'male' and 'female' gongs which gave different sounds.

The 'white copper' (*po-t'ong*) mentioned by a fourteenth-century writer seems to have been a form of 'German silver', for it contained zinc, nickel and copper, with traces of iron. It was smelted in Yunnan, refined at Canton, and whitened by the addition of unrefined zinc. Familiar in Europe by the name of *pétong* or *packfong*, it was imported from China in the nineteenth century and soon imitated in Berlin, where it was known as 'white metal' by 1824.

The supervision of the rivers was still one of the Government's foremost concerns. It was indispensable in order to avert terrible famines and to ensure the delivery of the rice tribute from central China to Peking. Sea transport should be used when the Grand Canal was partly out of operation. In 1826, 1,633,000 piculs of rice were conveyed in 1,562 junks from Shanghai to Tientsin. Sea transport was abandoned, however, despite its obvious technical advantages, under pressure from the officials who lived along the Grand Canal and who saw their interests endangered. Supervision of the Yellow and Blue rivers, which was particularly important, was entrusted to high officials, some of whom were severely punished for their failure to prevent floods which were occasionally disastrous (1757). Other officials have left excellent descriptions of the methods used to keep the rivers within their beds. This was done by building embankments and digging overflow channels—measures which were merely palliative, not curative. In the twenty-third year of the Tao-Kuang period (1823), the Yellow River reached its highest recorded rate of discharge (36,000 cubic metres per second). It is easy to imagine the terrible calamities that resulted.

Porcelain (*ts'e*) is differentiated from pottery (*t'ao*). The great problems relating to raw materials (clay, rock), colours and firing had been virtually solved by the Ch'ing period, and the technique was thus almost perfect. Characteristic features of this period include deeply incised and complex *lace* engraving, the 'grain of rice' style of decoration which consisted in piercing holes in regular patterns and covering them with a transparent coating, the 'cracked' glaze obtained by the use of pegmatite or by rapid cooling, and the *orange-peel* surface which came from the systematic repetition of an 'accident' already known in the fifteenth century. The 'powder blue' effect characteristic of the K'ang Hi period was obtained by blowing the colouring matter through a bamboo tube, the lower end of which was covered with thin gauze. Painted decoration was becoming immensely popular. The secret of colouring-matter with a basis of copper, lost since the fifteenth century, was now rediscovered.

Much colouring-matter of animal origin was used, such as the 'golden purple' discovered by Andreas Cassius at Leyden about 1650 and known to the Chinese as 'the foreign colour' (*Yang-ts'äi*). By their extraordinary skill in handling enamels (sometimes superimposing them), and in glazing and firing, the Chinese were able to imitate wood, bronze, jade, bamboo and cloisonné enamel in their ceramic work. They even attained to a degree of virtuosity at which they could cover white porcelain with a coat of black lacquer and encrust it with mother-of-pearl, gold or silver.

One of the great manufacturing centres was King-te-chen, which after being partially destroyed in 1680, had been rebuilt in 1682. King-te-chen, which stood on the southern bank of the river Ch'ang, was connected by water, via Lake Po-yang, with Kieu-kiang on the Yangtse. Hence the name of Kieu-kiang (porcelain transhipped at Kieu-kiang) which was given to the imperial porcelain (*Kwan-yao*) sent twice a year along the Grand Canal to Peking. The work was subdivided to a remarkable extent, and one fine-quality object might have passed through the hands of 70 workers by the time it was finished.

The furnaces consisted either of one very large chamber or of several long, narrow chambers with a chimney at the back and a domed roof. The floors sloped, and were wholly or partly below ground-level. A temperature of approximately 1,450° C was reached in firing hard porcelain, 700 to 800° C for unglazed (biscuit) porcelain and 800 to 900° C for muffle firing. Firing took place by 'reduction' (with limited admission of air) or by oxygenation (free admission of air), according to the colour desired. Incidentally, wastage amounted to something like 50 per cent, and the rejected products piled up through the years into little mounds, the archaeological investigation of which is by no means concluded as yet. Destroyed during the Tai-ping rebellion (1853), the King-te-chen 'manufactury' was rebuilt in 1864. It continued to turn out very beautiful pieces, but there were no technical improvements during the Ch'ing period.

Ever since Marco Polo's time, Europeans had been fascinated by Chinese ceramics, with its obvious technical superiority, its highly vitreous glazes and its fine porcelains. From the sixteenth century onwards, the history of Western ceramics is a succession of attempts to imitate the Chinese work, technically and artistically. But a singular combination of chance and methodical experiment was needed before the last alchemists and the earliest chemists (nearly all of whom were physicians) could advance from pottery to porcelain.

Western science and technology had been familiar to a minority since the Ming period, through various objects (watches, clocks, automata, firearms, barometers, thermometers, microscopes, etc.) and from works translated, usually by the Jesuits or their Chinese friends. Outstanding among these is Wan Cheng (1571–1644). He was particularly interested in the applied sciences, and in collaboration with Father Terrenz he translated and illustrated several European works on mechanics. A book by him, entitled *Yuan-si ki-ki t'u-shuo lu-tsui*, was published at Peking in 1627, and led to the permanent admission of certain mechanical terms into the Chinese language. It was reprinted in 1830 and 1844. Generally speaking, however, Western technological achievements were regarded as amusing toys, until the Opium War gave the Chinese a practical demonstration of the fundamental importance of technology, both from the military and economic standpoints.

From then onwards, translations of Western works and the activities of reform societies unquestionably played an important part. The reform societies included that at Fukien, led by Lin Siu (1875–98), that at Szechwan, led by Yang Jouei (1857–98) and that at Hunan, led by T'an Sze-t'ung, Yang Wenhwei (1831–1911), Ch'en Pao–chen (1831–1900), Siu Jen-chou (1863–1900) and Huang Tsuen-hien. Many Cantonese had long been converted to Western methods, which were more readily acceptable in the seaboard provinces of the south than in the continental provinces of the north, the cradle of Chinese civilization. But Westernization raised many psychological, religious and political problems, and questions of protocol. Railways, bridges and factory chimneys destroyed the geographical balance of a town. They also threw certain corporations out of employment, and it was realized after a time that the concessions made to foreigners were merely a disguised method of extending their respective 'spheres of influence'.

The difficulties of industrialization included those resulting from the workers' objection to the use of machines which, while increasing output, were likely to cause unemployment. This was a widespread phenomenon, already manifested in Europe during the industrial revolution, and had nothing specifically Chinese about it. In point of fact the majority of provincial authorities, who knew the Western peoples only by hearsay, had no wish to alter the traditional techniques. The Imperial Court was more favourable to change, but it followed rather than led a handful of officials, intellectuals and businessmen (nearly all Cantonese) who appreciated the superiority of Western techniques and wished to use them for their own benefit. The Court still insisted on the primordial importance of forms and ceremonies; Tuan Fang (1861–1911) was dismissed from his post as Governor-General of Che-li because he photographed the funeral procession of Tse-Hi.

The advocates of reform had realized that to equip China with heavy industry meant more than recruiting a few engineers and buying some machinery. It was equally necessary to set up offices to translate technical books, to open schools which would teach Western technological methods, to send young intellectuals to study abroad, and to establish arsenals and factories to manufacture the equipment required for the expansion of heavy industry. Thanks to the tenacity of a few men, this programme was carried out.

Lin Tso-siu (1785–1850) was a member of the Imperial Academy (*Han-lin*) and a determined opponent of the foreign opium merchants; but he was the first mandarin to decide that his country could learn something from the West and that foreigners' knowledge should be respected and disseminated. As a high-placed official he encouraged the translation of Western books (*Hai-kwo t'ou-che*, 1875) and ordered new types of guns and ships to be tested. After his time his experiments were continued by friends of his who became Viceroys of Fukien and Chekiang. Teng T'ing-chen and Kung Chen-lin launched paddle-steamers at Amoy (1840–1). Tsiang K'ing-ts'iuan, Governor of Kwantung, had ships built to new designs, so did Siu Siang-kwang, while P'an She-cheng was particularly active in this respect. He had three ships built to American designs at Canton, and in collaboration with an engineer he constructed submarine mines powerful enough to blow up a warship (1842). The great engineer Ting Kung-chen, a native of Fukien and superintendent of the Canton manufactury, wrote and illustrated a treatise on the manufacture of heavy guns (*Yen-p'ao t'ou-shwo*, 1841), made advances in ballistics, and built paddle-steamers and locomotives. New types of warships were designed by Admiral Wu Kien-sien. Tseng Kwo-fan (1811–72) showed an early interest in geography, science and educational methods. Like Lin Tse-siu, he had the advantage, towards the end of his career, of close contact with Europeans (Sir Robert Hart, S. R. Brown, Halliday, Macartney, Anson Burlingame) and with Chinese who had lived abroad (Yung Hong, Pin Chwen, Swen, Kia-ku, Che Kang). He also had some outstanding assistants—Chang Sze-kwei, Li Shan-lan (1810–82), Hwa Heng-feng, Syu Sheu (1818–84) and Hou Lin-yi. During the last ten years of his life he was the 'steamboat boss'. It should be remembered that the first steamboat ever to reach China came from India in 1828; not until 1853 was there a regular steamboat service in Chinese waters. Ten years later (1863) the first Chinese-built steamer came into service on the Yangtse-kiang. A little later, between 1868 and 1871, the Kiang-nan arsenal built five steamers, one of which was called *Chow-kiang* (Master of the River). A school of engineering grew up in connection with the Kiang-nan arsenal, at the same time as the interpreters' college at Peking and the Shanghai school.

Tseng Kwo-fan's work was continued by his protégés, Tso Tsung-t'ang (1812–85) and Li Hong-chang (1823–1901). Li Hong-chang founded the School of Navigation (*Pei-yang schwei-she hiue-t'ang*) at Tientsin in 1880, and appointed Yen Fu as director of studies, as the Foochow school specialized in shipbuilding. Tso Tsung-t'ang (1812–85) and his successors, Shen Pao-chen (1820–70), with the co-operation of Paul d'Aiguebelle and Prosper Giquel, established the arsenals of Ma-wei and Foochow (1866). A naval college (*Ch'wan-cheng hiue-t'ang*) was added to this, and had as its most brilliant pupil (and afterwards professor) Yen Fu (1835–1921).

Side by side with these high-placed officials who were in favour of Westernization (*Yang-wu-p'ai*) it is only right to mention the industrialists, an entirely new social category, one of whose most typical representatives was Sheng Siuan-hwai (1849–1916).

In 1872 the first Chinese students to come to the United States on scholarships began to arrive at the rate of 30 a year. In the space of four years, 140 students were sent abroad on research projects. They included an engineer,

Chan T'ien-yu (1861–1919), a railway pioneer; administrative officials—Liang Tuen-yen (d. 1924), T'ang Shao-yi (1860–1938), the Prime Minister of the Republic, Wu T'ing-fang; and navigators—Lieu Pu-shan, Lin T'ai-tseng, Fang Po-k'ien, Lin Yung-sheng, Ye Tsu-kwei, Sa Chen-ping (1859–?) who later became the Navy Minister, and Yen Fu.

Some of these travelling intellectuals deserve fuller mention. Ma Kien-chung (1845–99), who came from Tan-t'eu (province of Kiang-su), the Tai-ping headquarters, first studied at Shanghai, where he revealed a remarkable gift for languages. In addition to mastering classical Chinese, he learnt Latin, Greek, English and French. He was also a fascinated student of history, geography, astronomy, mathematics, physics, chemistry, biology and geology. In 1875 he held the post of Secretary of the Ministry (Lang-chung) and Li Hong-chang sent him to study in France (1877). In France he became chargé d'affaires, and translated Kuo Sung-tao. Returning to China, he perceived that the great arguments about international law which were carried on by the Western powers were not due to a different way of looking at things, but to different interests. They resorted to international law merely to serve their selfish ends. He thus adopted an attitude hostile to Westernization, and severely criticized it. Conscious of being a member of the lettered mandarin class, he agreed with Chen Che, Sie Fu-cheng (1838–?) and Cheng Kwan-ying (1841–?) in favouring private capitalist enterprise, advocating a constitutional monarchy, and opposing bureaucracy and the slavish copying of foreign ways. Ma Kien-chung wrote some celebrated 'Memoirs' and produced the first modern Chinese grammar (*Ma-she wen-t'ung*, 1898).

Ho Wu-sheng, a Cantonese from Nanhai, studied in England for over ten years. Back in China, he settled at Hong Kong, where he practised both as lawyer and doctor. He was among the organizers of the University of Hong Kong, and a companion of Sun Yat-sen. Most of Ho's works were written in English and adapted into Chinese by one of his contemporaries, Hu Li-yuan (1847–1916), a Cantonese from San-shwei, a tradesman's son, who worked for the revolution at Hong Kong and in Japan.

At the end of the nineteenth century, heavy industry appeared in China. The stages of its development are indicated by the following dates: 1882—first spinning-mill opened at Shanghai; 1883—establishment of the first Chinese firm with Chinese capital, the Yuan-Chang Metal Factory, founded by Chu Ta-k'wen; 1892—mining output considerably increased thanks to modernization by the Europeans of mining methods and transport. In 1877–90 the output of the Yunnan tin-mines, which had been worked intensively for 30 years, was almost negligible. In 1892 it rose to 2,000 tons, and between 1902 and 1905 to 4,000 tons.

The construction of the first railway was undertaken by Jardine Matheson, over a distance of about 9 miles from Shanghai to Wu-sung, in 1876; it had a 30-inch gauge. The project was encouraged by the British authorities, in the hope of further penetration into China, against which the Chinese protested.

In 1877 Li Hong-chang bought the line, and the equipment was transferred. to Taiwan. The North China Railway (Tang-shan siu-ko-chwang) was built in the same year, to carry coal to the sea. This line was extended to Tientsin in 1890. Sheng Huai-syuan, an industrialist with a keen interest in telegraphy, navigation and mining techniques, was appointed Director-General of Railways in 1892. This office was first attached to the navy (1896) and then to the Ministry of Posts and Communications (Yu-ch'wan-pu), set up in 1906. In 1896 the Russians organized the railway from Manchuria to the south, and the Eastern Railway. In 1897 the English tried to establish the Yangtse line and the French that of Yunnan. The Germans gained control of the Shantung Railway.

After an unsuccessful experiment in 1878, the imperial postal service was set up in 1896 and entrusted to Sir Robert Hart. The first telegraph line was put into service between Tientsin and Taku by Li Hong-chang in 1879, when he was Viceroy of Che-li (Hopei). The Tientsin–Shanghai line was set up in 1881. In 1884 Chekiang and Fukien were linked with Kwantung, and the central telegraph service was transferred from Tientsin to Shanghai. In 1906 the telegraph service was operated by the Yu-ch'wan-pu.

Medicine was one of the foremost Western techniques to arouse interest during the Ch'ing period. Western medicine had been known in China from the practical standpoint ever since the seventeenth century, through the presence in Peking of Jesuit physicians and of English doctors who arrived in the wake of the Russian embassies. Chinese doctors gradually began to realize that their doxology was inadequate and their anatomy erroneous, as is shown by the case of Wang Ts'ing-jen (1768–1831), corrector of medical errors.

However, a mere handful of people had access to this information, and the readiness of the Japanese to alter their earlier medical practice stands in marked contrast to the Chinese refusal.

It was in the treaty ports that the first chinese practitioners use to Western methods, Yau Hoghun (1850) and Kwan A-tou (1818–74), were trained by a team of doctors from the English-speaking countries, of whom some were missionaries, others laymen. Western medicine was not taught officially until much later.

Wu Lien-te (1878–1959) gives us some interesting particulars concerning this period in his autobiography.

In the fourth year of the T'ung-che year (1865) a scientific section was opened at the Interpreters' Institute (T'ung-wen kwan) at Peking, in which prominence was given to modern medicine, the subject being taught by Dudgeon. At Tientsin the School of Medicine (Yi-hiue kwan), was founded in 1881, under Kwang-Siu, and the first group of Western-trained students graduated from here, in 1885. In 1893 the school was reorganized by Li Hong-chang—its name being changed to the Peiyang School of Medicine—and brought under the Government service, with Lin Lien-hwei as its first director. In 1898, Suen Kia-nai was in charge of the School of Medicine (Yi-hiue t'ang) of the Ta-hiue t'ang University. Chang Pai-hi, who established the faculties drafted the rules of the medical faculties and decreed three years' specialized training (1902).

In 1903 the Kin-she ta-hiue-t'ang, or University of Peking, founded its Yi-hiue she-ye-kwan (School of Medicine), to which it admitted ten students who specialized in Chinese and Western medicine. In 1905 this school was transformed into a Faculty of Medicine (Yi-hiue kwan). There were also many foreign institutions, such as the Hong Kong Medical College, where Sun Yat-sen studied from 1887 to 1892, as the pupil of Sir James Cantlie (1851–1926).

Thus it was that many Chinese of various origins, from the Emperor to the modest employees of the Indian Company, developed an interest in foreign technology and science. It is worth noting that some of the lettered mandarins, more open-minded than the majority of State officials, were at the head of the modernist movement, which was much more advanced in south China than in the north.

Hence, thanks to many favourable factors, technology was enabled to make progress in China in the latter half of the nineteenth century.

3. CULTURAL LIFE IN NINETEENTH-CENTURY CHINA

Education

Education (the word *kiao* means both education and religion) still had the importance, the almost religious character, attributed to it by all previous dynasties, which had caused it to be described as the 'blood and veins' (*hiue-mo*) of the Empire. K'ang-hi declared that laws restrain for a time, but that education alone is permanently binding—meaning that only respect for moral law could uphold a social system maintained by a mere handful of officials and by a sovereign who was the arbiter of disputes rather than a dictator. Seen thus, the acquisition of knowledge was the lesser part of education, and indeed the State took less pains to propagate it than to keep control over the examination for admission to the Government service. At the same time it subjected literary output to relentless censorship and placed on the index anything that might suggest direct or indirect criticism of the dynasty and its official philosophy.

There was thus considerable political and cultural importance in the fact that the true path (*cheng-lu*) of knowledge and wisdom was no longer to lead through the hitherto unalterable stages of the *Sieu-tsai* (first-degree examinations), the *Kiu-jen* (second-degree examinations) to the rank of *Tsin-she* (erudite) and to membership of the academy (*Han-lin*), and in the further fact that the youth of China was now called upon to break away from the narrow circle of clan and family and go to study abroad. The reform of the educational system went far beyond the bounds of scholastic innovation. It was to shake the already decrepti structure of the Empire. The history of education is the subject of studies by Hwang Shao-ki (1854–1908).

The syllabus of the competitive literary examinations was very mediocre even from the point of view of Chinese culture. From 1622 to 1905 the *Pa-ku wen-chang* was the sole model for the dissertations (*wen-chang*) required for the literary examinations. It was imbued with the narrowest Neo-Confucianism. The *Yu-hiue* (1757), together with the *San-tseu king* and the *luen-wen*, made up the entire scientific teaching of the schools. The mandarins who dealt with the examinations had long since (1744) proposed that they be reformed. In 1756–8 a second attempt at reform was made by Chwang Ts'wen-yu (1719–88).

In 1869 the Governor of Fukien asked the Emperor to have a mathematics paper added to the syllabus of the triennial examinations, and in 1875 Li-Hong-chang suggested that candidates should be allowed to choose between a literary paper and one on mathematics. In 1878 the monarch agreed to the inclusion of mathematics, thus giving rise to disturbances in the Yangtse valley in 1891.

Not until 1898 did Chang Che-tong (1837–1909) in his *Exhortation to Study* (*Kiuan-hiue pyen*) launch an attack on the literary competitions which effectively stirred public opinion—as a result of which they were abolished in 1905.

The traditional schools were set up privately by wealthy families, singly or in groups, for the benefit of their own children. As poor families could not afford this, their children had nothing better than the very primitive country or town schools. Except in the family circle education was reserved in principle for boys; the idea of girls' schools would have seemed preposterous. The tuition was essentially moral and literary. The aim was not so much to instruct as to educate, not so much to open and train the mind as to inculcate mental attitudes and moral principles which would apply to every situation in life. Wisdom and the worthy life were placed above science and knowledge.

After leaving these primary schools, pupils went on to pursue their studies in the provincial literary clubs and studios or at the Han-lin Academy. Generally speaking this venerable system, which in the old days had developed a high level of culture, had become obsolete by the early nineteenth century. But the fact was not realized in China until the end of that century.

The destruction of the traditional system of education began with an apparently harmless development, the opening of mission schools. In 1818 Robert Morrison opened the first foreign school for Chinese children, at Malacca. Numerous similar schools were set up later in the treaty ports, to teach English and mathematics. Since they made no attempt to teach the classics they gave their pupils no possibility of sitting for the literary examinations. But they could offer them the prospect of lucrative business careers in the treaty ports.

The missions also took the initiative of opening girls' schools, where the pioneers of the Chinese feminist movement were educated. The first university for women was established by Li Hong-chang at Tientsin in 1898. Incidentally, it should not be assumed that this movement was essentially a foreign one. There were Chinese feminists such as Yu Chang-sie (1775–1840), who disparaged bound feet and condoned women's jealousy and the remarriage of widows. The Tai-pings had a programme for the emancipation of women, including a ban on exposing girl babies and on the sale of child brides; the abolition of dowries and bound feet; enforced monogamy; and the admission of women to the civil service and the army.

A number of Chinese women attained distinction in the nineteenth century, otherwise than through feminist or political activities. Among them were Wang Chow-yuan (1763–1851), distinguished as the collaborator of her husband, Hao Yi-hing (1757–1825); K'ong Lu-hua (1777–1833), the wife of Yuan Yuan (1764–1849), who was a granddaughter of Confucius in the 73rd generation and left a collection of poems; and Sai Kin Hua (1874–1936), the concubine of Hong Kium (1840–93), who was also a poetess and a leading figure in Shanghai political and literary circles; she had some influence with Graf Waldersee (1832–1904), commander of the international occupation corps, and persuaded him to protect certain sections of the Chinese population.

From 1860 onwards the Protestant and Catholic missionary schools went ahead quickly. Timothy Richard, a kind of Protestant Ricci, threw himself heart and soul into a campaign to spread Christianity and propagate Western learning. He established Shanghai's first public school and planned to organize higher education (one college in each province) under the auspices of the Baptist Missionary Society (1885). Subsequent foundations included the University of Communications (1897) and the National University of Peking (1898), St John's College of Hong Kong, the University of Shansi (c. 1900), the Catholic University of Peking, etc. Ma Siang-po (1840–1939) took his Doctorate in Theology in 1870, devoted himself to the translation of the Bible (c. 1900), founded, in collaboration with Tsai Yuan-pei, the Catholic Centre at Shanghai (Siccawei) and the Aurora University (*Chen-tan ta-hiue*, 1903), and became Chancellor of the University of Peking in 1913.

The missionary universities played their part in the education of a number of prominent Chinese statesmen, including Cheng King-yi (d. 1940), Swen Wen and many others. They were violently criticized, but they did much to awaken public opinion. Under the influence of the Empire's political and military reverses, and more particularly after the Japanese victory in 1894, educational reform advanced from the technical and cultural level to become a burning political question. A torrent of pamphlets intended for the general public and of petitions to the throne demanded radical changes in the public educational system. *Exhortation to Study*, a book which became a classic, clearly illustrates the attitude of the erudite mandarins at that time.

The names of a few progressive educationalists deserve mention. Among these were Fong Kwei-jen (1809–74), a keen student of economic and social problems, a mathematician and an astronomer, who drew up a map of the heavens; Kieu Fong-kia (1864–1912), who was the first headmaster of the T'ang wen hieu t'ang school at Swabow (1899) and afterwards directed a secondary school and a foreign language institute at Canton; Suen Yi-jang (1848–1908), who opened over 300 primary and secondary schools in his province after the Sino-Japanese War (1894–5) and founded a school of chemistry at Wenchow in 1905; Chang Po-hi (1847–1907), who was Superintendent of Education (1902); Wu Ju-luen, who founded a Western-style school in Cheli with Ho T'ao (1849–1912); Fan Tang-she (1854–1904), and Wang Shu-nan (1851–1936), who was Rector of the University of Peking (1902) and employed Japanese and English professors.

A few Chinese intellectuals even went so far as to approach some Western intellectuals with a view to setting up study circles, technical schools or institutes of higher education or to undertake the translation of foreign works. It was chiefly in the treaty ports that this kind of co-operation found auspicious conditions. To quote only one instance: the *Wu-si* club was founded under the influence of the *Manual of Natural Philosophy* written by Dr Hobson, of the London Missionary Society, and published at Shanghai in 1855. The total number of copies issued was 31,111, comprising 83,456 volumes.

Culture

The Ch'ing dynasty had two official languages, Manchu and Chinese. From 1647 onwards books were printed in the former of these. From the reign of Kien Lung onwards, however, Manchu was merely the private language of the imperial clans. Li Wen-t'ien (1834–95) is one of the few Chinese authors to take an interest in it.

Thus literature was, broadly speaking, written in Chinese for Chinese. Our best guides were Lu Siun, Fung Yuan-kiun and Wan Chung-min.

In the eighteenth century and the first part of the nineteenth, few writers rallied to the school of Tung Ch'eng, the last great post-classical literary school. But fresh developments soon made themselves felt in literary language and style, under the influence of two factors, one external and the other internal.

On the one hand the translation of Western and Japanese works introduced a simple style and a considerable number of philosophical, political and economic neologisms; such concepts as that of the author's own personality (*tseu-wu*) or those of equality (*ping-teng*), liberty (*tseu-yeu*) rights (*kong-k'iuan*), law (*kong-fa*), debate (*kong-yi*), etc. On the other hand, changes were taking place in the Chinese language itself. Hampered by the accepted literary styles (*Wen-t'i*), with their artificial antitheses and rhetorical tropes, it had exhausted its powers of expression. It was therefore compelled to renounce the verbal equipment relied upon by candidates at the triennial competitive examinations and develop simpler forms, nearer to the speech of the common people and better suited to the new cultural problems. Hence the She-wu-ti style, which led to the famous movement known as 'clear language' (Pai-hua yun-tong), 'the new tide' (Sin szeu-chao) or 'the renaissance' because it took up forms which had been forgotten or disdained since the Han and Tang periods.

Philosophy was divided into two principal schools. The Neo-Confucianist or Sung school (Sung-hiue), faithful in spirit and letter to Chu Hi (1130-1200) had achieved its two-thousand-year-old ambition by becoming the State creed, as a result of the promulgation of the holy edict (1671) and the commentary thereon (1724). Represented by Huang Tsung-hi (1610-95) and Fang Tong-shu (1772-1851), it enjoyed the support of the dynasty until the very last, and as late as 1894 a book hostile to Chu Hi was banned by Kwang-Siu (1875-1908) (who saw himself as China's Peter the Great).

Nevertheless, the Sung school found a vigorous opponent in the Han school (Han-hiue), whose members despised literary elegance and wished to revive the spirit of the great classics and to reissue them, freed from the accretions of commentators (as the Western humanists had done at an earlier date). This movement had no taste for metaphysical speculation on Buddhist or Taoist lines. Its interests lay in philology, historical criticism, certain social and economic aspects of communal life, and science.

The greatest philosopher of the Ch'ing period was undoubtedly Tai Chen (1723-77). He wrote two commentaries on the *Shuai-king chu* (1775 and 1776). He shows some influence of the teachings of Yen Yuan (1635-1704) and Ku Yen-wu, and his unconventional attitude also singles him out as an early revolutionary thinker. Tai Chen's ideas were never properly understood, even by the Emperor K'ien Lung, whose favourite he was. His disciples, Hung Pang (1745-1819), Chang Hiue-ch'eng (1738-1801) and Yuan Yuan distorted his teachings, and their importance was not recognized until our own time.

His influence on his contemporaries was kept down to a minimum, for he was never successful in a competitive literary examination. Like all members of the Han-hiue, Tai Chen criticized the Neo-Confucian Sung school, and undertook important historical and philological research. But he was an astronomer and a mathematician as well, and strove to apply astronomical forecasting and methods of analysis to other fields of knowledge. He also believed that specialized research should not be aimed solely at adding to scientific knowledge in all its spheres, but should be used in the elaboration of a new philosophy which would improve the conditions of daily life. At all events, the Han-hiue were often the concealed pioneers of a renaissance which did not come to flower until the late nineteenth and early twentieth centuries.

At the end of the nineteenth century the leading Chinese thinkers were Confucianists, disciples of Wang Yang-ming (1472-1528). They were still asserting the supremacy of ideals, of the mind and of moral perfection; they were the last group of statesmen-philosophers.

K'ang Yiu-wei (1858-1927) ranks with Wang Mang (25) and Wang An-she (1021) among the few reformers imperial China ever produced; but he was hostile to science and democracy and wished to set up Confucianism as the national religion of China. All he achieved was the deification of Cunfucius himself (1907). He was the master of Liang Ki-chao (1873–1929), who advocated a syncretism between Confucianism and Buddhism, and of T'an Sze-tung (1865–98), one of the six martyrs of the movement for reform and the author of a synthesis between Western science and Cunfucianism, Buddhism and Christianity. He knew French and admired the revolution of 1789. Tseng Kwo-fan (1811–72), who defeated the Tai-ping revolt (1865), was typical of the writers who regarded war as a shameful necessity.

Side by side with these national systems there were small groups of Western-minded thinkers who introduced certain elements of foreign philosophy.

Between 1892 and 1905 Yen Fu, a very elegant stylist, translated or adapted T. H. Huxley's *Evolution and Ethics* (1894–6, published in 1898). *The Study of Sociology*, by Herbert Spencer (1898–1902, published in 1903), *On Liberty*, by John Stuart Mill (1899, published in 1903), Adam Smith's *Wealth of Nations* (published in 1901), *A History of Politics*, by E. Jenkins (1903 published in 1904), *L'Esprit des Lois*, by Montesquieu (1903–4, published in 1904), and J. S. Mill's *System of Logic* (1900–2, published in 1905).

Chang Che-tong wrote the *Shu-mu ta-wen*, (1875), an excellent and practical index to literature. The chief prose writers included Wang Sin (1775), Yuan Mei (1716–98), Tuan Yu-tsai (1735–1815), Yao Nai (1732–1815), Pao She-chen (1775–1855), Wei Yuan (1794–1856), Cheng Kwo-fan (1811–72) and Chang Chen-tung (1919). Each dynasty, at least in its early stage, was ambitious of being a great dynasty and remodelling the world out of the chaos left behind by its predecessor. This is what prompted K'ang Hi and K'ien Lung to compile encyclopaedias containing the whole sum of Chinese thought and learning.

The *Kou-kin t'ou-shu si-sheng* (a compilation of ancient and modern writings and drawings) is a famous encyclopaedia composed by order of the Emperor K'ang Hi (1662–1722). It was completed in 1725, and comprised 10,000 parts. The encyclopaedia in four sections (*Sze-kou* or *S'yuan-shu*), thus called because it was arranged in four divisions (canonical books, philosophy and science, history, literary) was compiled between 1772 and 1790, in 36,000 volumes.

The Imperial Library at Peking had 36,275 volumes housed in the *Wen-yuan ko* (1782), and new premises were built to contain the two new encyclopaedias. The largest of the other libraries, after the Wenyuan ko (in the Summer Palace) were the Wen-tsin ko at Jehol, the Wen-so ko at Mukden, the Wen huei ko at Yangchow, the Wen-tsung ko at Sinkiang and the Wen-lan ko at Hangchow. Here the lettered class could consult the latest treatises on mathematics, astronomy, cosmography, engineering and medicine.

Huang Suen-hien (1848–1905) advocated a 'revolution' in poetry. He was one of the first to criticize the conventional forms and to introduce free rhyme which was related to the spoken language. His 'Lamentation on Pyongyang' was prompted by the defeat suffered at Pyongyang in Korea in 1894.

Since Chin and Tang days, short stories had been a vigorous branch of literature. Countless public story-tellers of the Ch'ing period have been lost to history.

Successful novels included the famous *Kin-hwa-yuan* (*The Mirror of Flowers*, or *Mirror of Women*), by Li Ju-chen (1763–1830). This novel was one of the earliest of propaganda novels, dealing with the social problems of women. After the failure of the reform movement (1898) and the suppression of the Boxers, novels were used as an indirect means of criticizing the imperial policy and its abuses. The principal representatives of the 'social novel' were Li Pao-kia, Wu Wo-yao and Liu Ngo. Li Pao-kia (1867–1906), who wrote under the name Nan-ting chang-ting, gives subtle descriptions of sycophantic mandarins and arrogant missionaries. Having failed to pass the local examinations in his province, he went to Shanghai where he edited two magazines whose titles are in themselves indicative of change: *The Guide* and *Let's Have a Laugh*. He was also an excellent engraver of seals. His *Kwan-chang hien-hing ki* (Memorial on the present-day mandarin class) was a gigantic undertaking, intended to comprise 120 chapters, of which only 60 had been written when he died.

Lieu Ngo (*c.* 1850–1910), in addition to being a doctor, collector, engineer, scholar and mathematician, was a writer on social subjects. His finest work, *Lao-sian yiu-ki* (Travels of the Aged Outcast) denounces the faults of the Ch'ing régime.

Wu Wo-yao (1866–1910) became a well-known journalist at Shanghai. In 1902 he was at Yokohama, publishing a magazine, *New Romances*, in collaboration with Liang Ki-chow. He described all classes in the Chinese community, including the inefficient civil servants, in a masterly work entitled 'Strange Events Witnessed for Twenty Years' (*Eul-she nien mou-tou ti kwai-hien-chouang*). In 'Sea of Regrets' (*Hen-hai*) he expressed his reformist sympathies and raised the problem of national humiliation.

Historical studies were highly popular at the end of the nineteenth century. Historians fell into two schools. One of these, the Kin-wen, which included K'ang Yiu-wei (1858–1927) and Liang Ki-chow (1874–1929) represented the views held in philosophy by the Han school, while the Ku-wen school supported the Neo-Confucian philosophers in their attachment to the letter of the canonical books. The latter were eliminated by their adversaries just as the writers who clung to the *wen-ti* style were defeated by the *she-wu-ti* writers.

Huang Tsuen-hien (1848–1905) left a *History of Japan* (*Je-pen kwo-che*, 1887) in 40 chapters, which had a great vogue in the years 1890–8.

The earliest translations were frankly bad. The works were ill chosen (at least half dealt with military and technological matters) and gave no true idea of Western culture, and the translators were unprofessional in their attitude, resorting without hesitation to pirated copies and producing wildly inaccurate versions. Matters were even worse when Western material was rendered at second hand, by way of an earlier Japanese translation. This state of affairs was violently castigated by Chang Che-tong and Liang Ki-chow (1898). Gradually a body of Chinese neologisms was built up to deal with technical, philosophical and religious subjects. In the last years of the nineteenth century the Chinese discovered that Western literature had its poetry, novels and dramatic works. Some Western authors learnt to write Chinese, as the seventeenth- and eighteenth-century Jesuits had done. The younger generation was tremendously influenced by translations of novels and plays (300 in 20 years), even more than those of scientific works. The most-translated Western authors included, Scott, Dickens, Victor Hugo, Stevenson, Dumas *père* and *fils*, Balzac, Ibsen, Conan Doyle, Cervantes and Tolstoy in the field of literature; Huxley and Adam Smith in that of Science; and J. J. Rousseau, Montesquieu, Kant, Schopenhauer, Nietzsche, Comte, Kropotkin, Herbert Spencer and John Stuart Mill in philosophy.

Lin Shu (1852–1924) was as prolific a translator as Yen Fu. He introduced Dickens, Washington Irving and Alexandre Dumas to the readers of *The Dream in the Red Pavillon* and *At the Water's Edge*. His translations of *David Copperfield* and *La Dame aux Camélias* are particularly good.

Traditional China had no periodicals. But the first newspaper, printed from woodblocks, was produced in China in the reign of the T'ang Emperor Kai Yuan (713–41)—hence its title, *Kai-yuan ji-pao* (Official Gazette of the Kai-yuan Period). Ancient China also had bulletins (imperial decrees and memoranda) known as *Ti-pao*, similar in character to Julius Caesar's *Acta Diurna*. The modern press was introduced in 1815, when the *Chinese Monthly Magazine* began to appear at Malacca. This was produced by three missionaries, Robert Morrison, W. Milne and Walter H. Medhurst (1796–1857), helped by one of their converts, Leang Ya-fa, the first Chinese editor. Later, from 1858 onwards, several papers printed in Chinese were founded under foreign management in the treaty ports. Young J. Allen (1836–1907) was one of the missionaries turned journalist. He built up a Western press, printed chiefly in English, one of his best-known papers being the *Review of the Times* (1868). With its campaigns against bandaged feet, concubinage, child marriage enslavement of women, it did more to reform social conditions than any Government measures. The Reverend Timothy Richard (1845–1919) founded a newspaper which became celebrated, the *Wan-kwo kong-pao*. Chinese journalism was initiated in 1873 by Wang Tao (1828–97), a modern-minded Chinese who launched the *Tsun Wan Yat Pao* at Hong Kong in 1874.

Earlier than this, in 1873, a daily paper, the *Chow-wen-sin-pao*, had been started by a Chinese group at Hankow, but it had a small circulation and a very brief career. A group known as 'the three Shanghai friends' (Wang Tao, Li Shan-lan and Tsiang Touen-fu) played an important part in the reform movement during this period. Other pioneer Chinese journalists included Wang She-to (1802–89) and Wu Ting-fang (1842–1922). After the Sino-Japanese war of 1894–5, the reformers tried to use the press as a political weapon. Their success reached its apex in 1897, when they were in control of more than 30 newspapers. The most important of these was *She-wu-pao* (Current Affairs), published for the first time at Shanghai in August 1896 with Liang Ki-chow (1874–1929), the assistant of Kang Yeu-wei (1858–1927), as its director. This paper campaigned for a constitutional monarchy and the development of capitalism in China. Other early Chinese papers were the *Tung-pao* (1877), a Shanghai daily paper interested in foreign countries (it had a circulation of 6,000), the *Lieu-fen* ('Six Minutes'), the *King-pao* or Peking Gazette, which was the official gazette of the Empire; and the first illustrated paper, *Hua-pao* (1884), which reproduced amusing caricature-sketches of European soldiers by Tientsin artists. As well as these news-sheets there were the 'mosquito' papers, or tracts, many of which appeared in Shanghai. The first newspaper in Honan (*Hiang-hiue sin-pao*) was founded in 1897.

The press was widely read by the intellectuals. Chen Tou-sieu (1880–1942) and Wu Yu (1871–1949) used it as a vehicle for evolutionary teachings and for their views on equal rights. Tseu Yong, Chen Tien-hua and Wu Yue published their anti-dynastic sentiments in the papers; the first of the three published *Armed Revolution* (1903) and the second *Awakening* (1904), and both articles were reprinted in the Kiangsu newspaper.

In 1899 Sun Yat-sen (1866–1925) founded the first Chinese revolutionary paper, *Chong-kwo ji-pao* (The Chinese Daily) at Hong Kong, and in November 1905 the *T'ong-meng hwei* (Chinese Revolutionary League) began to issue the *Min-pao* (People's Journal) in Japan.

4. RELIGIOUS LIFE AND THOUGHT

First come the three great religions, Taoism, Buddhism and Confucianism. At the period with which we are concerned they were of no more than historical interest, though they still had their own clergy and temples. The general population did not observe them, either collectively (in accordance with the ill-conceived concept of a triple religion, *san-kiao*) or individually. The lack of co-ordination on an empire-wide scale had led to the gradual development of a popular religion which had borrowed from all three of the great organized, recognized churches, but which must nevertheless be regarded as a separate system with considerable local variations, such as those to which Father Dore devoted his eighteen volumes. Nothing could be more mistaken than the widespread assumption that all the Chinese were Buddhists.

Alongside this popular religion there were also forms of guild worship, centring on tutelary figures chosen as patrons by the mandarins, the craftsmen, the tradespeople, the sailors, the peasants, the soldiers, the doctors, etc.; secret or semi-secret societies established for social, political or shamanistic purposes (these sought to create states of trance, possession or hysteria, sometimes associated with social, religious and sexual promiscuity, practices denounced in the imperial decrees as 'vicious cults'); the official worship paid by the imperial family to the patrons of the dynasty, Kwan-ti and Kwan-yin. This outline gives some idea of the manner in which the various religions overlapped and had become inextricably entangled.

It should also be realized that any human being, man or woman, could be deified. The gods were human beings, endowed after their death with super-natural powers, so that they all passed through life on earth. The highest-ranking divinities retained their functions in perpetuity, while the lesser gods were celestial officials, who could be replaced in their posts, promoted or reduced, and be reborn as men.

The official religion had as its ministers the Emperor, the Empress and their representatives throughout the Empire, the mandarins of the civil service. Rather than priests these were masters of the ceremonies held in honour of Confucius, his disciples, and the historical figures who had been deified for outstanding services to the country or the dynasty. Since the celestial and imperial worlds were identical, these ministers could also promote or down-grade certain genii or lesser divinities. As well as this pontifical role the mandarins had a negative part to play; for as R. Stein has shown clearly, they were required to impede the expansion of Buddhism and Taoism by a display of hostility based solely on political and social considerations (tax evasion, the non-productivity and non-fecundity of the clergy, the sterile accumulation of real estate and personal property). Priests were officially called in only as specialists in certain essential rites (prayers for the dead, healing sickness, or obtaining rain) and no religion was given preference. The leaders of the 'vicious cults', because of their efforts to communicate with the supernatural world, were even more exposed to the hostility of official circles than were the bonzes and the *Tao-she*. The mandarins always strove to counter the 'Diony-siac' attitude and hysterical tendencies of the 'exuberant' cults by their own 'Apollonian' tendencies, which concentrated on the establishment of the 'golden mean' and of a prudently balanced mentality.

At the end of the nineteenth century Kang Yiu-wei, disturbed by China's lack of a properly organized religion, tried to establish a Confucian church, based on an alliance between the dynasty and religion. By an imperial edict of 1906, Confucius was raised to the same rank as Tien and Hiu Tou (Heaven and Earth), whose worship was reserved for the Emperor.

By the end of the eighteenth century, Taoism and Buddhism had developed so many similar features and borrowed so extensively from each other that it seems natural to study them together. Comparatively little was now being written about Taoism, but it still provided the inspiration for a few major works, including a collection of short stories and a *Summary of Ethics*. Chang Tai-yen tried to bring Confucianism into harmony with Taoism. Buddhism was a stimulus to artists and still deserved its title of 'doctrine of images' in all three of its forms—the Lamaist, the Hinayanist and the Mahayanist. Lamaism was to be found in the north-west and extended as far as Peking.

There was little activity in Buddhism of the Lesser Vehicle or among the Vedantists. The worship of Amida was, however, very popular and gave rise to a fairly considerable literature. The monks were not so dynamic as their Japanese counterparts, who went to Europe to study the scriptures or the functioning of the Christian churches (Shimaji Mokurai, 1873–4; Nanjo Bunyu, 1878), or their Indian brothers who founded the *Maha bodhi* (Society of the Great Awakening) in 1891 in Ceylon, whence it spread to all parts of the world.

Nevertheless, Buddhism was a subject of interest to Yang Wen-hwei, ambassador to Paris and London, and T'an Sze-tung, one of the six martyrs of the reform movement. And there were still a few great figures among the monks, such as Wang Wen-she (1730–1802), a scholar, calligrapher and poet who had at one time been a senior official in the imperial service, and P'eng Shao-sheng (1740–96), a member of the 'Pure Earth' sect. The latter's asceticism and mysticism did not lead him to neglect the Buddhist, Taoist and Confucian classics, and he tried to reconcile Confucianism and Buddhism. He wrote biographical studies of the Buddhists of the 'pure' sect (*Ts'ing-t'ou sheng-hien lu* and *Kiu-she-chwan*) and of the Buddhist nuns (*c.* 1770–5).

The *Jewish* religion, probably imported from Iran, was confined to small communities, to be found at Nanking, Peking, Ning-po and Kai-fong-fu (the capital of Honan). Its adepts were more Chinese than Jewish, having forgotten the Hebrew language, and were not among the more cultivated groups in the Empire. Their cultural and political significance was very slight.

Moslems (*ts'iao-men, hwei-hwei*) had been known in China since the T'ang period, but were of comparatively little importance until the nineteenth century, when several Chinese translations of the Koran were published (1827, 1828, 1831 and 1862). Lieu Che (*c.* 1770) was the best Moslem writer of this period, during which many works of propaganda appeared in Yunnan, Kansu and the Tarim. Ma An-li of Yunnan made a Chinese adaptation of the *Qasidat el-Burdat* by the celebrated Egyptian poet Al-Busiri (1212–96), in the style of the *Book of Odes*. He called his translation *Tien-fang she-king* (the Book of Arab Odes) and it was published at Chengtu (Szechwan) in 1890. In 1775 Kien Lung subdued Kashmir, Tibet and various parts of Burma, and made what appeared to be a successful attempt to establish Chinese civilization in Turkestan. From 1840 onwards, however, there was a progressive awakening of the Chinese Moslem community, which was seething with excitement during the Crimean War and during the serious disturbances in 1856. This was a period of rebellions in Yunnan (1818–19, 1826–8, 1834–40, 1856, 1861, 1863, 1864, 1875). The leaders included Ma To-sin (d. 1874) and Tou Wen-siu (d. 1872), who ruled at Ta-li-fu from 1856 to 1872 under the name of Sultan Soliman, and was defeated by Ts'en Yu-ying (1829–89). Sinkiang too was the scene of disturbances (1873–7), which were put down by Tso Tsung-t'ang (1812–85). His adversary was Yakub Beg (*c.* 1820–77), Emir of Kashghar, who had obtained diplomatic recognition from Turkey, Russia and England.

The total number of Moslems must have been less than 20 million. Their influence was limited and few of them rose to a high level in the Imperial service—one of the exceptions being Ma Sin-yi (1821–70), who was assassinated by chauvinists when he was Governor-General of Nanking. Turkestan had its own decorative arts (carpets, metalwork and painting), represented by Kao Tsu (1752–1827) and by a celebrated imperial concubine who was forced by the Dowager Empress to commit suicide. Thus the Moslems constituted an important minority, designated by one of the five horizontal bands on the flag of the first Chinese Republic.

Orthodox Christianity was introduced into China by a religious mission headed by Hilarion Lejaiskii (d. 1718). This had come to Peking in 1768 to attend to the prisoners from Albazine (the *albazintzi*) who had been brought to Peking. It remained there after the departure of the Catholic Mission (1826), which left it part of its library, now at the University of Kazan. In 1861 it was replaced by a secular mision. Nevertheless it remained fairly active and included in its ranks an eminent sinologist, Palladius Kagarov (d. 1878). The Russian clergy were well liked by the Chinese populace, and seem never to have been disturbed.

Catholicism made a flying start, but under the Ch'ing emperors, who regarded the cultural role of the Catholic church as much more important than its religious mission, Catholicism suffered an eclipse. Except at Peking and Macao, Catholic worship was prohibited until 1860, and Kia-K'ing (1796–1820) issued an edict for the persecution of Christians in general (1805). Thereafter, missionaries were tolerated only in the imperial circle, as scientists, artists or craftsmen. But they were not actually banished, as in Japan, until 1826. The Jesuits had been succeeded by the Lazarists in 1783, and the last Lazarist died at Peking in 1838.

About 1905 the number of Catholics approached the million mark and was steadily increasing. They were in charge of many schools and hospitals and of important universities.

The first Protestant missionaries—the Englishman Robert Morrison (1782–1834) and Gutzlaff (1803–51) and the Americans Bridgman and Parker—had not made more than a hundred Chinese converts by 1840, the first of these being Liang A-fa (1789–1855) who was converted at Macao in 1814. Later, protected by the treaties, they made considerable progress under the leadership of men like Timothy Richard and C. W. Matteer. By 1897 there were 50,000 Chinese Protestants. The missions controlled 1,819 primary schools, 170 high schools and 257 hospitals. Like their Catholic counterparts, the Protestant missionaries were active in the field of culture, doing pioneer work in education, the popularization of science, the translation of Western books and the press, while their medical activities were of prime importance. Mention must at least be made, among these pioneers, of Parker (1842) at

Canton, Lockhart (1844) at Shanghai, Holson (1843) at Hong Kong and MacGowan (1843) at Ningpo.

T'an Sze-tung (1865–98), in his *Jen-hiue* (Study of Benevolence), advocates a combination of Confucianism, Buddhism and Christianity with elements of Western science. His refusal of aid from his Japanese friends and his death as one of the six voluntary martyrs of the reform movement—on the principle that innocent blood must be shed so that the new China could come into being —illustrate the noble ideal which inspired certain forms of Chinese religious syncretism.

Later on, disputes broke out within and between the various Protestant churches. Some of those concerned failed to appreciate the great complexity of the task the missionaries had taken up, or to perceive the value of the schools and hospitals, which were expensive to maintain and which they regarded as useless or even highly dangerous. They underestimated the obstacles to be overcome and overestimated the dynamic force of Christianity as a factor in the reconstruction of China. There was also considerable controversy as to the relative importance of the civilizing, social and strictly religious roles under-taken by the msisions. This was particularly acute in English Protestant circles about 1863. The missions gradually found that they could not confine themselves to their original aim, that of saving souls from hell without regard to the conditions of life on earth.

Towards the end of the nineteenth century, under the joint influence of progress in sinological studies and changes in Western ideas, a new source of conflict made its appearance, dividing the American and English evangelical laymen, the traditional supporters of the missions, from the more modern tendencies of the younger missionaries, denounced as 'diabolical signs of the spirit of the century'. It became apparent to Protestants and Catholics alike that Christianity was not necessarily bound up with Western civilization and its languages, but that certain other cultures were sufficiently advanced to provide a vehicle for it. The logical consequence was to set up independent churches to keep pace with the development of nationalism in politics, to train Chinese as clergy and to encourage the use of the Chinese language for purposes of worship. All this gave rise to considerable difficulties, and was not achieved until much later, after sometimes impassioned debate. A few European missionaries went so far as to adopt Chinese nationality.

Similar changes took place in the attitude it was thought fit to adopt towards non-Christians. In the early nineteenth century the unchallenged prestige of Western residents in China gave them a sense of superiority from which some of the missionaries were not immune. They showed no more respect for the heathen Chinese state than their European brethren displayed towards governments hostile to their own churches. The 'pagans' were often harshly described as 'barbarians' and 'sinful vessels', and some of their forms of worship were even denied the name of religion. Buddhism was among these, and not until much later did it come to be regarded with something better than objectivity—with real understanding, sometimes coupled with a desire to adopt its values in the intellectual and moral training of Christians.

Though the Chinese were curious about foreign religions (and in some cases embraced martyrdom in their cause), many of them underestimated the importance of the religious factor as a basic element in Western civilization and in individual life in the West. K'ang Yiu Wei and Liang K'i-chow were essentially scientists, unshakably convinced that science was the principal cultural value in Europe and that it could eradicate religion without undesirable repercussions in other cultural spheres. They were apt to regard religion as the handmaid of politics. Argument on the subject was sometimes envenomed by the inferior quality of certain Chinese Christians ('rice-bowl Christians') who used their faith as an excuse for claiming protection or material advantage from the missionaries. The missionaries did not always suit their activities to the views of their respective consuls, and this created difficulties for the provincial mandarins, whose instructions were contradictory. Even the tenor of life in orphanages and hospitals might be disturbed by rumours (Tientsin massacre, 1870) which, though totally unfounded, found belief among a population completely unprepared for scientific medicine and unable to grasp the fact that even charitable foundations must have a budget, however small its receipts. Moreover, there is evidence of a frequent time-lag between Chinese criticism and the changing Western ideas. At the very time when the young missionary teams had succeeded, not without difficulty, in convincing their superiors that religious problems must be approached with fuller and more friendly understanding, they were being judged unfairly for attitudes they had outgrown, but which the Chinese believed to be still prevalent. Lastly, as foreigners (for whose benefit taxes were levied and humiliating conditions imposed) the missionaries became scapegoats for the nation's resentment.

Neither the Chinese nor the Indian civilizations ever experienced the religious wars which are almost inevitable in cases where belief is rigorously defined by laws set forth in a sacred book. The 'book' religions (Judaism, Christianity, Islam) are obliged to attribute to the letter of the law an importance the Chinese never attached to it. The Chinese inclined to the opinion that all forms of religion had their value and could be placed on an equal footing; and furthermore, that they all deserved study. Thus it is that we have certain Taoist interpretations of Christianity. The Chinese went even further than this, however, pushing the idea of reconciliation to the point of attempts at syncretic religion. A good present-day example of this is Caodaïsm in south Vietnam. But an excellent illustration of it was provided long before by the Tai-ping religion, which was a mixture of Bible texts—unaccompanied by any form of gloss, vestiges of the most ancient field-cults; and rationalism.

In a prison in Peking in 1912, one conference-room was hung with portraits of Christ, Lao-tse, Confucius, John Howard and Mahomet.

5. THE GENERAL SITUATION OF CHINA ABOUT THE YEAR 1905

Li Hong-chang, the 'Iron Chancellor', and his 'War Lords' represented the views of continental China in its traditional anti-revolutionary, anti-democratic and chauvinistic aspects. They wished to preserve the heritage of the past (*ti-pao*), Confucian paternalism and the hard-and-fast laws which made class struggle impossible, since they recognized only the duties of the individual. They had taken credit for the extermination of the *Tai-ping* and for the 'health treatment' which had a few industrial and economic achievements to its credit.

They were not to maintain their hold very long, however, for the Chinese feudal system had been overthrown once and for all by Western capitalism. The closed, aristocratic China of the big landowners now had to confront a China whose trade and sea-power were expanding, a Westernized China. Prominent in this were the international-minded *compradores* who had a stake in the success of foreign firms, the prosperity of the 'concessions' and the division of the Empire into zones of influence. They were the successors of the Han merchants, except that the national authorities had virtually no control over them. Another factor was the 'overseas China' composed of emigrants, originally from Canton, who had settled at Batavia, Honolulu and San Francisco and, from 1860 onwards, had been filling all available territory in south-east Asia. This was first of all an economic power, but later developed political leanings of a strongly anti-dynastic character, favourable to the Ming dynasty as the Tai-ping had been, but systematically anti-Manchu. Though nationalistic in sentiment it was not chauvinist in the Boxer sense, for it established bases in Japan and the British colonies. Moreover it had accepted the Western views as to the rights of the individual, social revolution and democracy. A final factor was the emergence of a Chinese capitalist and a Chinese proletarian class, due to the activities of certain Chinese industrialists, whose interests were seriously prejudiced by the presence of foreign industry and who looked to Chinese independence as the one hope of normal expansion for their firms.

The great mass of workers and peasants were not yet ready to overthrow the political and social structure; but the intellectual middle classes, with their interest in trade and industry, had at last begun to play a not unimportant role in the economic and political life of the Empire.

They revived some of the aims of the Tai-ping, more especially the concept of 'government by the people'. The word *min* (people) was now much in vogue. The 'People's Newspaper' (*min-pao*) was founded at Tokyo in 1905 by Leang Ki-chow (1874–1929), and talk about how the new 'people' (*sin-min*) would save the country was the order of the day. This idea was harped on by a number of secret societies. They were much more than mere partisans of dynastic reform, for they were losing their religious aspects and becoming more and more exclusively nationalist and anti-dynastic. In 1905 they managed to unite. There is an appreciable contrast between the severity with which they were hunted down in the early nineteenth century and their situation at the end of that same century. True, Liu Kwen-yi (1830–1902), Governor-General at Hankin, confiscated the weapons of the anti-missionary *Ko-lao-hwei* Society and, in agreement with Chang Che-tong (1837–1909), Governor of Hopei and Hunan, neutralized the Boxers in 1900. But in many other provinces the societies were encouraged, on the instructions of the Imperial Court, and established their own cells in the militia created in 1898.

An important part was played by Tseu Yong (1885–1905), on his return from studying in Japan. In 1902 he wrote *Ko-ming kiun* (The Revolutionary Army), which marked an important stage in the anti-Manchu revolution, for which it laid down a practical doctrine. Tseu died in prison a month before he was to have been released. Other names to be remembered are those of Tao Cheng Chang (1911) and Siu Si-lin (1873–1907), the latter of whom was the leader of the *Kwang-fu hwei* movement; of Sun Yat-sen (1866–1925), founder of the *Hing-chong hwei* at Tokyo; of Hwang Hing (1873–1916), leader of the *Hwa-hing hwei*, and of Mrs Tsiu Kin (1879–1907). Revolutionary activity was conducted not only in China and Japan but abroad, in South-East Asia and in Europe.

Li She-tseng (alias Li Yu-ying), born in 1882, studied biology at Montpellier and translated Kropotkin in a magazine founded in Paris in 1905 by himself, Wu Che-hwei and Wang Tsing-wei. The foundation of the Université d'Outre-mer at Lyons was due to this group. Shortly afterwards, Li joined the Kuomintang.

Peking had lost much of its cultural and political influence, which had passed to Tientsin and Shanghai. In those two cities publishers and journalists were protected from the spies of the imperial Government by the operation of concessions, which also favoured the spread of new ideas, afterwards smuggled into the rest of the Empire.

In 1905 all the secret societies amalgamated into a group called the *Chong-kuo tong-meng huei*, a revolutionary party from which the Kuomintang issued later. They were already imbued with a lofty spirit, and though they sometimes resorted to Russian-style terrorist methods, they had their martyrs too. Among the population their prestige had by this time outshone that of the dynasty. In 1904 Sun Yat-sen published his 'Abridgement of the Revolution', in which he foretold the end of imperial rule, a democratic constitution, a Republic in which all Chinese would be equal, and a form of socialism in agriculture. He formulated the three essential points of his programme, the 'three *min*' (people). a single people, all power for the people, everything for the benefit of the people.

In an article entitled 'To our Readers', he set forth the three principles of the people—Nationalism, Democracy and Life. He called upon the people to rise against the monarchy. His newspaper, the *Ming-pao*, ran a series of studies of the French Revolution of 1789, and some reports, illustrated by photo-graphs, on the budding revolution of 1905, which had considerable reper-cussions not only in Russia but in the Far East. Journalism flourished in this way chiefly in places where the censorship and the imperial police were power-less, such as the Western concessions in China and the Chinese 'colonies' in Japan. Between 1903 and 1907 seven separate magazines, each running to 80 pages, were published by Chinese students in Japan. In addition to political contributions, they carried Chinese translations of Western literary articles already translated into Japanese.

After the war between China and Japan in 1894, Kang Yeu-wei, Liang Ki-chow and others began to advocate the reform of the state. When Russia was defeated by Japan in 1905, the victory of the latter was attributed to its constitution, by virtue of which a little country like Japan had been able to overcome Imperial Russia, that vast and absolute monarchy. The result was a movement in favour of a constitution for China. The Ch'ing Court was obliged to send a diplomatic mission to Europe and America in 1905, to study the principles of a constitution. The President of the Ministry of Ceremonies visited 9 countries.

The armed forces were a power to be reckoned with. The Wu wei yu kiun, one of the four armies defending Peking, which was commanded by Yuan She-kai, formed the nucleus of a regular army (Pei-yang lu-kiun). Its numbers were raised by stages to six divisions (1905). Notable generals became prominent political figures. The new army drew its officers from a special military founded in 1900. Its ranks were not filled by conscription. It retained as its basis the old provincial militia, the organization of which had been amended by Lieu Kuen-yi in 1898. Some of the larger units were drilled and armed in the Western manner, and their military qualities were unquestionable. One such was the army corps led by Yuan She-kai (1859–1916), which was trained on European lines.

The nationalist drive engendered a militaristic spirit in which revolutionaries and conservatives could all participate. The Chinese army was represented in the German manoeuvres of 1905.

Cadets were sent to Japan, Germany and France for training. And, astonishingly enough, the soldiers were cheered in the theatre. Clear-sighted observers were uneasy, however. Without a modern army the nation was at the mercy of its foreign creditors. With a modern army it was at the mercy of the 'Warlords'. There could be no escape from this dilemma except by a revolution in the country and a complete transformation of foreign policy.

But education remained backward. In some provinces 98·5 per cent of the peasants had received none at all. In the vicinity of the towns illiteracy amounted to between 75 and 87 per cent—the rate being higher among women than among men—and there could be no question of arranging adult education classes. As a result of the educational reform (1902–4) and the abolition of the triennial competitive examinations (1905) the classical system of education had collapsed; but it could not be immediately replaced. In 1903 scientific studies had been put on the same footing as literary ones. But this had not sufficed to change the mental attitude of the pupils so that they could reap the full benefit of the change. Some members of the Government still clung to the old idea that the purpose of education was to train civil servants. For them, the abolition of the competitive examinations merely meant that the Government now needed civil servants of a different type. The idea that education was the right of every child and should be provided at the nation's expense was not generally accepted, though it was gaining ground.

The crux of the problem was how to organize the educational system and recruit teachers. Most of the latter had never been outside their own country. A few of them had visited the Western countries or Japan and were now, with the best of intentions, trying to apply a system of teaching devised for foreign peoples, which had no appeal for the vast majority of Chinese, whose requirements differed from those of the intellectuals who formed their only link with the outer world. Although these intellectuals belonged to a social élite of high professional quality, they tended to imbibe only one selected foreign culture, whereas respect for their country's intellectual autonomy should have prompted them to seek out what was best in every modern civilization. And in their attitude to the one they selected they were apt to be insufficiently critical, content to imitate instead of assimilating what was useful in it. Generally speaking, therefore, they formed a group which, though very useful from the technical standpoint, was too limited in its activities and in its individual interests to understand the broader aspirations of their pupils and acquaint them with the fundamental values of their own national history and literature. Sun Yat-sen (1866–1925) showed a clear awareness of this when he wrote (San-min chu-yi) that 'Chinese culture should be the essence of our education, and Western teaching methods should be merely the vehicle for purveying that education'.

All these schools were independent bodies, constructed on social foundations that were too restricted and with a view to a form of public life that had no reality. They were incapable of playing any role in the community.

Modern schools were still few in number, because of the lack of teachers of whom there were only 4,222 for 102,767 pupils.

The educational establishments opened by foreigners were nearly all of the secondary or higher type rather than at primary level. They were not intended for the humble classes but for the privileged circles which produced the ruling élite.

In 1905 the relationship between China and the West was very hard to define. In order to visualize it more clearly it is by no means superfluous to stress the radically different mentality of the two parties. The constant scientific and technological advances made by the West during the nineteenth century had increased the expectation of life, stabilized the national currencies, enhanced the prestige of science and steadily augmented Europe's technical capacities. Europe had thus developed a deep-rooted sense of security and an intoxicating conviction of its own intellectual and material superiority. Hence it was that ever since the Opium War every conflict between China and the West had ended in a treaty considered by the Chinese to be 'inequitable' and 'unilateral', because China had no effective national army or political representatives to pit against the foreign powers. The history of the treaty ports had been one long succession of mutual recriminations.

China soon came to be treated no longer as a sovereign state but (though the word was never pronounced) as a 'supercolony', more enslaved than the real colonies. It was therefore not surprising that these seventy years of tension and conflict should have culminated in the Boxer disaster (1900). This ended with a treaty that was particularly ill-conceived, since it forced the Chinese people to pay dearly for the errors of a foreign dynasty maintained on the throne by other foreigners. As a result, thousands of students left for Japan, where Liang Ki-chow and Sun Yat-sen themselves were living at that time.

China kept in touch with the West through the foreigners then living in China (who in 1905 numbered less than 20,000) and through her diplomatic and cultural relations with the Western countries. The enthusiasm felt by the Chinese reformers of 1898 and thereabouts, which paralleled that of the Indian liberals around 1880 and of the Western-minded among the Japanese, was now beginning to fade. But though the surface of things was deceptively calm there were still many occasions of conflict, owing to the existence on both sides of that unfailing spirit of indulgence, that serenity of mind, which induces acceptance and comprehension and is known to the Hindus as *mantu*.

While the Western visitors complained that there was a barrier which prevented them from penetrating into the country and effecting more rapid changes, the Chinese were indignant at the ascendancy gained in their land by newcomers whom until recently they had openly scorned as barbarians. It exasperated them to see that the Western influence, which in ordinary circumstances might have been useful, was on the contrary endangering their nation. The Western visitors, on the other hand, overestimated their material strength and even more their intellectual and moral prestige. Few of them could see that their greatness was deceptive and that the Chinese weakness was equally so. For in spite of its forty years of intercourse with these foreigners, including two invasions and three draconian treaties, its appalling disintegration and its manifest decrepitude, old China had kept its independent spirit intact and was determined never to abandon it.

In 1899 Liang Ki-chow (1874–1929) declared that he was trying to discover the soul of China. China had, in point of fact, achieved self-awareness since 1894 and 1898. But that awareness flowed like a subterranean river, which would not rise to the surface until about 1900–8. That was the time when

China, with a rapidly increasing population, tired of being not merely subdued but subjugated by foreigners and swamped with ideas which were enforced rather than accepted, followed Japan, India and other Asian countries by taking up the challenge flung at it by the West. Soon after the Boxer episode the dynamic elements among the nation were swept by a mighty intellectual, moral, political and social wave into a revolution which has not yet been brought to a standstill.

CHAPTER XXVIII

THE DEVELOPMENT OF JAPAN

I. WESTERN INFLUENCE ON JAPANESE CULTURE[1]

DURING the Tokugawa period (1603–1868) Japan was cut off from external influences and was able to consolidate her national culture, which had already been subjected to, and had assimilated, the Confucianism of China and the Buddhist culture of India. Her attitude to the West during this long period of seclusion was a blend of curiosity, respect, and fear. European imports, such as paper screens decorated with European figures, which came through the 'permitted' port of Nagasaki, were much prized by the *daimyôs* and the wealthy and even by the ordinary people. The words *Nanban torai* (imported from the West) exercised a powerful attraction. Western knowledge—especially astronomy, geography, botany and medicine —was viewed with great respect, but only by those who were sufficiently educated to understand its importance. After the Meiji restoration, however, the study of the natural sciences made great progress.

Finally, the ordinary people were afraid of the West, and particularly of Christianity. The tragic happenings at Shimabara (1638–9), when 37,000 Christians besieged in Hara Castle fought to the death against the armies of the Shogun, had made a terrible impression; it led to the isolationist policy of the Shogunate and to the severe repression of Christianity which made the masses regard Christianity as somehow accursed. The Russian threat from the north, and that of England from the south added to the feeling that the West was dangerous and terrifying. The final result of all this was the decision of Japan to enter into competition with the West, and, if possible, to outclass it; this decision was to lead to the risk of Japan's becoming a militarist and imperialist nation, so strong was her attitude of pride and independence in face of the occidental menace.

In 1804 Russia was threatening the north of Japan and twenty years later England threatened the south. The utter defeat of China in the Opium War of 1840–2 was a terrible shock to many Japanese who had previously thought of Western power as something rather unreal. Following Chinese history books, which were familiar to them, the Japanese of the late Tokugawa period regarded the new menace from the West as 'barbarians' from across the frontiers, who should be expelled from the soil of their country. A book written in 1825 by Aizu Seishisai (1782–1863), the *Shin Ron* or New Theory, reflects this attitude. It begins:

'The holy land of Japan is the place where the sun rises and where the spirit is born. The descendant of the Sun ascends the throne without a break from generation to generation. He is the ruler of the earth, the orderer of the world, whose dominion should be universal—for no place is too remote to be blessed by his royal grace. But in recent times the barbarians of the Western wastes have rampaged all over the world, invading country after country and attempting to overthrow the High Country despite their poor resources. What arrogance!'

Here we see the two main ideas of the divine nature of Japan and its Emperor and the expulsion of the inferior barbarians from the West.

Yet Japan was forced to open her ports to the rest of the world and, upon contact, the Westerners were found to be quite different from what they had been supposed (Pl. 91) as the following passage illustrates:

'Nine out of ten Japanese look upon Europeans as dogs or horses and some dare to kill them. But the Europeans are different: they regard foreigners as their brothers. In the United States, a new country, people have mild tempers. As we said, they love the Japanese more than their brothers. Although we cannot understand them completely. they seem frank and honest. If the Japanese knew this, they would not wish to kill them. Moreover, in the United States even presons of high rank do not despise their inferiors or abuse their authority, so that the ordinary people do not have to kowtow to them. The country is wealthy and the people live in peace; if the foolish people of Japan saw this, they would certainly be touched by it, even the great ones, since it is the result of a real spirit. At this time only 77 Japanese travelled in the United States, and all hated the Americans; they will change their minds and be sorry for their lack of understanding—it will be like waking up from a nightmare.'

This passage comes from a diary written in 1861 by a Japanese sent to the West by the Shogunate. As the country became more open, such ideas gained wider currency. In 1870 a review even advocated the improvement of the race by intermarriage with the West. Within about ten years contempt and fear had changed into respect and the desire to imitate the West.

But this was not sufficient to make it possible for an independent Japan to play a part in international affairs. It was not until the twentieth century that Japan established her equality with the West strongly enough to be able to insist on the revision of the treaties. This treaty problem had been the central difficulty of the Meiji period, and had led to the tragicomedy of the Rokumaikan years (late 1880s) when Japanese politicians resorted to masquerade to strengthen their diplomacy. Japan's aim, after the opening of her ports, was to become *Fukoku Kyohei* (a wealthy state with a strong army) in Western style, but opinions were divided as to the method of achieving it. Some, like Fukuzawa (1834–1907), declared that 'the independence of man leads to the independence of the country', and wished to concentrate first on wealth; the army circles, however, wished to make Japan militarily strong, without necessarily making her aggressive.[2] The Sino-Japanese and Russo-Japanese wars were not in fact wars of aggression, but were caused by competition with

China in Korea, and Russian pressure in Manchuria respectively, although it is true that military influence was later to become dangerous. However, all Japanese were agreed on their aim, and on the necessity for imitating the West.

This imitation, however, was not to be allowed to go too far, so that Japan would become a 'cultural colony' of the West. When, as during the Roku-meikan period, this did occur, there was at once a reaction in favour of things Japanese, which became even ultra-nationalist. In fact the *Tennô Sei* (emperor system), a modern state which recognized the absolute authority of the Emperor, was Japan's answer to Western political influence.[3]

The Meiji restoration was the negation of the Tokugawa feudalistic régime; it was made possible by two almost contradictory movements—the 'progressive' one of public emancipation and the opening of the ports, and the 'conservative' one of the *Osei Fukka*, the restoration of imperial rule. When in 1868 the Emperor Meiji (*Meiji Tennô*) came to the throne he took an oath of which the first clause ran: 'Public councils shall be organized, and all governmental affairs shall be decided by public opinion.' The fifth and last clause said that 'Knowledge shall be sought the world over, and thus the foundations of the Empire shall be strengthened.' The other three clauses were all concerned with liberation and the foundation of a new Japan. This gave rise to the expression *Meiji ishin* (*Meiji*, restoration; *ishin*, quite new), and the people enjoyed using the phrase *Go ishin* (graciously new). Yet one must not overstress the new elements, since the centre of the restoration was the abolition of the Shogunate and the replacement of the Emperor at the centre of the Government as in ancient Japan.

In the first clause of the Emperor's oath there existed the germs of parliamentary government. The passage 'Public councils shall be organized' was originally drafted as 'Councils of magnates shall be organized'. When it became public, the wording was changed, but it is impossible to tell what it was meant to imply, although when an agitation for parliamentary government began about 1873 it was based on the phrase in question. On the other hand, the sacred and inviolable emperor, the descendant of the gods, was now to have actual political power. These two ideas, difficult to harmonize, were enshrined in the Meiji constitution of 1889.[4]

The position of the emperor was not definitely decided at the beginning; there were, in fact, three different trends of thought. In the first place, there were those who wished the emperor to be a religious authority—the scholars of the *Kokugaku* (National Learning) and the Shintoists—and this was the main ideological basis of the restoration as a result of which the *Jingi-Kan* (the administrator in charge of Shintoism) was placed above the *Dajê-Kan* Cabinet or Supreme Council) after the restoration. But this was changed within a year, for the politicians were well aware that the Shinto idea of the coincidence of religion and politics would not suit the new political conditions in Japan.

A second group, influenced by Confucianism, believed that it was the emperor's task, according to the will of heaven, to diffuse morality among the people, and that it was from this that his dignity derived. This was clearly expressed in the Imperial Rescript (1890) but had a certain irrelevance to politics.

The third group, which regarded the emperor's power as a political one, were largely those who had taken an actual part in the restoration and in the Government which followed; they were in political contact with the West and had some idea of Western political thought. Their ideas became embodied in the Meiji constitution which, while declaring the emperor to be sacred and inviolable, vested in him political prerogative. Before this could be settled there had been, however, much discussion. Some small groups favoured the French system and disapproved of imperial absolutism, others wished to imitate England. In the end the Prussian system found the greatest favour. Finally, although the idea of the emperor's political authority was enshrined in the constitution, it must be emphasized that this did not automatically exclude the other two points of view: that in fact the religious and moral views of the emperor's authority were also accepted as presupposed or implicit. This meant the possible danger of deification of the emperor, which was accentuated by the fact that he stood for the spirit of Japan in a new age. (Pl. 88).

Certainly this belief in the absolutism of the emperor was a factor in the progress of Japan. The Emperor Meiji was, in fact, also a first-class statesman, and took a prominent part in the development of his country. It was probably after the Taisnô era that respect for the emperor became an empty formality. To summarize the state of Japan in the Meiji period, one might say that it was rather a combination than a synthesis of ancient and modern—centred upon the emperor, yet containing some elements of a modern parliamentary state. This was Japan's political reaction to Western influence.

The breakdown of Tokugawa feudalism in politics was bound to lead to far-reaching social changes. After the restoration in the 1870s the feudal lords were deprived of their hereditary status and transformed into an official class, appointed by the Government. The rest of the populace—*bushi*, farmers, artisans and merchants—all became citizens. The nobles of the court and the *daimyôs*, now called the flower class, were allowed to retain their privileges. The *bushi* class, whose status was very complex, were now called *Shizoku* (the warrior class), while the farmers, artisans and merchants were classed as *Heimin* (the people). The warriors and farmers were allowed to trade. Thus the closed 'caste' society was effectively abolished, with its social distinctions of *Shi-nô-kô-shô* (*bushi*, farmer, artisan, merchant) in favour of an open modern society.

Politically, the influence of the West had resulted in a combination of the two systems; socially, neither synthesis nor combination occurred, but rather a mixture of Japanese and Western culture. Changes in clothing first occurred in military uniforms: in fact, one may say that Westernization in Japan occurred in general first in the military field. Towards the end of the Shogunate both the Shogun and the powerful clans realized the needs of improved defence; warships were purchased from the West, and the clans attempted to construct modern weapons. (Pl. 94). Although suspect, those who understood Western science were respected. Takashima Shûhan (1798–1866) of Nagasaki was invited to Edo (Tokyo) by the Shogunate to train soldiers on Western lines. During the wars connected with the restoration the superiority of Western arms became evident. When the *bushi* class was abolished and conscription introduced, military uniforms on a Western pattern were adopted, because of their convenience. Civil servants wore Western dress and sat on chairs in their offices; policemen, too, wore uniforms. Court robes became Westernized, and to dress in Western style became not merely useful but a matter of prestige. Similarly men began to cut their hair, women to dress it in European styles, and watches and umbrellas became widespread. There was, of course, a movement of reacton against the abandonment of the national dress, but most people began to wear European clothes at school and at the office. On returning home, however, most of them changed into Japanese clothes—perhaps because of their comfort in that particular climate, perhaps because of tradition. Most Japanese today possess two sets of clothes, differing slightly according to their sex: women, for example, wear Japanese dress for ceremonial occasions, men European.

Food, too, became rather a mixture than a synthesis of Eastern and Western dishes. In the Tokugawa period meat was regarded as impure: this was not a result of Buddhist influence, since the Chinese Buddhists willingly ate pork and beef. From the restoration onwards, however, the eating of beef and the drinking of milk became signs of 'civilization'. The expression 'he stinks of butter' came to be used of someone who was superficially Europeanized! Today most homes eat some Western and some Japanese dishes, more or less indifferently.

The first Western-type houses were built of fireproof brick in Tokyo after the great fire in 1872 in the Ginza quarter. On the whole, Westernization in building started with the Government and was confined at first to offices and schools, only later extending to private houses. During the Taishô period (1912–26) a compromise known as a 'cultural house' became popular: this consisted of a traditional building with a Western-style drawing-room. The larger cities, especially Tokyo, now consist of a mixture of Japanese and European building. Kitamura Tôkoku (1869–94) summarized this development by saying 'It is not a revolution but a move', and his friend Shimazaki Toson (1873–1943) wrote similarly in his novel *Spring*:

'Look! There are painted houses and brick houses as well as old Japanese ones. The present age has been robbed of its spirit by the material revolution.

It is a civilization moved by an external stimulus—not a true revolution but a move.'

This was also true of changes in the social structure.

During the Meiji period the population of Japan rose from 30 to 50 million, but the growth of the urban population was even more rapid. Tokyo rose from 1 to 3 million during the period, and Osaka from 400,000 to a million. The same was true of industrial towns like Nagoya and ports like Yokohama and Kobe, as the following table illustrates:

Increase in number of cities, towns and villages

Year	1888	1898	1908
Size town			
Under 10,000	70,272	13,794	12,084
Under 50,000	110	213	344
Under 100,000	8	12	19
Over 100,000	6	8	10

During the period between the Muromachi era and that of the Tokugawa there were many *Jôka-machi* or castle-towns built for feudal protection. In 1731 Edo was estimated to contain 500,000 chônin (artisans and merchants) and rather more than the same number of *bushi* with their families—a total of 1 million. The former produced for the latter, and one of the great changes of the Meiji period was the transformation of consuming into producing towns. A glance at Japanese light industry will illustrate this. The typical light industry of Japan is cotton-spinning, and between 1870 and 1880 the size of these establishments quintupled (from 2,000 to 10,000 spindles on an average), while the production of cotton yarn rose from 12,000 bales in 1883 to 105,000 bales in 1890. Thus the late 1880s are considered by economists to be the period of Japan's industrial revolution. Heavy industry, however, was behindhand by ten years, and the year 1901, when the Yawata Ironworks opened, is generally considered the turning-point. In the shipyards the annual output in 1890 was only 3,000 tons, in 1900 it was 10,000, but by 1908 it was 70,000 tons.

Two points are worthy of note: firstly, the development of Japanese industry occurred under the protection and guidance of the Government. Between 1882 and 1885, for instance, ten spinning mills equipped with modern machinery were established by the Government and later sold to private owners. In heavy industry the great munition factories of the Tokyo and Osaka arsenals, and the shipyards of Yokosuka were all run by the Government. The Yawata Ironworks, however, the biggest enterprise of its kind in Japan, does not seem to have been connected in any way with the Government.

Secondly, a paternal relationship—traditional and human—remained in the large new industries of which the State railways are an interesting example.

Here the employees were regarded as a single large family, and were given other work in the same 'family' when they retired from one position. Another, even more cogent example is the women workers in the spinning-mills; these were mostly farmers' daughters, either training before their marriage or working in the winter when they were not needed on the farms. As they were still dependent on their parents they were able to work for low wages and this enabled Japan to compete in the world market—an interesting example of the 'mixture' of paternalism and new competitive industry.

In fact, it would be wrong to describe Japanese industry as modern 'free' industry in the stricter sense since there were so many relics of paternalism, a close relation between entrepreneurs and politicians and an absence of class antagonism, at least before the Second World War.[5]

2. SOCIAL AND ECONOMIC DEVELOPMENT

For Japan, the nineteenth century was one of transition: in about the middle of the century the country changed over from the feudal system of production to the capitalist system and the economic, political, social and cultural life of Japanese society was transformed accordingly.

At the beginning of the nineteenth century, Japan was still a typical feudal country, with the agrarian, artisan-type of economy. The basic wealth of the country, the land, belonged to the feudal lords who, profiting by their monopoly as landowners, exploited the producers, the peasant serfs. In the towns there was as yet no large industry, still less machine industry. Most production was of the artisan type and there was a very small number of factories manned by serfs.

Supreme power was in the hands of the most powerful member of the ruling family, the Tokugawa, known as the Shogun. This military-feudal dynasty had ruled in Japan from the beginning of the seventeenth century, completely usurping the power of the nominal head of the state, the emperor (*Tennô*) who was reduced to the role of titular head of the Japanese national religion, Shinto.

Japan at that period ranked officially as a united, centralized state with the Shogun Government—Bakufu—ruling over the whole of the country. But apart from the Shogun who, as the foremost feudal lord, owned approximately one-third of the whole of the land of Japan, there also existed over 250 feudal princes, exercising considerable power over their own domains, the extent of their power depending on their wealth and military strength.

Those who were hereditary vassals of the Tokugawa dynasty bore the title of *fudai daimyôs*; and the Shogun put them in charge of the entire State administration, both in the centre (in Yedo the capital of the Tokugawa Shogunate) and in the rest of the country. The remaining *daimyôs* (about 100 in number) were known as *tozama daimyôs*; they were not trusted by the Shogun, and therefore played no part in the Bakufu. On the other hand, they wielded considerably greater economic power than the *fudai daimyôs* and enjoyed a substantial degree of political independence in relation to the Bakufu, especially since their domains were situated at some distance from Yedo, being in south and south-west Honshu and on the islands of Kyushu and Shikoku.

The social basis of the Shogunate was formed by the Samurai (*bushi*), the ruling landowning class. The rest of the population consisted of three classes possessing no rights—peasants, artisans and merchants, the peasants having the least rights of all. The artisans and merchants, though legally below the peasants on the social ladder, had by this period, owing to their wealth, acquired considerable privileges, even in comparison with the lower ranks of the Samurai.

The first half of the nineteenth century, like the previous centuries, was marked by repeated peasant risings against the feudal lords. These risings were frequently accompanied by hunger riots (*utikowasi*) on the part of the urban plebs in protest against the oppression of the authorities and the rich, and the speculation of merchants and usurers. The revolt of the toiling masses undermined the feudal power.

The Shogun, the *daimyôs* and the leading Samurai did eveything in their power to strengthen the feudal system. As early as the seventeenth century, in the early years of the Shogunate, the feudal lords felt that their position was threatened not so much by their own still very weak capitalist elements as those of the European states where, at that period, capitalist relations in production were developing fast. The Tokugawa régime reacted to this danger by isolating Japan from the outside world, a measure which naturally resulted in prolonging the period of feudalism in Japan for more than 200 years, though the course of historical development could not be arrested for ever. Slowly but steadily, the capitalist elements within the feudal society increased.

The end of the seventeenth and beginning of the eighteenth century, known as the Genroku era (1688–1703) was at once the apex of the development of Japanese feudalism and the beginning of its decline. The developing money-and-goods system undermined and broke down the primitive economy characteristic of a feudal country. The growth of industrial production (still at the artisan level) increased the wealth of the representatives of the third estate (in Japan, the third and fourth estates); and the feudal lords—the *daimyôs*, the Samurai and even the Shogun himself—came to be more and more dependent economically and, in particular, financially, on the trade and usury capital system.

The growing economic power of the urban third estate influenced the development of Japanese culture. Even during the Genroku period there grew up alongside the traditional feudal culture a new type of urban, 'burgher' culture, in literature, drama, art, and so on. Fantastic luxury existed not only at the Shogun court in Yedo, in the palaces of the *daimyôs* and the high

Buddhist, Shinto officials, but also in the houses and families of the rich merchants. This was the period of activity of such outstanding representatives of Japanese culture as the writer Saikaku, the poet Matsuo Basho, and the historian Arai Hakusaki.

The cultural development of the urban population at that time was incompatible with the isolation of Japan from the outside world, and in particular from the culture of other countries. Little by little, cultural contacts were established with the outside world. This process was specially marked during the reign of the eighth Shogun, Yoshumune (1716–45). In 1720, the law against the importation into Japan of foreign books (Dutch, because the Shogunate maintained some trade with Holland through Nagasaki), was repealed. In 1741, the Shogun gave instructions to a number of Japanese scholars to study the Dutch language, thus laying the foundations for the dissemination of what was called *rangaku* (Dutch science). The Shogun Yoshimune himself was interested in astronomy. On his orders an astronomical observatory was constructed at Yedo in 1744. Japanese scholars of the 'Dutch school' began to study European sciences, starting with medicine and astronomy. Some of these scholars such as, for example Hiraga Gennai (1728–79) made a study of the applications of natural sciences to agricultural and industrial production.

Apart from the development of interests in European science, the first half of the nineteenth century in Japan was marked by the development of the national school (*yagaku*). As opposed to the ideologists and teachers of Chinese feudal culture and in particular of Confucianism, the representatives of the national school turned their attention to all aspects of distinctive Japanese culture. They began to make a study of Japanese chronicles (*Kojiki, nihonsyoki*) and Japanese history; and preached the dogma of the Japanese national religion, Shinto. The most eminent representatives of this school were the seventeenth-century scholars Kamo-no-Mabuchi (1697–1769) and Motoori Narinaga (1730–1801).

To this period, too, belongs the work of the Japanese scholar and materialist philosopher, atheist and democrat Shyoeki Aido, whose works have only recently become known. Aido strongly condemned the régime existing in Tokugawa Japan and, in particular, the isolation of the country. His opinions resembled those of the Utopian socialists and, like them, he dreamed of a society where exploitation would be non-existent, and every man would live by the fruits of his labour. The works of Aido bear witness to the fact that the progressive people of feudal Japan were already deeply imbued with the new theories.

The feudal lords, however, were reluctant to yield to the pressure of the new, capitalist forces. A number of eminent representatives of the Bakufu (the Shogun Yoshimune, Okitsugu Tanuma, Shadanotu Matsudaira, Tadokuni Mijuno, etc.) took all kinds of measures to reinforce the tottering feudal structure. To this end they introduced in the eighteenth and the first half of the nineteenth century a number of economic and social reforms which were, however, nothing more than palliatives which did not, indeed could not, stave off the crisis of the feudal system.

Meanwhile capitalism, in the first half of the nineteenth century, developed fast especially in the princedoms in the south and south-west, belonging to the *tozama daimyôs*—Satsuma, Choshū, Hisen, Toas.

In the middle of the nineteenth century, Japan came face to face with the capitalist countries of the west, beginning with America, which demanded that the Shogun Government abandon the policy of isolation and open the country to trade. At pistol point, America forced Japan to sign various one-sided agreements, giving Japan unequal status. (Pl. 91). After the U.S.A. came other European capitalist countries. The result of this was an upsurge, particularly amongst the Samurai, of anti-foreign sentiment, directed also against the Shogunate, which had been responsible for the conclusion of these inequitable agreements. The unrest among the Samurai was aggravated by numerous peasant risings and 'rice' riots in the towns.

The *tozama daimyôs* of the princedoms in the south and south-west decided to take advantage of the weakening of the Shogunate; and there developed in those regions and in Choshū in particular, a strong movement in favour of driving out all foreigners, overthrowing the Tokugawa Shogunate and setting up in its place an alliance of these princedoms designed to restore the power of the emperor. In 1863–5, naval squadrons of Western powers bombarded Kagoshima and Shimonoseki, the main towns of Satsuma-Choshū. The Shogun, for his part, sent a punitive expedition against the 'rebellious' province of Choshū; but it proved unsuccessful. Foreign powers also intervened in this internecine strife, France supporting the Shogun, whilst England helped the opposition in the hope that this faction would help her to strengthen her position in Japan.

The bourgeois elements in Japan, grown considerably stronger as a result of the country's isolation being broken down, supported the anti-Shogun faction, since they regarded the Shogun as an obstacle to the development of capitalism. Thanks to their help and in particular to that of the financial magnate Mitsui, the anti-Shogun faction, after a long struggle, got the upper hand. The last Tokugawa Shogun was forced to abdicate in favour of the young Emperor Mitsuhito (Meije) in Kyoto. This event, known in the history of Japan as the restoration of the Meije ranks, on the historical plane, as a bourgeois revolution, since the new imperial régime when it came into power put through, in the period 1868–73, a series of bourgeois reforms which transformed Japan from a feudal country into a capitalist one.

The reforms covered every aspect of Japanese life. The *daimyôs* and the Samurai were deprived of their feudal rights; the princedoms were eliminated and replaced by prefectures with prefects nominated by the central authorities. All strata of society were given the same rights under law. The old feudal regulations governing trades and occupations were annulled; and universal military service was introduced, so breaking the Samurai monopoly as the privileged military class.

Another very important measure was the land reform. Feudal ownership of land was eliminated and replaced by private, bourgeois ownership. The peasants, the hereditary holders of land plots, now became the owners. But those peasants who had mortgaged their land lost it; and the law did not recognize the right of tenants to private ownership of land. As a result, many peasants received no land, and were obliged to rent land from the new landowners in iniquitous conditions. A land tax, so heavy as to lay a crushing burden on small and even medium landowners, was imposed; with the result that they ran into debt, so losing their land and having to become tenants. Very soon, 70 per cent of the agricultural population were tenants. Thus the land reform was neither radical nor democratic, but simply perpetuated the iniquitious exploitation of the peasantry, partly on a new, capitalist basis and partly on the basis of a system representing a combination of feudal and capitalist exploitation.

The bourgeois reforms, limited though they were, greatly accelerated the development of Japanese capitalism. The Government itself began building industrial enterprises, railways, dockyards, telegraph lines, and so on; universal primary education was introduced, and secondary and higher education colleges were instituted. The works of numbers of European and American writers were translated into Japanese. But at the same time there were, in this new capitalist Japan, many survivals of feudalism which affected all sides of Japanese life.

Many of the Samurai disliked the new régime and failed to adapt themselves to the changed conditions. They organized various anti-government risings, the most serious of which was the Satsuma rebellion of 1877, led by Takimori Saigo. But all these risings were put down by the armed forces of the Government.

The new Japan, in the economic field, was extremely backward in relation to many of the large capitalist countries; and its leaders were determined from the outset to win for Japan the same status that those countries had acquired by resorting to war, the seizure of foreign territory and the enslavement of other peoples. To this end, one of the first steps of the Japanese Government was to put the country on a military footing. It built armaments works, created a large army and navy with the help of foreign instructors—French for the army, British for the navy—sent many young men abroad to study military science, and so on. The Japanese militarists, after thus equipping themselves for war with great haste, now began to prepare for foreign aggression. In 1874 the Japanese attempted to seize the island of Formosa from China, but were unsuccessful. In 1876 they forced an unequal treaty on Korea: this was the first step towards turning that country into a Japanese colony.

All this time Japan was undergoing a rapid process of industrial development. In the ten years between 1868 and 1877 some 500 industrial enterprises were built in the country, more than in the preceding two centuries. In 1880 the Government sold all State enterprises—with the exception of military enterprises and parts of the railway system—for a trifling sum to be paid in instalments over a long period, to private capital, in most cases large companies and banks closely connected with the Government, such as Mitsui, Mitsubishi, Sumitomo, Fujita, etc. Already at this time the production and sale of commodities in many branches of industry began to be put on a monopoly footing.

As capitalism developed, the young Japanese proletariat emerged as a class. The labour force was supplied by the impoverished peasants, who contracted their children, girls in particular, to manufacturers for what was virtually slave labour; by craftsmen and artisans ruined by the competition of machine production and the flooding of the market by cheap foreign goods; and by the mass of urban poor. The exploitation of the workers was particularly bad: wretched wages, work from early dawn till late at night, incredible overcrowding in the factory hostels, semi-starvation, military discipline, corporal punishment for the least offence, or even for no offence at all . . . Employers 'trained' the workers in a spirit of feudal paternalism, to regard the boss as their father, to whom they owed submission and respect.

The development of capitalism led to the growth of socialist contradictions. The Government, from 1868 onwards, was in the hands of the Samurai of the princedoms (clans) of Satsuma and Choshū—which, as is known, played an important part in the overthrow of the Shogunate and the creation of the new capitalist Japan. This Government, known as the 'clan' Government, now installed throughout the country a reactionary, bourgeois-landowner dictatorship, run by semi-feudal landowners and the rich bourgeoisie. Not only the workers but also the middle strata of the urban and rural population and even the members of the bourgeois-landowner class, excluded by the 'clan' Government for government service, expressed their dissatisfaction with the political régime.

This dissatisfaction led, in the second half of the 1870s and the first half of the 1880s, to a widespread movement known as the *jiu minken undo* (Movement for people's freedom and rights). This movement, which was led by Itagaki and Okuma, was originally a liberal, bourgeois-landowner opposition to the 'clan' Government. Before long, however, there grew up within it a leftist faction under the leadership of Kantaro Oi and Tyomin Nakoye. The principal demand of the *jiu minken undo* was that a constitutional type of government should be set up. There was a mass movement throughout the country for the institution of a parliament, and the repeal of unequal treaties. The Government replied by repression, but was nevertheless obliged, in the end, to make certain concessions. In 1881 came the publication of the imperial decree for the establishment of parliament in 1889.

The opposition elements began to prepare for parliamentary activity by organizing political parties. In 1881 Itagaki formed the *Jiyuto* (liberal) party; and in 1882 Okuma organized the *Kaishinto* (progressive) party. These were both landowner-bourgeois parties, the first composed mainly of landowners and rural bourgeoisie, the latter of urban bourgeoisie engaged in commerce and industry. The *Jiyuto* party, however, also included members of the petty bourgeoisie and peasantry, small landowners and even tenants—which is what gave this party, especially in some places, its radical character.

In 1882–84, agrarian risings occurred in a number of prefectures. At the same time the young proletariat, led by the miners (Minke, Takasima, etc.) began to strike; and the new workers' associations (builders, printers, metallurgists) in the form of mutual insurance funds, were formed.

On 11 February 1889 the Government, acting on behalf of the Emperor, proclaimed the new constitution. It was modelled on the Prussian constitution, and strongly reactionary in character. It proclaimed the Emperor to be 'sacred and inviolable' and conferred immense power on him. It was to him (and not parliament) that the cabinet of ministers as a body and each minister individually was responsible. The people continued to have virtually no rights. Only a very small fraction of the adult population, mainly members of the landowning class and the top and middle strata of the bourgeoisie, had the right to vote. In the first parliamentary elections, held in 1890, only 1 per cent of the population voted. Over half of the deputies elected belonged to the parties opposing the 'clan' Government—the *Jiyuto* and *Kaishinto*. During the first few years the meetings of parliament were very stormy; and the Government repeatedly dissolved it. But before long the opposition of the landowners and bourgeoisie died down because the members of these groups were at one with the Government on the subject of an aggressive foreign policy.

The targets of Japanese aggression, as before, were Korea and China. Korea had long been a feudal vassal of China; and Japan decided to 'liberate' Korea from the yoke of China, and then take China's place. After forcing Korea to sign an unequal treaty, Japan proceeded to occupy all the positions of power, both economic and political, in that country. The Japanese Government acquired the right to keep its garrison in Seoul, ostensibly for the purpose of protecting its mission there; and installed in Korea a puppet government which complied with all Japan's demands. This resulted in a wave of anti-Japanese feeling throughout the country, which had to be repressed by force.

In Tientsin, on 18 April 1885, Japan and China signed a convention, whereby both countries undertook to withdraw their troops from Korea; in the event of 'serious disorders' in Korea, both countries undertook to send troops only after notifying the other party thereof in writing, and to withdraw such troops immediately after the liquidation of the affair'. The signing of this convention represented a diplomatic triumph for Japan, since it gave her equal rights with China to intervene in the domestic affairs of Korea. But it did not satisfy the Japanese militarists, and they sought a pretext for starting a war with China over Korea.

In 1894 there was a peasant rising in Korea against the feudal Government, which had now acquired a religious bias—the *Tong hak* rising (Eastern teaching). The Korean Government appealed to China for help; whereupon the Chinese Government, in compliance with the Tientsin convention, informed Japan that it was sending a certain number of troops to Korea to put down the rising. The Japanese quickly sent troops of their own. After peace had been concluded with the insurgents, the Korean Government requested both China and Japan to withdraw their troops. The Japanese declared that they would not evacuate Korea until the requisite 'reforms' had been introduced in the country; and used this as a pretext for staying in Korea.

Japan then decided to go straight ahead, and start a war with China. On 25 July 1894, the Japanese fleet sank a British naval transport which was carrying Chinese troops; at the same time the Japanese, without declaring war, started operations against Chinese troops in Korea. This was the beginning of the Japanese–Chinese war of 1894–5.

A few days before the beginning of this war, Japan had righted the inequalities imposed by earlier treaties by concluding a treaty on equal terms with England, and this was followed by other similar ones with other capitalist countries. She owed this success not so much to the skill of her diplomats as to the development of the international situation and the growing antagonism between England and Russia: England was endeavouring to use Japan as an ally in her drive to arrest the spread of Russian influence in the Far East.

The war between Japan and China ended in a victory for Japan. Under the terms of the treaty of Shimonoseki (Pl. 92b), the Chinese Government recognized the 'independence' of Korea, ceded to Japan the Liaotung Peninsula and the islands of Formosa and the Pescadores, opened a number of ports to trade with Japan, granted Japanese ships the right to navigate Chinese internal waterways and gave them various other privileges. (At the insistence of three Great Powers—Russia, Germany and France—Japan was soon forced to hand the Liaotung Peninsula back to China.)

At the end of the nineteenth and beginning of the twentieth century, Japan passed into the monopolist stage of her capitalist development. Japanese industry continued to develop, the process of the concentration of production and the centralization of capital was intensified, and foreign trade expanded. An increasingly important role was played by the financial oligarchy headed by such magnates as Mitsui, Mitsubishi, Yashuda, Shumitomo, and so on. For all this, Japanese imperialism, economically speaking, was still far behind the imperialistic countries of Europe and the U.S.A. Japan was to catch up with them in this respect in the course of the next century, the twentieth.

3. INSTITUTIONAL REFORMS

I.

During the period 1775–1905 two major reforms took place. The first was the *Taisei-hôkan* of 1867—the restoration of the governing power to the Emperor by the 15th Shogun, Yoshinobu Tokugawa—and the reforms which accompanied it such as the *Hanseki-hôkan* (return of land and people to the emperor) and the *Haihan-chiken* (abolition of the clans and establishment of 'prefectures'). The second was the promulgation of the imperial constitution in 1890 and its attendant reforms. Between the two occurred individual reforms which must not be neglected.

2.

The period from 1775 to 1867 represents the decline of the Tokugawa Shogunate. In the early eighteenth century the reformer Yoshimune Tokugawa, the 8th Shogun, an orthodox financier and reactionary, carried out the Kyôho reforms; subsequently the Shogun Government became less rigid, but in the latter half of the century, a member of the Council of Elders, Okitsugu Tanuma, attempted to reconstruct the Shogunate through an alliance with commercial and finance capital. He was succeeded by Sadanobu Matsudaira, an imitator of Yoshimune who had little success, and the nineteenth century opened with a decadent period under Ienari, the 11th Shogun. Tadakuni Mizuno, another member of the Council, again resorted to tight finance without success, and the situation of the Shogunate went from bad to worse, complicated, as it now was, by American demands for the opening of the country. The conclusion of commercial treaties with the United States involved a revolution in the now age-old policy of isolation of the Shogunate. Other curious incidents occurred: in 1858, for example, the Shogun asked the Emperor's permission to conclude these treaties, an action quite unprecedented and possibly foreshadowing the latest power of the Emperor. Again the Shogunate consulted in the same matter all the *daimyôs*, including those (*Tozama-daimyô*) who were not hereditary feudatories of the Tokugawa, and other officials of the Government. Finally, the Government signed the treaties without imperial permission, and this added fuel to the *Sonni-jôi* movement (reverence for the Emperor and expulsion of foreigners). Groups hostile to the Shogunate, together with the Choshû clan whose lands had been largely confiscated after the battle of Sekigahara (1600) attempted to overthrow the régime; they were joined by some other great clans such as the Satsuma. The 15th Shogun, Yoshinobu Tokugawa, on the advice of the Tosa clan which was greatly indebted to the Shogunate for past favours, voluntarily surrendered the Government to the Emperor Meiji on 9 November 1867 (the *Taisei-hôkan*).

The Emperor, who since the Middle Ages had gradually lost all political authority, had during the Edo period lived in retirement in the imperial palace at Kyoto; his only power was to confer imperial rank (which was purely honorary), to determine the names of regnal years and construct almanacs. The entire governing power had passed into the hands of the Shogunate, not by any grant from the Emperor, but as a consequence of the latter's gaining supremacy over the feudal lords by force of arms. In the early Edo period scholars, who were forced to explain how the power had been transferred, considered the Shogun as the Emperor's deputy; later, in the decadent period, both at the Shogunate and at the Court the idea arose that he held the governing power as the Emperor's delegate, and from this it was an easy transition to the theory of the imperialists (*Sonno-ronsha*) that the Emperor should cease to delegate it. No act of delegation could, however, be proved, and it would therefore probably be more correct to regard the Meiji 'restoration' as a mere practical transfer of power.

Yoshinobu's party had hoped that his surrender to the Emperor would be followed by a renewed grant of power to him by the Emperor, for instance, by making Yoshinobu chairman of the *Daimyô* Council. These hopes were disappointed when on 3 January 1868 the Emperor issued the *Daigôrei* (great declaration) of restoration, which abolished the regency (Sesshô), Kwanpaku (the Chief State councillor) and the Shogunate, and declared that government should be conducted through the *Sôsai* (President), the *Gijô* (Councillor) and the *Sanyo* (Consultant) as things were in the time of the first Emperor, Jinmu. On the same day a council held at Kogoshu (the small palace) decided that Yoshinobu, who was a very high-ranking minister at the imperial court, should resign and return his lands to the Emperor, who was badly in need of both land and men to support his authority. This threat, though never fully carried out, provoked the Shogunate to resistance, and a battle (Toba-fushimi) took place between its forces and those of the Satsumu and Choshû clans. The Emperor thereupon declared all the lands of the Shogunate forfeit, and thus succeeded in fact as well as in name to the position of Buke-no-Tôryô (Leader of the Samurai). This, for the moment, established a feudal structure with the Emperor at its head. However, there were certain important changes: it became a custom to decide all important matters at the *Reppan-Kaigi* (Council of all the Clans) and later, when it became necessary to pursue Yoshinobu to Edo with an army, the Emperor confirmed this with his five-point imperial covenant aimed at the support of the clans. Yoshinobu submitted and the Castle of Edo surrendered. The city was renamed Tokyo, and in 1869 the Emperor moved the seat of government there.

The lands of the ex-Shogun and of his ex-vassals and the confiscated lands of his supporters were all turned into prefectures (*Ken*), while cities such as Tokyo, Osaka and Kyoto became metropolitan prefectures (*Fu*). The latter were governed by *Chifuji*, the former by *Chikenji*, all imperial officials, but the rest of the country was governed, as formerly, by daimyôs or clan-chiefs. Thus the old clan system and the new prefectoral system existed side by side. Yet the clans themselves did not remain unchanged. In the first place their rulers participated in the Government, and in the second central control was strengthened by each clan being compelled to choose an administrator (*Shissei*) to help the chiefs to understand imperial policy, and also to set up deliberative bodies. The imperial Court however remained weak, and the clans were still often quasi-independent in practice. This led to the *Hanseki-hôken* of July 1869, by which, although the clans retained their names, they were henceforth to be ruled by *Chihanji* as prefectures. In theory this should have made the Emperor more or less absolute, but in fact many clan-chiefs were made *Chihanji* and much of the feudal structure remained untouched.

A further change was clearly necessary, and in preparation for this the Imperial Guard was strengthened and the magnates at the Court were changed Takamori Saigô of the Satsuma clan and Takayoshi Kido of the Choshû clan were made central figures in the Government as Sangi, to strengthen it. Thus fortified, the Emperor on 29 August 1871, carried out the *Haihan-chiken*, dismissing the *Chinanji*, who were ordered up to Tokyo, and replacing them by prefects chosen and appointed by the central Government. This meant the effective end of the feudal system in Japan.

This was accompanied by other major changes, such as the abolition of the complex ancient system of status and its replacement by a simpler three-class system: *Kazoku* (noblemen), *Shikoku* (ex-Samurai) and *Heimin* (commoners). *Heimin* were allowed to have surnames, and indeed were later compelled to do so. Control stations (*Sekisho*) and goodwill of wholesale stores (*Toiya-kabu*) were both abolished; the ban on perpetual sale of land (*Eitai-baibai*) was removed; farmers were permitted to change their occupation. In 1877, after many smaller changes, the system of fiefs was also abolished, and Samurai were given bonds (*Kinroku-kôssi-syôsho*) in compensation. The Government also assisted them in finding employment.

3.

The *Daigôrei* of 1868 set up the three offices of *Sôssi*, *Gijô* and *Sanyo*. The government office of *Sôsai* was called *Dajôkan-dai* (after the old Japanese administrative council) which gave some colour to the idea of a restoration; but the three names just quoted had nothing old about them. On 11 June the *Seitaisho* was published, which detailed the new form of the Japanese Government, and this was succeeded by many changes. The legislative, administrative and judicial authorities were separated, higher government officials were to be elected by the lower, etc. (Some influence can here be noted from the eighteenth-century notion of the separation of powers.) It was at this point, too, that the clans were ordered to set up deliberative councils. But ideas of reform and restoration alternated, and soon an ordinance introduced government organization on the lines of *Ritsu* and Ryô (ancient Japanese laws made under the influence of Chinese *lü* and *ling*) by which an office in charge of Shintoism (*Dajôkan* and *Jingikan*) was set up. But as a result of the *Haihan-chiken* of 1871 the latter was abolished and the former altered into three institutions (*Seiin*, *Sain* and *Uin*, the front, right and left offices), with eight *shô* or departments under them. In *Seiin* the emperor conducted all State affairs with the assistance of *Daijin* (chief minister) and Nagon (ministers), with the *Sangi* participating. *Sain* was the legislature, and in *Uin* the heads of departments conferred. The system was again reformed in 1873, when power became more concentrated in *Seiin*. This meant increased centralization, and *Sangi* were made active members of the cabinet at the same time. (By now the cabinet had become the centre of administration.) Formerly many court nobles and ex-daimyôs had been members of the Government, but by now it consisted mainly of members of the Satsuma and Choshû clans. However, as we shall see later, the imperial rescript of 1875 which urged the gradual establishment of constitutional government abolished *Sain* and *Uin*, set up a Senate of officially elected members as the legislature, the *Daishinin* as the highest court of law and the *Chihôkan-kaigi* (conference of local officials) as a means of informing the government of local conditions. This continued for ten years until another complete change.

A landmark in local government was the issue of regulations concerning prefectoral assemblies and local rating in 1878. These set up *Gun* (districts), *Ku* (wards), *Chô* (towns) and *Son* (villages), and thus enabled some uniformity of government in the localities to be enforced. *Fu* and *Ken*, which had been merely administrative divisions, were now considered self-governing bodies; some town and village assemblies (*Shê Son-Kai*) were established. Later, in 1880, ward, town and village assemblies were made compulsory.

During the period 1873–81 there was an important reform of the land-tax system, which had come down unchanged from the Edo period and in the early Meiji epoch formed 70–80 per cent of the Government's revenue. Land-taxes varied according to district and were mostly paid in kind, so that the Government was chronically short of cash. The reform undertook a nation-wide land survey, with a reassessment according to the class of the owner, and finally a collection of a standard rate (3 per cent) from the whole of Japan. This left untouched, however, the relation of landlord and tenant, and rents in kind remained as before.

In 1873 conscription was adopted, thus robbing *Shizoku* of employment, and in 1878 soldiers recruited from the Heimin played a prominent part in the suppression of the Satsuma rebellion. As regards the judiciary, the *Seitaisho* of 1868, which was based on the theory of the separation of powers, set up *Keihô-kan*, or officials of the criminal law, but did not forbid administrative officials to judge crimes; hence the Ministry of Justice at the centre and the prefectoral governors in the localities continued to exercise the same jurisdiction as before. An attempt to separate judiciary and administration in 1872 by Shinpei Etô had little success. In 1875 for the first time *Daishinin* and the inferior courts were overhauled, and the independence of the judiciary recognized, but it was not until 1877 that local administrators were forbidden to be judges.

In 1870 there was an attempt at codification of the law by simply translating and adapting the French civil code. Later a Frenchman, Gustave Emile Boissonade, was charged with the task of compiling a Japanese civil code. This was promulgated in 1890. The criminal code, however, had been issued already in 1868—the *Kari-kei-ritsu*, based on Chinese ideas; thereafter the criminal regulations of the Tokugawa Government were to guide the courts until a new code could be compiled. In 1870, after consulting the *Yôrôritsu* (an ancient Japanese criminal code) and the precedents of the Tokugawa regulations, a new criminal code, patterned on the laws of Ming and Ch'ing was issued (the *Shinritsu-kôryô*). A further code was issued in 1873, called the *Kaitei-ritsurei*; this was influenced both by Chinese and by Western ideas, and both codes remained in force together.

4.

By 1890 Japan had an official constitution. The movement for a constitution and that for a deliberative assembly had gone hand in hand. A number of draft constitutions were attempted, including the *Kokken* of 1880, which was turned down as being too much influenced by Western ideas in its attitude to the Emperor. When it became essential to convene a Diet in 1890 (in connection with the 'Affair of the Articles of the Commissioner of Colonization sold by the Government', the new constitution became urgent. In 1882 Hirobumo Ito was sent to Europe to study various constitutions, and he consulted Rudolf von Gneist, Lorenz von Stein and other authorities who convinced him that the imperial constitution should be based on that of Prussia. This also accorded with the opinion of Tomomi Iwakura, then Minister of the Right Office. Ito revised an original draft by Kowashi Inoue and Karl Friedrich Hermann Rösler, and this, after deliberation in the Privy Council, was promulgated on 11 February 1889, and came into force the next year at the opening of the Imperial Diet on 29 November. This *Dainihonteikoku-kenpô* (imperial constitution of Great Japan) consisted of seven chapters and seventy-six articles. It was both concise and elastic. Japan was to be governed by an unbroken line of emperors who were to superintend all three branches of government, although the courts were to exercise judicial authority in the name of the emperor. The imperial prerogative was wide: much could be done without the Diet's sanction, e.g. if the budget were rejected, the previous year's budget could be adopted; to the emperor alone belonged the initiative to revise the constitution, and he could issue a wide range of independent decrees (emergency, delegated, etc.). Some articles touched on the rights and duties of the people, but these had a certain unreality as there was no idea of human rights and these mostly dealt with riots or could be limited by law. The Diet, which had two chambers, consisted of a House of Representatives popularly elected, and an Upper House consisting of nobles and officially elected members. The two houses had equal powers except that in matters relating to the budget the Lower House had priority of discussion. Military matters also belonged to the imperial prerogative and were customarily considered to be untouchable by ministerial advice. Thus the constitutional nature of the Japanese Government had serious limitations although the establishment of a constitution was a landmark.

Various subsidiary reforms were carried out at this time. *Shô*, or heads of departments, had until now been mere subsidiary officers under the *Dajôkan*, and only *Dâjo-daijin* (the chief minister) and *Sa-* and *U-daijin* (Ministers of the Left and Right Offices) had assisted the Emperor. But now *Shô-kyo* also became ministers of state, assisting the Emperor and constituting a cabinet. The cabinet was responsible to the Emperor alone, and was supposed to remain aloof from the Diet, but the realities of politics intervened, and it began about 1898 to be based on political parties.

Although nothing about local self-government appeared in the constitution, certain changes had taken place. In 1890 the *Fu-ken* prefectoral system was established, and by the revisions of 1899 *Fu* and *Ken* were made local bodies. *Chiji*, the officials appointed to govern the prefectures, were at the same time the 'directors' of *Fu* and *Ken* as self-governing bodies. *Gun* (districts) which were sub-prefectures, were also made self-governing bodies by an order (*Gun-sei*) of the same year. In 1888 regulations concerning towns and villages drafted by Albert Mosse, a German, were promulgated.

Under the criminal code set up by Boissonade in 1882 separate civil and criminal courts were to be established. In 1890, however, the law for the constitution of the courts abolished this separation and established the system of three instances. In the same year the code was amended and transformed into the criminal procedure code, from the draft of a German Hermann Techow. The civil code, drafted by Boissonade in 1880, was first amended by the Committee for Legal Research (Hôritsu-torishirabe-iinkai) and the Senate, and the chapters on persons (*Jinji-hen*) and succession (*Zaisan-shutokuhen*) inserted by Japanese drafters, and then promulgated in 1890. But then ensued a long debate about when it should come into force (the 'code controversy'), so that finally it was postponed, with the commercial code, until 1896. Then in 1893 the Committee for Codification (Hôten-chôsa-kai) was formed and this, under strong German influence, drew up a new civil code which was enforced in 1898. While this was regarded formally as the revised edition of the earlier civil code (Kyû-minpô) it is clearly of German origin.

Work on the commercial code had begun in 1881. It was drafted by Rösler and was to have been promulgated in 1890 and brought into force in the following year. But it became involved with the postponement of the civil code of Boissonade, and in fact only the most necessary articles came into force in 1893. The Codification Committee then worked on it, and the new draft was enforced in 1899. This completed the codification of Japanese law and brought it all into force. The desire for revision of unfair treaties was a stimulus to law reform, and it is significant that the year of enforcement of the commercial code was also that of treaty revision.

In sum, it is clear that before the imperial constitution Japanese law was strongly under French influence; after the constitution German law was preponderant.

4. INTELLECTUAL AND ARTISTIC DEVELOPMENTS IN JAPAN

After the Meiji restoration Western culture poured rapidly into Japan.

Between 1868 and 1905 there were some movements of reaction against this, but neither those who were in favour of the West nor those hostile to it showed great originality. During the later Tokugawa period Confucianism had flourished as never before under official patronage. Chinese influence was also strong in the arts. The rather academic Tosa school of Japanese painting, inspired by earlier Chinese paintings, had become lifeless and formal. A new inspiration, known as the Literate or Southern-style painting, now came from China via imported albums of paintings and Chinese books of art-criticism: this was much less conventional and showed considerable literary taste. Ikeno Taiga, Yosa Buson, Tanomura Chikuden, Watanabe Kazan and others were members of this school. Flower-and-bird paintings, based on sketches from Nature, were introduced by Shên Nan-p'in, a Chinese realist painter who visited Japan in 1731, and others who succeeded him. Japanese painters of this genre included Maruyama Okyo and Ganku. Western art was also introduced to Japan either directly, through imported illustrated books, or via China. Hishikawa Moronobu, who lived in Edo (Tokyo) during the later seventeenth century, began to mass-produce *Ukiyo-e* (genre paintings), usually portraits of beautiful women or of Kabuki actors, by wood-block printing. (Pl. 90). Suzuki Harunobu in 1765 invented a method of polychrome block printing which was known as *Nishiki-e* (brocade pictures). Kitagawa Utamaro and many other Japanese artists also worked in this field, until *Ukiyo-e* prints became a widespread form of popular art.

Among these various schools the Literate school was perhaps the most characteristic. During the second half of the eighteenth century and the first half of the nineteenth many discussions on their fundamental aesthetic principles were published, including the *Gadan Keiroku* of Nayakama Koyo, the *Kaiji Higen* and *Gyokushu Gashu* by Kuwayama Gyokushu, the *Gado Kongosho* by Nakabayashi Chikudo and the *Sanchujin Josetsu* of Tanomura Chikuden, as well as unpublished letters of Watanabe Kazan to his pupil Tsubaki Chinzan, and of Chinzan in turn to his pupils. These works, besides discussing theories of painting, expatiate on the essence of Literate painting— subjectivism—and emphasize the importance of spiritual profundity, which they believe to be attainable through literary erudition and freedom from worldly concerns.

The painters of the Ukiyo-e school were craftsmen of a high order but far from being theorists. The sole exception is Nishikawa Sukenobu who worked in Kyoto. In his *Ehon Wabigoto*, published in the early eighteenth century, he criticized a slavish imitation of Chinese art and urged the awakening of the Japanese spirit. The rest did sometimes discuss the realism and accuracy of perspective of Western art, but their theories were merely derivative and based on imported books. In fact, to sum up, one may say that although Confucians, scholars and artists had expressed some views on aesthetics in the late eighteenth and early nineteenth centuries, neither philosophy nor aesthetics had really developed.

It was in the middle of the eighteenth century that Western ideas began to be accepted by Japan. In 1774 Johann Adam Kulmus's *Anatomische Tabellen* was translated and published, and this strongly impressed people with the development of Western knowledge. The Copernican theory, introduced about the same time or a little later, helped to shake the foundations of traditional thought and led to humanistic and anti-feudal notions. The Institute of Research into Foreign Books which the Tokugawa Government maintained was enlarged in the mid-nineteenth century and its scope now included the natural sciences, foreign languages and Western painting. The social sciences were, however, in their infancy. The first serious students were perhaps Tsuda Shin'ichiro and Nishi Amane (1829–97) who were sent to the Netherlands by the Shogunate and studied politics under Professor Simon Vissering at Leiden (until 1865).

Philosophical studies also began about the same time. Nishi Amane in his book written in 1875 introduced Kant's *Critique of Pure Reason*; he also translated John Stuart Mill's *Utilitarianism* and Joseph Haven's *Mental Philosophy*. Public education in philosophy began in 1878, when Ernest Fenollosa (1853–1908) was invited from America to the Chair at Tokyo University. He lectured on Mill and Herbert Spencer, but also introduced the theories of Kant, Fichte, Schelling and Hegel. The standpoint of his lectures was the evolutionism in vogue at that time, diluted with some Hegelian ideas. Fenollosa was later appointed Professor at the Tokyo School of Arts (now Tokyo Arts University) and Ludwig Busse (1862–1907) replaced him lecturing from 1887 to 1892. Busse was a critical realist strongly influenced by R. H. Lotze; though not a follower of either Kant or Hegel his influence prepared the way for Japanese acceptance of German idealism.

Busse was followed by Raphael von Kober, who came to Japan in 1893 and until 1914 lectured on Western philosophy, German literature and the classics. His humanism and learning attracted many Japanese writers and philosophers. He himself was influenced by Schopenhauer and E. V. Hartmann, and called his own philosophy 'transcendental pantheism'.

Although public lectures in philosophy, especially in German philosophy, did not begin until 1878, books outlining the essentials of German philosophy had been available much earlier. Takegoshi Yosaburo (1865–1950) had written a survey of German philosophy in his *Diotsu Tetsugaku Eika* and the theories of Kant and others had been discussed in Nake Chomin's (1847–1901) book *Rigaku Kogen* (An Outline of Philosophy). During the last decade of the nineteenth century German philosophical ideas became widespread, partly as a result of the growth of nationalism, partly as a reaction against the materialist utilitarianism of the preceding period. Two strong advocates of German idealism were Miyake Setsuei (1860–1945) and Inoue Tetsujiro (1855–1944) who studied in Germany and later lectured at Tokyo University. Nakajima Rikizo (1858–1913) wrote articles on Kant and Hegel and in his ethical teaching followed T. H. Green. Kiyono Tsutomo was also an exponent of Kant. An outstanding thinker was Onishi Hajime (1864–1900), who wrote *Rinrigaku* (Ethics) and *Seiyo Tesugaku-shi* (A History of Western Philosophy), etc. Under the influence of his teacher, Busse, he took the side of R. H. Lotze and developed a critical idealism. His promising career was cut short by an early death.

Thus the tendency of the 1890s was an idealism tending to be flavoured with religion or ethics; this factor was common to philosophers of the most divergent schools. Philosophic studies on Buddhism and Confucianism did not begin to develop until the twentieth century, with the work of Takase Takejiro and Inoue Tetsujiro on the Yang Ming, the Confucian ideal which emphasized the unity of knowledge and action; these researches went back to the Taoist philosophy of Lao-Tse, and Chuang Tse. The most important writer on Buddhist philosophy in the period was Murakani Sensei (1851–1929), a pupil of Inoue Enryo, who sought for truth in religion, especially in Buddhism, rather than in Western philosophy.

In aesthetics Nishi Amane played an important role through his lectures at his own school in 1870, where he introduced aesthetics as an integral part of philosophy. In 1872 he presented his lectures to the Emperor, but they were not published. In his *Hyakuichi Shin-ron*, published in 1874, he discussed aesthetics, and dealt with the subject more systematically in his translation of J. Haven's *Mental Philosophy*, which was published by the Ministry of Education in 1878. He developed no original ideas and no pupils. In 1883–4 Nakae Chomin's translation of E. Veron's *Esthetique* was also published by the Ministry of Education.

Fenollosa, who had been so important in philosophical teaching in general, also took a great interest in Japanese art, and later wrote his famous *Epochs of Chinese and Japanese art: An Outline History of East Asiatic Design* (London, 1913). He recognized the worth of Japanese art and attempted to revive it. When he arrived in Japan, traditional painting was in decline, overpowered by the Literate painting and the Western influence which had been coming in since the Meiji restoration. In 1882 Fenollosa delivered a noteworthy lecture at a meeting of the *Ryuchi-kai*, a group of artists organized for the preservation of traditional art. The original lecture has been lost, but a Japanese translation exists in a pamphlet called *Bijutsu Shinsetsu* (A True Theory of Art). In conformity with his general views on philosophy, Fenollosa emphasized the idea as the essential in art and, classifying the fundamentals of painting into eight principal elements, he proved the superiority of Japanese art. However, he rather illogically omitted the Literate school of painting. This lecture, which greatly impressed painters and art critics, led to the movement for the revival of indigenous art which has borne such valuable fruit in the present century. He trained a number of Japanese to follow him, among whom the most important were perhaps Ariga Nagao and Okakura Tenshin (1862–1914). Ariga translated Fenollosa's lectures, and later also his *Epochs of Chinese and Japanese Art*. Okakura, in collaboration with Fenollosa, established in 1884 the *Kanga-kai* (Society for Art Appreciation) which produced such geniuses as Kano Hogai and Hashimoto Gaho. He also laboured at the foundation of the Tokyo School of Arts (later the Tokyo Arts University) of which he subsequently became principal.

Busse also taught aesthetics and art history, using as his textbook Wilhelm Lübke's *Grundriss der Kunstgeschichte*. Among his pupils who specialized in aesthetics were Otsuka Yasuji (1868–1931), later professor at Tokyo University, and Tachinbana Eizaburo (1867–1901) who taught aesthetics at the Gakushuin. Busse's successor, Köber, also taught art history and aesthetics; he published a book called *Lectures on Aesthetics and History of Art* (Tokyo, 1894) which he also used as a textbook. He lectured on Kant's aesthetics as expounded in the *Critique of Pure Reason*, and then proceeded to the more modern aesthetics evolved by Schelling, Krause, Hegel and Hartmann. Takayama Chogyu (1871–1902) and Fukada Yasukazu (1878–1928), who lectured in aesthetics at Kyoto University, were also his pupils.

Köber was succeeded by Otsuka Yasuji who, after graduating at Tokyo in 1891, did research in aesthetics, then lectured on Hartmann's aesthetics at the Tokyo *Semmon Gakko* (now Waseda University), then travelled widely in Germany, France and Italy during 1892, and finally returned to Tokyo as professor in 1900. Dissatisfied with Hartmann, he attempted to modify aesthetics along psychological and sociological lines. He was the founder of aesthetics as a science in Japan and wrote several articles on contemporary painting.

Onishi Hajime, a lecturer at the *Semmon Gakko*, also advocated the psychological developments in aesthetics. Among his pupils were Shimamura Hogetsu, Tsunashima Ryosen and Hasegawa Tenkei, who all became art or literary critics.

Mori Ogai (1862–1922) and Takayama Chogyu were also important. Ogai was surgeon-general of the Japanese army. He went to Germany in 1884 and spent three years attending lectures at various universities. His talents and interests were wide, and he interested himself in literature and art. He wrote articles on Hartmann's aesthetics in books and periodicals and for a time taught aesthetics at the Tokyo Art School and the Keio Gijuku University. He was also a prominent art critic, and wrote on exhibitions of Western-style paintings. When Kuroda Seiki brought back from France the ideas of the *pleinairiste* movement, it was Ogai who popularized it. Chogyu graduated from Tokyo in 1896: he was an able art critic and lectured at Tokyo and Waseda Universities. In 1900 he was due to visit Germany to study aesthetics, but he fell ill and died soon after. In the first half of his *Kinsei Bigaku* (Modern Aesthetics) he gave an historical account of Western aesthetics; in the second half he discussed contemporary aesthetics theories centring on Hartmann. He also wrote criticisms of Western- and Japanese-style paintings, and frequently had heated discussions on the subject with Ogai. In later years he tended to favour the indigenous style.

Okakura Tenshin worked on the history of Chinese and Japanese art and lectured on the history of Oriental art at the Tokyo School of Arts and at Tokyo University. His idealism in art is expressed in his book *The Ideals of the East* (London, 1903), and in *The Awakening of Japan* (1904) and *The Book of Tea* (New York, 1906) which were all written in English. He was at the head of various groups of artists all working for the restoration of traditional Japanese art. His most important activity was the establishment of the *Nihon Bijutsu-in* (Art Academy of Japan) after his retirement as principal of the Tokyo Art School in 1898. This Academy produced many distinguished artists, including Yokoyama Taikan, Hishida Shunso, Shimomura Kanzan and Yasuda Yukihiko, and its traditions are still important today.

5. RELIGION IN JAPAN BETWEEN 1775 AND 1905

During the Tokugawa period Buddhism was the most prominent of the various religions which flourished side by side. The Government had been seriously alarmed by the Catholic missions to Japan and by the Shimabara rebellion in 1637. Christianity was banned, and Buddhism was used by the Government as a means of exterminating it. All Japanese were ordered to register as adherents at some Buddhist temple; land was given generously for temple-building, and Buddhist priests stood high in the social scale. Buddhism, in fact, had almost become a State religion. But, in fact, all this political protection was unhealthy for the inner life of Buddhism and, indeed, although the Shogunate was using Buddhism, it did not wish it to acquire too much social power. New sects, new interpretations were discouraged and, despite its apparent prosperity, Buddhism was slowly losing its real hold on the people.

The basic philosophy of the Shogunate system was not Buddhist but Confucian. Here an interesting fact must be stressed: religion and ethics were regarded as separate. Buddhism and Shinto governed the religious aspects of life, Confucianism the ethical. It is not necessary to believe that the Tokugawa Government deliberately encouraged such a separation, yet to maintain its power both the institutional strength of Buddhism and the philosophy of Confucianism were necessary. This was the origin of the Japanese cultural tradition of dividing religion from ethics; it drove Buddhism back on purely religious matters such as life after death.

Despite the prominence of Buddhism Shinto was a close competitor which had not been eradicated during the centuries-old spread of Buddhism. Hundreds of thousands of Shinto shrines showed how lively the faith of the villagers still was. It was common to profess both faiths without any feeling of contradiction. Yet this vague, customary Shinto had not sufficient impetus in it to challenge Buddhism. A new movement was necessary and was, indeed, developing among the scholars working on ancient Japanese poems and manuscripts. This work had been going on for a century and the oldest Japanese writings, the *Kojiki* (Record of Ancient Things), compiled in 712, had just been deciphered. The aim of these scholars was to find the original indigenous Japanese culture before it was 'spoiled' by the continental influences of Buddhism and Confucianism. Now the religion of Japan in those ancient times was Shinto, and the problem was how to revive the true, ancient Shinto. Groups of 'Restoration Shintoists' began to emerge, among them being Motoori Norinaga (1730–1801) and Hirata Atsutane (1776–1843). When, after 250 years, the Shogunate at last fell, 'Restoration Shinto' was logically the most useful religion and indeed played an important ideological role in the Meiji restoration.

An event such as the restoration could not fail to have tremendous implications for religious life. The three most important changes which occurred were (1) a breach between Buddhism and Shinto, (2) an attempt to make Shinto the State religion, (3) the reintroduction of Christianity. During the Shogunate, as we have seen, there was a good deal of Buddhist–Shinto syncretism, which was displeasing to the Shinto priests who were unable at that time to remedy the state of affairs. However, after the Meiji restoration the new Government ordered a readjustment of the relations between Buddhism and Shinto: Buddhist elements were to be eliminated from Shinto sanctuaries, syncretism was to cease, and the ancient type of Shinto sanctuary was to be restored. At this the long-suppressed dissatisfaction of the Shintoists burst out: Buddhist temples built within Shinto precincts were destroyed, their images thrown out and their holy writings burned. This outburst, which was a disaster for Buddhism, spread all over Japan and raged for three years. Buddhism, which had lost much of its spiritual vitality under the Shogunate, now lost its external protection from the Government; it was thirty years before it fully recovered.

At first the 'restoration' side of the Meiji Government was so strong that its structure was almost that of a theocracy, modelled on the first Tennô Jimmu's time. Government functions were twofold: the secular administration and the performance of Shinto ritual. But this system did not wear well, and the Government decided to set up a central office for religion; all religions were asked to unite in acting and teaching in such a way as to enhance the spiritual happiness of the people. Here the resistance of Buddhism proved too strong and, after various failures, the central office was abolished in 1875. Thereafter, every religion except Shinto remained free of government control and could develop on its own lines; as for Shinto, the way was being paved for it to become the State religion.

Meanwhile Christianity was returning to the country with the reopening of the ports. In the sixteenth century Christianity had meant the Catholic missions from Europe; now they were mainly Protestant missions from the United States. The Japanese, however, could not yet distinguish between them; Government and people alike were afraid of them and attempted to resist them—the former legally, the latter emotionally. But it soon became clear that this was not the correct policy to adopt if Japan wished to take her place among the Western nations. Very reluctantly, the Government admitted Christianity to Japan.

It was an unfamiliar type of religion to the Japanese. In contrast with the pantheism of Buddhism, the ritual and nature-mysticism of Shinto, it was a rigorous, monotheistic, *ethical* religion. It was therefore bound to have a revolutionary effect on Japanese minds. However, at the same time its militant, missionary spirit drove the other religions into a defensive alliance.

Finally, in the early Meiji days, the average Japanese could not make a clear distinction between the modernization, the Westernization, and the Christianization of Japan. Christianity was often admired because it was a product of Western civilization, and some people were converted because they wished to learn English and come into contact with Western ideas. In other words, Christianity was accepted not only as a religion but as a channel of communication with the West.

By now Shinto was the leading religion in Japan, but the situation was slightly more complex: beside State Shinto, under government protection, there were other manifestations, collectively known as 'Sectarian Shinto' and consisting of a multitude of new Shinto sects often founded by leaders sprung from the masses. Though they were classed as Shinto sects most of them showed traces of the syncretism which represented the general religious background in Japan. Some of the sects, such as *Tenri-kyo* and *Konko-kyo*, were later to develop into powerful religious bodies. Buddhism was slowly recovering from its low ebb. Christianity made great strides in the early Meiji era, and since it spread mostly among the town intellectuals its strength was much greater than its statistics showed. The great difference in Christianity was that it contained its own ethical programme as an integral part of its religious teaching; thus, as it began to spread, not merely Shinto and Buddhism were driven on to the defensive, but also Confucianism, which had supplied Japan with ethical principles. At first it appeared that Christianity would sweep the whole country, but this early rapidity of growth did not last more than a few decades.

In 1889, when the constitution was promulgated, the right to freedom of belief was stated for the first time officially. However, there was a curious exception: State Shinto. It was still the duty of the people to reverence the Shinto sanctuaries. The Government reconciled this apparent contradiction by declaring State Shinto as not a religion, but a cult, and treating it so administratively. Both this interpretation, and the application, lasted until 1945. Meanwhile a considerable amount of latitude was permitted to other religions —Buddhism, Christianity and Sectarian Shinto.

In the following year (1890) the imperial rescript of education was issued —a short document of only 2,500 words in its English translation, but full of significance. It laid down a moral code based on Shinto ideals and Confucian ethics, with a strong emphasis on loyalty to the Emperor and on filial piety, and this moral code was to be accepted by the Japanese as the basis of their moral life as well as the educational ideal. Copies were to be kept in every educational establishment in Japan, and on ceremonial occasions it was to be recited by the head of the institution before the Emperor's picture, while staff and students bowed deeply. Its influence was widespread and it is possible that the imperial rescript played a greater part than State Shinto in the ethico-religious life of the people.

By the end of the 1880s Japan's first wave of enthusiasm for Westernization was over. Leaders and intellectuals were becoming seriously concerned about national integrity and the Japanese cultural traditions. A national reaction was setting in. In the mid-1890s the arguments about the conflict between education and religion illustrate the struggle between nationalism and Christianity in the field of education. Basing themselves on the rescript, Japanese educationalists attacked Christianity on the grounds that supernatural allegiance was incompatible with loyalty to the Emperor and world brotherhood with the spirit of nationalism. State education banned Christian ideas and this may have helped to deepen the irreligious tendencies of the Meiji era.

Japan won two wars (the Sino-Japanese, 1894–5, and the Russo-Japanese, 1904–5) in which her whole fate was at stake; by these two victories she won an international position which enabled her to feel complete confidence. Yet internally a sense of inferiority and the new self-confidence formed an unstable mixture, in which religion had to find a foothold. Some of the Shinto sects were growing quietly but rapidly. Buddhism was slowly recovering, not so much on her former lines, but as a result of the achievements of scholarship and lay interest in Buddhist thought. Stimulated by Christianity both Shinto and Buddhism were turning slowly to social work. A Christian socialist movement was germinating in the basement of the only Unitarian church in Japan; this was to be the beginning of the socialist movement and the socialist party in Japan. When the twentieth century opened, both national feeling and religious zeal were strong in Japan, and they were to grow stronger still.

APPENDIX

AN ANALYSIS OF THE REVIVAL

Despite the fact that China was the most highly developed country in Asia it was Japan which took the lead in modernization. Although this modernization is associated with the Meiji era, it is pertinent to inquire whether Japan had not some particular resources, associated with earlier epochs, which made her particularly adapted to progress and reform. When we look back on Japanese history it is clear that, unlike the Greeks, the Chinese and the Indians, Japan had no creative culture of her own which was capable of export: her own peculiar culture, in fact, throve best under the stimulus of foreign influences. This can be seen as far back as the Asuka period (552–645) and that of the Nara (710–84). Between 645 and 650 a reform took place (the Taika reform) which was modelled on the legal system of Tang China, and occurred at a time when the Japanese clan system was in a thoroughly disorganized condition and when foreign relations with south Korea were in a critical state. As a result of the reform Japan became a unified state. The actual reform was brought about by a *coup d'état* of the Nakatomis (a family of Shinto priests) in alliance with Prince Nakano Oe against the Buddhist Soga family, which was strong enough to endanger the imperial throne. Like the Meiji 'restoration', this was a blend of restoration and the adoption of new ideas from China. As a result of this political reform, it is interesting to note that there also appeared a remarkable flowering of Japanese culture as well as a revival of Shintoism. Two famous books—the *Kojiki*, an historical account of Shintoism, and the *Nihon Shoki*, a similar account of Confucian influence—were compiled by order of the Imperial Court. Two anthologies also appeared—the *Manyô-shû*, an anthology of Japanese poems still greatly loved, and the *Kaifûsô*, a book of poems written in the Chinese style. The common phrase *Wakon kansai* (Japanese spirit and Chinese knowledge) sums up this acceptance of Chinese civilization without the loss of Japanese feeling which was characteristic of the period. Here again there is a parallel with the Meiji era, when the phrase *Tôyô Dôtoku Saiyô Geijutsi* (Oriental morality and Western arts) was advocated by Sakuma Shôzan (1811–64). Thus it might be said that the fundamental pattern for acceptance of a foreign culture had been established a thousand years previously.

We might further examine the period between the Sengoku (sixteenth century) period and the Togukawa period, when Japan first came into contact with the West, at that time with Spain and Portugal (later Holland and England). This, too, was a critical period for Japan, which, after the civil war of Onin (1467) underwent a social upheaval called the *gekokujô* (lower versus upper), as a result of which the Ashikaga Shogunate fell and the country was ravaged by 260 feudal lords all fighting one another. This Sengoku or war period came at the end of what Japanese historians call 'the first feudal age'. Contact with the West contributed to ending these wars and to the unification of Japan. Firearms imported from Spain and Portugal considerably facilitated the suppression of the rebellious feudal lords by Oda Nobunaga (1534–82), while the technique of castle-building is said to have been improved. Such sciences as astronomy and medicine began to enter Japan from the West, and their superiority was recognized.

The contact with Spain and Portugal also meant the importation of Christianity, and some *daimyôs* (feudal lords) were converted. Nobunaga, who burned the Buddhist monks of Mount Hiei and quarrelled with the priests of the Honganji temple, though apparently irreligious and a rationalist, supported the Christians against the Buddhists. Hideyoshi (1536–98) was more cautious about Christianity and it was finally banned by the Tokugawa Shogunate, when suspicion of the missionary activities of the Jesuits led to the closing of the country for 250 years. The rebellion of the Shimabara farmers led to the death of 37,000 Christians, which shows what deep roots Christianity already had among the people. Later, the Tokugawa Shogunate relaxed its ban on Western learning but Christianity was not officially permitted until the Meiji period.

These examples of Japan's contacts with the West underline three interesting conclusions: Japan was well aware of the superiority of foreign civilizations and prepared to adopt features concerned with law, administration, art or technology; she was much more hostile to religious influences from abroad, whether Buddhist or Christian; and finally, her goal was the adoption of useful knowledge from abroad together with the maintenance of her independence and her own civilization. This was only partially successful.

Japan's confidence in her own powers was partly due to the fact that she had never been conquered by a foreign invader, which was in turn due to her unusual island situation. When, in the Meiji period, she found herself again confronted with European civilization, she felt herself to be the guardian of Oriental culture and, probably unconsciously, fell back upon the traditions of earlier contact-eras. Yet things were not quite the same. Uchimura Kanzô (1861–1929), a leading Christian of the Meiji and Taisho periods, wrote in one of his early articles

'As a result of our national temperament we are easily attracted by foreign things; perhaps no country is more apt at adopting the civilization of other countries than Japan. Japan alone of Oriental countries can understand the civilization of Europe and America. Japan is the only civilized country which can think in an Oriental way. The two currents of world thought flow together in Japan to create a sound mode of thought capable of influencing the rest of the world.'

This may sound like megalomania, but the leading Japanese of the Meiji age were all alike in possessing the same faith, the same hope, and the same ideals concerning the mission of

Japan. This was the motive force behind the progress of the period. Yet many of the realities of the situation had already been prepared during the preceding (Tokugawa) epoch.

Japanese feudalism in that epoch had been similar to feudalism elsewhere in that it was based upon status and inheritance, its quasi-independent local lords, and the close relationship of politics and the military order. Yet it had some original features: it was the Emperor who formally appointed the Tokugawa Shogun as Seii Taishogun (Generalissimo), and though both the Emperor and his Court aristocracy were powerless politically, it was not the Shogun but the Emperor who stood for Japan with its long history and its traditions. Although the Shogun tried to use the Emperor to maintain his own dignity, it was not at the expense of the Emperor's; he carefully prevented him from having any political power, but respected his religious authority. Foreigners who visited Japan in this period noticed that the country really had two rulers—the religious ruler at Kyoto, the Emperor, and the political ruler at Edo (Tokyo), the Shogun: this paradox was resolved at the Meiji restoration by the elimination of the Shogunate. There was also even at the time of the Taika reform a consciousness of racial unity, and that unity was felt to centre on the Emperor.

Another point to be remembered is that the rule of the Shogunate was more centralized than many feudal systems. While there were 200 mainly independent *daimyôs* the Shogunate could issue orders to the Fudai *daimyôs* (who were descendants of the Tokugawa) and could move them about at will; they also controlled the Tozama *daimyôs*, former enemies who had become vassals. All this was reinforced by the *sankin-kôtai* system, by which the *daimyôs* were ordered to live in Edo every other year, or for several months in each year, and to leave their families in the town all the time. Thus feudalism in the Tokugawa period was not as strong as it might have been. Even more important was the modification of the *bushi* or military element; the Shogunate, to prevent rebellions, deprived the *daimyôs* of as much of their fighting forces as possible, and adopted a pacific internal policy based on Confucianism. The policy of national isolation also made few demands on the military strength of the country, and the *bushi* became less and less men of war and more like civil servants. This was again a step away from feudalism towards a modern state. Japan's later failure was also implicit in the feudal age, resulting as it did from the deification of the Emperor, bureaucratization and militarism.

Modern economic development also begins in the period of isolation. It is estimated that land under cultivation increased from 1·5 million chôbu (about 2·4 acres) in 1600 to 3 million chôbu in 1700; this was due partly to irrigation, fertilization and other agricultural improvements. By 1700 much silk and cotton was being produced by the peasants as a domestic industry, and in a list of goods sent from Osaka to Edo cloth amounted to three times the value of rice. Fishing, mining and other industries were also developing. During the later part of the period some of the clans began to engage in monopolistic production (e.g. sugar) and a money economy made its appearance even in the villages. In his *Seidan* (Treatise on politics) Ogyû Sorai (1666–1728) writes:

'In the country in the old days everything was bought not for money but for rice and wheat (on account of the acute shortage of coin). Now I hear that recently a money economy has penetrated also into the country, since about the time of Genroku, and that people buy things for money.'

Another modern feature was the rise of a merchant class. According to the Shi-nô-kô-shô hierarchy the merchants held the lowest rank in society, but in actual fact they were regarded as next in rank to the warriors, and the wealthier ones were as powerful as *daimyôs*. These latter exchanged the rice, which the farmers paid in taxes, for cash; Osaka was the centre of this business and it was the granary of the whole country. The merchants of Osaka were national figures, and *daimyôs* were known to borrow money from them: it was even said that 'when the Osaka merchants become angry, the *daimyôs* are afraid.' This mercantile capital formed the fortunes of great families such as the Mitsui and the Konoike who were to play an important role in the Meiji era.

Already in the Tokugawa period, despite certain inconveniences due to the existence of dialects, it was possible to travel round the country for 2,000 miles and find the same language spoken. From this point of view, compared with India and China which still have the problem of diversity of languages, Japan's problem was a simple one. Elementary education, given by the private schools (*terakoya*) was also spreading among the people. Travel also became easier under the Tokugawa, for despite the highway-barriers (*Sekisho*) which were necessary for the maintenance of feudalism, the system of *sankin-kôtai* led to the spread of trunk roads through-out the country. Though by present-day standards these would be regarded as quite in-sufficient, their sensible planning, in a country of which 77 per cent was mountainous, was a considerable achievement.

Certain features of modern civilization such as rationalism, utilitarianism and humanism were also to be found in the Tokugawa period. Between the Kamakura and the Muromachi epochs (i.e. from the twelfth to the sixteenth centuries) Japan developed a particular form of Buddhism which spread rapidly among the people and came to hold political power. It was often opposed to the feudal lords—hence the quarrel of Nobunaga with the Honganji temple in Kyoto and his setting fire to the temple on Mount Heii. When Tokugawa Teyasu became ruler of Japan he adopted the Confucian ethic and prevented the Buddhists from wielding political power. Thus he soothed down the fighting spirit aroused by the earlier civil wars, and at the same time preached the virtues of obedience and status, as expounded by Confucius, as a means to social order. This strengthened the feudal system.

The adoption of Confucianism by the Shogunate meant an abandonment of religion and the supernatural for the ethical, political and earthly—a change characteristic of the development from the medieval to the modern world. Furthermore, Confucianism, which was recognized as an official science in the Tokugawa period, belonged to the Sung epoch and the Chu Hsi school of thought, which (since it was opposed to Buddhism though influenced by it) was highly abstract and philosophical. Its metaphysic, based on the two principles of *ri* (reason) and *ki* (spirit) illustrate this. The methodology of *Kakubutsu Chichi*, the attainment of knowledge by mastering the essence of things, was even positivist. When the missionary Sidotti entered Japan illegally Arai Hakuseki (1657–1725), a scholar of the period, was frankly astonished at his knowledge of astronomy and geography, saying that it would be impossible for the Japanese. Yet he frowned on the Christian idea of the creation and advocated 'astronomical geography'; he further criticized Sidotti's preaching as 'listening to two people, one wise and the other foolish, whose positions are changeable'. This illustrates the rationalistic attitude induced by Confucianism and its readiness to receive Western science. In effect, influenced by Hakuseki, the Shogun Yoshimune removed the ban on the import of books on medicine and astronomy.

As economic development moved from country to town and people's minds became more secular and realistic, the idea of practical learning (*Jitsugaku*) became increasingly popular. In addition to the Chu Hsi school of Confucianism, which might have become purely formal and intellectual, there existed another called Wang Yang Ming which advocated *Chikô Gôitsu* (or harmonizing knowledge and action) and denounced unpractical knowledge. This school was of course far more progressive, and appealed more to the people, while the Chu Hsi school remained an official learning, but both were utilitarian in basis.

The new school of Wang Yang Ming was also humanist: the dignity of man, freedom from tradition and respect for humanity were among its principles. In the older school, too, the Way was thought of as something intended for the peace and happiness of mankind, and not merely a metaphysical affair, and this also led to respect for the human being. An interesting movement was that of 'National Learning', led by Kamo Mabuchi (1697–1769) and Motoori Norinaga (1730–1801) which sought the roots of modern Japan in mythology. It was owing to the efforts of this group that many of the Japanese classics were at last understood correctly.

Three points are of particular interest in this movement when we are considering the mod-ernization of Japan. Firstly, there was the objective tendency which studied the facts of ancient history and compared them with the Confucian theories. Mabuchi, pointing out many dis-crepancies between Confucianism and Chinese history, showed that the former was often irrelevant, and urged a return to the old gods of Japan, a kind of naturalism. Though one may consider it strange that he sought support for his factualism and naturalism in the mythology of Japan, it must be admitted that both these are modern traits.

Secondly, the importance of the emotions was affirmed and man's emancipation preached—two modern factors closely linked with naturalism. Mabuchi stated that the true way should be neither abstract nor artificial, that it should be expressed by art, by ancient poems, rather than by theories, while Norinaga urged the charms of Nature. The *Genji Monogatari* (Tales of Genji) was denounced by the Confucians as an unethical book, and was only accepted by the Buddhists because of its ideas on cause and effect. Norinaga, however, saw in it a positive value, since it expressed naturally the emotional foundation of human nature.

Thirdly, the National Learning played a part in arousing the national consciousness of the Japanese, by stressing the original Japanese culture as opposed to the Chinese which centred on Confucianism. The *Kannagara no michi*, or divine way, although it glorified ancient Japan, was modern (as we have seen) in its objectivity, naturalism and humanism. Its criticism of Confucianism, the spiritual basis of feudalism, and its enhancement of the national consciousness, also prepared the way for the Meiji restoration. It can be seen to be linked with the *Sonno Jôi* (respect for the emperor and expulsion of foreigners) which emerged from the Confucianism of the Mito school.

In sum the realism and positivism, that is, the secular character of Japan, enabled her to adopt so easily modern European civilization, especially its technical aspects. This is particularly clear when Japan is compared with such Asian countries as Thailand and Burma, where Buddhism flourishes. But this is another story. Although Japan successfully adopted the material civilizations of the West, she was unable to resist completely certain more intangible influences which were liable only to be superficially absorbed. There was, too, the danger of her acquiring a militaristic and imperialist outlook, as the tragedy of the Second World War illustrated.

NOTES TO CHAPTER XXVIII

1. Dr K. T. Eidus considers that here the influence of Western culture on Japan in the Tokugawa period is exaggerated. Since ordinary Japanese people did not make wide use of imported goods they could not value them highly.

   The outbreak of the Shimabara rebellion cannot be attributed to the desire of the rebels to defend Christianity alone. It was an anti-feudal peasant rising, which was used by the southern *daimyôs* in the struggle against the Shogunate under a religious flag. The author fails to note the class character of this rebellion.

   The isolationist policy of the Tokugawa period had many causes, not only fear of the spread of Christianity in Japan.

2. Dr Eidus is not in agreement when the author says that at the end of the nineteenth century the Japanese army circles carried out the militarization of the country without having any aggressive aims. He does not regard the Sino-Japanese and Russo-Japanese wars as aggressive from the Japanese side. He has to take this attitude because the British and Americans gave every possible material and moral support to Japan in these wars. It is in any case a well-known fact that these wars were aggressive and imperialist from the Japanese side (and from the Tsarist side in the Russo-Japanese War) and that Japan had already become an imperialist power by the turn of the century.

3. Dr Eidus does not believe that the *Tennô Sei* can be regarded as Japan's answer to Western political influence. This is of course not true, as the *Tennô* cult was the product of Japan's internal development.

   The author interprets Meiji Ishin in the same way as most conservative Japanese and Western historians, i.e. as merely the overthrow of the Shogunate and the restoration of imperial power. But he gives no social background to this event.

4. Dr Eidus feels that the author does not stress sufficiently the reactionary nature of the Japanese constitution of 1889.

5. The author, speaking about Japanese industrial development, is wrong in disregarding class antagonism as one of its characteristic features.

ILLUSTRATIONS

(a)

73

THE MOSLEM WORLD I

(b)

(a) *The Royal Square, Isphan. From E. Flandrin, La Perse moderne*

(b) *The Bazaar of Kachan. From E. Flandrin, La Perse moderne*

(a)

(b)

74

THE MOSLEM WORLD II

(a) *An Arab Council*

(b) *A view of Cairo in the middle nineteenth century*

75
OCEANIA
The village of Manevia, Wanikar Island. Astrolabe expedition of 1833

(a) [LF

(b) [LF

(c) [LF

(d) [LF

(a)

(b)

77

SOUTH-EAST ASIA I

(a) *Pnom-Penh, Cambodia, in the late nineteenth century. From E. Cotteau's* Un Touriste en Extrême Orient, *1884*

(b) *Saigon, Vietnam, ca. 1885. Woodcut*

Opposite

(a) *Englishman on an elephant shooting a tiger. Indian folk art ca. 1830*

(b) *An English judge with two Indian experts at a trial for murder. Indian folk art ca. 1845. Coll. of O. W. Samson*

(c) *An Indian husband slaying his Westernized wife who has returned home with an umbrella and a handbag. Drawing by Nirbaran Chandra Ghosh, ca. 1880*

(d) *Gurkha soldiers from Nepal. From Dr Gustave le Bon's* Voyage au Népal, *1886*

(b)

78
SOUTH-EAST ASIA II

(a)

[LF

(b)

[LF

79
(a) *Java. 'Gamelang' orchestra. From the Comte de Beauvoir's* Voyage autour du monde, 1869
(b) *Palm leaves decorated with legendary scenes. Bali, nineteenth century. Coll. Louis Frederic*

Opposite
(a) *Java. The Sultan of Jogakarta. From Comte de Beauvoir's* Voyage autour du monde, 1869
(b) *Burma. A nobleman and his retainers. From Henri Yule's* Voyage au royaume d'Ava,
Empire des Birmans, 1855

[LF

80

SOUTH-EAST ASIA IV

(a) *Siam. King Mongkut by the royal palace in Bangkok. From the Comte de Beauvoir's* Voyage autour du monde, 1869

(b) *Siam. The entrance to the royal harem, Bangkok. From the Comte de Beauvoir's* Voyage autour du monde, 1869

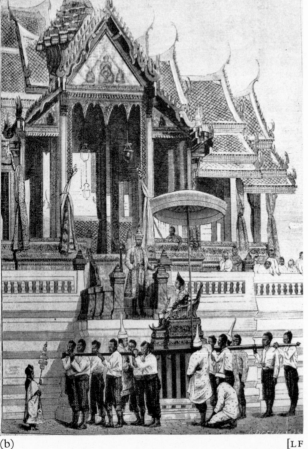

(b) [LF

(a) *Part of a bronze chandelier from the royal palace at Mandalay, representing a protective angel. Nineteenth century*

(b) *Vietnamese women inlaying mother-of-pearl. From E. Cotteau's* Un touriste en Extrême Orient, 1884

(a)

[LF

(b)

[LF

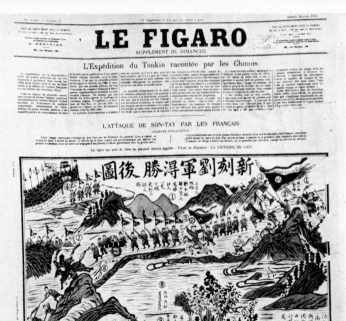

(a) *The French expedition in Tonkin*, 1884. *A Chinese view of the storming of Son-Tay. From* Le Figaro, *Paris*, 28 *June* 1884

(b) *The French expedition in Tonkin; the storming of the forts of Huê*, 1883

[LF

(b)

[LF

[LF

[LF

83
CHINA I

(a) *A formal reception at the Imperial Court of China. From G. Panthier's* L'Universe pittoresque, 1837

(b) *The retinue of a Chinese mandarin. From E. Cotteau's* Un touriste en Extrême Orient, 1884

(a)

(b)

84
CHINA II

(a) *A view of Peking in* 1885. *From G. Panthier's* L'Univers pittoresque, 1837

(b) *The Beggar's Bridge, Peking. From E. Cotteau's* Un touriste en Extrême Orient, 1884

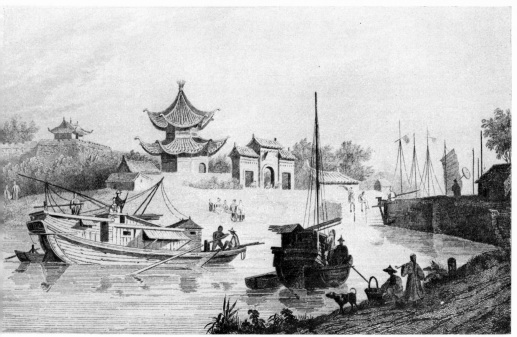

[LF

b) [LF

85
CHINA III

(a) *A lock on the Grand Canal of China. From G. Panthier's* L'Univers pittoresque, 1837

(b) *The French Legation in Shanghai in* 1874. *From the Abbé David's* Journal

(a)

[L

(b)

[LF

86

CHINA IV

(a) *The Tai-ping rebellion, 1864. The imperial troops attacking the rebels in Nanking*

(b) *Chinese regulars in Korea, 1884*

87
CHINA V

(a) *The treaty of Tien-Tsin,* 1858. *A Chinese view*

(b) *A French view of the same*

(a) [LF (b) [

88

JAPAN I

(a) *The Emperor of Japan, Mutsu-hito (Meiji) in 1875*

(b) *The Empress of Japan, wife of the Emperor Mutsu-hito (Meiji) in 1875*

Opposite

(a) *The imperial palanquin in Yedo (Tokyo) ca. 1875. Japanese woodcut from L. Metchnikov's* L'Empire japonais, 1878

(b) *The Chamber of Commerce in Kyoto, ca. 1880. Japanese engraving from* Kyoto Meisho Meguri (A Visit to the Monuments of Kyoto)

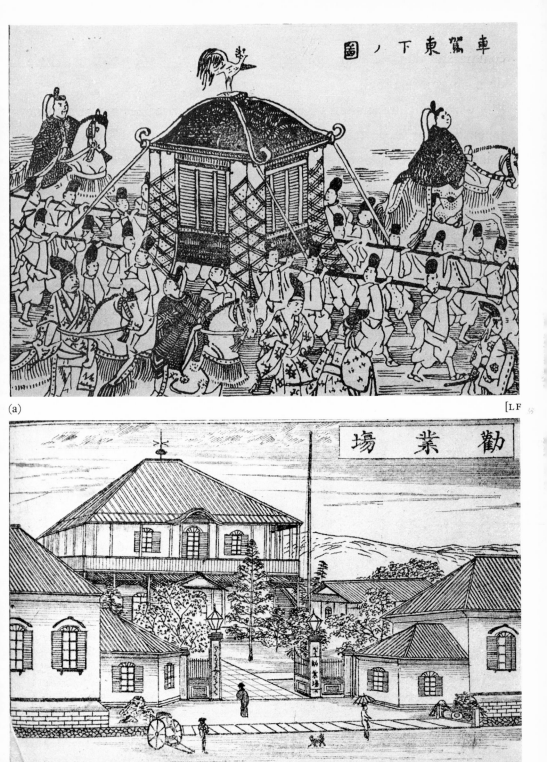

(a)

(b)

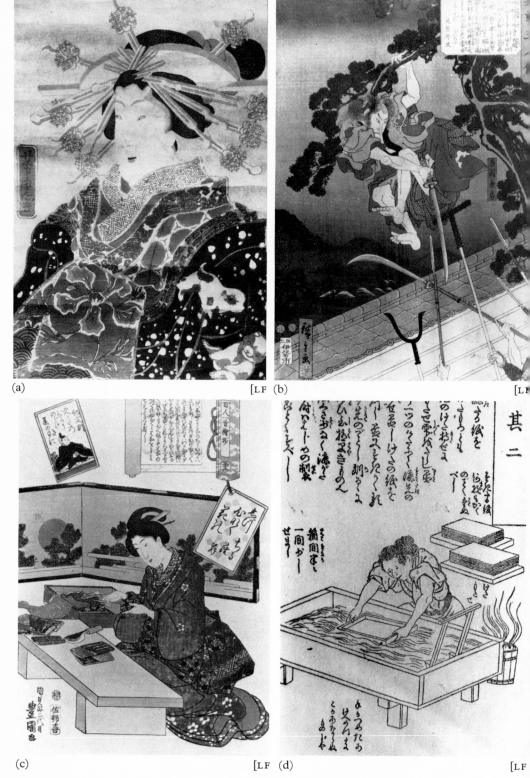

(a) [LF (b) [LF

(c) [LF (d) [LF

90 JAPAN III: SOCIAL LIFE (a) *Japanese lady, ca. 1850. Colour print by Yoshitora,*
Paris (b) *Kabuki actor by Hiroshige, 1796–1858* (c) *Japanese woman sewing sacks.*
Nineteenth century. Coll. J. P. Hanchecorne (d) *Paper making. Nineteenth century. From*
the Shiroku Chō hōki. *Coll. J. P. Hanchecorne*

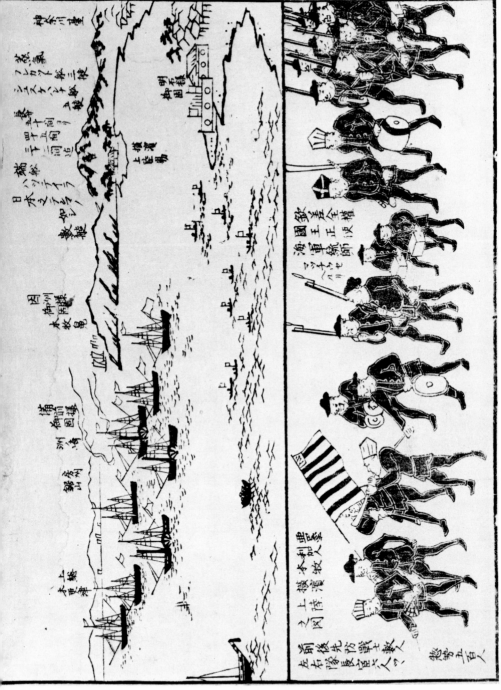

JAPAN IV:
THE OPENING
OF JAPAN

*Japanese impression of
Commodore
Matthew C.
Perry's squadron
and the American
landing party at
Yokohama on
8 March 1854.
From Philip K.
Lundeberg's
'Japanese Prints
of the Perry
Expedition' in The
Smithsonian
Journal of
History, II,
151967*

(a)   [LC

(b)   [LF

92

JAPAN V: FOREIGN RELATIONS

(a) *The Ministry of Foreign Affairs in Tokyo, ca.* 1875

(b) *The signature of the Treaty of Shimonoseki,* 1895, *between China and Japan.*
Contemporary Japanese engraving

93
JAPAN VI

(a) *Tokyo in* 1884. *From G. Deffing's* Le Japon
(b) *Yokohama in* 1884. *From G. Deffing's* Le Japon

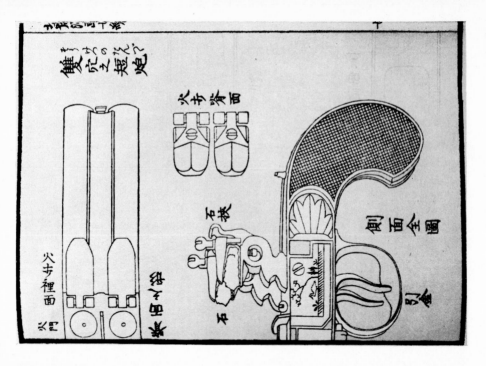

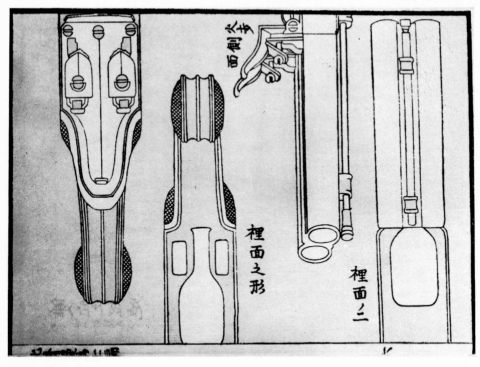

A two-barrelled flint pistol. Japanese woodcut by Hokusai (1760–1848). From Manga, Vol. XI, ca. 1834

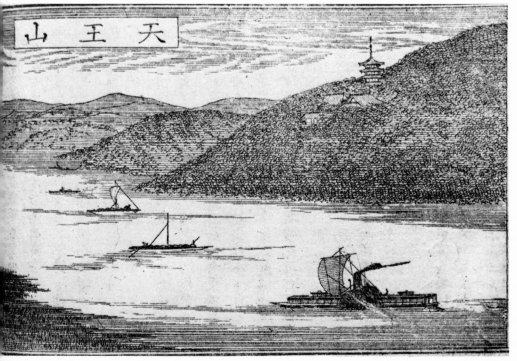

95
JAPAN VIII

(a) *The railway line by the Shinto temple of Imari, Kyoto. End of the nineteenth century. Japanese engraving from* Kyoto Meisho Meguri

(b) *Japanese ship cruising by the Takara-Dera pagoda near Kyoto. Late nineteenth century. From* Kyoto Meisho Meguri

(a)

(b)

96 JAPAN IX: RELIGIOUS LIFE

(a) *Ikkyu Osho preaching on the rarity of things of this world. Engraving by* Shō Gyōsai (1831–89)

(b) *The temple of Asakusa in Tokyo. Photograph dated* 1878

INDEX